Peter
Thank you for everything —
your friendship, advice,
support, and insights.

With much appreciation
and respect,
Ken
10/18/90

Federal Courts and the International Human Rights Paradigm

Kenneth C. Randall

Federal Courts and the International Human Rights Paradigm

Duke University Press
Durham and London   1990

For Susan and our children,
Gregory, Meredith, and Douglas

© 1990 Duke University Press
All rights reserved
Printed in the United States of America
on acid-free paper ∞
Library of Congress Cataloging-in-Publication Data
appear on the last page of this book.

CONTENTS

v

II

═══

Domestic Jurisdiction
in the World Legal Order

═══

ACKNOWLEDGMENTS

This book partly stems from my doctoral work at the Columbia University School of Law, and I am very grateful to my dissertation committee — Oscar Schachter, chairman, and Alfred Hill, and Lori Damrosch — for their earlier guidance. Peter Strauss, who heads Columbia's graduate legal program, also provided important and considerate support. My international law teachers at the Yale Law School, Myres McDougal and Michael Reisman, beneficially helped me to think about my present topic some years ago. More presently, Dean Nathaniel Hansford and the University of Alabama Law School Foundation have generously provided research funding. Susan Brown's word-processing support has been superb, as has Susan Sheffield's research assistance. The Alabama Law librarians, particularly Penny Gibson, Robert Marshall, and Paul Pruitt, have greatly helped my research, which was completed in the summer of 1989. Three friends and colleagues, Peter Alces, Tony Freyer, and Wythe Holt, have provided valuable insights on a few chapters. Luke Harris, my former colleague at Simpson Thacher & Bartlett, has offered encouragement and friendship while I wrote this book. Above all, I wish to thank my wife, Susan Lyons Randall, who, with both abundant patience and a Columbia J.D., has greatly helped to nurture and edit my manuscript. Finally, the notes indicate when this book draws upon my previous essays.

There is a subtle interaction between theory and practice in politics, not always easy to trace because the actors themselves may easily be unconscious of theoretical prepossessions which, nevertheless, powerfully influence their whole attitude towards practical affairs; and at no time has it been so important, as it is today, that we should see the facts of international life as they really are, and not as they come to us reflected in false or outworn theories.

The Basis of Obligation in International Law and Other Papers by the Late James Leslie Brierly 2 (H. Lauterpacht & C. Waldock eds. 1958)

INTRODUCTION

International human rights law is often commended for its worthy aspirations, but criticized for its lack of enforceability. Some critics even claim that the continued brutalization of individuals around the world belies the very idea that human rights law is really "law." The past decade has developed a new legal strategy, however, to help bridge the gap between the theory and practice of human rights norms. A 1980 federal case, *Filartiga v. Pena-Irala*,[1] triggered an innovative genre of civil litigation: cases involving human rights violations and terrorist acts committed outside of the United States, usually brought by alien victims against other aliens or foreign nations.

Filartiga concerned one Paraguayan's torture of another Paraguayan in Asunción. To quiet Dr. Joel Filartiga's outspoken criticism of the Stroessner regime, a police official, Pena, kidnapped Dr. Filartiga's son and tortured the teenager to death. Pena then brought Dr. Filartiga's daughter to see her maimed brother's body, shouting: "Here you have what you have been looking for for so long and what you deserve. Now shut up."[2] Dr. Filartiga's legal action in Paraguay was halted when Pena shackled Filartiga's attorney to a wall in police headquarters and threatened him with death. The attorney was subsequently disbarred without just cause. When later living in Washington, D.C., Dr. Filartiga and his daughter learned of Pena's presence in New York and commenced a wrongful death action against the torturer in federal court. Creative lawyers invoked an arcane, 200-year-old jurisdictional statute, the Alien Tort Statute, and convinced the Second Circuit Court of Appeals to sustain jurisdiction in the case. Although faced with a host of unique and difficult legal issues, the court concluded that torture violates international law

3

and is actionable by individual litigants. A $10 million judgment was eventually awarded to the Filartigas.[3]

The Filartigas' victory ignited the human rights era of federal litigation. In the case's aftermath, federal courts have been inundated with dozens of human rights cases. The new civil litigation has included the following: actions concerning human rights violations committed by the former military junta in Argentina; a class action against the German Reich's henchman in Croatia, who committed war crimes and crimes against humanity, executing tens of thousands of Jews; and several human rights actions against the deposed Philippines president, the late Ferdinand Marcos.[4] Related litigation has involved the innocent victims not only of human rights violations, but of extraterritorial terrorism. These cases include an action brought by a United States serviceman held hostage in Iran and a suit brought on behalf of a Swedish diplomat whom Soviet officials illegally imprisoned and probably murdered.[5] As just this small sampling of cases indicates, many important international events occur one day and end up in federal court the next.

The judiciary's response to human rights and terrorism cases has varied greatly. Jurisdiction has been sustained sporadically in *Filartiga*'s progeny, and judgments have been rendered inconsistently. Undoubtedly, the fact that the cases raise many questions of first impression for the circuits accounts for these diverse results. As with any new or changing legal field, confusion predates clarity.

Exemplifying the judiciary's disagreement over human rights and terrorism cases is the 1984 decision of the D.C. Circuit Court of Appeals in *Tel-Oren v. Libyan Arab Republic*.[6] This case was commenced by Israelis and others who survived, or represented innocent persons murdered during, a terrorist attack in Israel. Allegedly with Libya's support, the Palestine Liberation Organization seized civilian vehicles on the highway between Haifa and Tel Aviv and tortured or seriously wounded or killed 121 civilian hostages, including 26 children. *Tel-Oren* presented the D.C. Circuit with far-ranging questions of domestic and international law. Although the court dismissed the case, the three-judge panel was unable to agree about why it had done so. The court rendered a cursory three-paragraph *per curiam* decision, but each judge went on to write a lengthy concurring opinion, explaining why he, and not the other judges, understood the correct rationale for dismissing the action.

This judicial debate led then Judge Bork to conclude: "[T]he three opinions we have produced can only add to the confusion. . . . [I]t is impossible to say even what the law of this circuit is. Though we agree on nothing else, I am sure my colleagues join me in finding that regrettable."[7] Another member of the panel, Judge Edwards, correctly concluded that "[t]his case deals with an area of the law that cries out for clarification by the Supreme Court. We confront at every turn broad and novel questions about the definition and application of the 'law of nations.'"[8] The Supreme Court's clarification of this area is still awaited.

The academy has also extensively debated the use of federal court authority over human rights and terrorism cases. Given the diverse array of commentators' views, a federal judge usually can find some scholarly support for any decision he or she wishes to make in this area of the law. At least one member of the bench, however, Judge Robb, the third jurist in *Tel-Oren*, expressly rejected academe's advice. He caustically commented that "[c]ourts ought not to serve as debating clubs for professors willing to argue over what is or what is not an accepted violation of the law of nations."[9] The thrust and parry among federal judges and commentators has also generated legislative proposals designed to clarify the law, but such legislation itself remains subject to congressional debate.[10] In short, *Filartiga* and its progeny sorely requires clarification, especially if that case is to fulfill its deep and important potential.

How should litigants, judges, lawmakers, and others approach *Filartiga*, *Tel-Oren*, and their offspring? The modern cases raise numerous and difficult legal issues. But I suggest that most, if not all, of those issues are actually subissues of the following inquiry: In the human rights and terrorism context, what is the legitimate authority and appropriate role of federal courts within both the United States legal system and the international legal system? That is essentially a jurisdictional inquiry, since *jurisdiction*, correctly conceived, refers to an institution's proper authority within a given system.[11] Jurisdictional questions are at the threshold of every lawsuit and they lie at the heart of the *Filartiga* debate.

The reference, in my touchstone inquiry, to two legal systems foreshadows this book's organization. Part one examines the federal judiciary as an institutional constituent in the nation's governance. It considers the relationship between the federal and local state courts under federalism concerns; it also considers the relationship between the judicial branch and the executive and legislative branches under separation-of-powers concerns. Such governmental "relationships" refer to the relative authority of the federal courts vis-à-vis the state courts, and to the relative authority of the federal judiciary vis-à-vis the executive and legislative branches, in matters involving the individual victims of human rights violations and terrorism. Certain federal jurisdictional statutes and judicial abstention doctrines provide vehicles for theoretically assessing federal court authority in this context. While those statutes and doctrines must be applied on a case-by-case basis, I will demonstrate that federal judicial authority exists and should be exercised in most human rights and terrorism cases—at least as that authority relates to the national system.

Part two examines the federal judiciary as an institutional actor within the international legal system or "world legal order," that is, the legal system that regulates foreign relations and enforces the rights and obligations recognized by international law. This part considers the permissible and proper scope of domestic court authority when such tribunals essentially act as agents or representatives of the world legal order. This topic was also the focus of Richard Falk's renowned work, *The Role of Domestic Courts in the International Legal Order* (1964). Although deservedly much utilized by judges, lawyers, commentators, and teachers—and although its thesis was ultimately adopted by the Supreme Court—Professor Falk's book is some twenty-five years old. Falk's book illuminated domestic court authority in the cold war atmosphere and disputes endemic to that era, such as the uncompensated nationalization of private property. But it is hoped that the present text will illuminate more current disputes. The actors, events, and law involved in human rights and terrorism cases present truly international disputes and demand as global and as cosmopolitan a perspective as was needed in the cold war cases. Depicting the proper role of domestic courts in the modern setting is actually as relevant to the United States' tribunals as it is to any other nation's tribunals. The vehicles for assessing domestic court authority within the world legal order include certain jurisdictional principles of international law. Although, again, every human rights and terrorism case demands ad hoc jurisdictional treatment, I will demonstrate that the universality principle supports federal court authority in most of these cases, in relation to the international legal system. My thesis, moreover, argues that post-World War II human rights and antiterrorism developments may have structurally or paradigmatically altered the world legal order. Although nation-state sovereignty remains the legal order's hallmark, it is now meaningful to speak of a "human rights paradigm," by which the conventional statist perspective has yielded to the creation of individually enforceable rights. Ultimately, the human rights paradigm obligates domestic courts, including the federal judiciary, to assume authority over violations of international rights.

Before proceeding, a common understanding of the terms *human rights* and *terrorism* is necessary. Various legal sources create international law. Focusing momentarily, however, upon the treaties created after World War II, human rights norms include those found in the International Covenant on Civil and Political Rights ("Covenant").[12] Nation-states that are parties to the Covenant are obligated to confer and protect certain fundamental liberties, including the right to live; not to be summarily executed; not to be subjected to torture or to cruel or inhuman treatment or punishment; not to be held in slavery or servitude; and to be treated equally before the law. Other relevant humanitarian treaties are the four Geneva Conventions of 1949,[13] which prohibit certain war crimes; the Genocide Convention,[14] which prohibits the destruction of a national, ethnic, racial, or religious group; the Apartheid Convention,[15] prohibiting racial segregation and discrimination practiced in South Africa; and, finally, the Torture Convention.[16] The United States is a party to the Geneva Conventions and the Genocide Convention, but not to the Covenant or the Apartheid Convention. Although the nation is also not a party to the Torture Convention, President Reagan transmitted that treaty to the Senate for its advice and consent. As will be discussed, however, the norms contained in the latter three instruments may still bind the United States under customary law and other international law sources.[17]

Regarding terrorism, a pair of hijacking treaties is significant: the Hague[18] and Montreal Conventions,[19] which together prohibit the seizure of civil aircraft and violence committed against a person on board an aircraft. Another tandem of terrorism conventions is the Hostage Convention[20] and the Internationally Protected Persons Convention.[21] While the former prohibits hostage taking as a means of coercing a nation-state's behavior, the latter prohibits violent acts committed against certain representatives of nation-states and international organizations.

These four treaties, also created after the Second World War, share their derivation: the legal order's evolving condemnation of force and violence committed against the world's public and private actors. The United States is a party to each of these conventions, which are thus part of federal law. But since those treaties are primarily criminal or regulatory in character, their utilization in civil matters must particularly be addressed.[22]

The human rights and terrorism concepts share not only their historical and normative derivations from the postwar decades, but as I suggest they are also linked in substance and character. One might argue against the parallel treatment that I give to human rights violations and terrorism. That argument might focus upon the political nature of terrorism; the difficulty of defining terrorism; and the problem of distinguishing between the use of force by terrorist organizations and by the United States and other countries.[23] Granted, terrorism may sometimes be motivated by political goals or ideological values more "legitimate" than those underlying human rights violations. That is to say, the goals of terrorism may legitimately be freedom fighting (or self-determination), whereas the goals of human rights violations can simply never be legitimate.

My thesis and my proposals, nevertheless, maintain that federal courts should usually adjudicate terrorism as well as human rights violations. To some extent, political and ideological values and motivations underlie both human rights and terrorist offenses. The act of torture in *Filartiga* and the terrorism in *Tel-Oren* were both motivated by the defendants' politics and ideologies, for example. Indeed, it is the political nature of human rights violations that especially subjects those offenses to international attention and condemnation. So even if terrorism is somewhat more politicized than human rights violations are, all of these international offenses have political overtones and implications. The purportedly unique political character of terrorism thus should not preclude the adjudication of acts such as hijacking, hostage taking, and offenses against internationally protected persons. In addition, the modern hijacking and terrorism treaties provide federal judges with a relatively well defined conception of terrorism. These positive sources of law explicitly and extensively define the crimes at issue. The acts that constitute terrorism are as clear as those that constitute human rights violations; all of these acts are equally well codified. The hijacking and terrorism treaties also identify the criminals that may be held internationally responsible. In light of those treaties, some federal judges have already assumed jurisdiction over not only terrorist organizations, but over nation-states that sponsor terrorism.[24] Moreover, the hijacking and terrorism treaties permit, if not obligate, federal courts to adjudicate civil cases against hijackers and terrorists.[25]

As part of the United Nations' overall program against the use of force, international law has tried to curtail terrorist acts as a means of implementing even legitimate political goals. This is indicated, for instance, by recent UN instruments, promulgated with overwhelming support, condemning certain terrorist acts and appealing to nation-states to become parties to the hijacking and terrorism conventions.[26] As a diverse multinational committee on terrorism recently reported: "Certain acts are so reprehensible that they are of concern to the international community, whether they are perpetrated in time of peace or war, irrespective of the justice of the cause which the perpetrators pursue, and regardless of political motivation."[27] In the final analysis, irrespective of the goals at hand, terrorism and human rights violations often equally affect the lives and physical integrity of individual persons. Terrorism victims may be as innocent as the victims of human rights violations, and their assailants just as reprehensible and culpable.[28] It is thus fitting that federal courts should hear civil suits brought by the victims of either humanitarian violations or terrorism. Terrorism and human rights violations deserve parallel treatment in this book and in federal courts.

Finally, it cannot be pretended that the recent flurry of federal litigation will put an end to human rights violations or terrorism. Just the practical problems of service-of-process and judgment collection significantly reduce the utility of the human rights and terrorism cases. Nevertheless, the adjudication of these lawsuits, at least incrementally and in conjunction with other legal strategies, lends support to the enforceability of human rights and terrorism norms. As with all important social and legal movements, the human rights and antiterrorism platform must receive juridical support to flourish. And only by studying and thus understanding this new genre of civil litigation can the human rights and terrorism cases correctly advance the values of peace and human dignity.

I

Judicial Authority
in the National System

International law is part of our law, and must be ascertained and administered by the courts of justice of appropriate jurisdiction as often as questions of right depending upon it are duly presented for their determination.

Justice Gray, *The Paquete Habana*, 175 U.S. 677, 700 (1900)

The greater the degree of codification and consensus concerning a particular area of international law, the more appropriate it is for the judiciary to render decisions regarding it.

Justice Harlan, *Banco Nacional de Cuba v. Sabbatino*,
376 U.S. 398, 428 (1964)

In the modern age, humanitarian and practical considerations have combined to lead the nations of the world to recognize that respect for fundamental human rights is in their individual and collective interest. Our holding today, giving effect to a jurisdictional provision . . . , is a small but important step in the fulfillment of the ageless dream to free all people from brutal violence.

Judge Kaufman, *Filartiga v. Pena-Irala*, 630 F.2d 876, 890 (1980)

We will teach [Fawaz Yunis and other terrorists] a lesson far beyond what the threat of force could convey. We will get them on our turf: On the law.

Noel Koch, former head of Pentagon's Counterterrorist Unit,
U.S. News & World Report 26 (Sept. 12, 1988)

CHAPTER 1

Foreign Relations as Shared Federal Relations: Eighteenth-Century Prologue

America's independence in 1776 meant not only liberation from one foreign nation, but new obligations to all others. As a member of the international community, the Confederacy was bound by the existing law of nations. The Confederacy also soon would make treaty commitments to other nations on a variety of important subjects. Meeting those responsibilities would be critical to the development of successful foreign relations, especially given the wary existence of a nation in infancy.

Federalism: National versus State Control

The question thus arose of how to satisfy America's treaty commitments. Under the Articles of Confederation, which created neither an executive nor a judiciary of which to speak,[1] Congress was given the national government's primary international responsibilities. Congress was empowered to declare war, send and receive ambassadors, enter into treaties, grant letters of marque and reprisal, and appoint courts to try pirates.[2] The states, however, also were afforded quite similar authority over international matters. The states could establish embassy relations with foreign nations at home and abroad, enter into treaties, and even engage in war, although Congress's consent to each of those activities was usually necessary.[3] Therefore, while Congress was to conduct foreign relations for the national government, the several states were permitted substantial authority to deal independently with foreign nations.

It was soon evident that this arrangement was not up to the task of guarding the United States' international obligations and foreign relations. Simply put, the deficiencies stemmed from unilateral state action negatively affecting foreign affairs and Congress's feebleness in responding to those problems. Rather than articulating the Confederacy's foreign policy through a single voice, the individual states conveyed mixed messages to foreign sovereigns. The states even violated the Confederacy's treaties and, against the law of nations, failed to give special protection to foreign dignitaries invited by Congress.[4] Without departments to adjudicate and redress such offenses, the weak central government's verbal retorts were ineffective. Indeed, the Confederacy's main defect, wrote James Madison, was its inability to "cause infractions of treaties, or of the law of nations to be punished," and thus "particular States might by their conduct provoke war without control."[5]

Such problems were a motivating force behind the Constitutional Convention of 1787, aimed at establishing a truly strong national government.[6] Running rampant through both the Federalist Papers and the Convention's records is the idea that the new federal government must correct the Confederacy's foreign affairs defects. As Federalist John Jay succinctly put it: "It is of high importance to the place of America that she observe the laws of nations . . . and . . . it appears that this will be more perfectly and punctually done by one national Government than it could be . . . by the thirteen separate States."[7] Accordingly, when the various plans were presented at the Constitutional Convention, a burning question concerned each scheme's international ramifications. For instance, when considering and eventually rejecting the New Jersey plan, Madison poignantly inquired:

> Will it prevent those violations of the law of nations [and] of Treaties which if not prevented must involve us in the calamities of foreign wars? The tendency of the [s]tates to these violations has been manifested in sundry instances. The files of Congs. contain complaints already, from almost every nation with which treaties have been formed. Hitherto indulgence has been shewn to us. This cannot be the permanent disposition of foreign nations. A rupture with other powers is among the greatest of national calamities. It ought therefore to be effectually provided that no part of a nation shall have it in its power to bring them on the whole. The existing confederacy does not sufficiently provide against this evil. The proposed amendment to it does not supply the omission.[8]

Such sentiments produced a constitution significantly strengthening the central government's powers over foreign affairs. While the states continued to influence foreign affairs through their representation in Congress, their individual meanderings in the international arena were stopped. Under article I, section 10 of the Constitution, states specifically are prohibited from entering into treaties and engaging in war with foreign nations. Other provisions implicitly preclude states from maintaining embassy relations with foreign nations and carrying on foreign relations.[9] Those powers are exclusively delegated to the federal government's legislative and executive branches. In addition, the new federal government was given remedial authority to redress international law violations, including those that state governments commit. This result satisfied the wishes even of someone ever-cautious about strong central governance, Thomas Jefferson: "My general plan would be to make the States one as to everything connected with foreign nations."[10]

"Federalism"— the relationship between and relative authority of the federal and state governments — was further altered by the Constitution's supremacy clause. The Articles of Confederation contained a precursor to the supremacy clause. As the Articles provided: "Every state shall abide by the determinations of . . . congress assembled, on all questions which by this confederation are submitted."[11] That provision was intended to confer supreme national authority over certain legal issues, international questions ostensibly among them. The provision was without bite, however, owing to its lack of concreteness and the absence of federal enforcement machinery. In order to ensure that federal legal authority thereafter would be paramount, some delegates to the Constitutional Convention went so far as to propose that military force be used against states that took action or maintained laws in contravention of national legislation and treaties.[12]

A more moderate, though still effective, supremacy clause was eventually adopted to replace its early counterpart. Article VI, section 2 of the Constitution specifies that the "Constitution, . . . the Laws of the United States . . . and all Treaties made, or which shall be made, under the Authority of the United States, shall be the supreme Law of the Land." In the hierarchy of American law, treaties, the most prolific source of international law, are thus superior to inconsistent state laws and behavior. The supremacy clause is silent about sources of international law other than treaties. Nevertheless, it is now accepted or assumed that the phrase "Laws of the United States" tacitly includes all of the international law that the federal government recognizes. For instance, customary law, international law's second most prominent source, is viewed as part of, or similar to, federal common law.[13] Customary law thus also is supreme. Other nontreaty legal sources — from general principles of international law, to binding United Nations resolutions, to federal judicial precedent on international issues — are likewise superior to contravening state acts.[14] Adding to the supremacy clause's efficacy, the provision concludes that "the Judges in every State shall be bound [by federal law], any Thing in the Constitution or Laws of any State to the Contrary notwithstanding." State judges periodically may still misconstrue international law, but the federal judiciary, which was virtually nonexistent under the Confederation, possesses appellate jurisdiction to correct state court errors.[15] Therefore, from the coalescing of limited state jurisdiction and the supremacy clause, foreign relations are federal relations, and international law is supreme national law. This constitutional achievement led the Supreme Court to conclude broadly, in a 1937 case upholding an international compact over inconsistent New York State policy: "[I]n respect of our foreign relations generally, state lines disappear. As to such purpose the State of New York does not exist."[16]

Connecting that conclusion to the present subject, it is evident that international human rights and terrorism fall within the ambit of federal authority. The globe's human rights and terrorism concerns are properly addressed by the national government, and the laws and principles regulating those problems are national in scope and supreme. While that proposition may seem straightforward, federalism remains essential to delineating federal court authority. Indeed, federalism concerns will repeatedly be important to our discussion of human rights and terrorism, dictating expansive federal court jurisdiction in that context. Perhaps the most significant point to be made is that if federal court jurisdiction does not extend over a human rights or terrorism case, state courts are the only forum available to adjudicate that action in the United States. That result would be anathema to the prevailing intentions of the Constitution's framers: "If we are to be one nation in any respect, it clearly ought to be in respect to other nations."[17]

Distribution of Federal Authority: A Primer on
Congressional and Presidential Powers

Although the Articles of Confederation centered national foreign affairs authority in the solitary Congress, the Constitution distributes that authority among the three branches of the federal government. The distribution of international authority includes express, implied, and even vague and debated powers. While some federal powers are distinctly within the province of one branch, others are shared. As with all subjects of federal control, the delimitation and commingling of foreign affairs and international law jurisdiction within the national government is encompassed by the rubrics of "separation of powers" and "checks and balances." In order to evaluate judicial authority in the federal system over international cases, we should first briefly describe the executive and legislative branches' international authority.

Congress and the president possess vast authority relating to the nation's international concerns. Under article I, section 8 of the Constitution, Congress is empowered, for instance, to "provide for the Common Defence" (clause 1); "to regulate commerce with foreign Nations" (clause 3); to establish naturalization rules (clause 4); "[t]o define and punish Piracies and Felonies committed on the high Seas, and Offenses against the Law of Nations" (clause 10); "[t]o declare War, grant Letters of Marque and Reprisal, and make Rules concerning Captures on Land and Water" (clause 11); and to raise and maintain armies and a navy (clauses 12 and 13).[18] Several of those powers were previously subject to the concurrent jurisdiction of the Confederacy and the individual states. Of course, by its nature, only the Constitution's "great outlines [are] marked, its important objects designated, and the minor ingredients which compose those objects [must] be deduced."[19] Congress's express international authority is augmented by at least the implied authority that clause 18 permits; that clause allows for the enactment of any laws that are "necessary and proper for carrying into Execution the foregoing Powers."[20]

Article II of the Constitution delineates the executive department's authority. Although Congress is the nation's legislative body, the president's international lawmaking authority at least equals Congress's. The president is empowered to negotiate and make treaties (section 2, clause 2), ranging from bilateral trade and arms agreements to multilateral human rights and terrorism conventions. Since treaties become law only with the Senate's advice and consent, the president and Senate share control over treaties, with each checking and balancing the other.[21] Treaties are the only international compacts that the Constitution explicitly mentions. But presidents, from Washington to Bush, have entered into "executive agreements" with foreign sovereigns on myriad subjects,[22] recently including human rights and terrorism.[23] The president plays a further legislative role regarding customary international law, that is, the general and consistent practices of nation-states, which they follow by a sense of legal obligation (*opinio juris*).[24] The executive department, with its numerous agencies at home and abroad, may significantly influence customary law[25] on all subjects, including human rights and terrorism.[26] Apart from the president's international lawmaking authority, article II confers other powers intimately linked with foreign relations: acting as the commander-in-chief of the Army and Navy (section 2, clause 1); appointing ambassadors and consuls to other nations, with the Senate's advice and consent (section 2, clause 2); and receiving foreign ambassadors and public ministers (section 2, clause 2). Of course, the president must faithfully execute federal laws (section 3), including international law. Moreover, the president's foreign affairs powers are not, in either constitutional theory or reality, tightly limited to those that article II expressly sets forth. Whatever unwritten foreign relations powers that the Congress has claimed, the president has claimed more.[27]

From this primer on congressional and executive foreign affairs authority, what lesson relevant to human rights and terrorism should be brought to the subsequent discussions of federal judicial authority? To be sure, the president's and the Congress's vast powers over international law and foreign relations encompass the subjects of human rights and terrorism. Accordingly, an analysis of federal court jurisdiction over human rights violations and terrorism must take into account the substantial authority of the judiciary's coordinate branches. Arguments about the appropriate scope of judicial authority must recognize and be reconciled with legislative and executive efforts in the human rights and terrorism arena. Judicial participation in that arena, however, may often further the goals of the political branches. Particularly when this is true, the federal judiciary acts in concert with the executive and legislative branches to redress human rights violations and terrorism. This idea may remind one of Justice Jackson's famous concurrence in the "*Steel Seizure Case*": "While the Constitution diffuses power . . . , it also contemplates that practice will integrate the dispersed powers into a workable government. It enjoins upon its branches separateness but interdependence, autonomy but reciprocity."[28] That opinion concerned presidential versus congressional authority. But its underlying thesis — that the powers of one federal department "are not fixed but fluctuate, depending upon their disjunction or conjunction with those of" the other departments[29] — is also relevant to the judiciary's authority vis-à-vis the president and the Congress. Hence by assuming jurisdiction over civil cases, federal courts may sometimes help to implement the political branches' human rights and antiterrorism agenda.

Federal Judicial Authority over Cases with International Components

That the president and the Congress possess broad powers, moreover, should not suggest that the federal judiciary is without its own jurisdiction in all or most cases involving international law or affecting foreign relations. To the contrary, the Constitution's drafters contemplated an important role for federal courts in cases containing international components. Even if international law is primarily composed, and foreign relations primarily influenced, by the national government's political branches, the federal judiciary legitimately participates in both processes. Such judicial participation importantly serves separation-of-powers concerns and actually helps to satisfy the nation's international commitments.

Constitutional Antecedents

The Articles of Confederation created very limited national judicial authority. Only parts of three articles bore any relation to judicial power, and such authority was limited to specific and discrete cases: those involving piracy, admiralty issues on appeal, and interstate border disputes.[30] Even that narrow authority was underutilized.[31] Independent state courts thus handled the great bulk of the nation's adjudication, including most international law disputes and cases possibly influencing foreign affairs. As with the legislative function, the Confederacy's adjudicatory shortcomings posed serious foreign relations difficulties for post-Independence America.

Most basically, international law issues demanded a forceful and uniform judicial response. The varied and even parochial judgments of separate state courts could hardly meet the nation's international law commitments. John Jay, as Publius, explained:

[U]nder the national government, treaties and articles of treaties, as well as the laws of nations, will always be expounded in one sense, and executed in the same manner—whereas adjudications on the same points and questions, in thirteen States . . . will not always accord or be consistent; and that as well from the variety of independent courts and judges appointed by different and independent governments, as from the different local laws and interests which may affect and influence them.[32]

Apart from their disparate interpretations of substantive international law, state judicial institutions sometimes displayed an inability or unwillingness to provide effective remedies even for significant violations of the law of nations.[33] The federal government was virtually powerless to remedy such offenses. Blackstone's influential eighteenth-century treatise identified "[i]nfringement of the rights of ambassadors" as a principal offense against the law of nations.[34] Especially at that point in history, the maintenance and improvement of intercourse among nation-states depended upon the physical presence of ambassadors in foreign nations. The host nation had a special obligation to protect ambassadors and other foreign dignitaries and to provide a judicial remedy for violations of ambassadorial rights.[35] The host was also obliged to ensure the "safe-conduct" (or passport) of ambassadors and other invited guests.[36] According to Blackstone, violations of safe-conducts were another principal law of nations offense.

The national government was aware of such obligations, but without sufficient adjudicatory authority itself to ensure that those commitments were met. Instead, under a 1781 resolution, the Continental Congress recommended that the several states punish violations of the law of nations, including transgressions of ambassadorial rights and safe-conducts.[37] It was resolved, moreover, that each state should create or designate a specific tribunal "with power to decide on offences against the law of nations."[38] As recommended, such tribunals would have not only criminal jurisdiction, but also civil jurisdiction over "suits to be instituted for damages by the party injured."[39] With only one exception, however, the states did not establish the specific adjudicative machinery that the resolution proposed.[40] That the states remained unwilling, and the federal government unable, to remedy law of nations violations was highlighted by a few causes célèbres, concerning the rights of foreign dignitaries.

The first, occurring in Pennsylvania in 1784, involved an assault and battery committed against Francis Barbe Marbois, the secretary of the French legation and consul general to the United States. Both in the street and in the French ambassador's home, Marbois was attacked by another Frenchman, the Chevalier de Longchamps.[41] After his arrest and release on bail, de Longchamps threatened to assassinate Marbois. Naturally, the Marbois affair greatly angered France and other foreign nations; it was viewed as concerning the entire diplomatic corps. Certain foreign ministers "demanded that Congress declare the law of nations to be part of the common law of each of the states."[42] Of course, the Continental Congress lacked both adjudicative and enforcement power to respond effectively to the Marbois affair. Congress could only offer a reward for de Longchamps's apprehension and weakly press Pennsylvania to try the offender in state court. It was resolved that the Confederation's secretary for foreign affairs apologetically explain to Marbois the "difficulties that may arise on this head from the nature of a federal union in which each State retains a distinct and absolute sovereignty in all matters not expressly delegated to Congress leaving them only that of advising in many of those cases in which other governments decree."[43] Fortunately for the nation, de Longchamps was eventually prosecuted and sentenced in Pennsylvania state court.[44] While the Congress, in an understatement, "highly approved" of Pennsylvania's trial, the national government's incompetence in the matter was threateningly clear.

Similar ramifications sprang from an incident in New York City in 1788. A constable entered the house of P. J. Van Berckel, the Dutch ambassador, and arrested the ambassador's servant.[45] As a member of the Dutch mission, the servant should have been immune from criminal arrest and prosecution. In addition, the ambassador's residency should have been inviolable by the local police. Van Berckel was quite right when, in a protest to John Jay, the foreign affairs secretary, he characterized the arrest as "a most notorious and direct violation of the rights of nations."[46] Jay's response explained that "the federal Government does not appear . . . to be vested with any judicial powers competent to the Cognizance and Judgement of such Cases."[47] Jay was limited to trying to convince the New York governor to bring judicial proceedings against the constable, "as Justice and the Law of Nations may require."[48] The foreign affairs dangers of the Van Berckel incident were abated when the constable was finally charged and prosecuted in New York court for having violated the law of nations, as incorporated in the common law.[49]

The Marbois affair, preceding the Constitutional Convention, and the Van Berckel incident, occurring during the ratification process, displayed the need for federal court jurisdiction over cases touching upon foreign relations. Even if Pennsylvania and New York, after some prodding, had made criminal jurisdiction available, civil jurisdiction was also necessary in such instances.[50] In either the criminal or civil context, a failure to provide justice to any alien, not just a foreign dignitary, was and is considered to violate international law.[51] Hamilton argued that, since the "denial or perversion of justice by the sentences of courts, as well as in any other manner, is with reason classed among the just causes of war, it will follow that the federal judiciary ought to have cognizance of all causes in which the citizens of other countries are concerned."[52] To Hamilton, that conclusion was true whether a case involving an alien arose under substantive international law or purely domestic law.[53] As he reasoned: "So great a proportion of the cases in which foreigners are parties involve national questions that it is by far most safe and most expedient to refer all those in which they are concerned to the national tribunals."[54]

In sum, the Confederation's judicial deficit confronted the Constitutional Convention with the need for centralized and consistent judgments on international law issues; the need for federal civil and criminal jurisdiction over international law violations; and the need for federal court jurisdiction over cases involving foreign dignitaries and all other aliens. While those needs arose over eighteenth-century international law violations and foreign relations concerns, they remain quite relevant to modern offenses, such as human rights violations and terrorism, and current foreign affairs.

The Constitutional Outline

Enter the Constitution, which is quite responsive to the problems experienced under the Articles of Confederation. Article III of the Constitution outlines the permissible scope of federal court jurisdiction. Judicial authority is vested in the Supreme Court and those inferior federal courts that Congress establishes. Certain aspects of that authority are particularly significant to international disputes.

Article III extends judicial power over "all Cases, in Law and Equity, arising under the Constitution, the Laws of the United States, and Treaties made, or which shall be made" (section 2, clause 1). That clause, in essence, provides federal jurisdiction over all cases "arising under" international law. Granted, the clause mentions only treaties and not all international law sources. But related to the prior discussion of the supremacy clause,[55] article III's reference to "the Laws of the United States" is read to encompass all nontreaty sources of international law, including customary law, that the United States recognizes. "Arising-under jurisdiction" is sometimes called "federal question jurisdiction," since every case invoking that jurisdiction somehow involves questions of federal law. The Supreme Court is permitted only appellate jurisdiction over federal question cases (section 2, clause 2), although original or appellate jurisdiction over such cases may be granted to the lower federal courts. Owing to Anti-Federalist sentiments, however, federal question jurisdiction is not exclusive to the federal judiciary.[56] Nothing in article III stops the state courts from maintaining concurrent jurisdiction to adjudicate cases involving international law, although such decisions may be subject to federal appeal.

Article III also extends jurisdiction where the nature of the litigants — and not necessarily the nature of the substantive dispute — may affect foreign relations. Federal jurisdiction is available in actions involving nation-states, foreign dignitaries, and other aliens. More specifically, jurisdiction exists over "all Cases affecting Ambassadors, other Public Ministers and Consuls; . . . to Controversies between . . . Citizens of different States; . . . and between a State, or the Citizens thereof, and foreign States, Citizens or Subjects" (section 2, clause 1). The Supreme Court possesses original jurisdiction over those cases affecting ambassadors, public ministers, consuls, and states; it has appellate jurisdiction in all other cases (section 2, clause 2). The lower federal courts may hold original or appellate jurisdiction over all of the cases mentioned. Again, however, due to concessions made to the Anti-Federalists, federal jurisdiction is not exclusive over any of these types of cases.[57] Even though, as Hamilton suggested, cases involving foreign dignitaries and other aliens may have serious foreign affairs ramifications,[58] article III does not prohibit concurrent state court jurisdiction over those cases. Nevertheless, the concurrent jurisdiction represents a significant step forward from the virtually exclusive state court jurisdiction existing over such cases under the Articles of Confederation.

The correlation between the Confederacy's foreign affairs problems and article III's solutions is quite evident. Under article III, federal jurisdiction is assured over cases involving international law and cases involving foreign actors. Both the Marbois and the Van Berckel incidents, for example, if litigated today in civil suits, would fall within the federal jurisdiction that article III contemplates.[59] The plaintiffs' access to justice in those cases would not be limited to state tribunals. Article III, then, exemplifies the transformation of federalism governing international matters; it is part and parcel of the federalization of such matters in the national government. Just a brief glance at article III indicates the judiciary's substantial role in the federal governance of situations having international implications; federal jurisdiction over international cases may stem from the nature of a claim or from the character of the litigants. That role should prove relevant to today's international disputes — modern human rights and terrorism cases.

Conclusion

Within the domestic legal system, the Constitution is the ultimate source by which to evaluate judicial authority over any set of disputes. This early chapter, therefore, has briefly offered a constitutional backdrop for evaluating federal court jurisdiction over human rights and terrorism cases. Providing a federal forum for those disputes is counseled by the very reason compelling the Constitutional Convention to have federalized international matters: ensuring uniform, appropriate, and effective resolution of issues having important foreign relations implications for the nation. With their vast authority, the president and the Congress often resolve such issues. Article III, however, expressly contemplates the judiciary's involvement in cases arising under international law or involving foreign actors. The judiciary is not an impotent, but an important, component in the federal control of international matters. Judicial involvement may even reinforce the political branches' international commitments, including the president's and the Congress's condemnation of terrorist and human rights offenses. In sum, federalism compels the national government's attention to those offenses; article III may permit the federal judiciary's jurisdiction over those offenses; and the separation of powers may actually support the judiciary's adjudication of those offenses.

CHAPTER 2

From Constitutional to Statutory Authority: Federal Jurisdiction over Nonstate Offenders

Federal court jurisdiction depends not only upon the constitutional allocation of power. It also depends upon Congress's statutory implementation of the judicial authority that article III permits. With the relevant historical and constitutional lessons at our disposal, we next connect constitutional authority with statutory authority. That linkage may be illuminated by first thinking conceptually about "jurisdiction."

Conceptualizing "Jurisdiction"

"Jurisdiction" should not be a euphemism for naked power. It, instead, should refer to the legitimate authority that different institutional actors possess, as distributed systemically. As we have seen, the delimitation of international law and foreign affairs authority within the United States encompasses both "vertical" and "horizontal" dimensions. Those dimensional terms help to describe the relative authority, that is, the jurisdiction, of different entities and thus the way in which a system seeks to achieve order.[1] They here, in part one, define federal adjudicatory authority within the United States legal system; they later, in part two, will define domestic authority within the international legal system.

As between the federal and state governments, international authority is mostly ordered vertically. The Constitution centralizes almost all foreign affairs matters in the federal government and denotes international law as federal and supreme. State authority, as a result, is vertically or hierarchically subordinate and almost nonexistent in international matters. Of course, the states may assert some unchecked influence on foreign relations. State courts, for example, are not prohibited from

26

maintaining concurrent jurisdiction over judicial disputes involving ambassadors and other aliens; unless a federal question is involved, a state
court decision in such a matter is not appealable in federal court.[2] In
this regard, labeling the federal-state jurisdictional relationship as "vertical" evokes a faulty metaphor. Nevertheless, for the most part, the Constitution's federalism vertically orders international authority, with the
states being subject to federal control.

International authority within the federal government is, by contrast,
less vertically and more horizontally arranged. To be sure, the three federal branches do not possess the same international authority, either
qualitatively or quantitatively. Assuming that quantification is possible,
the executive, legislative, and judicial branches probably rank first, second, and third, respectively, in international jurisdiction. The legislature
and even more so the judiciary are vertically subordinate to the president
on a short-term basis. The Congress and the federal judiciary, nevertheless, do possess substantial authority over international law and over matters affecting foreign relations. For instance, the Senate gives its advice
and consent to the treaties that the president has negotiated. The courts,
in turn, have jurisdiction over cases arising under those treaties.[3] As Alex-
ander Hamilton wrote, it "seems scarcely to admit of controversy that
the judicial authority of the Union ought to extend . . . to all those cases
which arise out of the laws of the United States,"[4] including international
law. "If there are such things as political axioms," continued Hamilton,
"the propriety of the judicial power of a government being *coextensive*
with its legislative may be ranked among the number."[5] The panoply of executive, legislative, and judicial international authority, of course, was
described earlier. The present point is simply that the sharing, checking,
and balancing of that authority demonstrates that the federal government's international jurisdiction is not vertically deposited in just one or
even two branches. Rather, to a significant degree, international jurisdiction is distributed horizontally among all three branches. Therefore,
while federalism and separation-of-powers relationships may both involve a mixture of vertical and horizontal components, the former is
ordered vertically in most situations, whereas the latter is structured
horizontally in many instances.

Connecting Constitutional and Statutory Jurisdiction

The Constitution mandates the legal or structural arrangements between the federal and state governments and among the federal branches. Regarding any international subject or dispute, therefore, jurisdiction must be grounded in the Constitution's vertical and horizontal parameters of legal order. Jurisdiction otherwise amounts to whatever power is simply grabbed by any legal institution. As Justice Chase once concluded: "Without jurisdiction the court cannot proceed at all in any case. Jurisdiction is power to declare the law, and when it ceases to exist, the only function remaining to the court is that of announcing the fact and dismissing the cause."[6] Hence in every legal context, an institution's jurisdiction depends upon the authority that a system distributes to it. Jurisdiction "is both an assertion and a circumspection, both a practice and a syntax."[7]

Under our conceptualization of jurisdiction, if the victims of human rights violations or terrorism seek a federal judicial response, they must demonstrate that the national system's vertical and horizontal beams support the federal court's authority. There are two principal components to such a demonstration, both bottomed on the Constitution: a federal jurisdictional statute, enacted pursuant to article III, must encompass the case; and if such jurisdiction exists, certain judicial abstention doctrines must not counsel against exercising that authority. Both the statutes and legal doctrines are essentially the means or techniques by which to assess the legitimacy and appropriateness of federal court jurisdiction in any given case; they are the vehicles by which the courts' constitutional authority is defined and demonstrated in concrete situations. The jurisdictional statutes primarily reflect the federalism boundaries of judicial authority, while the judicial abstention doctrines fixate upon judicial authority under the separation-of-powers guidelines.

We will begin by considering certain federal jurisdictional statutes. Determining whether those statutes cover a particular human rights or terrorism case, however, is neither mechanically simple nor simply mechanical. The proper construction of the relevant statutes is particularly subject to debate in this gestational set of human rights and terrorism cases. The indeterminacy of most mechanical analyses leads not only to debate about what *is* the scope of federal court jurisdiction, but also about what it *should be*. At the risk of bastardizing Rawls, jurisdictional statutes perhaps contain a sense of "reflective equilibrium": they are supposed to represent conclusions about judicial authority, an aggregate of the vertical aspects of constitutional order.[8] But when leading to debated or debatable results, jurisdictional statutes become vehicles for reassessing, for reflecting about, the constitutional system's pursuit of international justice. The Constitution thus provides a starting point, not a talisman, for defining federal statutory jurisdiction.

Tying these abstractions to the more concrete, statutory jurisdiction will be examined first over nonstate defendants—e.g., individuals, government officials, terrorist groups, and hijackers—and second over nation-state defendants. The initial inquiry considers three provisions of title 28 of the United States Code: sections 1332 and 1350 are logically considered together in this chapter, to be followed by a consideration of section 1331. The second inquiry considers only one statute, the Foreign Sovereign Immunity Act of 1976. Each statute confers original subject matter jurisdiction to the federal district courts.[9] We will eventually propose legislative prescriptions, recommending revisions to those statutes.[10]

Diversity and Alienage Jurisdiction

Under 28 U.S.C. section 1332(a), district courts have jurisdiction over any civil action where the amount in controversy exceeds $50,000 and is between "(1) citizens of different States; [or] (2) citizens of a State and citizens or subjects of a foreign state."[11] Section 1332(a)(1) confers "diversity jurisdiction," that is, jurisdiction where the plaintiff and defendant hail from diverse (or different) states. Section 1332(a)(2) confers "alienage jurisdiction," that is, jurisdiction where a party is an alien from a foreign nation. Putting aside the amount-in-controversy requirement, both the diversity and alienage provisions draw upon the constitutional language found in article III, section 2, clause 1.[12] Both jurisdictional bases have been in place since the first congressional enactment conferring federal jurisdiction, the Judiciary Act of 1789.[13]

Diversity Jurisdiction

The original purpose of diversity jurisdiction was straightforward: protecting out-of-state litigants from the favored treatment that a state tribunal might show toward citizens of the state in which the court sits.[14] Relatively disconnected with local concerns and interests, federal district courts are to provide an alternative and hopefully unprejudiced forum for disputes between diverse parties. The federal alternative provides nationalized and perhaps more capable adjudication. Although the qualitative differences between state and federal adjudication may not be as great today as they were originally, the lack of parity between federal and state courts, and the potential for bias by the latter, is still deemed sufficient enough for diversity jurisdiction to continue to exist.[15] The assumed need for diversity jurisdiction has overridden modern calls for the abolition of section 1332(a)(1).[16] Granted the statute sometimes provides federal jurisdiction over garden-variety contract and tort cases, normally thought to be the stock of state court adjudication. But the provision exists due to the federal interest in the fair and uniform judicial treatment of diverse citizens; that interest is important to the vertical relationship between federal and state court authority over this group of cases.

As might be expected, diversity jurisdiction has not proved relevant in most human rights and terrorism cases. Terrorist acts and violations of basic human rights, thankfully, are not often committed by one United States citizen against another. Of course, one could conjure up examples of diverse United States citizens committing egregious, internationally condemned offenses against each other: an anti-Semite from one state sets out to destroy the Jewish population in the metropolitan area of another state; a police officer tortures and brutalizes a person of color from another state, hoping to elicit a confession. Assuming a sufficient amount in controversy, such victims of genocide and torture (or their survivors) could invoke the federal district court's diversity jurisdiction.

International norms would have been violated in such hypothetical cases. Section 1332(a)(1) jurisdiction, however, is not predicated upon the nature of the dispute, but on the character of the parties. It thus simply could be alleged that the defendants were responsible for the domestically recognized torts of assault, battery, or wrongful death. Whether an individual commits a human rights violation or commits negligence in driving a car, diversity jurisdiction exists in any $50,000 tort case between diverse parties. International normative standards, then, are not central to diversity cases. The presence of an international law violation is critical to other jurisdictional statutes, such as the alien tort and federal question provisions, soon to be encountered; but it is not really pertinent to a section 1332(a)(1) tort case between diverse parties.[17]

Hence diversity jurisdiction is not a particularly relevant match with human rights violations and terrorist acts. Modern cases involving those acts typically have not postured United States citizens — from either the same or different states — against each other. But even if a human rights or terrorism case between diverse American citizens were to occur, the case simply would sound in tort, thus rendering the international law violation as subsidiary to the district court's authority.

Alienage Jurisdiction

The alienage statute is one of various jurisdictional provisions aimed at conferring federal court authority over cases specifically involving aliens.[18] The constitutional antecedents of those provisions — including the incidents surrounding Marbois and Van Berckel's servant — were set out earlier.[19] At least in certain situations, the federal government aspires to provide justice to aliens, lest the states fail to do so. Although that aspiration is motivated by foreign relations concerns, alienage jurisdiction is limited by the amount-in-controversy requirement.[20] (Perhaps as with all else in the world, even worthy foreign relations intentions have a bottom line: $50,000.) Section 1332(a)(2) is also limited to provide judicial authority where there is an alien on only one side of a lawsuit, but not on both sides. That conclusion was crystallized in an 1809 Supreme Court opinion, *Hodgson and Thompson v. Bowerbank*.[21] The opinion, terse and until recently obscure, apparently rests upon a simple reading of article III's language: "The judicial Power shall extend . . . to Controversies . . . *between* a State, or the Citizens thereof, *and* foreign States, Citizens or Subjects."[22] Alienage jurisdiction thus exists only over suits between a United States citizen and an alien. Since all federal laws must be reconciled with the Constitution, the alienage statute can go no further than to grant jurisdiction where a foreigner and citizen litigate against each other.[23] *Hodgson's* validity has recently been confirmed.[24]

Hence in a human rights or terrorism case, where an alien and a United States citizen are opposite parties, alienage jurisdiction may exist. So an American soldier held hostage in Iran could sue the individual

Iranian captors under alienage jurisdiction, perhaps claiming a violation of the Hostage Convention.[25] Likewise, a Sandinistan soldier allegedly injured by war crimes that United States citizens committed or
directed hypothetically could sue the citizens under alienage jurisdiction.[26] In such alienage cases, the fact that the defendants had violated
international law, as well as municipal law, would actually be unessen-
tial to the district court's jurisdiction. Alienage jurisdiction, like diversity
jurisdiction, is premised upon the litigants' identity (and the requisite
amount in controversy), not upon the nature of the plaintiff's cause of
action. If the requirements of alienage jurisdiction were met, the American plaintiff's suit might simply sound in the domestic tort of false imprisonment; the Sandinistan's suit might sound in the domestic tort of
battery.

The American and Nicaraguan soldiers' suits, however, do not typify
the human rights and terrorism cases commenced during this decade.
Since alien is usually postured against alien, federal courts are without
authority in most current disputes under alienage jurisdiction. Therefore, in *Filartiga v. Pena-Irala*,[27] the Paraguayan torture victim's representatives could not successfully invoke the federal court's alienage jurisdiction over the Paraguayan torturer. And a Tibetan tortured by a national
of the People's Republic of China, for example, could not utilize section
1332(a)(2).[28]

This lack of federal authority over alien-versus-alien suits may contradict the ultimate intention behind alienage jurisdiction — ensuring
United States justice to aliens. If federal jurisdiction is unavailable, a
state court may mistreat an alien on one or both sides of a lawsuit, potentially injuring the United States' foreign relations. The possibility surely
exists that a state court might favor one alien over another: one Mexican
over another, for instance, or a Canadian over a Libyan. Where an alien
sues another alien, however, it is probably less likely that a state court
will show bias against an alien than it would if the alien were countering
a United States citizen. In addition, although foreign relations are federal relations, it has been noted that the federalism relationship is not
entirely vertical in all matters having international implications. Here,
as the Federalists and the Anti-Federalists compromised, the constitutional allocation of international authority does not empower the federal
judiciary to act simply on the basis of aliens suing aliens. In the universe

of disputes conceivably affecting foreign relations, cases simply between aliens—but not necessarily involving foreign dignitaries as parties and not necessarily involving international law violations on the merits— may be the least needy to keep within federal authority.

Although *Hodgson*'s rule may occasionally have a negative impact on foreign relations, the Constitution's alienage provision does not support section 1332(a)(2) jurisdiction over suits between aliens. Such cases are thus subject to state control, despite the more normal vertical structuring of federal foreign relations, unless they can ride an alternative jurisdictional vehicle. We turn, then, to the Alien Tort Statute, a jurisdictional cousin of section 1332. It hopefully will prove more hospitable and relevant to human rights and terrorism cases than either alienage or diversity jurisdiction have been.

Alien Tort Statute

The Alien Tort Statute burst into prominence in 1980, when used to uphold jurisdiction in *Filartiga v. Pena-Irala*.[29] Codified as 28 U.S.C. section 1350, the statute confers original district court jurisdiction over "any civil action by an alien for a tort only, committed in violation of the law of nations or a treaty of the United States."[30] Truly a case of landmark proportions, *Filartiga* ruled that the statute provides federal judicial authority when the mistreatment of aliens anywhere in the world constitutes a violation of the law of nations or a United States treaty.[31] The court more particularly held that "deliberate torture perpetrated under color of official authority violates universally accepted norms of human rights, regardless of the nationality of the parties. Thus, whenever an alleged torturer is found and served with process . . . , 1350 provides federal jurisdiction."[32]

The *Filartiga* decision caused lawyers (litigators, commentators, lawmakers, judges, all) to ponder the Alien Tort Statute's past, present, and future. Hardly a new jurisdictional vehicle, the Alien Tort Statute originally was a provision in the Judiciary Act of 1789. But unlike the diversity and alienage bases of jurisdiction, countlessly invoked by lawyers on a daily basis, the Alien Tort Statute was apparently utilized in only twenty-one published cases in the 190 years prior to *Filartiga*.[33] That dearth of precedent, coupled with the Judiciary Act's lack of legislative history, led a noted judge to conclude: The statute is "a kind of legal Lohengrin; although it has been with us since the first Judiciary Act . . . no one seems to know from whence it came."[34]

Early disuse has led to modern misuse. Federal judges, bemoaning the Alien Tort Statute's obscurity and unfamiliar language, have diversely interpreted and misinterpreted section 1350. The statute's inconsistent application has been aggravated by numbers: section 1350 has figured significantly in more than twenty post-*Filartiga* cases.[35] Although the statute is pertinent to all disputes when a tort and any international law violation is committed against an alien, the bulk of the recent litigation has centered upon heinous human rights violations and depraved terrorist attacks. So, too, the perplexity over the statute has centered upon human rights violations and terrorist attacks. Some cases involving these offenses have prospered under the Alien Tort Statute, while other indistinguishable cases have not.

Regarding the very relevant Alien Tort Statute, the task, therefore, is to examine the statute's origin and purpose and to analyze its contents and requirements. We must consider how the statute horizontally and vertically channels federal judicial authority over human rights violations and terrorism — and how the statute might be revised to rechannel that authority. Of course, the ultimate inquiry concerns the statute's ability to fulfill the dream of which the *Filartiga* court spoke: "Our holding today, giving effect to a jurisdictional provision enacted by our First Congress, is a small but important step in the fulfillment of the ageless dream to free all people from brutal violence."[36]

Origin and Purpose

A common tool for fathoming a statute's contemporary meaning is to discover the law's origin. Unfortunately, the Alien Tort Statute's legislative history is scant. Senate debates over the Judiciary Act of 1789 were not transcribed, and the correspondence between the senators who drafted the Judiciary Act barely mentions the Alien Tort Statute. Records were kept of the House debates, but they are bereft of reference to the Alien Tort Statute.[37] Despite such a lack of evidence, however, other legislative and historical sources may be tied together to reveal the Alien Tort Statute's derivation. The statute should be viewed as one piece in the Judiciary Act's mosaic of federal authority over matters having international ramifications.

The embarrassing situations involving Marbois and Van Berckel undoubtedly were fresh in the minds of the Alien Tort Statute's drafters.[38] Those who responded to such national dilemmas overlapped with those who authored the Judiciary Act of 1789. Indeed, early drafts of the Judiciary Act contained various references, some more explicit than others, to the Marbois and Van Berckel disputes. For example, a bill that the Senate drafting committee prepared would have vested the Supreme Court with "original, but not exclusive jurisdiction of all suits for trespasses brought by ambassadors, other public ministers or consuls, or their domestics or domestic servants."[39] This provision, although never adopted in quite that form, appears to be a direct response to the matters involving Marbois and Van Berckel. It would have conferred Supreme Court authority over civil cases involving those matters, since the plaintiffs would have been an ambassador or an ambassador's servant and the actions would have sounded in trespass or tort.

As finally conceived, however, the Judiciary Act established the circuit courts as the principal trial courts — rather than the Supreme Court, as in the Senate bill,[40] and rather than the district courts, as is the case today. The circuit courts were provided with alienage jurisdiction under section 11, but that provision would not have supported jurisdiction in a civil action brought by Marbois, since Marbois and his assailant both were Frenchmen. The alienage provision would have supported civil jurisdiction in a suit commenced by Van Berckel or his servant against the New York constable, but only if $500 or more, the amount in controversy then required, was at stake in the case. Under section 13 of the Judiciary Act, the Supreme Court ended up with "original, but not exclusive jurisdiction of all suits brought by ambassadors, or other public ministers, or in which a consul, or vice consul, shall be a party."[41] That provision would have offered judicial authority in Marbois's case, but not in Van Berckel's, unless Van Berckel rather than his servant was named as plaintiff. In fact, section 13 never allowed original jurisdiction when an alien other than a dignitary was injured by a law of nations violation, even when it was a violation such as piracy.[42] Section 13 also was problematic in that the Supreme Court's abilities and workload have caused it to serve the nation better as an appellate court than as a trial court. Such were the shortcomings of the circuit courts' alienage jurisdiction under section 11 and the Supreme Court's original jurisdiction under section 13. Those provisions did not adequately respond to the foreign affairs implications of the Marbois and Van Berckel scenarios or, more generally, of cases containing international components.

Enter the Alien Tort Statute. As first enacted, in language virtually unchanged today, section 9 of the Judiciary Act provided that the district courts "shall . . . have cognizance, concurrent with the courts of the several states, or the circuits courts, . . . of all causes where an alien sues for a tort only in violation of the law of nations or a treaty of the United States."[43] This provision is the apparent successor to the jurisdictional grant contained in the Senate draft mentioned above.[44] But somewhat broader in scope than the early bill, section 9 recognizes federal judicial authority where any alien — not just a dignitary or a dignitary's employee — sues any defendant, who or which has committed any tort and a violation of the law of nations or a United States treaty. On its face, section 9 also provides jurisdiction irrespective of the location of the defendant's behavior, within or without the United States. Section 9 is surely more expansive than would have been necessary to provide federal civil jurisdiction over the Marbois and Van Berckel disputes, even if its creation was instigated by such incidents. The Alien Tort Statute, therefore, more than helped to fill the lacunae left by sections 11 and 13 of the Judiciary Act in matters involving aliens and international law violations.

The derivation of a few particular aspects of the Alien Tort Statute deserves further mention. To begin, although the statute established an important basis of federal jurisdiction, it did not create exclusive federal authority. Aliens injured by a tort and an international law violation still could (and can) sue their assailants in state court. The nonexclusivity of federal jurisdiction was probably due to a compromise forged between the Federalists and the Anti-Federalists. International authority, again, is not purely vertically arranged, and each provision in the Judiciary Act represented some negotiation between those favoring an omnipotent federal government and those favoring states' rights. As Professor Warren's seminal study concluded, the Judiciary Act "cannot be properly understood, unless it is realized that it was a compromise measure, so framed as to secure the votes of those who, while willing to see the experiment of a Federal Constitution tried, were insistent that the Federal Courts should be given the minimum powers and jurisdiction."[45] As a result, the Alien Tort Statute contains concessions to the Anti-Federalists: its federal grant is not exclusive and it confers authority over alien tort actions only when involving international law violations.

Another noteworthy aspect of the statute is its requirement that aliens may sue "for a tort only." Since the Marbois and Van Berckel situations had involved torts, the statute's drafters were cognizant of the particular need for federal jurisdiction over civil tort claims. In addition, they may have specifically intended to exclude jurisdiction over commercial actions. Subsequent to the American Revolution, many British merchants pursued commercial claims on debts owed by American citizens.[46] The Britons' ability to collect those debts in state courts should have been ensured by the Definitive Treaty of Peace, which concluded the war and which provided: "Creditors on either Side shall meet with no lawful Impediment to the Recovery of the full Value in Sterling Money of all bona fide Debts heretofore contracted."[47] That treaty obligation was not kept, however, as the courts of the several states imposed obstacles to the British commercial claims.[48] Such treaty violations were anathema to the nation's foreign policy and represented the very type of problem that cried out for vertically ordered federal judicial authority.

Nevertheless, the states' hostility to the British claims raged strongly enough that the Alien Tort Statute was drafted to exclude all commercial claims. The statute's "tort only" language is peculiar to section 9 of the Judiciary Act. But without that limitation, British creditors would have been able to invoke the Alien Tort Statute. Their commercial actions would have been governed by the law of merchants, which in 1789 was subsumed by the law of nations.[49] Hence without the tort limitation, the federal courts would have had jurisdiction over violations of the law of merchants and probably would have treated the British merchants more fairly than the state courts did. The federal courts still possessed alienage jurisdiction over suits between Britons and Americans. Recall, however, that the alienage provision contained a $500 amount-in-controversy requirement. The majority of British claims fell below that amount,[50] a fact not lost on the Judiciary Act's principal drafter, Oliver Ellsworth, a former state court judge.[51] Hence with section 9's tort limitation and section 11's amount-in-controversy requirement, British commercial claims were relegated to unfriendly state courts. While explicit legislative evi-

dence on this point does not exist, it seems quite likely that the antagonism against the British commercial suits was a limiting force against the
Alien Tort Statute's otherwise expansive contours.

Constitutional Basis

In instances where an alien sues a United States citizen, jurisdiction
under the Alien Tort Statute is legitimate under the same constitutional
provision that supports alienage jurisdiction.[52] Such suits, after all, are
simply suits between the citizens of a state and citizens of a foreign nation-state. In the more typical human rights or terrorism cases between
two aliens, however, support must come from article III's arising-under
clause.[53] All section 1350 tort actions are predicated upon the existence
of a treaty violation or a law of nations violation. As such, they may be
characterized as arising under treaties (which article III specifically mentions) or as arising under the law of nations (which article III impliedly
includes).[54] Just as a case involving a violation of one's freedom of speech
arises under the Constitution, a case involving a violation of one's human
rights arises under international law.

It has been suggested by certain judges and commentators, however,
that section 1350 cases between aliens may be illegitimate under article
III. Their argument is that "if the substantive law of the *situs* defines the
cause of action, federal courts cannot constitutionally hear the case under
article III, since it does not 'arise under' the Constitution or the laws or
treaties of the United States."[55] For example, if Paraguayan law is applied
to the merits of a case between Paraguayans concerning an offense in
Paraguay, the case does not arise under international law, and the federal judiciary is without arising-under authority.

That argument is wrong. As elaborated upon below, the Supreme
Court has very broadly interpreted article III's arising-under component.[56]
That component legitimizes federal jurisdiction where a federal question merely "forms an original ingredient" in a case.[57] Since every section
1350 recipe involves a preliminary determination of whether the law of
nations or a treaty was violated — clearly, federal question ingredients —
every case arises under federal law for purposes of article III. As the *Filartiga* court correctly concluded, applying Paraguayan law on the merits "would not retroactively oust the federal court of subject matter juris-

diction, even though plaintiff's cause of action would no longer properly be 'created' by a law of the United States."[58] The Supreme Court tacitly validated this conclusion in *Verlinden B.V. v. Central Bank of Nigeria.*[59] In *Verlinden,* the Supreme Court held that jurisdiction under the Foreign Sovereign Immunities Act of 1976 (FSIA) is constitutional where an alien corporation sues an agency of a foreign government on a contract claim to be governed by the Netherlands law.[60] That case arose under federal law because, at the jurisdictional level, or at "the threshold of every action . . . against a foreign state, the court . . . must apply the detailed federal standards set forth in the [FSIA]".[61] Although foreign law (not federal law) would be applied on the merits, *Verlinden,* like every FSIA case, also raised "sensitive issues concerning the foreign relations of the United States, and the primacy of federal concerns is evident."[62] That *Verlinden* involved the FSIA does not distinguish it from a case involving the Alien Tort Statute, since cases under either jurisdictional grant must satisfy the very same article III arising-under standard. Just as every FSIA case presents a preliminary jurisdictional question of federal statutory law, every section 1350 case presents a preliminary jurisdictional question of federal international law, even if federal law is not applied on the merits. FSIA and alien tort cases also jointly raise sensitive foreign relations issues.[63] Questions regarding section 1350's constitutionality, therefore, should be dashed.

Alien Torts, Human Rights, and Terrorism

Now versed in the Alien Tort Statute's historical and constitutional background, we may turn more specifically to *Filartiga* and its checkered progeny. The modern human rights and terrorism cases may be organized most profitably according to four questions that have arisen repeatedly in the disagreement over section 1350.

1. Do individuals and other nonstate actors have the legal personality to possess rights and responsibilities under humanitarian and terrorism law? Intrinsic to the *Filartiga* debate is the issue of whether individual plaintiffs may hold legal rights under international law. The reciprocal side of this issue is whether individuals and other nonstate defendants may have legal responsibilities under international law. Essentially, this threshold inquiry concerns the concept of "legal personality," denoting the legal capacities that different legal actors possess. Legal personality is a concept perhaps analogous to jurisdiction, in that each essentially delineates the authority, rights, and responsibilities of distinct entities in a given system.

The concern over legal personality was forcefully raised in *Tel-Oren v. Libyan Arab Republic*, a case briefly noted earlier.[64] *Tel-Oren* involved terrorism committed on the Israeli coast in 1978. Thirteen members of the PLO, allegedly with Libya's support, landed by boat in Israel and began "a barbaric rampage" along the main highway between Haifa and Tel Aviv.[65] Having seized two civilian buses, a taxi, and a passing car, the PLO held hostage and tortured scores of civilians on one of the buses, which they drove south toward Gaza. When the bus was eventually stopped by Israeli police, the PLO terrorists opened fire on their hostages and finally destroyed the bus with hand grenades. Thirty-four adults and children lay dead and eighty-seven others had been seriously wounded when the smoke cleared. While the majority of victims were Israeli citizens, a few were American and Dutch nationals. The torture and terrorism victims or their representatives sued the PLO, Libya, and other defendants in the district court for the District of Columbia, with the alien plaintiffs primarily alleging jurisdiction under the Alien Tort Statute. The district court dismissed the case, ruling that neither the Alien Tort Statute nor any other provision supported subject matter jurisdiction in relation to the PLO; that Libya had sovereign immunity from the suit; and that claims against other defendants had not been substantiated.[66] The court of appeals unanimously affirmed, although each member of the three-judge appellate panel saw fit to explain the "correct" rationale for the dismissal.

The concept of legal personality figured importantly in two of the judges' separate opinions, each concurring in *Tel-Oren*'s dismissal. Judge Robert Bork's opinion is predicated upon a "statist perspective" of international law.[67] Under this view, nation-states are the exclusive actors and "subjects" of international law; nonstate entities, including individuals, are the mere "objects" of international law, bereft of any legal capabilities. Judge Bork drew upon Lassa Oppenheim's early appraisal: "[T]he Law of Nations is primarily a law for the international conduct of states, and not of their citizens. As a rule, the subjects of the rights and duties arising from the Law of Nations are States solely and exclusively."[68] Under this doctrine, even rights that benefit individuals are held corporately by the individual's state of nationality. This results, in Judge Bork's words, in a "general relegation of individuals to a derivative role in the vindication of their legal rights."[69] Hence, "[i]nternational law typically does not authorize individuals to vindicate rights by bringing actions in either international or municipal tribunals."[70] This is so, thought Judge Bork, even though he recognized that the Alien Tort Statute was intended to confer individual remedies for at least the eighteenth century's principal law of nations violations — piracy, offenses against ambassadors, and violations of safe-conducts.[71]

Judge Bork's opinion also cited *Dreyfus v. Von Finck*,[72] which the Second Circuit Court of Appeals decided before *Filartiga*. *Dreyfus* involved a claim by a Swiss citizen, a Jew and former German resident, against West German citizens for the wrongful confiscation of property in Nazi Germany. Alleging jurisdiction under the Alien Tort Statute and other provisions, the plaintiff claimed that the defendants had violated the law of nations and several instruments to which the United States was a party or an adherent. The court dismissed the suit, partly based upon a legal personality rationale.[73] It held that international law sources do not usually confer individual legal rights. Moreover, the court opined that the law of nations "deals primarily with the relationship among nations rather than individuals. 'It is termed . . . International law . . . because it is relative to States or Political Societies and not necessarily to individuals, although citizens . . . of the earth are greatly affected by it.'"[74]

While Judge Bork's opinion and *Dreyfus* focused upon the legal personality and rights of individual plaintiffs, Judge Edwards's separate opinion in *Tel-Oren* emphasized the legal personality and responsibilities of nonstate defendants.[75] Judge Edwards was the only *Tel-Oren* judge to embrace some of *Filartiga*'s tenets, including the ability of individuals to sue when tortured or injured by certain other international law violations. But the cases were distinguishable, he argued, due partly to the different legal obligations that the different defendants owed. The police officer in *Filartiga* committed torture on Paraguay's behalf, "*under color of state law,* although in violation of it."[76] On the other hand, in *Tel-Oren,* the PLO, "not a recognized member of the community of nations," had acted in a private capacity.[77] Judge Edwards was unwilling "to venture out of the comfortable realm of established international law—within which *Filartiga* firmly sat—in which states are the actors."[78] He recognized that individuals, acting in even a purely private capacity, had been held liable for a few universally condemned offenses, such as piracy.[79] Judge Edwards concluded, however, that "non-sovereign torture" (i.e., torture that a nation-state has not encouraged or supported) lacked sufficient international condemnation to justify the PLO's responsibility. This conclusion partly derived from reading the Torture Convention restrictively to encompass only acts that nation-states sponsor.[80] Although Judges Edwards and Bork significantly disagreed about several aspects of the *Tel-Oren* case, their opinions jointly demean the legal personality (rights and responsibilities both) of nonstate actors under international law.

The statist perspective of international law, however, suffers from significant flaws. To some extent, *Filartiga* and every other decision sustaining jurisdiction under the Alien Tort Statute has necessarily recognized the problems with that perspective. At the outset, the rigid subject-object dichotomy between sovereign and nonstate actors is simplistic and misleading. Legal personality need not be an all-or-nothing concept; rather, it is a relative concept. As Professor Lissitzyn aptly observed two decades ago, legal personality is "merely a short-hand symbol which denotes that an entity is endowed with *some* legal capacities, but does not tell us what particular capacities it has. Different kinds of 'international persons' have different capacities."[81] Actually, in every system, domestic and international, legal personality is relativistic.[82] That nation-states are the primary actors in the international legal system, having full legal personality, does not dictate that all other actors are without any legal personality. Evidence instead suggests that individuals and other nonstate actors possess at least basic legal rights and responsibilities under international law; nonstate actors are legal subjects, not objects, where those rights and duties are at issue.

The very drafters of the Alien Tort Statute obviously understood that individuals are capable of possessing enforceable rights under international law. After all, the statute was created in response to international law offenses committed against individuals; it confers judicial authority where an alien alleges a tortious injury flowing from a law of nations or treaty violation. Judge Bork actually acknowledged the statute's derivation when he spoke of Congress's intent to provide tort jurisdiction over eighteenth-century international law violations.[83] But if individual aliens were capable of suing for piracy, offenses against ambassadors, and violations of safe conducts two hundred years ago, why are they without the same legal capacity to sue for human rights violations and terrorism today? The Alien Tort Statute's broad language surely does not permit such a reading. The modern international offenses that directly affect and injure individuals are the counterparts of the eighteenth-century offenses. Since individual rights are at the forefront of the global agendum even more today than in the eighteenth century or at any other historical point, it is dubious to argue that individuals presently are less capable of possessing international rights than in the past. Judge Bork's position cuts against the vertical federalizing intentions of the statute's framers, leaving section 1350 virtually without relevance to any current international disputes.[84] Under this position, when the victims of modern offenses seek solace from a court in the United States, it must be from a state court, not from a federal court; the Alien Tort Statute thus will not correct the federalism problems that the Marbois and Van Berckel incidents posed.

Even though Judge Bork utilized *Dreyfus* to support his statist degradation of individual rights, *Dreyfus*, if ever correct, is old law. The *Filartiga* decision, handed down after *Dreyfus* by the same circuit court, recognized that individuals possess certain international legal rights, including the right to be free from torture. This conclusion, according to *Filartiga*, renders *Dreyfus* to be "clearly out of tune with the current usage and practice of international law."[85]

Filartiga's rejection of *Dreyfus* is punctuated by *Forti v. Suarez-Mason*,[86] a 1987 California federal district court case. *Forti* was commenced by Argentine citizens residing in the United States, suing for themselves and on behalf of their families. They had been subjected to acts of torture, summary execution, prolonged arbitrary detention, and governmentally caused "disappearance." Those human rights violations were committed under the direction of the defendant, a former Argentine general, who had overseen Buenos Aires during Argentina's "dirty war" and when it was declared to be in a "state of siege."[87] The court sustained jurisdiction under the Alien Tort Statute. In doing so, it rejected the statist view of international law. The court summarily found "defendant's contention that the law of nations extends only to relations between sovereign states [to be] unsupported."[88] The defendant had relied upon *Dreyfus*. But the *Forti* court relied upon the later case of *Filartiga*, in which the Second Circuit "expressly disavowed" *Dreyfus*'s view of legal personality, "at least insofar as it concerns individual injuries under the international law of human rights."[89] Hence, as *Forti* decided, reliance upon *Dreyfus* is misplaced, and *Filartiga*'s conception of individual rights should be extended to encompass summary execution, prolonged arbitrary detention, and causing the disappearance of individuals.

Both international and domestic law support the *Filartiga-Forti* view of individual rights. Modern treaty and customary law have referred with increasing clarity to the rights that individuals hold. To take just one example, the Covenant on Civil and Political Rights ("Covenant"), which has generated customary norms recognized throughout the world, explicitly speaks in terms of individual rights. Article 6, for instance, provides that "[n]o one shall be arbitrarily deprived of his life," and article 7 provides that "[n]o one shall be subjected to torture or to cruel, inhuman or degrading treatment or punishment."[90] These provisions surely sound indistinguishable from various clauses in the Constitution's Bill of Rights that so obviously confer individual rights: the Fifth Amendment's double-jeopardy clause, for example, provides that "[n]o person shall be . . . subject for the same offense to be twice put in jeopardy of life or limb." Along with other contemporary international sources, the Covenant dispels the positivist fiction that human rights are not individual rights. And an obvious fiction it is, since individuals, not sovereigns, directly benefit when basic rights and liberties are inviolable.

Individuals also derive their legal personality from particular nations' domestic law. International humanitarian norms and values are part of the United States' federal law. Just as the government may recognize individual rights under constitutional or statutory law, it may recognize individual rights under the international norms incorporated in federal law. If the government can say that individuals have the right of free speech or the right to receive public assistance, there is nothing to stop it from saying that individuals have the right not to be tortured or summarily executed. In other words, since international law is domestic law, the federal government, like other national governments, surely can recognize and enforce individual rights when violations of that law injure private parties. The renowned British scholar Hersch Lauterpacht articulated this vision of incorporating international human rights law into domestic law: "[I]n the criticism of the doctrine that only States are subjects of international law, full use . . . [has not] been made of the fact that according to the law of many States rules of international law form part of their domestic law."[91] Hence "[t]he principle that international law is . . . part of municipal law means in effect that rights and duties created by international law are directly applicable to individuals through the instrumentality of municipal courts and that, to that extent, individuals are subjects of the law of nations."[92]

Concrete embodiments of this view are found in various federal decisions recognizing individual rights that emanate from international law, but are incorporated into federal law. These decisions include, even apart from the successful alien tort cases, *Fernandez v. Wilkinson*[93] and *Lareau v. Manson*.[94] *Fernandez* was a habeas corpus action brought by an excludable Cuban refugee who had arrived in the United States aboard the "Freedom Flotilla." He was being detained indeterminately in a maximum-security prison without bail and without having been charged with any crime in this country. At the federal district court level, it was decided that "international law secures to petitioner the right to be free of arbitrary detention and that his right is being violated."[95] While the alien's detention "cannot be said to violate the United States Constitution or our statutory laws, it is judicially remedial as a violation of international law."[96] *Lareau* was commenced by a class of inmates against prison officials, alleging that various conditions of confinement at the facility—from overcrowding to inadequate food—violated the Eighth Amendment's ban on cruel and unusual punishment and the Fourteenth Amendment's due process clause. In finding that the inmates' rights had been transgressed, the federal court utilized international law, although in a manner different from that in *Fernandez*. Following a notable judicial trend, the district court cited to international instruments, particularly the UN Standard Minimum Rules for the Treatment of Prisoners, in defining the inmates' constitutional rights.[97] Even if the international standards were not directly applicable in the case, they constituted "an authoritative international statement of basic norms of human dignity," which "are relevant to the 'canons of decency and fairness which express notions of justice' embodied in the Due Process Clause."[98]

While international individual rights in *Fernandez* were directly incorporated into federal law, the individuals' constitutional personality in *Lareau* was informed and defined by international guidelines. In its own way, each case illustrates how the domestic incorporation of international law may give rise to individual rights. Since federal law encompassing or informed by international law may embody individual legal personality, Judge Bork's statist perspective is misguided. Again, this perspective skews the federal judiciary's vertical responsibility of providing justice to foreign actors victimized by terrorism or human rights violations. As a result, the judiciary abrogates the governmental ideal of extending federal authority to international matters.

As with Judge Bork's view of individual rights, Judge Edwards's narrow view of nonstate duties somewhat similarly misses the mark. For centuries, individuals and other nonstate actors have often been held responsible for international law violations. Indeed, when Marbois's assailant was eventually brought to trial in 1784, the Pennsylvania chief justice understood that an individual is capable of violating the law of nations. Addressing the defendant in no uncertain terms, the chief justice said: "The first crime in the indictment is an infraction of the law of nations. . . . The person of a public minister is sacred and inviolable. . . . *You then have been guilty of an atrocious violation of the law of nations.*"[99] The eighteenth- and nineteenth-century case reporters also contain numerous actions against those who committed the international offense of piracy.[100] The fact that pirates are often called "stateless" emphasizes the conclusion that individuals were and are capable of violating international law. Not only do pirates act without governmental authority, but perhaps with exaggeration they are even said to lack a nationality and are thus without a state.[101] Analogously, in recent years, some federal courts, without much, if any, hesitation about legal personality, have held individuals responsible for hijacking and terrorism.[102] The majority of these hijackers and terrorists have violated international law as incorporated into federal law without sovereign support. The PLO has been stateless, in some sense, for decades. Particularly when the PLO commits offenses without the assistance of a nation-state, its international law responsibility may be analogous to that of a pirate ring.[103]

Judge Edwards erred by refusing to add nonsovereign torture to piracy and the list of other universal offenses that nonstate actors are today capable of committing.[104] Various instruments and a contextual analysis of torture evidence his error. For instance, the Covenant, which grants the right not to be tortured, explicitly prohibits any "State, *group or person*" from committing torture or any other acts prohibited by the Covenant.[105] The Covenant thus bars sovereign and nonstate actors alike from committing torture. Admittedly, a second instrument, the Torture Convention, less expressly prohibits nonsovereign torture. That Convention defines torture to include certain violent acts aimed at punishing, coercing, or intimidating a person or a third person, committed by a "*public official*" or any other "person acting in an *official capacity*."[106] This means that if, hypothetically, a Palestinian beats his wife in the West Bank, a simple battery, not international torture, has occurred. But to read the Torture Convention's definition hyperliterally, as Judge Edwards did,[107] to exclude all but sovereign-sponsored torture, seems incorrect. The PLO and other groups that commit violent offenses often act in a "public" or "official" capacity, whether or not supported by nation-states. As in *Tel-Oren*, the PLO's acts of torture were not committed in a private setting. Instead, those acts arguably satisfy the Convention's definition of torture because they were intended to intimidate Israelis and Israel on a very public level; the offenses were part of a continuous effort to coerce Israel to accept the PLO's political and international agendum. The distinction between every-day battery and international torture should depend on the *context* in which the act is committed, not simply upon *who* commits the act. Logically, battery becomes torture when committed by either nation-states or nonstate actors in a public and global context, undertaken to have international implications and repercussions.[108] Since, as noted earlier, neither the Covenant nor the Torture Convention is yet in force in the United States, the liability that those instruments encompass may be binding as a matter of customary law.

As a factual matter, the line is often gray between torture that is sovereign-sponsored and torture that is not. For example, in *Filartiga*, a Paraguayan police officer committed torture—which makes the offense seem sovereign in nature—but the torturer acted in violation of Paraguayan law and possibly even without the direct approval of his superiors—which makes the offense seem nonsovereign. In *Tel-Oren*, a nonsovereign actor committed the actual acts of torture, but Libya allegedly supported the PLO's offenses—possibly giving the torture a sovereign character. *Filartiga* and *Tel-Oren* thus may not really be factually distinguishable on the issue of whether the torture in each case was nation-state sponsored. Even more conceptually, however, the "statist line" to which Judge Edwards clings inadequately delineates between the offenses that constitute international torture and those that do not. The Covenant does not draw that line. And the Torture Convention's reference to "public" and "official" acts is not necessarily predicated upon whether an offender had the support of a nation-state. When undertaken in a political or public context, either a sovereign or a nonstate battery becomes or constitutes international torture under the Covenant and, logically, under the Torture Convention as well.

But let us even put the Covenant and the Torture Convention completely aside for a moment, in a further effort to see the forest through the trees. On a very basic level, Judge Edwards's distinction between official and nonofficial torture suffers from the weakness that any legal fiction suffers: the failure to grasp reality. Despite the statist myth, modern international law violations are simply committed by whomever (individuals, public officials) or whatever (the PLO, Libya, the Druses, the Red Brigades) commits them. When the PLO alleges that Israel has encouraged its army to commit human rights violations in the occupied territory, the response is not that Israel is without the legal personality to sponsor those offenses. In turn, when the PLO tortures Israelis, the response should not be that the PLO is legally incapable of committing such acts. Indeed, the International Military Tribunal (IMT) at Nuremberg squarely grasped the reality that individuals and other nonstate actors are capable of violating international law. Prosecuting and sentencing major war criminals, the IMT's opinion poignantly ruled: "Crimes against international law are committed by men, not by abstract [sovereign] entities, and only by punishing individuals who commit such crimes can the provisions of international law be enforced."[109] To differentiate between the war criminals and the PLO on the ground that only the Germans acted under a nation-state's authority misses the IMT's very point. Moreover, is it not conceptually illogical to view the nonstate torture victims in *Tel-Oren* as the subjects of international law and yet their nonstate assailants as objects of the law? Yet that is exactly the stance that Judge Edwards assumed by his particular combination of accepting and distinguishing *Filartiga*. If nonstate actors are capable of deriving benefits from the norm against torture (as *Filartiga* held, and Judge Edwards agreed), it follows that nonstate actors are also capable of bearing obligations under that norm (to Judge Edwards's disagreement). Benefits and obligations, rights and duties, are reciprocals, the flip sides of legal personality; it is difficult to fathom how a nonstate actor can have one without the other.

Finally, as is true of legal rights, legal duties may also be recognized as a matter of domestic law.[110] Through its incorporation of international law, federal law is free to hold individuals and other nonstate actors responsible when customary or treaty law is violated. In this way, torture, piracy, war crimes, and other fundamental offenses actually violate domestic law. Federal law defines and encompasses the legal personality of nonstate actors to commit those offenses. The panoply of international offenses that may give rise to nonstate duties and rights under domestic law will be elucidated below.[111]

Akin to the problems with Judge Bork's view of individual rights, Judge Edwards's view of individual duties undermines the Alien Tort Statute's very purpose: to ensure federal judicial authority when defendants commit a violation of international law against an alien. Just as that authority was needed in the Marbois and Van Berckel situations, in which, after all, individuals had committed international law violations, it is needed today when individuals and other nonstate actors commit human rights violations and terrorism. The Constitution's vertical federalist structure of international matters demands such federal jurisdiction over such modern violations of federal law.

2. *What elements must be established by the victims of human rights violations and terrorism for jurisdiction to exist under the Alien Tort Statute?* Assuming that individuals can sue and nonstate actors can be sued regarding international law violations, the specific language of section 1350 must be examined. Many federal judges consider the statute's phraseology to be cryptic and perplex. Their interpretative problems may legitimately stem from the statute's unfamiliar terms, sounding somewhat unorthodox to the jurisdictional ear. Or their problems may really be a smoke screen for rejecting a set of cases that they wish not to adjudicate. One judge even accused another of having intentionally misconstrued section 1350 "simply to void a statute of which he does not approve."[112] In any event, once pared of obscurity and other baggage, the statute's elements should seem rather straightforward.

The Alien Tort Statute has three requisites. Simply enough, the first is that the plaintiff must be an alien. At least this one element has not stirred any juridical confusion or debate. By definition, an alien is "any person not a citizen or national of the United States."[113] Either an individual alien or an alien corporate entity may invoke the statute. Citizens who are injured by human rights violations and terrorism, of course, must try to invoke a jurisdictional provision other than section 1350.

The alien's action must be "for a tort only, committed in violation of the law of nations or a treaty of the United States." As read by many courts and commentators, that language requires the defendant to have committed an "international tort."[114] Such a reading is typically followed by befuddlement about the meaning of the term *international tort*. An alternative and correct interpretation of section 1350, however, is that the defendant's behavior must have constituted a domestic tort (the statute's second requisite) as well as a violation of the law of nations or a United States treaty (the third requisite). Hence, rather than requiring international torts, the statute requires a domestic tort *plus* an international law violation.[115]

Even though international law permits nations to provide private remedies for certain offenses, the term *tort* does not actually exist in the international legal system. Instead, a tort is a legal construct of the Anglo-American system, conceptualized at least as early as the eighteenth century.[116] Human rights and terrorism victims, therefore, must frame their injury in terms of a tort cognizable under the law of the forum in which the federal court sits. When and if a judge adjudicates the *merits* of a case, choice-of-law principles may dictate the application of a foreign situs's tort law,[117] which may, in varying degree, be somewhat comparable to the tort law of the United States. But at the *jurisdictional level*, the victims of human rights violations and terrorism must explicitly speak of torts recognized in the United States. As a few examples of this point: torture victims would allege the torts of assault and battery; former hostages would allege the false-imprisonment tort; and representatives of perished victims would allege the tort of wrongful death.

The tortiously injured alien must additionally establish that the defendant violated the law of nations or a treaty of the United States. Read literally, the plaintiff is given two options: to allege a violation of *either* the law of nations *or* a United States treaty. But alas, both alternatives have been misunderstood.

One federal district judge wrote that "the concept of 'law of nations' is an elusive one."[118] Another concluded that even those "judicial decisions recognizing and enforcing the 'law of nations' under 1350 do not fully explain or define that phrase."[119] Although of sixteenth-century vintage, however, the law of nations has always encompassed a variety of international legal sources, applicable in the absence of a binding treaty that directly regulates a given dispute. As the Supreme Court articulated in an early piracy case: "[T]he law of nations . . . may be ascertained by consulting the works of jurists, writing professedly on public law; or by the general usage and practice of nations; or by judicial decisions recognising and enforcing that law."[120] Accordingly, aliens complaining of human rights violations or terrorism must show that customary practice, as buttressed and documented in part by judicial precedent and scholarship, prohibits the defendant's behavior. The modern law of nations against certain human rights violations and terrorist acts may also be augmented by international instruments that standing alone do not create legal obligations for the United States or other nations. Both the *Filartiga* and *Forti* courts, for instance, looked to various declarations, resolutions, and even treaties not signed by the United States in determining that the law of nations prohibited the acts at issue in those cases.[121]

Judge Bork, in *Tel-Oren*, seemed insistent upon confining the law of nations to the offenses recognized in the eighteenth century (namely, acts against ambassadors, violations of safe-conducts, and piratical acts).[122] Straitjacketing the law of nations in that manner, however, is not supported by either the Alien Tort Statute's unrestricted language or by any jurisprudence that views the law as living, breathing, and evolving. That the law of nations must be kept current has long been understood. Judge (eventually Justice) Joseph Story, for instance, observed, in an 1821 slave-trading case: "It does not follow . . . that because a principle cannot be found settled by the consent or practice of nations at one time, it is to be concluded, that at no subsequent period the principle can be considered as incorporated into the public code of nations."[123] The *Filartiga* court and others have echoed that sentiment: "[I]t is clear that courts must interpret international law not as it was in 1789, but as it has evolved and exists among the nations of the world today."[124] Construing the law of nations in its modern form and as it relates to the current litigation, there is a strong consensus that the law of nations prohibits genocide, slave-trading, apartheid, torture, murder or causing the disappearance of individuals, prolonged arbitrary detention, piracy, war crimes, hijacking of aircraft and other violent acts committed aboard aircraft, hostage taking, and offenses against internationally protected persons.[125]

There remains the option that the defendant violated a United States treaty. On its face, the Alien Tort Statute demands only that the treaty must be in force in the United States. Section 1350 ostensibly does not require the defendant to have any affiliation with a given treaty. So a citizen of a country that is not a party to a particular treaty may still be considered to have violated that treaty, for the statute's purposes. That situation does not regularly arise in human rights and terrorism cases, however, since most of the relevant treaties have garnered significant multinational support. Those treaties may also provide customary law rules for nation-states that are nonparties. The citizens of many or most nations, therefore, are regulated by the norms at hand under treaty or custom. Similarly, nonstate coalitions or groups — the PLO or the Red Brigades, for example — may violate United States treaties, at least in the sense of section 1350. It may appear paradoxical that a group that is neither recognized as a nation nor is a party to a particular treaty may violate that treaty. But especially if one sheds the statist perspective, there is logic in the idea that at least certain treaties may encompass universal norms binding upon all global actors. One is otherwise left with a true paradox: Terrorism treaties are inapplicable to nonstate terrorists; and when terrorism bleeds into torture, summary execution, and other heinous acts, the terrorists can continue to act with impunity against international law, unregulated by otherwise very pertinent treaties. Terrorism and human rights treaties should logically govern all terrorists and human rights offenders.

There is another reason why United States treaties are relevant to both nonstate coalitions and to the citizens of nonparties to a given treaty. For jurisdiction to exist under the Alien Tort Statute, the federal court first determines that the defendant has committed a tort. Since the defendant has violated a domestic legal right and owes a remedy under municipal tort law, his or her legal responsibility does not solely depend upon having violated a United States treaty. A state court would have jurisdiction over the case if the action simply sounded in tort. The fact that the defendant also violated a treaty norm, however, makes the case worthy of federal jurisdiction. Viewed in this light, a United States treaty need not even directly regulate the defendant. The treaty, instead, may represent a set of values or principles, which, if violated, gives rise to federal, not just state, jurisdiction. Hence a nonstate faction or the citizen of a nonparty may already be liable under tort law, but is subjected to federal court authority by having violated a norm or value that the federal government embraces. This point relates to federalism concerns and the vertical structuring of federal authority over the areas of international human rights and terrorism. The *Forti* court perfectly understood the propriety of federal jurisdiction in these areas:

> The international character of plaintiffs' claims may militate in favor of exercising federal jurisdiction. State common law courts can hear aliens' tort suits. . . . [But] . . . Congress intended 1350 to provide concurrent federal jurisdiction over alien tort claims alleging treaty or customary international law violations *in order to facilitate federal oversight of matters involving foreign relations and international law.* . . . Such an intent would of course be furthered by the adjudication of alien tort claims in federal district court rather than in a state court of general jurisdiction.[126]

Of course, not every United States treaty is pertinent to the Alien Tort Statute. Even though nonstate actors are not international law's mere objects, they have rights and responsibilities only under those treaties that sufficiently govern nonsovereign as well as sovereign behavior. A violation of a territorial boundary treaty or of an agreement on foreign debt repayment, for example, relates primarily to national, not private or nonstate, concerns. Normally, such treaties do not directly create enforceable rights or duties for nonstate actors[127] — even though individuals obviously implement, and receive some benefits from, those treaties. On the other hand, the Geneva and Genocide Conventions, for instance, are framed more in terms of both sovereign and nonsovereign interests. Since they have established individual rights and sovereign and nonstate responsibilities, they are applicable in alien tort litigation. Those humanitarian treaties are also "self-executing," that is, capable of being applied by a court without domestic implementing legislation. The self-executing treaty doctrine will soon be discussed.[128] It suffices presently to note, however, that any human rights or terrorism instrument relied upon under section 1350's treaty component must be self-executing. After all, since non-self-executing treaties simply command execution, they are violated only when not implemented by the nations that are parties; such violations directly relate to sovereign, not private, concerns.

Finally, while the law of nations and treaty components are separate on section 1350's face, they are, in practice, often integrated. Of the treaties most relevant to human rights and terrorism cases, the United States is a party to the Geneva, Genocide, Hague, Montreal, Hostage, and Internationally Protected Persons conventions. When a case implicates one of those specific treaties, there may actually be no reason to refer to the law of nations. Nevertheless, given the judicial uncertainty about how those treaties apply to civil disputes, judges sometimes rely upon those instruments to help evince norms that regulate private behavior under the law of nations. Although that judicial practice may benefit plaintiffs, it is often unnecessary, for reasons to be clarified further below.[129] Integrating treaties and the law of nations is appropriate, however, when a case implicates an instrument to which the United States is not a party, such as the Covenant and the Torture and Apartheid conventions. Again, it is not uncommon to inform the law of nations through instruments not directly binding upon a country. The law of nations, which binds all countries not objecting to it on a given subject, includes customary law; custom may be codified, crystallized, or created by treaties to which a country is not a party. Hence the commingling of treaties with the law of nations is jurisprudentially sound when a relevant instrument is not in force in the United States. In fact, courts in several alien tort cases have already used the Covenant and the Torture Convention to establish private rights and duties under the law of nations,[130] although none have yet used the Apartheid Convention in this fashion.

3. *When the Alien Tort Statute is invoked, how does the victim of terrorism or a human rights violation derive a cause of action?* This question, also a source of judicial infighting, concerns the derivation of the plaintiff's cause of action. The term *cause of action* (or "right of action" or "civil remedy") refers to "the alleged invasion of 'recognized legal rights' upon which a litigant bases his claim for relief";[131] it alternatively refers to the "question of whether a particular plaintiff is a member of the class of litigants that may, as a matter of law, appropriately invoke the power of the court."[132] Certain opinions have found that the Alien Tort Statute itself confers a private cause of action. For instance, in a

1907 dispute between Mexicans and an American corporation, Attorney General Bonaparte's opinion concluded that the statute provides "a right of action and a forum."[133] Likewise, a 1795 attorney general's opinion, concerning alien tort jurisdiction over United States citizens who helped attack the Sierra Leone colony and plundered private British property on the high seas, determined: "[T]here can be no doubt that . . . the individuals who have been injured by these acts of hostility have a remedy by a civil suit in the courts of the United States."[134] Several recent human rights and terrorism cases also suggest this conclusion.[135]

Conversely, other opinions have held that the Alien Tort Statute does not confer a cause of action. *Jaffee v. Boyles*,[136] a bizarre 1985 case, provides one example of this viewpoint. *Jaffee* involved an individual who had skipped bail in Florida and was allegedly kidnapped later in Canada by the defendants, including a bonding company, its officers, and the Florida state attorney's office, allegedly in violation of international law. In disavowing authority under the statute, the court held that "[t]he provisions of 28 U.S.C. (§) 1350 are jurisdictional; they do not create a cause of action for a plaintiff seeking recovery under a treaty."[137] The plaintiff, according to this view, must, instead, establish that international law itself (either the law of nations or a United States treaty) provides plaintiff with a cause of action.

We can, however, short-circuit the disagreement over the plaintiff's cause of action because it is misguided and misplaced. As a jurisdictional provision, the Alien Tort Statute does not really itself confer a cause of action; *Jaffee* is correct in this regard and the two attorney general opinions are wrong. But the statute does not require the plaintiff to establish an international law cause of action; so *Jaffee* is also incorrect. 28 U.S.C. section 1331, to be considered shortly, may require an international cause of action, since it provides jurisdiction only over cases that arise under international law.[138] So if the arising-under concept is synonymous with the cause-of-action concept, then section 1331 may require an international cause of action. Section 1350, however, does not statutorily require that plaintiff's claim arise under international law; it requires only that the defendant must have *violated* the law of nations or a United States treaty. In section 1350 cases, the victims of human rights violations and terrorism may thus derive their cause of action from domestic tort law. The tort constitutes an invasion of a recognized legal right and certifies the plaintiff's ability to invoke a state court's authority. By alleging an international law violation in addition to a tort, the plaintiff is permitted to bring the municipal-right violation to the attention of a federal court.[139]

An analogy may be made to 28 U.S.C. section 1332, which permits plaintiffs to bring garden-variety tort or contract causes of action (involving $50,000 or more) into federal court, not just state court, if the alienage or diversity requisite is met. The alienage/diversity requisite is comparable to the requirement of an international law violation in section 1350 cases, in that both signify the presence of a national interest and the propriety of a federal forum.[140] The national interest in section 1332 cases depends upon the character of the litigants, while the national interest in section 1350 cases stems from the character of both the litigants and the plaintiff's claim. As with section 1332 cases, plaintiff's cause of action in alien tort cases springs from nonfederal law, providing plaintiff with a tort right that is enforceable in state court. Authority or jurisdiction over the cause of action is also distributed to federal courts under section 1350 because the alien plaintiff has additionally been injured by a law of nations or treaty violation. The debate over plaintiff's cause of action, therefore, is misguided — since neither of the two prevailing positions is really right — and misplaced — since it is really relevant to section 1331 cases.

4. Does the Alien Tort Statute confer jurisdiction over extraterritorial acts? The statute may originally have been a reaction to incidents occurring within the United States, such as those involving Marbois and Van Berckel. Nevertheless, at least as drafted, the statute facially does not limit jurisdiction to offenses committed territorially. The drafters apparently understood that cases involving international law violations vertically belong in federal court, not state court, irrespective of the situs of the offense. Indeed, some of the earliest usages of the Alien Tort Statute involved acts occurring outside of the United States. Exemplary of this point is the Sierra Leone incident mentioned above, in which alien tort jurisdiction was said to exist over the plundering of private property on the high seas, off the coast of the African colony.[141] Moreover, the "transitory-tort" doctrine permits jurisdiction in any forum that achieves personal jurisdiction over the defendant, wherever the tort occurs. Conceivably, the drafters of the Alien Tort Statute were aware of this legal doctrine, since many were lawyers and the doctrine was recognized in the eighteenth century. Federal courts have recently cited to the transitory-tort doctrine when upholding section 1350 jurisdiction over extraterritorial human rights violations and terrorism.[142] A federal judge may decide to apply the tort law of the situs — be it Paraguayan, Argentinian, or Israeli law — when actually adjudicating the case. But this does not affect the legitimacy of subject matter jurisdiction under the Alien Tort Statute, as supported by the transitory-tort doctrine.

In short, section 1350 confers jurisdiction over extraterritorial human rights violations and terrorism. Judicial abstention doctrines, discussed below, relating to separation-of-powers concerns, may conceivably counsel a court not to exercise its jurisdiction in a particular case.[143] And federal authority must also be squared with international law's jurisdictional principles, another topic considered below.[144] Both the judicial abstention doctrines and the international principles, however, should be kept analytically separate from the availability of extraterritorial jurisdiction under the Alien Tort Statute itself. The statute arranges federal judicial authority over international claims vis-à-vis state judicial authority — and not in relation to the president or Congress (as do the judicial abstention doctrines) and not in relation to the world legal order (as do the international jurisdictional principles). Given the statute's federalism underpinnings, section 1350 should support federal court authority over international offenses occurring either within or without the United States; otherwise, such offenses may be adjudicated only in whatever state tribunal ascertains personal jurisdiction over the defendant. The key is to ensure vertical federal jurisdiction over cases involving federal interests and concerns.

Conclusion

After conceptualizing "jurisdiction" and connecting constitutional and statutory authority, we examined the first three bases of jurisdiction over nonstate offenders. The diversity and alienage statutes have not proven relevant to most of the modern human rights and terrorism cases. The Alien Tort Statute, however, should provide a jurisdictional vehicle of great utility. If pared of juridical confusion and baggage, section 1350 is actually of straightforward, although admittedly broad, proportions.

It grants judicial authority when an alien anywhere suffers from a tort and a human rights violation or a terrorist act recognized as illegal under the United States treaty or customary law. The statute's wide girth, deriving essentially from its own language, reasonably fits the vertical dimensions of federal judicial authority. Section 1350 ensures what section 1332 may often not: a federal judicial forum for cases very deserving of national and centralized adjudication. The Alien Tort Statute serves important federalism concerns and is a significant component of the judiciary's responsibility to entertain cases involving international law. Just as federal jurisdiction over the Marbois and Van Berckel situations was needed in the eighteenth century due to the normative and foreign policy implications involved, it is needed today over human rights and terrorism cases for the very same reasons.

CHAPTER 3

Federal Questions, Human Rights, and Terrorism

The difficulties (mostly unwarranted) that some judges have had with the Alien Tort Statute mandates an examination of additional bases of jurisdiction over nonstate offenders. Most pertinent among these bases is 28 U.S.C. section 1331, the statutory provision of "federal question" or "arising-under" jurisdiction. The statute confers original district court jurisdiction over "all civil actions arising under the Constitution, laws, or treaties of the United States."[1] Such jurisdiction extends not only to federal questions arising under treaties, but under all international law sources; the term *laws* in section 1331 includes customary law and other international sources.[2] Federal question jurisdiction has the advantage of being a statute more familiar to judges and lawyers than section 1350. Nevertheless, section 1331 is not without its own judicial confusion and its specific application in human rights and terrorism cases is relatively new and unchartered.

Constitutional and Statutory Overview: Judicial Myths

The language of section 1331 (just quoted) echoes section 2, clause 1 of the Constitution's judiciary article: "The judicial Power shall extend to all Cases, in Law and Equity, arising under this Constitution, the Laws of the United States, and Treaties made, or which shall be made under their Authority." That clause encompasses both original and appellate jurisdiction, although we will focus on the former. The *raison d'être* for federal question jurisdiction is to provide centralized and relatively uniform adjudication of cases arising under federal law, since the supremacy clause designates federal norms to be the "Supreme Law of the Land."[3] The federal question component is vital to article III's vertical federalism scheme: it acknowledges the need for national judicial fora when cases involve national law.

Despite the constitutional significance of federal question jurisdiction, Congress did not confer *general* original jurisdiction over *all* actions arising under federal law until 1875. The statutory lineage of section 1331, encompassing all cases arising under federal law, thus dates just over a century. Prior to 1875, the Constitution's federal question provision was relevant only where Congress granted statutory jurisdiction in more narrow contexts over specific federal questions. The courts, in these more restricted cases, had to decide whether jurisdiction was in keeping with article III's federal question provision; that is, they had to decide whether specific cases legitimately arose under constitutional, international, or other federal law.

Within such a context, the earliest significant interpretation of original federal question jurisdiction came from Chief Justice Marshall's pen in the 1824 companion cases of *Osborn v. Bank of the United States*[4] and *Bank of the United States v. Planters' Bank.*[5] A federal government bank, suing under its charter, commenced both cases. The charter gave the bank "the right 'to sue and be sued,' 'in every circuit court in the United States,'"[6] which Chief Justice Marshall viewed to be a federal jurisdictional grant. *Osborn* truly involved a constitutional law issue, whereas *Planters' Bank* involved a mere contract issue, likely to be governed by Georgia law.[7] The chief justice, nevertheless, found sufficient federal questions to uphold jurisdiction in both cases. In fact, Chief Justice Marshall broadly opined that article III would support federal jurisdiction in any case in which the bank was a party. Since a federal charter created and governed the bank's right to sue (and be sued), questions about that right would theoretically appear at the outset of every case involving the bank, to be decided by federal law. The chief justice was unconvinced that a challenge to the bank's right to sue might be resolved by a single case, never to reappear, because a defendant, hypothetically, could revive such questions in any case. Hence a federal question "forms an *original ingredient* in every cause. Whether it be, in fact, relied on or not, in the defense, it is still part of the cause and may be relied on."[8] Under *Osborn* and *Planters' Bank*, then, article III's arising-under clause supports jurisdiction whenever a federal question may theoretically arise as an ingredient of a case, even a case essentially involving nonfederal contract law on the merits.

Chief Justice Marshall's "original-ingredient test" took on increased importance when the Judiciary Act of 1875 was passed.[9] The bank's charter had provided jurisdiction only in cases involving the bank—and other enactments had also provided jurisdiction only over limited sets of federal questions—whereas the 1875 Act provided original jurisdiction over *all* cases arising under federal law.[10] The available legislative history indicates Congress's intention to grant federal question jurisdiction over the full expanse of cases that article III's arising-under clause encompasses.[11] Therefore, it would be logical to assume that section 1331 (the present statutory equivalent of the 1875 provision) provides jurisdiction over all cases hypothetically involving an original ingredient of federal law. That assumption would draw ample support from Chief Justice Marshall's still-prevailing view of article III jurisdiction; from the Congressional intent behind statutory arising-under jurisdiction; and from section 1331's own language, being nearly verbatim to that of its constitutional counterpart.

Throw logic to the wind. As Chief Justice Burger described in 1982 in *Verlinden B. V. v. Central Bank of Nigeria*,[12] *Osborn* does remain the "controlling decision on the scope of Art. III 'arising under' jurisdiction."[13] But while "the language of 1331 parallels that of the 'Arising Under' Clause of Art. III, the Court never has held that *statutory* 'arising under' jurisdiction is identical to *Art. III* 'arising under' jurisdiction."[14] According to Chief Justice Burger, the upshot is that "Art. III 'arising under' jurisdiction is broader than federal-question jurisdiction under (§) 1331."[15]

Chief Justice Marshall's approach thus applies only when the Constitution's arising-under clause is drawn upon to support a statutory grant of jurisdiction *other than* section 1331. *Verlinden* supplies an example. In that case, a Dutch corporation sued the Central Bank of Nigeria concerning a letter of credit established in connection with a cement contract. The parties' agreement had selected the Netherlands law to govern disputes over the transaction. Since the defendant was an instrumentality of the Nigerian government, subject matter jurisdiction was alleged under the Foreign Sovereign Immunities Act of 1976 (FSIA).[16] Article III's alienage provision does not support federal jurisdiction where an alien corporation sues a nation-state.[17] The issue before the Supreme Court, therefore, was whether article III's arising-under provision would support FSIA jurisdiction in the case. Answering that issue in the affirmative, Chief Justice Burger's opinion rang true to Chief Justice Marshall's opinions in *Osborn* and *Planters' Bank:* "At the threshold of every action . . . against a foreign state, the [district] court must satisfy itself that one of the [FSIA's] exceptions [to sovereign immunity] applies. . . . Accordingly, an action against a foreign sovereign arises under federal law, for purposes of Art. III jurisdiction."[18] Hence similar to *Planters' Bank*, in which Georgia contract law applied, *Verlinden* legitimized federal jurisdiction under the FSIA over a mere contract case, in which nonfederal foreign law was applicable on the merits. Preliminary jurisdictional questions about suing a foreign nation — akin to questions about a federal bank's ability to sue or be sued — justify FSIA jurisdiction under article III's arising-under clause; that conclusion disregards the source of law (federal or nonfederal) that creates the rights and remedies at issue in the case.

On the other hand, when original jurisdiction is predicated upon section 1331, an original or threshold ingredient of federal law purportedly does not suffice.[19] Something more is necessary. The Supreme Court's justification for reading section 1331 more narrowly than article III — or article III more narrowly in section 1331 cases than in bank charter or FSIA cases — is question begging and fuzzy: It is due to the "demands of reason and coherence, and the dictates of sound judicial policy which have emerged from [section 1331's] function as a provision in the mosaic of federal judiciary legislation. It is a statute, not a Constitution, we are expounding."[20]

The Court's categorical distinction between section 1331 and article III — and between section 1331 cases and other arising-under cases — is ill-guided, however. In actuality, that distinction is nothing more than a judicially created myth.[21] Distinguishing the statute from its constitutional counterpart, of course, cuts squarely against their similar language as well as against the former's legislative history. Reading section 1331 narrowly may also undermine the vertical federalism goals that the statute should serve. Moreover, no relevant, inherent difference exists between section 1331, the FSIA, or a bank's charter; each is merely a jurisdictional statute; each is predicated upon the same clause of article III. Irrespective of the particular jurisdictional statute invoked in a given case, a court should always perform the same function. It should always determine whether the *case* arises under federal law. Federal judges are thus faced with a common and consistent inquiry in every case: Do the allegations of law or fact involve an issue of national interest, encompassed by principles or norms of constitutional, international, or other federal law? The judicial standard used to answer that question need not vary depending upon the specific jurisdictional statute at issue. Whether section 1331 or another statute is invoked, a single functional analysis (be it Chief Justice Marshall's or another) may determine whether any case's factual and legal circumstances cause it to arise under federal law. Although cases vary, the meaning of "arising under" need not.[22] In short, if the mythological and skewed distinction between section 1331 cases and other arising-under cases is discarded, it can be seen that federal questions are federal questions are federal questions.

The Supreme Court, however, does not seem poised to give up its distinction between section 1331 cases and other arising-under cases. So rather than directly criticize that dichotomy any further, we, instead, will try to analyze what section 1331 requires beyond an original ingredient of federal law. That analysis, unfortunately, is not simple. Courts and commentators alike consider the section 1331 caselaw to be a morass. By the Supreme Court's own admission (or fault), "the statutory phrase 'arising under' . . . has resisted all attempts to frame a single, precise definition for determining which cases fall within, and which cases fall outside, the original jurisdiction of the district courts."[23]

The thorny task, therefore, is to try to give some organization to the section 1331 caselaw. Human rights and terrorism cases must then be analyzed under the conceptual framework that will be constructed. Our analytical framework, admittedly, will be innovative, but it does draw support from the caselaw. Within that framework, we will demonstrate that jurisdiction under 28 U.S.C. section 1331 has been recognized over four conceptual genuses of disputes.[24] The first to the fourth genuses generally move from narrow to broad interpretations of arising-under jurisdiction; in fact, the final species of the caselaw is reminiscent of the purportedly inapposite original-ingredient test. The more specific organizing principle concerns the relationship between the notion of a "cause of action"— the buzzwords for federal question jurisdiction — and "positive" federal law. As we move through the genuses, the plaintiff's cause of action becomes increasingly removed from positive federal law, although section 1331 jurisdiction remains legitimate. While the genuses sometimes intersect and sometimes contradict, each is constitutionally supportable and each extends federal question jurisdiction over at least certain human rights and terrorism cases. Of course, determining how those cases interface with the four genuses is the ultimate goal. For the reasons mentioned earlier, we will argue for expansive federal question jurisdiction equally over human rights violations and terrorism. The comparable nature of human rights and terrorist offenses makes federal adjudication appropriate over all of these acts, subject to the terms of whatever treaty is relevant to a given case.

First Genus: Causes of Action under Positive Federal Law

Section 1331 jurisdiction exists over the first genus of cases where plaintiff's cause of action derives from positive federal law. "Positive law" here encompasses constitutional, federal statutory, and international law, in comparison to the judicially formulated sources that will be considered under the second genus.[25] Justice Holmes's 1916 opinion in *American Well Works Company v. Layne and Bowler Company*[26] provides the origin of the first genus. Although that case involved certain business torts to be governed by Arkansas law, it also involved an essential issue of federal patent law. Despite that federal issue, Justice Holmes rejected statutory arising-under jurisdiction because Arkansas law provided the plaintiff's cause of action. Justice Holmes opined: "A suit arises under the law that creates the *cause of action*."[27] Hence at least in this genus, arising-under jurisdiction must be predicated upon a federal cause of action, not upon an Arkansas or other nonfederal cause of action. *American Well Works* thus put distance between statutory arising-under jurisdiction and Chief Justice Marshall's conception of constitutional arising-under jurisdiction, the latter of which requires only a federal question or issue, not a federal cause of action.

Apart from whatever other infirmities it suffers, the *American Well Works* approach has proven to be problematic because it fixates upon the term *cause of action*. As the Supreme Court has remarked: a "'cause of action' may mean one thing for one purpose and something different for another";[28] and "[o]ne of the most theory-ridden of legal concepts is a 'cause of action.'"[29] Essentially, one amorphous term (cause of action) defines another (arising under). About the best one can do, therefore, is to focus upon a few of the more accepted definitions of *cause of action*, adhere to those definitions, and apply them to human rights and terrorism cases.

In the 1979 decision of *Davis v. Passman*,[30] a Fifth Amendment case in which a woman lost her job to a man due to sexism, the Supreme Court identified two definitions of "cause of action." That term, first, may *"refer roughly to the alleged invasion of 'recognized legal rights' upon which a litigant bases his claim to relief."*[31] Apparently, according to this definition, plaintiff must possess only a *right* under positive federal law for section 1331 jurisdiction to exist.

Davis's second definition corresponds to the *"question of whether a particular plaintiff is a member of the class of litigants that may, as a matter of law, appropriately invoke the power of the court."*[32] This definition is applied particularly liberally when constitutional law is at issue in a given case. Although the Bill of Rights does not expressly allow individuals to invoke federal jurisdiction, "[a]t least in the absence of 'a textually demonstrable constitutional commitment of [an] issue to a coordinate political department,'" courts should *"presume* that justiciable constitutional rights are to be enforced through the courts."[33] This is particularly true regarding litigants who "have no effective means other than the judiciary to enforce these rights."[34]

When the positive law involved in a case is other than constitutional law — that is, when federal statutory law or international law is relevant — federal law may either explicitly or implicitly authorize an individual to invoke judicial authority, thus satisfying the second cause-of-action definition. Little confusion should ensue when federal law explicitly confers plaintiff's cause of action. But when the relevant federal law is primarily criminal or regulatory in nature, courts must determine whether the drafters implicitly intended to confer a private cause of action for civil litigation. In making that determination, courts may focus upon four criteria connected to legislative intent, as enunciated in *Cort v. Ash*:

First, is the plaintiff "one of the class for whose *especial* benefit the statute was enacted," . . . that is, does the statute create a *federal right* in favor of the plaintiff? Second, is there any indication of legislative intent, explicit or implicit, either to create such a *remedy* or to deny one? . . . Third, is it consistent with the underlying purposes of the legislative scheme to imply such a *remedy* for the plaintiff? . . . And finally, is the cause of action one *traditionally relegated to state law*, in an area basically the concern of the States, so that it would be inappropriate to infer a cause of action based solely on federal law?[35]

In summary form, the first of those criteria refers to the implication of a federal *right*, while the second and third consider whether federal law implies a *remedy*. Federalism concerns underlie the final criterion of whether to imply a private cause of action. In applying those criteria, however, the Supreme Court does not require evidence that Congress, in enacting a statute, "actually had in mind the creation of a private cause of action," since under that requirement, "[t]he implied cause of action would be a virtual dead letter."[36]

Human Rights and Terrorism Cases
under Davis's First Definition

How do human rights and terrorism cases interface with the *American Well Works* genus of section 1331 jurisdiction? Under *Davis's* first definition of cause of action, federal question jurisdiction would seem to exist straightforwardly over many or most of those cases. Since the first definition fixates simply upon the legal right that was violated, jurisdiction exists whenever the plaintiff possesses an international law right that the federal government recognizes.[37]

Individual rights are primarily recognized under treaties or from combinations of treaty, custom, and other international legal sources. Initially, we should focus upon the International Covenant on Civil and Political Rights ("Covenant") and the Torture Convention, each of which clearly provides that individuals themselves possess legal rights.[38] (Other human rights and terrorism treaties — which less explicitly acknowledge individual rights — are considered below under *Davis's* second definition to determine whether they imply a private cause of action.) Article 6 of the Covenant, for instance, provides that "[n]o one shall be arbitrarily deprived of his life"; article 7 provides that "[n]o one shall be subjected to torture or to cruel, inhuman or degrading treatment or punishment"; and article 8 provides that "[n]o one shall be held in slavery." The Torture Convention speaks somewhat less explicitly of an individual right not to be tortured and more in terms of a criminal prohibition of torture. Nevertheless, the Torture Convention goes on, as does the Covenant, to oblige the parties to provide judicial recourse to the victims of torture and other human rights violations.[39] This obligation obviously indicates that the victims must possess individual rights that they can enforce. After all, possessing a right is preliminary to possessing a remedy; there is no point in conferring a remedy upon individuals unless it is first assumed that individuals also hold rights. Therefore, individuals, at a minimum, clearly possess the human rights that the Covenant and Torture Convention recognize.

Those international rights, however, must also be enforceable directly and specifically under the United States' federal law for section 1331 jurisdiction to exist. This requires human rights victims to clear two hurdles.

Initially, it must be shown that the Covenant and the Torture Convention are "self-executing." The self-executing treaty doctrine concerns whether a treaty, in whole or in part, is complete and may be applied by a court without further implementing legislation.[40] When treaties are heavily relied upon to establish customary norms, it is possible that only self-executing treaties can give rise to self-executing customary law that individuals can directly enforce in court. Fathoming whether an instrument is self-executing depends upon the treaty's language; the nature of the rights and duties that the treaty encompasses; the treaty makers' intentions; and whether the parties are just encouraged or are actually mandated to comply with the treaty's provisions.[41] Under those considerations, the norms that the Covenant and the Torture Convention encompass appear to be self-executing. There is, to begin, a presumption that treaties are self-executing, unless the contrary intention is clearly shown.[42] The instruments' very language illuminates the absence of such a contrary intention; the instruments acknowledge that individuals hold certain fundamental rights. The Covenant provisions quoted above, for instance, are every bit as self-executing as the constitutional provision adjudicated in the *Davis* case itself, the Fifth Amendment: "No one shall be . . . deprived of life, liberty, or property, without due process of law."[43] Indeed, the very same style of language is used in the Constitution and the Covenant. As Oscar Schachter has concluded, many of the Covenant's provisions "are capable of direct application by the courts . . . without any legislative action."[44] The same is true regarding the Torture Convention. The parties, moreover, are not just permitted, but are obligated to comply with the norms in those instruments. In other words, the instruments recognize individual rights, and the parties must enforce those rights. The Covenant and the Torture Convention do require the parties to adopt whatever domestic legislation is necessary to implement those instruments.[45] This requirement, however, does not broadly render the instruments to be non-self-executing because such legislation must be created only to the extent necessary. Where criminal and civil statutes, such as section 1331, are already in place to enforce the relevant norms judicially, new legislation is unnecessary.[46]

The second hurdle for human rights victims is that the United States is not a party to either the Covenant or the Torture Convention. In 1988 President Reagan transmitted the Torture Convention to the Senate for its advice and consent,[47] and the United States may well become a party to the Torture Convention. In the meantime, however, if the Covenant's and the Torture Convention's substantive norms are to raise federal questions, they must enter federal law through alternative international law sources.

Such norms are part of the United States' customary international law. According to the American Law Institute's *Restatement (Third) of Foreign Relations Law (Restatement)*, customary law prohibits torture, genocide, slavery, murder, inhuman or degrading treatment or punishment, systematic racial discrimination, and causing the disappearance of individuals.[48] The United States, in the *Restatement*'s view, is subject to those customary norms due partly to its support for the Universal Declaration of Human Rights.[49] Along with a plethora of other resolutions and pronouncements, the Declaration "creates an expectation of adherence," according to the court in *Filartiga v. Pena-Irala*, "and 'insofar as the expectation is gradually justified by State practice, a declaration may by custom become recognized as laying down rules binding upon the States.'"[50] Although the Torture Convention was just in draft form when *Filartiga* was decided, commentators' statements and various instruments, even though not independently conclusive or binding on the United States, collectively indicated a customary norm against torture recognized under federal law.[51]

Customary human rights law, moreover, may even derive from instruments to which the United States is not a party. Drawing upon the lexicon of the *North Sea Continental Shelf Cases*, the Covenant and the Torture Convention may codify, crystallize, and even create customary law.[52] Certain provisions in the Covenant and the Torture Convention may have codified or crystallized the post–World War II practice condemning crimes against humanity, including the Allies' prosecution of those crimes. Through its instrumental involvement in that postwar customary law development, the United States clearly indicated its intention to recognize as legally binding certain principles that the instruments now contain. Rather than objecting to those principles, the nation has indicated an affirmative *opinio juris* as to those principles. The Covenant and the Torture Convention also expanded the quantity and quality of human rights norms addressed at the war's conclusion. That expansion may be viewed as having generated human rights norms "which, while only conventional or contractual in . . . origin, [have] since passed into the general *corpus* of international law, . . . so as to have become binding even for countries which have never, and do not, become parties to [a] [c]onvention."[53] The Vienna Convention on the Law of Treaties also recognizes this jurisprudential concept: "Nothing . . . precludes a rule set forth in a treaty from *becoming binding upon a third state [a non-party] as a customary rule* of international law, recognized as such."[54] Hence, just as if the United States was a party to the Covenant and the Torture Convention, it may be bound by those instruments' norms under customary law.[55] Indeed, in certain instances, the failure to grant "an effective remedy under [domestic] law for violation of the customary law of human rights might itself be evidence that a violation of rights is state policy."[56] The Covenant and the Torture Convention thus exemplify certain human rights norms and values, but nation-states may be obligated to follow those principles without having ratified those instruments.

There is, then, ample customary law support for the norms that the Covenant and the Torture Convention include. Since those instruments are self-executing—and to the extent that customary norms particularly draw upon those instruments—it logically follows that the customary law affiliated with those instruments is likewise self-executing. Unless the United States becomes a party to the Torture Convention and/or to the Covenant, customary federal law may satisfy *Davis's* first definition of cause of action, supporting federal question jurisdiction over at least the individual rights found in those instruments. Since those are federal rights, they should give rise to federal judicial authority. Section 1331 can thus serve as an important vehicle to provide a federal forum for international matters; this comports with the vertical federalist authority that the Constitution ordains over such matters.

Human Rights and Terrorism Cases under Davis's Second Definition

Can the victims of human rights violations and terrorism satisfy *Davis's* second cause-of-action definition and thus, "as a matter of law, appropriately invoke the power of the court"?[57] To answer that question, we should analogize international law claims to the three types of federal law claims that *Davis* mentioned: constitutional law claims; claims where statutory law explicitly grants a cause of action; and claims where the statutes, at most, implicitly grant a cause of action.

Analogy to Constitutional Claims. Recall *Davis's* ruling that its second definition should be applied more liberally to actions involving constitutional law. At first blush, it may seem that international law claims do not merit as lenient a jurisdictional treatment as constitutional law claims. Since the supremacy clause makes constitutional law superior to international law,[58] one might broadly conclude that international law claims are not analogous to the perhaps more important constitutional law claims. Constitutional and international law claims are particularly comparable, however, if the latter is narrowed to claims only involving human rights violations and terrorism. Human rights and terrorism claims parallel individual constitutional claims due to the primacy of the rights at issue. Indeed, there is a clear overlapping between the first principles involved in both types of claims. At a minimum, every human right is subsumed by a constitutional right; human rights and terrorism cases may even involve more basic and compelling rights than constitutional cases. For example, it is loathsomely sexist to deprive a woman of her job because she is a woman and to give it to a man instead — the constitutional scenario at issue in *Davis*. The international rights involved in torture and terrorism cases, however, are at least as significant and fundamental as the constitutional right involved in *Davis*. In a word, the right to be free from torture and terror emanates from instruments as basic to the international system as the Constitution is to the domestic system.

Assuming that a cogent analogy exists between constitutional cases and human rights and terrorism cases, then *Davis's* more liberal conception of a cause of action applies to both. That analogy creates a presumption that human rights and terrorism claimants may invoke the federal court's authority. Rebutting that presumption is the defendant's burden. Since *Davis* found federal question jurisdiction to be appropriate over a Fifth Amendment claim — despite the Fifth Amendment's lack of express language to that effect — jurisdiction is likewise appropriate even over those human rights and terrorism norms that say nothing about civil judicial enforcement. Claims involving the rights found in various treaties and custom may thus trigger cause-of-action's more liberal version, thereby justifying section 1331 jurisdiction. Human rights and terrorism cases are perfectly tailored to *Davis*'s recommendation that federal jurisdiction should especially exist when victims "have no effective means other than the judiciary to enforce [their] rights."[59] Hence alleged violations of both international humanitarian rights and constitutional rights deserve a federal judicial forum, not just a state tribunal. Both sets of rights should invoke vertical federal authority.

Analogy to Explicit Statutory Causes of Action. Satisfying *Davis*'s second cause-of-action definition should also be easy when either international or statutory law explicitly authorizes individuals to invoke judicial authority. At least the Covenant and the Torture Convention expressly indicate the propriety of a judicially enforceable private cause of action. Article 2(3) of the Covenant obligates each party to provide remedies, particularly of a judicial nature, to individuals whose rights have been violated.[60] Similarly, the Torture Convention obligates each party to examine allegations of torture promptly and impartially[61] and to "ensure in its legal system that the victim . . . obtains redress and has an enforceable right to fair and adequate compensation."[62] By expressly authorizing that judicial remedies should be provided to the victims of human rights violations, both the Covenant and the Torture Convention satisfy *Davis*'s second cause-of-action definition. Logically, the customary law affiliated with those instruments, as recognized in the United States, likewise satisfies *Davis*'s second definition. The *Restatement* supports this conclusion.[63] Federal question jurisdiction offers the means by which the nation can meet its obligation to open the federal courthouse doors to the victims of the relevant human rights violations. Again this meshes with the vertical federalist structure that the supremacy clause and article III contemplate.

Analogy to Implied Statutory Causes of Action. Explicit authorization to invoke judicial authority, however, is not granted by the remaining treaties mentioned earlier: the Geneva, Genocide, Apartheid, Hague, Montreal, Hostage, and Internationally Protected Persons conventions.[64] Save the Apartheid Convention, the United States is a party to each of those treaties, and they directly constitute federal law. Nevertheless, all of the remaining instruments are primarily criminal in nature; they expressly address the criminal, not civil, liability of human rights offenders, hijackers, and terrorists. Under *Davis's* second definition, the prevailing issue, then, is whether those treaties imply a civil cause of action. The treaties should thus be analogized to federal criminal and regulatory statutes that have been examined under the *Cort* criteria. The analogy is on point, particularly since our analysis will contemplate criminal statutes created pursuant to some of these treaties. If the treaties or the corresponding legislation imply that individual victims may invoke judicial power, section 1331 jurisdiction is appropriate.

The initial *Cort* criterion examines whether plaintiff is "one of the class for whose *especial benefit* the statute was enacted,"[65] which essentially defines whether individuals have an implied federal right. Quite obviously, the treaties and corresponding legislation especially benefit individuals. Since war crimes, genocide, and apartheid involve acts committed against individuals, individuals are the most direct beneficiaries of the prohibition against those acts. Individuals likewise benefit from the proscription against hijacking and terrorism, even though other actors also benefit. Surely, if courts can infer private rights from certain provisions of the corporate and securities laws,[66] for example, they can infer private rights from humanitarian and antiterrorism laws. Although each case must be examined separately, the vast majority of human rights, hijacking, and terrorism cases probably will satisfy *Cort's* initial consideration. Against the myth that individuals are merely the objects of international law,[67] individuals unquestionably benefit from the norms at issue.

Cort's next two criteria consider whether a private *remedy* may be inferred from a law's legislative history and purpose; they consider whether the drafters of a law implicitly intended to provide a "remedy" to individuals and other private claimants. In this context, remedy simply refers to the idea that individuals are impliedly permitted to enforce their implied rights in a judicial forum.[68] To apply these criteria fully, of course, would require us to examine the complete *travaux preparatoires* (preparatory works) of each of the remaining ten treaties; we would also be required to examine each piece of corresponding domestic legislation and even each statute's legislative history materials. Without undertaking that truly herculean task — and rather than selectively examining just one or two treaties, which would not provide a model of exemplary value — we offer a few general observations and discuss a few key cases.

We begin with two maxims — one of treaty construction, one of international law — which may color the inquiry of whether the treaties and federal legislation imply a private remedy: Treaties should be liberally construed to satisfy federalism concerns;[69] and nations may usually meet their international obligations by the means that they choose.[70] The first maxim might suggest that private federal remedies should be expansively viewed to flow from treaties that are primarily criminal in character. This interpretation helps to ensure that federal jurisdiction exists over human rights and terrorism claims, since those claims involve quintessential federal issues and concerns.[71] The federal courts perpetuate the vertical structure of international authority when they infer a private remedy, with some treaty or statutory support; section 1331 jurisdiction conceivably might not exist without such a federal remedy, leaving only state court jurisdiction over what would amount to a tort claim. In a sense, the second maxim buttresses the first. Since a treaty normally affords parties some discretion in how to implement the treaty's norms, the relevant treaties presumably permit sovereigns to recognize a private judicial remedy. That the parties must provide criminal remedies against international offenders does not contradict, but actually supports the idea that nations also remain free to provide civil remedies against those outlaws. The treaties' overriding purpose — preventing and redressing human rights violations and terrorism — is well served when nations respond by choosing to recognize civil as well as criminal remedies.

We should further consider several federal court opinions that have interpreted the remaining treaties and federal legislation. While these opinions are one step removed from the actual treaties and statutes, they support an inference of private remedies for human rights violations and terrorism.

Regarding terrorism, *Von Dardel v. Union of Soviet Socialist Repub-*

lics[72] and *de Letelier v. Republic of Chile*[73] are relevant. *Von Dardel* was a civil action brought on behalf of Raoul Wallenberg, who was unlawfully seized, imprisoned, and perhaps murdered by Soviet officials outside of the United States. During the Second World War, the United States sought the assistance of neutral Sweden in an effort to save thousands of Jews in Hungary from Nazi extermination. A "counterforce to the notorious German Nazi — Adolph Eichmann,"[74] Wallenberg heroically helped with this endeavor as a member of the Swedish Legation in Budapest. The Soviet Union's mistreatment of Wallenberg occurred after it had overrun Hungary in 1945. In upholding jurisdiction in the case under the FSIA, section 1331, and other statutory provisions, the District Court for the District of Columbia determined that an implied private remedy was available for the violation of Wallenberg's rights.[75] Because Wallenberg was a diplomatic agent, the violence against him constituted a terrorist act under the Internationally Protected Persons Convention. The court specifically referred to the United States criminal statutes — 18 U.S.C. sections 1116 and 1201 (et seq.) — passed or revised pursuant to that Convention and to the Hostage Convention, respectively. The court ruled: "Congress has . . . enacted statutes designed to protect internationally protected persons, including diplomats, . . . *as to which a private remedy has been implied.*"[76] The two treaties and the corresponding statutes are expressly criminal in character. But the court interpreted them to encompass private civil remedies, thus permitting the plaintiff to invoke the federal court's authority.

The same court ostensibly suggested a similar conclusion in *de Letelier*. The representatives of de Letelier, the former Chilean ambassador to the United States, brought that action against Chile and certain terrorists. While driving in Washington, D.C., de Letelier and a companion were assassinated when an explosive device planted by the terrorists detonated under the driver's seat in de Letelier's car. The district court sustained jurisdiction under section 1331 and other statutes over several causes of action against the terrorists. For present purposes, most relevant was the extension of jurisdiction over the "tortious assault" of "an internationally protected person pursuant to 18 U.S.C. 1116."[77] The court apparently inferred a private remedy from section 1116, which, again, implements the Internationally Protected Persons Convention. Hence both *Von Dardel* and *de Letelier* recognized that the terrorism treaties and the corresponding criminal statutes may impliedly support federal question jurisdiction.

Regarding hijacking, *Chumney v. Nixon*,[78] decided by the Sixth Circuit Court of Appeals, found an implied cause of action under the federal criminal statute that corresponds to the Montreal Convention. *Chumney* involved an alleged physical assault by one United States citizen against another on an aircraft while flying over Brazil. On appeal, the issue was whether the federal assault statute, which, pursuant to the Montreal Convention, Congress had extended to apply to offenses committed on aircraft, implied a private cause of action.[79] The issue was answered affirmatively, particularly in light of *Cort's* second and third criteria, and federal question jurisdiction was upheld. Although the court found no legislative intent either to support or preclude a private remedy, it recognized that Congress's "clear-cut purpose" was to protect the safety of air travelers.[80] Contrary to some other cases, the court concluded that "[a] civil action for damages would certainly be consistent with the overall congressional purpose and we believe should be inferred therefrom."[81] The court significantly added: "Indeed the existence or nonexistence of a civil cause of action in this case may create a legal precedent which will affect other possible fact situations *(aircraft kidnapping or terrorism) some of which may well cry out for more than the criminal remedy.*"[82] Hence even if *Chumney* was just an assault-and-battery case between testy American air travelers, its holding has a deep potential for international violence aboard aircraft.

Filartiga[83] offers some support for implying a private remedy for human rights violations. As discussed earlier, the *Filartiga* court sustained jurisdiction under the Alien Tort Statute, having concluded that extraterritorial torture violates the law of nations. That conclusion drew largely upon human rights instruments that do not explicitly grant a private cause of action; the Torture Convention, which now expressly grants a cause of action, was only in draft form when *Filartiga* was rendered. In *dictum*, however, the *Filartiga* court "recognize[d] that our reasoning might also sustain jurisdiction under . . . 28 U.S.C. 1331."[84] That *dictum* may suggest that federal question jurisdiction is available over human rights violations for which an explicit private remedy does not exist. Since section 1331 jurisdiction over a torture claim in *Filartiga*—prior to the Torture Convention's completion—would have depended upon an implied cause of action, it may also be available today over other human rights claims when an explicit private remedy is lacking. Somewhat similarly, Judge Edwards's concurring opinion in *Tel-Oren v. Libyan Arab Republic* suggested "that persons may be susceptible to *civil liability* if they commit *either* a [universal crime] *or* an offense that comparably violates norms of international law."[85] The offenses that Judge Edwards envisioned include some of the acts that the remaining treaties prohibit.[86] Since the treaties do not explicitly grant a private remedy for those offenses, Judge Edwards seems to suggest that a civil remedy is impliedly available when such acts occur.

Finally, the fourth *Cort* criterion will help further to imply a private cause of action for the victims of terrorism and human rights violations. That criterion considers federalism concerns and whether inferring a federal cause of action would intrude "in an area basically the concern of the [domestic] States."[87] Such an intrusion will not occur in human rights and terrorism cases. Since matters involving foreign affairs and international law exemplify an area of vertical federal concern, this final criterion particularly supports federal question jurisdiction over the cases at hand. Therefore, under *Davis's* second definition, when the four *Cort* criteria imply a private cause of action, the first genus of federal question jurisdiction encompasses human rights and terrorism cases. In such instances, the invocation of federal judicial authority is appropriate.

Second Genus:
Causes of Action under Federal Common Law

The second genus of the federal question caselaw is but a variation of the first, since a federal cause of action is again needed. Under the second genus, however, the cause of action springs somewhat less directly from positive legislative or treaty law. It derives from federal common law, that is, substantive law that the judiciary discovers or creates. So if one concludes that a positive law cause of action is absent in a particular case, there is the option that federal common law will give rise to section 1331 jurisdiction.

In recent decades, however, with the onslaught of federal legislation, common law has become increasingly less independent of positive legislative pronouncements. Since federal judges today not infrequently refer to legislation and even treaties when crafting federal common law, the line between the first and second genuses of the caselaw is actually blurred. The distinction between inferring a cause of action from positive international or statutory law (under the first genus) and judicially creating one (under the second genus) really depends upon the breadth of the interstices of the positive law at issue and the amount of judicial creativity that is needed. As leading commentators have put it: "Statutory interpretation shades into judicial lawmaking on a spectrum, as specific evidence of legislative advertence to the issue at hand attenuates."[88]

Erie R.R. v. Tompkins,[89] the Supreme Court's famous 1938 decision, sometimes confusedly is read to have sounded the death knell for federal common law. In actuality, Erie only ruled that "[t]here is no federal general common law."[90] Indeed, on the same day that Erie was rendered, the Court, in another case, unanimously held that federal common law should regulate water apportionment in the specific context of interstate streams.[91] While a generalized federal common law was out — a federal common law in diversity cases — a more specialized federal common law was still in — a federal common law in nondiversity cases where federal interests are at issue, but where positive federal law is lacking. Judge Henry Friendly's noted commentary observed: "Erie led to the emergence of a federal decisional law in areas of national concern."[92]

The term laws contained in both article III and section 1331 includes reference to the federal common law. Accordingly, in several instances, the Supreme Court has held that federal common law may create a cause of action giving rise to federal question jurisdiction. This is logical because, from Justice Brennan's pen, "federal courts have an extensive responsibility of fashioning rules of substantive law. . . . These rules are as fully 'laws' of the United States as if . . . enacted by Congress."[93]

The Need for a Federal Common Law
of Human Rights and Terrorism

To sanction common law causes of action in human rights and terrorism disputes, it must initially be shown that the cases merit federal rules of decision. In general, most issues involving international law and foreign relations affect uniquely national interests.[94] "Specialized" federal common law, rather than state law, should thus regulate those issues. The Supreme Court's opinion in Banco Nacional de Cuba v. Sabbatino[95] well represents this conclusion. Although we will later consider Sabba-

tino in detail, the case primarily examined the act-of-state doctrine, a judicial abstention device that governs one sovereign's exercise of jurisdiction over another sovereign's behavior occurring within the latter's territory. The Court held that international issues may occupy one of the post-*Erie* "enclaves of federal judge-made law."[96] The act-of-state doctrine was one such issue, since it orders or affects the United States' "relationships with other members of the international community" and thus "must be treated exclusively as an aspect of federal law."[97] Indeed, the problems addressed by the doctrine "are uniquely federal in nature," and if "the state courts are left free to formulate their own rules, . . . the doctrine could be as effectively undermined as if there had been no federal pronouncement on the subject."[98] Since federal statutes did not govern the act-of-state doctrine in the case, federal common law governed. *Sabbatino*'s holding essentially derived from the vertical supremacy of federal courts over state courts in international matters. In fact, the *Sabbatino* perspective goes beyond just the act-of-state doctrine and speaks more broadly to federal judicial control over virtually all international issues. In Judge Friendly's words, the *Sabbatino* Court generally "found in the Constitution a mandate to fashion a federal law of foreign relations."[99] *Sabbatino* also exemplifies Alfred Hill's "constitutional preemption" theory. Certain areas, including international law and foreign relations, according to Professor Hill, are "federalized by the force of the Constitution itself "and thus" foreclosed to state action."[100]

In light of *Sabbatino*, human rights and terrorism claims should categorically be regulated by federal decisional law. Human rights violations and terrorism are particularly prominent subjects on the federal government's international agenda. Myriad laws, treaties, orders, speeches, and political messages evidence the executive and legislative devotion to those subjects. Even the United States' dealings on such topics as arms and foreign assistance often depend upon the other nation's human rights record and approach to terrorists. The need for federal decisional law may also derive from the fact that the executive department sometimes expresses its views to the judiciary concerning both jurisdictional and substantive aspects of human rights and terrorism cases. Since the executive is more accustomed to communicating with its coordinate judicial branch than with the state judiciaries, it can better affect the common lawmaking process when that process occurs in federal court than in state court. In short, the national government's very strong interest in human rights and terrorism mandates that these specialized areas be subject to federal rules. When a federal judge determines that, for whatever reason, positive international law does not explicitly or implicitly provide such rules of decision in a civil case, he or she needs to craft such rules. By supplying a federal cause of action, judges help to ensure that federal question jurisdiction is available to the victims of human rights violations and terrorism. Providing such access to the federal courts conforms with the Constitution's commitment of international law and foreign affairs to vertical centralized governance.

The Contents of a Federal Common Law of Human Rights and Terrorism

Assuming that federal common law should govern human rights and terrorism claims, the contents of that law must still be examined. Put differently, even if federal common law is necessary, how do federal judges actually create common law to produce a cause of action for human rights violations and terrorism? Depending upon both the character and status of the particular treaty relevant to a case, a cause of action may arise from one of two sources: the customary law that certain treaties generate; or the interstices of other treaties. The former source of common law is relevant to the Covenant and the Torture Convention, which expressly contain a private cause of action, but which are not in force in the United States. The latter source is relevant to the remaining humanitarian and terrorism treaties, which do not contain an express cause of action, but which are in force in this country. Although the judicial task of recognizing or crafting a cause of action may vary in different cases, this is consistent with the Supreme Court's conception of federal common law: "The range of judicial inventiveness will be determined by the nature of the problem."[101] The common law tasks at hand may be reminiscent of the first genus's functional analysis; this is due to the overlap between the first two genuses of federal question jurisdiction.

We begin with the Covenant and the Torture Convention. Since both instruments explicitly recognize a cause of action, the judge's common law task here is not really the traditional one of crafting individual rights and private judicial remedies. Instead, since neither the Covenant nor the Torture Convention is in force in the United States (although the latter may soon be), the juridical problem is to determine whether the Covenant and the Torture Convention support a customary law cause of action cognizable in the United States. If the substantive norms of those instruments are part of the nation's customary law, then the federal judge may recognize the causes of action from those instruments as representing federal common law. The judge's function here is the recognition or perhaps the establishment of federal common law, but not the true crafting of a human rights cause of action. As demonstrated earlier, the Covenant's and the Torture Convention's norms do seem to exemplify custom.[102] Indeed, since those instruments have codified and crystallized certain customary norms and have probably generated others, the federal government may even be obligated to recognize private causes of action for the human rights that those instruments protect. Such federal common law causes of action may well support section 1331 jurisdiction in cases of torture, as *Filartiga* suggested in *dictum*.[103] A similar suggestion was made in *Forti v. Suarez-Mason*,[104] concerning a former Argentine general's commission of prolonged arbitrary detention and summary execution; the Covenant prohibits both of those offenses. In short, federal common law jurisdiction may exist over human rights causes of action that the nation recognizes as a matter of custom.

On the other hand, the United States is a party to the Geneva, Genocide, Hague, Montreal, Hostage, and Internationally Protected Persons conventions. But again, those instruments, unlike the Covenant and the Torture Convention, are primarily criminal in character and lack an explicit private cause of action. Assume *arguendo* that these treaties also do not sufficiently provide an implicit cause of action—contrary to our argument in the first genus. That assumption forces the judge to play a more traditional common law role: discovering or crafting private rights and remedies.

Fortunately for plaintiffs, federal judges should be able to find individual rights in the interstices of the remaining treaties. The broad outlines of the treaties—or even the treaties' emanations—should support a common law cause of action for war crimes, genocide, hijacking, and terrorism. Despite their express criminal measures, the instruments are more broadly intended to protect individuals from heinous and depraved acts. Indeed, the treaties may be viewed as entitling individuals to be free from such offenses, and thus the very sentiments that underlie those instruments may support the judicial recognition of private rights. Crafting or discovering private rights under federal common law for these offenses is consistent with the very purposes and first principles of United States treaties. In other words, the treaties have established certain values, and judicial institutions remain free to implement those values through the creation of individual rights. Divining such rights is also supported by sources other than the treaties at hand, such as nonbinding international resolutions and declarations that condemn human rights violations, hijacking, and terrorism. Again, this type of common law jurisprudence — judges looking to positive law pronouncements and synchronizing their common law with positive law — has been well accepted in the recent decades.

Since judicial creation of individual rights seems appropriate, so does the creation of private remedies for violations of those rights. As the Supreme Court once wrote in a federal common law case, it is "not uncommon for federal courts to fashion federal law where federal rights are concerned."[105] One need only think of *Marbury v. Madison*'s admonition that the "very essence of civil liberty" is to provide "a remedy for the violation of a vested legal right."[106] To give full remedial effect to the rights at issue, human rights and terrorism claims should be enforceable in federal court. A common law remedy is particularly supported both by federalism concerns and by the discretion that international law allows nations in implementing their commitments. While the treaties oblige the parties to create criminal remedies for war crimes, genocide, hijacking, and terrorism, nations are also at liberty to create civil judicial remedies for those offenses. Providing private common law remedies will only further the commitment to prevent and redress those offenses. According to the *Restatement*, customary law also supports such common law remedies and thus federal question jurisdiction.[107]

Professors Hart and Wechsler have emphasized that "[f]ederal law is generally interstitial in its nature."[108] In this regard, the war crimes, genocide, hijacking, and terrorism treaties are not very different from other sources of federal law. Composing treaties with broad strokes, the United States and other parties have established fundamental humanitarian principles. When federal judges create private causes of action for behavior anathema to those principles, they properly work within the treaties' guidelines and fill in the treaties' lacunae. In this way, the common law dovetails with the federal government's ideals and it supports section 1331 jurisdiction over cases that require federal attention.

Finally, the Apartheid Convention, as a prospective source of federal common law, presents both sets of problems that the other treaties raise: It is not in force in the United States (and unlikely to become so) and it does not explicitly confer a private cause of action. The federal common law judge must, therefore, first recognize that the Apartheid Convention has generated customary law in the United States and then create a private cause of action from the interstices of that customary law. Given the distance between those judicial tasks and the positive law, federal judges will perhaps be reluctant to create private rights and remedies emanating from the Apartheid Convention. Since the Covenant, however, explicitly confers a private cause of action for at least certain types of racial discrimination, it may provide apartheid victims with a more viable basis of federal question jurisdiction than the Apartheid Convention itself would.

Third Genus: Protective Jurisdiction

Another possible basis of section 1331 jurisdiction is provided by the "protective jurisdiction" theory, which Professors Wechsler and Mishkin pioneered decades ago in other contexts. According to Professor Wechsler, federal jurisdiction should extend "to all cases in which Congress has authority to make the rule to govern disposition of the controversy but is content instead to let *the states provide the rule so long as jurisdiction to enforce it has been vested in a federal court.*"[109] Rather than enact substantive legislation in the areas of its authority under article I, section 8 of the Constitution, Congress may delegate its authority to the federal courts to adopt state law (i.e., domestic or foreign nonfederal law) as the rule of decision in an area. In those instances, "[a] case is one 'arising under' federal law within the sense of Article III whenever it is comprehended in a valid grant of jurisdiction as well as when its disposition must be governed by the national law."[110] Articles I and III thus together support the federal courts' use of nonfederal rules of decision, by which the judiciary adopts (or "federalizes") a nonfederal cause of action in areas of national concern.[111] Federal courts, in this way, regulate federal interests. Professor Mishkin offered a more narrow view of protective jurisdiction than did Professor Wechsler, extending it to only those areas "where there is an articulated and active federal policy regulating a field."[112] Within this more limited scope, however, "the 'arising under' clause of Article III apparently permits the conferring of jurisdiction on the national courts of all cases in the area — including those substantively governed by state law."[113] Assuming *arguendo* that a federal cause of action is wanting in a specific case under the first two genuses, the Wechsler and Mishkin theories may help to extend federal jurisdiction over nonfederal causes of action.

Despite some continuing and resourceful scholarly support for protective jurisdiction,[114] the third genus has received the weakest judicial embrace of the various genuses of federal question jurisdiction. In actuality, the protective jurisdiction theory may contain vestiges of *Osborn* and *Planters' Bank:* Given the mere existence of a federal jurisdictional statute (the bank's charter) and the hypothetical issues appertaining to that statute, Chief Justice Marshall upheld federal question jurisdiction.[115] Thus, as with protective jurisdiction, the presence of a federal jurisdictional statute supported arising-under jurisdiction even in *Planters' Bank*, in which Georgia law, not federal law, provided the cause of action. The Supreme Court, however, has not acknowledged the supportive nexus between those early cases and protective jurisdiction. Only a concurring opinion in one Supreme Court case has explicitly written that protective jurisdiction is constitutional,[116] while a dissenting opinion in that same case rejected the validity of protective jurisdiction.[117]

Perhaps some additional support for protective jurisdiction can be drawn from the jurisprudence of federal common law, considered under the second genus of arising-under jurisdiction. Once scrutinized, the second and third species really seem to overlap. Both genuses are intended to keep cases involving federal interests in federal court, even when legislators have not provided a federal cause of action. Moreover, judges sometimes refer to, or at least rely upon, nonfederal law when "creating" federal common law causes of action.[118] That practice is not much different from "adopting" nonfederal causes of action under the third genus. Therefore, the arguments underlying the federal common law genus may also give credence to the protective jurisdiction genus. The limited judicial acceptance of protective jurisdiction notwithstanding, credible support for the theory can be marshalled.

Protective Jurisdiction over Human Rights and Terrorism Cases

Let us, then, advance a thesis extending the protective jurisdiction theory to human rights and terrorism cases. The thesis assumes the theory's constitutionality in general,[119] but it requires two additional and dovetailed building blocks: protective jurisdiction is legitimate over at least certain section 1331 cases; and it is particularly appropriate where human rights violations or terrorist acts are at issue.

Under our starting point, protective jurisdiction must be as legitimate over certain cases involving the *general* federal question statute (i.e., section 1331) as it is over cases involving the more *specific* federal question statutes (e.g., the FSIA, at issue in *Verlinden*). As discussed earlier, under the Supreme Court's dichotomy, section 1331 cases receive a more narrow arising-under interpretation than do cases involving the more specific jurisdictional grants.[120] If that dichotomy also is employed to limit protective jurisdiction over section 1331 cases, then our thesis's starting point may be fragile. That is, even if protective jurisdiction supports FSIA jurisdiction, for example, it may not support section 1331 jurisdiction. It may be contended that Congress delegated less judicial authority to adopt nonfederal law under section 1331 than under the more specific grants of federal question jurisdiction. Otherwise, the protective jurisdiction theory would extend section 1331 to every garden-variety tort and contract case involving a nonfederal cause of action.

Despite these contentions, however, our starting point is sound. Protective jurisdiction should extend to section 1331 cases, just as in cases involving other jurisdictional grants, at least in certain areas in which federal interests are particularly strong. Recall that protective jurisdiction is predicated not only on the judiciary's authority under article III, but also on Congress's authority under article I. So even if federal courts choose to limit their article III authority in most section 1331 cases, their authority to adjudicate certain section 1331 cases is supplemented by Congress's article I powers. That additional article I support may even mandate that the judiciary assume its full authority or responsibility over cases entailing important federal concerns.

Cases implicating foreign relations surely constitute one such area of superseding federal interests. The delegation of foreign affairs powers to Congress is one of the most significant aspects of article I.[121] When these or other paramount article I interests are present in a case, courts should not narrowly interpret section 1331 cases under the statutory, nonconstitutional meaning of "arising under." Section 1331, instead, should be broadly interpreted under the protective jurisdiction theory. Hence at least those particular section 1331 cases deserve the full jurisdictional support of article III's arising-under component — the same constitutional support afforded the FSIA, for example. Under this limited application of protective jurisdiction, section 1331 does not excessively broaden federal jurisdiction. Rather it renders section 1331 as more similar to specific grants of federal question jurisdiction, so that the provision does not confer jurisdiction over everyday tort and contract cases.

This brings us, quite relatedly, to the second building block. Assuming that protective jurisdiction is legitimate over section 1331 cases that involve foreign relations and other strong article I interests, it is particularly appropriate over human rights and terrorism cases. Perhaps only with the exception of international law disputes in which the federal government itself is a litigant, there are no cases that have foreign policy implications as unique and significant as those involving human rights violations or terrorism. The subjects of human rights and terrorism concern issues that are central to Congress's international initiatives. The judiciary's handling of such issues directly implicates the federal government's response and commitment to those subjects.

Protective jurisdiction is appropriate over human rights and terrorism claims even under Professor Mishkin's more restrictive theory, which extends protective jurisdiction only to areas involving "an articulated and active federal policy."[122] Although the United States might condemn human rights violations and even terrorism more strongly and consistently, the federal policy against such acts is generally well articulated and promoted. For instance, the recent federal legislation implementing the hijacking and terrorism treaties commits the United States to prosecute (or extradite) individuals who have committed those crimes, even when the offense at issue bears no link whatsoever with the United States.[123] The Omnibus Diplomatic Security and Antiterrorism Act of 1986[124] and the Torture Victim Protection Act[125] are examples of other recent legislative efforts aimed at mitigating human rights violations and terrorism. One title of the former addresses the criminal punishment of terrorists, while another title dictates federal compensation for terrorism victims employed by the United States civil or military services.[126] The torture statute, currently pending, would provide a new basis of original district court jurisdiction over civil cases involving torture or extrajudicial killings.[127] Even if such positive federal law standing alone does not yet confer a private cause of action, it illustrates the federal government's "articulated and active" policy of meting out justice in the terrorism and human rights contexts.

In concert with that federal policy, and thus supported by article I powers, the federal judiciary should use the protective jurisdiction theory in section 1331 cases involving human rights and terrorism. Assuming that domestic and international lawmakers have provided insufficient rules of decision to govern those cases, federal courts should adopt nonfederal causes of action to regulate the claims at hand. The methodology for identifying such causes of action might draw upon choice-of-law principles. Civil disputes involving human rights violations and terrorist acts may be likened to tort cases. As such, under the *lex loci* choice-of-law approach, for example, the tort law of the situs of the offense (be it Chile's, Argentina's, or Israel's law) should provide plaintiff's cause of action. District courts then adopt and "federalize" such causes of action to support section 1331 jurisdiction. As a result, important federal cases are kept within the federal judiciary's vertical authority; this, of course, comports with the constitutional federalism of international matters. Hence the protective jurisdiction theory can and should significantly help to extend federal question jurisdiction to the human rights and terrorism context.

Fourth Genus:
Cases that Involve Substantial Issues of Federal Law

Within the final genus of the caselaw, the plaintiff's cause of action need not arise under federal law. As the Supreme Court recently indicated in *Franchise Tax Bd. v. Laborers Vacation Trust*,[128] section 1331 jurisdiction is available "where the vindication of a right under state law necessarily turn[s] on some construction of federal law."[129] Although nonfederal law provides the rule of decision, federal question jurisdiction is appropriate where "some substantial, disputed question of federal law is a necessary element of one of the well-pleaded state claims."[130] Jurisdiction is made available here essentially due to federalism concerns; the presence of an important federal issue in a case supports vertical judicial authority, even if a federal cause of action is lacking. The derivation of this genus is surely *Osborn* and its companion case, even though the Supreme Court has disavowed *Osborn*'s application to section 1331 litigation. *Osborn*'s analysis is perhaps different only in that a hypothetical federal issue there justified jurisdiction, whereas the fourth genus requires an actual and substantial federal issue. Most significantly, however, neither *Osborn* nor the fourth genus require a federal cause of action.

But having formally banished *Osborn* to a corner of the caselaw, the Court prefers to rest the fourth genus upon *Smith v. Kansas City Title & Trust Co.*[131] In *Smith*, a shareholder sued to enjoin the corporation's purchase of bonds issued under the federal Farm Loan Act. The plaintiff's cause of action arose under Missouri law, which as alleged prohibited the state-chartered corporation from investing in bonds that were unconstitutionally issued. Despite the state-created cause of action, the Court upheld jurisdiction under section 1331's statutory predecessor, due to the constitutional question concerning the bonds' issuance. According to the *Smith* Court, when "the right to relief depends upon the construction or application of the Constitution or laws of the United States, . . . the District Court has jurisdiction under [the statute],"[132] assuming that the federal issue is more than colorable and is reasonably in need of an answer. The similarities between *Smith*'s approach and that of the purportedly inapposite *Osborn* are obvious.[133] Moreover, *Smith* is virtually impossible to reconcile with *American Well Works* and the first genus, which requires a federal cause of action, not just a federal issue of law or fact. Indeed, Justice Holmes, the author of *American Well Works*, dissented in *Smith*. So here, the genuses of the law seem more to contradict than to converge. Nevertheless, *Smith* and its modern counterpart, *Franchise Tax Bd.*, will be divorced from the section 1331 quagmire and taken at face value. Since the Supreme Court seems to think that the first and fourth genuses can coexist, we will assume the same.

International Law Cases

A recent Second Circuit opinion, *Republic of Philippines v. Marcos*,[134] well illustrates the final genus's applicability to cases having international implications. The case involved the Philippines' attempt to enjoin its deposed president from transferring certain New York properties, which had allegedly been purchased from funds illegally appropriated from the Republic. Although the case was brought "under a theory more nearly akin to a state cause of action for conversion,"[135] the court sustained federal question jurisdiction. Apart from a possible federal common law basis, "the presence of a federal issue in a state-created cause of action" supported section 1331 jurisdiction.[136] More specifically, the conversion claim raised, "as a necessary element, the question whether to honor the request of a foreign government that the American courts enforce the foreign government's directives to freeze property in the United States subject to future process in the foreign state."[137]

The *Marcos* court seemingly took the same approach that was used in *Verlinden*, an FSIA case, which rested upon *Osborn*.[138] Recall, however, that *Verlinden* required only a federal issue, not a federal cause of action, because a jurisdictional statute other than section 1331 was involved. *Marcos*, in the heritage of *Smith*, is particularly significant because it involved section 1331. Hence, under *Marcos*, federal ingredients — not necessarily a federal cause of action — may satisfy section 1331 in international cases. Article III apparently supports section 1331 jurisdiction in every conversion case involving a foreign sovereign (which will always involve freezing property in the United States), just as it supports FSIA jurisdiction in every contract case involving a foreign sovereign. As *Verlinden* ruled, such actions "raise sensitive issues concerning the foreign relations of the United States, and the primacy of federal concerns is evident."[139] Issues of that ilk, *Marcos* echoed, must "be decided with uniformity as a matter of federal law, . . . regardless of whether the overall claim is viewed as one of federal or state common law."[140] With support from *Smith*, *Marcos* thus suggests a liberal approach to the fourth genus in cases that have significant foreign relations implications. *Marcos*'s view of section 1331, however, should not be limited just to cases in which a nation-state is a party. Since the court predicated its holding upon the case's foreign relations implications, any dispute satisfying that predicate should support section 1331 jurisdiction, whether or not a nation-state is a litigant. All such disputes deserve federal judicial treatment due to the vertical federal authority governing those disputes.

Virtually all human rights and terrorism cases can meet *Franchise Tax Bd.*'s requirement that there be a "necessary" and "substantial" federal issue, particularly if *Marcos* colors that standard in international cases.

In fact, the *Forti* human rights case,[141] although ultimately resting upon federal common law, referred to the generous section 1331 standard operable in cases implicating international law issues.[142] Accordingly, even if the cause of action arises under nonfederal law, numerous and significant federal issues must usually be resolved in human rights and terrorism cases involving section 1331. Those issues include the following, among others: whether a defendant is entitled to diplomatic, consular, or head-of-state jurisdictional immunity; whether judicial authority is legitimate under international law's jurisdictional principles; whether the act-of-state doctrine precludes judicial review of acts committed under the color of sovereign authority within that sovereign's territory; whether any procedural aspects of a case allegedly violate an individual defendant's rights under international law; and whether and how international law affects and informs nonfederal tort standards. Human rights and terrorism cases that present those and other substantial issues may forcefully impact upon foreign relations and are thus best suited to federal jurisdiction. Therefore, even if the rule of decision is not federal, but the situs's tort law, for example, section 1331 jurisdiction should avail in most human rights and terrorism cases when the fourth genus is utilized.

Conclusion

While varied and sometimes inconsistent, the federal question caselaw may be construed to offer four avenues to the courthouse — protective jurisdiction being the only relatively unpaved road. Federal judges may constitutionally utilize any of the genuses to extend their authority over human rights and terrorism cases. Where positive international law explicitly or implicitly confers a private cause of action, there is no need to go beyond the *American Well Works* approach. Nevertheless, where judges deem such a cause of action lacking in a specific human rights or terrorism case, the increasingly broader views of federal question jurisdiction are available. By giving meaning to "arising under," and by placing human rights and terrorism cases upon the model that we have constructed, section 1331 may provide a viable and significant alternative to alien tort jurisdiction. That alternative is much in keeping with the Constitution's vertical commitment of international matters to the federal judiciary.

CHAPTER 4

Judicial Authority over Nation-State Offenders

We turn now from cases brought against nonstate defendants to those against nation-states. Although most of the decade's human rights and terrorism cases have been commenced against nonstate actors, nation-states have been named as the defendant or a codefendant in a significant number of cases. Federal jurisdiction in human rights and terrorism cases, as in all cases against nation-states, depends upon the Foreign Sovereign Immunities Act of 1976 (FSIA).[1]

The FSIA's Exclusivity: *Amerada Hess*

Following the FSIA's passage, most judges and commentators had concluded that the FSIA was the exclusive vehicle of federal court authority over nation-states.[2] The Second Circuit Court of Appeals, however, bucked this juridical trend in 1987, in *Amerada Hess Shipping Corporation v. Argentine Republic*.[3] The case involved a suit by two Liberian corporations, one the owner and one the time-charterer of an oil tanker that Argentine aircraft attacked without provocation or warning during the Falklands War. Nearly $2 million of fuel was lost, and the tanker had to be scuttled at an estimated $10 million loss. In a split decision, the Second Circuit sustained jurisdiction over Argentina under the Alien Tort Statute: "The . . . Statute means what it says. If an alien brings a suit, for a tort only, that sufficiently alleges a violation of the law of nations, then the district court has jurisdiction."[4] Each of those requisites was met in the case, including the proposition that the attack, if proven, would "constitute a clear violation of international law."[5] While recognizing that the FSIA did not itself confer jurisdiction in the case (for reasons to be made evident shortly), Chief Judge Feinberg ruled that "the FSIA does not preempt the jurisdictional grant of the Alien Tort Statute."[6] Judge Feinberg was surely correct that *Amerada Hess* satisfied the Alien Tort Statute's terms, and his straightforward approach to the statute should be welcomed as uncommonly uncongested. Nevertheless, his very consideration of the Alien Tort Statute was dubious. As Judge Kearse's dissent convincingly demonstrated, "[T]he FSIA provides the exclusive framework within which the courts of the United States are to resolve a foreign state's claim of sovereign immunity."[7]

In a 1989 decision that most expected, the Supreme Court reversed the Second Circuit in *Amerada Hess*,[8] thus agreeing with Judge Kearse's viewpoint. The Court was unanimous in holding that the FSIA is jurisdictionally exclusive when nation-states are sued in federal court.[9] Chief Justice Rehnquist confidently concluded: "[T]he text and structure of the FSIA demonstrate Congress' intention that the FSIA be the sole basis for obtaining jurisdiction over a foreign state in our courts."[10] According to the chief justice, that conclusion does not permit an exception even when an alien has been tortiously assaulted by a blatant international law violation.[11] As a result, alien tort as well as federal question jurisdiction, however broadly construed, are wholly irrelevant when nation-states are sued.[12] Accordingly, when nation-states allegedly cause or sponsor human rights violations or terrorism, the victims may allege jurisdiction over those particular defendants only under the FSIA.

Preface to the FSIA

Under the Supreme Court's famous 1812 decision in *The Schooner Exchange v. McFadden*,[13] it was understood that nation-states enjoyed virtually absolute immunity from the jurisdiction of United States courts. Chief Justice Marshall enunciated the underlying premise of that conclusion: "One sovereign being in no respect amenable to another; and being bound . . . not to degrade the dignity of his nation, by placing . . . its sovereign rights within the jurisdiction of another, . . . [enters] a foreign territory only . . . in the confidence that the immunities [of] his . . . [nation] . . . will be extended to him."[14] This sovereign immunity, in turn, was reciprocated by the immunity that most foreign courts offered to the United States as a defendant.

Particularly during the twentieth century's latter half, however, it became necessary to reexamine the sovereign immunity doctrine.[15] Expanded commercial interaction was occurring between nation-states and private parties. If nation-states would continue to be jurisdictionally immune, there would be no United States judicial apparatus to keep sovereigns good to their ever-increasing bargains. Support thus mounted in the United States and elsewhere for restricting sovereign immunity. Early efforts toward a restrictive theory attempted to distinguish between a sovereign's "public" and "private" acts; immunity was to be maintained only where public acts were at issue. In practice, however, this distinction proved difficult to draw. For instance, when a nation-state allegedly fails to pay an American farmer for the wheat that it has purchased to feed its starving citizens, is the transaction not private in its nature but public in its purpose? Moreover, attempting sharp distinctions between public and private acts may be as facile an endeavor as drawing sharp distinctions between the legal personalities of public and private actors.[16] For an analysis to have any value, legal acts, like legal actors, deserve a functional and contextual examination, not superficial labeling. In any event, such difficulties with the public/private distinction plagued the courts, which in turn troubled the executive department about whether jurisdictional immunity should be accorded in a given case.

The FSIA was promulgated to clarify the restrictive sovereign immunity theory, providing some new content to the doctrine.[17] It also sought to reduce the politicalization of sovereign immunity, by having the judiciary make immunity determinations under statutory rules, without the executive department's input. Moreover, the FSIA tried to bring the United States more in line with the restricted sovereign immunity that other nation-states offered. Since international relations are significantly predicated upon reciprocal sovereign privileges and obligations, there was no compelling reason for the United States to offer more sovereign immunity than it was accorded abroad.

Under a type of alienage jurisdiction, article III, section 2, clause 2 of the Constitution clearly supports FSIA jurisdiction over cases between United States citizens and nation-states. That constitutional provision, however, does not provide judicial authority when an alien sues a nation-state.[18] In such instances, article III's arising-under clause, instead, permits jurisdiction (section 2, clause 2). As discussed earlier, *Verlinden B. V. v. Central Bank of Nigeria*[19] held that even when an FSIA case involves nonfederal rules of decision, the case preliminarily involves federal questions concerning the FSIA's regulations and thus sufficiently arises under federal law. *Verlinden*'s ruling reacted to the fact that all "[a]ctions against foreign sovereigns in our courts raise sensitive issues concerning the foreign relations of the United States, and the primacy of federal concerns is evident."[20] This passage echoes a now-familiar theme: Federal judicial authority should vertically extend to cases involving international matters, since those matters are constitutionally committed to the federal government. Hence, whether a United States citizen or an alien sues a nation-state, FSIA jurisdiction is constitutional.

Even though it is not without its difficulties and deficiencies, the FSIA has a certain, helpful simplicity. The statute creates a presumption that nation-states (and their agencies and instrumentalities) are immune from the jurisdiction of federal and state courts, unless a case involves one of the statute's fairly limited exceptions to immunity.[21] Where an exception applies, the federal district courts have jurisdiction under 28 U.S.C. section 1330.[22] Where the exceptions are inapplicable, the sovereign is immune, the judiciary lacks authority, and the case is over.

The task, then, is to consider how human rights and terrorism cases fare under the FSIA's exceptions to immunity. Irrelevant to these cases is the FSIA's most significant and most litigated immunity exception, the commercial-activity exception. In fact, only two immunity exceptions have any relevance to our context: the tort exception and the waiver exception. Most victims of extraterritorial terrorism or human rights violations have not successfully invoked either of those exceptions. But the waiver exception may have a somewhat greater potential utility when nation-states commit or sponsor such offenses. In addition, we should consider whether sovereign immunity is unavailable per se when international law violations are at issue. It must be kept in mind throughout, however, that the FSIA is a relatively new and fairly detailed piece of legislation, with a fresh legislative history to consult. Accordingly, in contrast to the archane and terse alien tort provision and the cryptic and purportedly ambiguous federal question provision, the FSIA provides less room for legitimate debate about its jurisdictional scope. Although one can argue about the authority that the FSIA should provide, one is relatively constrained when arguing about the authority that the statute does provide on its face and in its intent.

FSIA's Tort Exception

Most human rights and terrorism cases sound in tort. The tort exception to sovereign immunity is contained in 28 U.S.C. section 1605(a)(5). It permits judicial authority when money damages are sought for the plaintiff's "personal injury or death, or damage to or loss of property, *occurring in the United States.*"[23] Therefore, the tort exception is available in cases when terrorism or, somewhat less likely, human rights violations occur in the United States. For instance, the tort exception was used in *de Letelier v. Republic of Chile,*[24] in which Chile sponsored a terrorist's assassination in Washington, D.C., of its former ambassador to the United States. That exception also supported jurisdiction when a widow sued the Republic of China for having authorized Chinese nationals, including intelligence officials, to kill her husband in California, in *Liu v. Republic of China.*[25]

Nevertheless, since most of the recent litigation has involved offenses occurring extraterritorially to the United States, section 1605(a)(5) has not been a resource of much judicial authority. Hence neither the torture victim brutalized by government officials in Argentina nor the representatives of Israelis murdered by Libyan-backed terrorists in Tel Aviv could utilize the FSIA's tort exception when suing a nation-state as one of the allegedly responsible defendants.[26] Likewise, in *Amerada Hess,*[27] the tort exception was inapplicable because Argentina's attack on the Liberian tanker occurred on the South Atlantic high seas. For the same reason, the tort exception was irrelevant to *Martin v. Republic of South Africa,*[28] a recent case brought by a black American dancer on tour in South Africa, who was injured there along with a white companion in a one-car accident. An ambulance arrived and took the white to a hospital for treatment, but under apartheid, the black was left behind and he had to walk several hours to the hospital, only to find that the hospital would not treat him. Some twenty-four hours after the accident, he was granted "honorary White status" and transported sixty-five miles to another hospital. The black sued South Africa, alleging that he had become a quadriplegic during the transfer to the second hospital and that his original injury had become aggravated by the delay in medical service. Although the action more directly sounded in the torts of negligence and medical malpractice, section 1605(a)(5) did not provide judicial authority, since the torts occurred in South Africa. The plaintiff, instead, pressed the commercial-activity exception to immunity on appeal, but to no avail. South Africa was deemed immune from jurisdiction in the case.[29]

The tort exception has been narrowed even further by two additional limitations, both of which are illustrated by *Persinger v. Islamic Republic of Iran*.[30] *Persinger* involved a marine who had been stationed at the United States embassy in Tehran and was held hostage for almost fifteen months during 1979–81. The marine and his parents brought suit against Iran.

The United States ordinarily maintains substantial sovereign control over its embassies abroad, so the marine argued that the Tehran embassy was subject to the United States' territorial jurisdiction for purposes of the FSIA's tort exception. Judge Bork, for the District of Columbia's Court of Appeals, rejected this argument.[31] His holding was based upon an accurate interpretation of the FSIA's legislative history and a rather straightforward reading of the statute's definition of the "United States." Since section 1603 limits that term to the nation's "continental or insular" territory or waters,[32] torts committed at the United States' foreign embassies do not befit the tort exception to immunity. The *Persinger* court was correct, statutorily speaking, in rejecting the marine's claim. Nevertheless, *Persinger* illustrates a severe limitation of federal jurisdiction over nation-states in a potentially significant group of cases: disputes involving terrorism that nation-states sponsor at the United States embassies, consulates, and perhaps military bases and installations. When terrorism and even human rights violations occur at those locations, the federal courts lack statutory authority over nation-states.

Another limitation on the tort exception is demonstrated by the claim of the marine's parents in *Persinger*. The parents sought recovery for the mental and emotional distress that they had suffered as a result of their son's kidnapping. Making basically a textual argument concerning section 1605(a)(5) (quoted above[33]), they urged that *only their injury*, and not necessarily the defendant's tortious act or omission, must occur in the United States for the tort exception to apply to their claim. According to this argument, even if the tort against the marine, in both its commission and injury, occurred entirely in Tehran, FSIA jurisdiction attached to the parents' tort claim because their injury occurred in the United States.

The court ruled against the parents' argument. Judge Bork conceded that section 1605(a)(5) was textually "unclear [about] whether *both* the tort and the injury must occur here."[34] Congress, not illogically, may have intended the tort exception to apply to only those extraterritorial acts that cause effects within the United States; after all, since only those extraterritorial torts have a direct connection with the United States territory, it would not necessarily be paradoxical for a court to possess FSIA jurisdiction over the parents' claim, but not over the marine's claim.[35] Judge Bork's ruling, however, is consistent with that of virtually every other federal judge who has considered this point; it is arguably also supported by the FSIA's legislative history.[36] Hence in terrorism, human rights, and all other cases against nation-states, section 1605(a)(5) is effectively restricted to provide judicial authority only when both the tortious act and the injury occur in the United States. Although some might favor the availability of American justice against the likes of the late Ayatollah Khomeini's regime, the FSIA's tort exception, as written and interpreted, is unavailing in a case such as *Persinger.*

FSIA's Waiver Exception

Given the tort exception's restrictions, many human rights and terrorism plaintiffs have tried to invoke the FSIA's waiver exception. That exception, found in section 1605(a)(1), permits judicial authority in any case "in which the foreign state has waived its immunity either explicitly or by implication."[37] Some activists have forcefully argued that nation-states waive their jurisdictional immunity by participating in multinational human rights and terrorism conventions.[38] It is contended that these treaties waive sovereign immunity not explicitly, but implicitly. Their argument amounts to this: The parties to certain instruments, such as the Internationally Protected Persons Convention and the International Covenant on Civil and Political Rights ("Covenant"), impliedly or expressly recognize individual rights and remedies. In turn, and by implication, the parties to those instruments also waive their immunity from the enforcement of rights and remedies that they themselves have created.[39] Creating an enforcement scheme by treaty and then claiming immunity from that scheme are contradictory. Put another way, judges and other lawyers ordinarily try to validate and give meaning to all legal rights and remedies. If humanitarian rights and remedies are to be legitimized and aggrandized, they necessarily should be enforced against both nonstate and nation-state defendants. Immunity under the FSIA conflicts with that goal, and human rights and terrorism instruments can and should be read impliedly to waive that immunity.

At least one federal court has accepted this type of a waiver argument. *Von Dardel v. Union of Soviet Socialist Republics*,[40] discussed earlier, concerned the Soviet Union's mistreatment and probable murder of a Swedish diplomat, who had worked on the United States' behalf during the Second World War against the Nazi atrocities being committed in Hungary.[41] The District Court for the District of Columbia conceded that neither the FSIA nor its legislative history "makes clear how immunity can be implicitly waived" by agreement.[42] Nevertheless, the court ruled that the Soviet Union had implicitly waived its jurisdictional immunity by its subscription to the Internationally Protected Persons Convention and the Vienna Convention on Diplomatic Immunity.[43] As it concluded: "Any other result would rob each of those agreements of substantive effect, and would render meaningless the act of the Soviet Union in signing them."[44] Jurisdiction, accordingly, was upheld under the FSIA.

At the same time, a few courts have dismissed the implied-waiver argument outright, as exemplified by *Frovola v. Union of Soviet Socialist Republics*.[45] This case was brought by an American citizen and Stanford graduate student, who spent time researching her dissertation in the Soviet Union, where she met and married a Soviet citizen. The plaintiff returned to the United States when her visa expired, but the Soviet Union did not permit the husband to join his wife. Alleging mental anguish, physical distress, and loss of consortium rights, the plaintiff, heartbroken and hunger-striking with other Muscovites in the United States, sought monetary and injunctive relief against the Soviet Union for its refusal to permit her spouse to emigrate.[46] In ruling that it lacked authority under the FSIA, the Seventh Circuit Court of Appeals decided that the Soviet Union had not waived its sovereign immunity by signing either the United Nations Charter or the Helsinki Accords. Section 1605(a)(1)'s legislative history, according to the court, demanded that waivers must be inferred on a limited basis. The court concluded: "[T]here is absolutely no evidence from the language, structure or history of the agreements at issue that implies a waiver of the U.S.S.R.'s sovereign immunity."[47]

Are *Von Dardel* and *Frovola* simply inapposite decisions—one case to be cited in future plaintiffs' briefs, the other to be cited contradictorily in defendants' briefs—or can the decisions be logically distinguished from one another? The decisions may arguably be compatible if one focuses on the difference between the treaties utilized in each case. In *Von Dardel*, the Internationally Protected Persons Convention impliedly provided a private right and remedy to the victim.[48] In *Frovola*, however, the UN Charter and the Helsinki Accords, more hortatory in nature, did not provide the individual with a right or remedy. It may be concluded, therefore, that a sovereign implicitly waives its immunity only through treaties that expressly or impliedly contain a private remedial scheme. This is sensible because remedies obviously cannot be effectuated against a sovereign unless it has waived its immunity. As discussed earlier, a private cause of action may expressly or impliedly emanate from several human rights instruments (e.g., the Covenant and the Torture, Geneva, and Genocide conventions) and several terrorism instruments (e.g., the Hague, Montreal, Hostage, and Internationally Protected Persons conventions).[49] Arguably, then, each of those treaties implicitly may waive sovereign immunity; the *Von Dardel* precedent may support an implied-waiver argument when any of those treaties is at issue. *Frovola* does not necessarily contradict that suggestion, if *Frovola*'s ruling applies only to treaties that do not expressly or impliedly create private remedies. By interpreting and squaring *Von Dardel* and *Frovola* in this manner, the FSIA's waiver exception may be given a significant role in many human rights and terrorism actions against nation-states.

On the other hand, federal judges may be inclined to follow *Frovola* and to deny FSIA jurisdiction in most cases, since the human rights and terrorism treaties do not explicitly waive sovereign immunity. A waiver may reasonably be inferred from the Internationally Protected Persons Convention and the other treaties just mentioned. But a judge may be dissatisfied with such inferential evidence and may demand more concrete evidence of a waiver before assuming authority over a sovereign nation. It is one thing to infer a private cause of action in relation to a nonstate defendant, but perhaps another to infer a waiver of immunity by a nation-state defendant. Further, in other contexts, courts have frequently construed section 1605(a)(1) narrowly, in deference to sovereign defendants and wary of foreign relations difficulties that might otherwise result.[50] That restrictive construction draws some support from the FSIA's legislative history, as *Frovola* indicated. Judges thus may not care to distinguish between those treaties that contain a private remedial scheme and those that do not. They simply may reject the implied-waiver argument out of hand, even though section 1605(a)(1) specifically indicates that sovereign immunity can be waived by implication.

In sum, *Von Dardel* offers jurisdictional promise for the waiver exception. That promise may be fulfilled whenever a human rights or terrorism treaty expressly or impliedly contains a remedial scheme. But even when such treaties are at issue, some federal judges may choose to follow *Frovola*, practicing restraint particularly because a nation-state is before the court.

An Exception for International Law Violations

Finally, courts have been pressed with the argument that sovereign immunity is unavailable per se whenever a nation-state violates international law. This contention is not based upon the FSIA's express terms; the statute does not contain an "international-law-violation exception" to sovereign immunity. Instead, as argued, immunity simply should not exist over offenses such as human rights violations and terrorism. "To hold otherwise," contends Professor Paust, "would be to further illegality, give it legal effect. . . . This a court of law cannot do. Thus, a violation of law poses the one *necessary* exception to immunity, one *implicitly* necessary in any truly legal system."[51]

Disallowing sovereign immunity for international law violations is, indeed, a positive idea. If legal authority over nation-states is needed in any context, it is where sovereign actors sponsor human rights offenses and terrorism. The values and principles condemning these international law violations should override the legal tenets underlying sovereign immunity. Deference to sovereign authority should give way to respect for basic individual rights and liberties. Granted, an assumption of jurisdiction may negatively impact upon the United States' relations with the one sovereign defendant. But not assuming jurisdiction over an international law violation may breach the United States' obligations to all other members of the world community. In addition, even if immunity is not accorded, the act-of-state doctrine may counsel that jurisdiction should not be exercised when the adjudication of a specific case might have especially detrimental effects upon relations with a specific defendant, as we soon will discuss.[52] Although granting immunity in a case does not actually put the United States' imprimatur upon a sovereign defendant's illegal acts, it does cut against the global commitment to correct and deter human rights violations and terrorism. It is an obvious anomaly to outlaw an act and then grant immunity when the outlaw is brought to court. Professor Paust's argument is thus very well taken.

Perhaps not surprisingly, however, this argument has received only mixed reviews in federal court.[53] After all, the FSIA does not explicitly provide an immunity exception for international law violations; the statute's legislative history, too, does not expressly support that exception. Since the tort and waiver exceptions to immunity, which are contained in the FSIA, have often been narrowly applied, one would expect a lack of receptiveness to an immunity exception not expressly found in the FSIA. In fact, some of the same federal judges who have rejected implied-waiver arguments under section 1605(a)(1) have also rejected the argument that immunity does not attach to international law violations.[54] If a judge is unwilling to infer a waiver of immunity from a specific treaty that has been violated, he or she is probably even more unwilling to infer that sovereign immunity is generally unavailable whenever international law is violated. Again, federal judges usually practice particular restraint when a nation-state, in contrast to a nonstate actor, is sued in a human rights or terrorism action. That restraint has been put aside in a few cases, such as *de Letelier* and *Von Dardel*, which have bought the argument against immunity for international offenses.[55] Other courts have strongly rejected that argument, however, and individual plaintiffs cannot rest assured that sovereign immunity is unavailable per se when a sovereign sponsors even the most heinous international offenses.

Conclusion

Federal court authority over nation-states, under *Amerada Hess*, is contingent upon the FSIA. Hence nation-states are jurisdictionally immune unless one of the FSIA's exceptions to sovereign immunity applies. The tort exception, limited to sovereign acts committed entirely in the United States, is of no solace to the victims of extraterritorial terrorism or human rights violations. The waiver exception may possibly apply in those situations, if the relevant treaty expressly or impliedly encompasses a private remedial scheme and is interpreted implicitly to waive sovereign immunity. In addition, a few judges and commentators have read an exception into the FSIA, intrinsically applicable whenever a nation-state sponsors human rights or terrorist offenses. We should not exaggerate, however, the utility of either the implied-waiver exception or the international-law-violation exception. The former requires courts to infer a waiver of immunity, the latter to infer an immunity exception. Especially with nation-states before them, some judges may hesitate to draw such inferences. That restraint may contradict the commitment of international authority to the federal judiciary. But perhaps it is noteworthy that the FSIA governs the jurisdiction of both federal and state tribunals over nation-state defendants.[56] So if FSIA jurisdiction is absent in a human rights or terrorism case, a state court also cannot hear the case, which may partially help to satisfy federalism concerns.

CHAPTER 5

The Separation of Powers in Human Rights and Terrorism Cases

The prior pages have examined judicial authority under jurisdictional statutes, the contours of that authority primarily deriving from the vertical relationship between federal and state courts. Our goal was to comprehend the maximum jurisdiction that federal courts possess over human rights and terrorism cases under article III, statutory provisions, and federalism. Recall, however, that federal court authority should be legitimate not just vis-à-vis state courts, but also in relation to the authority of the executive and legislative branches.[1] In other words, even when a federal court constitutionally has jurisdiction under a statute and under federalism, the judge should further contemplate the propriety of exercising that jurisdiction under the more horizontal separation-of-powers concerns. There is a difference between *having* jurisdiction and *exercising* it. So before exercising jurisdiction in human rights and terrorism cases, federal judges should consider the political branches' international authority; we earlier provided a primer on that authority.[2]

The political question and act-of-state doctrines — both court-invented judicial abstention doctrines — encompass separation-of-powers concerns. Forming the crux of this chapter, those doctrines will provide vehicles for conceptualizing the separation of federal powers, just as the jurisdictional statutes provided vehicles for conceptualizing federalism. Certain aspects of the doctrines overlap, but they merit separate analysis. Despite the political branches' significant international authority, we will demonstrate that the political question doctrine is actually inapposite to most human rights and terrorism cases; alternatively, and at a minimum, the doctrine's requirements do not counsel judicial restraint in most cases. The act-of-state doctrine is at least relevant to human rights and terrorism cases, but it, too, should not normally result in judicial inaction. Finally, we will nod to another judicial abstention doctrine, *forum non conveniens*, which is predicated upon very pragmatic and not at all constitutional concerns.

Political Questions

Under the political question doctrine, certain issues are supposedly political in character; as such, they deserve resolution by the political branches of government and not by the courts. The doctrine stems from the separate authority that each federal branch possesses: "[I]t is the relationship between the judiciary and the coordinate branches of the Federal Government . . . which gives rise to the 'political question.'"[3] Unfortunately, as a leading critic reports, "[n]o branch of the law of justiciability is in such disarray as the doctrine of the 'political question.'"[4] The federal judiciary periodically contemplates and diversely applies the doctrine, but nary a defendant has convinced a majority of the Supreme Court to dismiss a case under the doctrine since 1946.[5] "[T]he recent history of the doctrine," Judge McGowan observes, "has been one of judicial indifference and scathing scholarly attack. The result has been to expose shortcomings in the doctrine."[6] Indeed, as renowned a scholar as Louis Henkin once posed these heretical questions: "Is there a 'political question' doctrine? Do we need one?"[7] He answered no on both counts. The doctrine, in actuality, often amounts to a decision on the merits that the president and the Congress did not violate the Constitution or that they acted within the discretion that the Constitution exclusively affords them. Rather than clarifying that decision, the political question doctrine unnecessarily obscures the decision.[8] This iconoclastic criticism of the political question doctrine might suggest that we should not consider the doctrine any further. Nevertheless, we will take the doctrine at whatever face value it can claim because the Supreme Court has not expressly disavowed the doctrine and because some lower federal courts have applied the doctrine in the human rights and terrorism context.[9]

Baker v. Carr,[10] which the Supreme Court decided in 1962, is the leading case on the political question doctrine. *Baker* involved a challenge by qualified voters to Tennessee's legislative apportionment of 1901, which allegedly had become obsolete and violated the Fourteenth Amendment. Rejecting the political question doctrine's application, the Court specifically found reapportionment to be justiciable.[11] But more generally, Justice Brennan's majority opinion provided something of an exegesis about the doctrine and its several attributes, which, "in various settings, diverge, combine, appear, and disappear in seeming disorderliness."[12] So true. Justice Brennan advised that the doctrine "is one of 'political questions,' not one of 'political cases,'"[13] and "the mere fact that the suit seeks protection of a political right does not mean it presents a political question."[14] The doctrine should be applied on a case-by-case basis under multiple criteria, the Supreme Court's bounty lacking no generosity:

Prominent on the surface of any case held to involve a political question is found a textually demonstrable constitutional commitment of the issue to a coordinate political department; or a lack of judicially discoverable and manageable standards for resolving it; or the impossibility of deciding without an initial policy determination of a kind clearly for nonjudicial discretion; or the impossibility of a court's undertaking independent resolution without expressing lack of the respect due coordinate branches of government; or an unusual need for unquestioning adherence to a political decision already made; or the potentiality of embarrassment from multifarious pronouncements by various departments on one question.[15]

Justice Brennan's opinion also considered the political question doctrine in several particular areas, one being foreign relations. As previously described, the president and the Congress hold vast authority over international matters.[16] Justice Brennan, however, rejected the sweeping contention that all international questions are political questions: "[I]t is error to suppose that every case or controversy which touches foreign relations lies beyond judicial cognizance."[17] Instead, courts should undertake "a discriminating analysis of the particular question posed, in terms of the history of its management by the political branches, of its susceptibility to judicial handling in the light of its nature and posture in the specific case, and of the possible consequences of judicial action."[18] Under such factors, the Court had previously found the following questions to be nonjusticiable: whether to recognize a foreign government; whether to recognize a belligerency abroad; and whether a person is a head of state. In contrast, the Court had previously found the following questions to be justiciable: whether the parties have correctly interpreted a treaty; whether a statute applied to a foreign sovereign's territory; and whether and how to construe the executive's head-of-state determinations in interpreting federal court jurisdiction.[19] This sampling shows that political question decisions contain both topical and functional components. The topics deemed nonjusticiable are particularly subject to the political branches' direct and exclusive control.[20] Functionally speaking, the justiciable items involve tasks for which the judiciary is particularly well suited: the interpretation, application, and construction of norms. Performing those tasks permits the judiciary to work with — and sometimes to check, balance, and even contradict — its coordinate branches in international matters.

Apart from *Baker*, a few more recent Supreme Court cases involving foreign relations deserve mention. Recall that the Constitution indicates how the president and the Senate together make treaties,[21] but it is silent about how to unmake treaties. *Goldwater v. Carter*[22] involved a challenge by members of Congress to President Jimmy Carter's termination of the Mutual Defense Treaty with the Republic of China (Taiwan) without senatorial or congressional consent. The president's action corresponded to the United States' shift of recognition from Taiwan to the People's Republic of China. The circuit court of appeals ruled in the president's favor,[23] but a very splintered Supreme Court vacated that judgment and dismissed the case.[24] Under an overly broad enunciation of the political question doctrine, then Justice Rehnquist opined that the case was nonjusticiable "because it involves the authority of the President in the conduct of our country's foreign relations and the extent to which the Senate or the Congress is authorized to negate the action of the President."[25] Important to Justice Rehnquist was the fact that *Goldwater* was not a private dispute, but one between coequal departments of government. Each political branch "has resources available to protect and assert its interests, resources not available to private litigants outside the judicial forum."[26]

Justice Rehnquist, however, was able to convince only three other justices to join his *Goldwater* opinion. Two additional members of the Court (Justices Powell and Marshall) agreed with the Rehnquist plurality's result to dismiss the case, but not with the plurality's reasoning. Indeed, Justice Powell, who thought that the case should be dismissed under the ripeness doctrine, argued that Justice Rehnquist's political question perspective was inherently confusing[27] and wholly unsupported by *Baker*'s various criteria: The case did not involve an issue textually committed to a particular political department; the Court was not without manageable standards to decide the case, but could apply normal principles of constitutional interpretation; and the case, if ripe and decided on the merits, would not cause the judiciary to embarrass its coordinate branches, but actually would eliminate, rather than create, multiple constitutional interpretations by the federal government.[28] The dissenting opinion of Justice Brennan, *Baker*'s author, wrote that the plurality opinion "profoundly misapprehends the political-question principle as it applies to matters of foreign relations."[29] Hence Justice Rehnquist's political question perspective broadly advocates judicial inaction and deference to the executive, but it is diluted by its plurality status and by the sharp criticism that it engendered.

Finally, *Japan Whaling Association v. American Cetacean Society*[30] was an action that wildlife conservation groups brought to compel the executive department to impose economic sanctions against Japan if Japan did not adhere to a zero quota on the harvesting of certain sperm whales. A commission had established that moratorium pursuant to the International Convention for the Regulation of Whaling (ICRW), to which the United States and Japan are parties. Federal legislation obligates the executive to sanction any offending nation.[31] The United States and Japan, however, concluded an executive agreement, which essentially allowed Japan a grace period in conforming to the commission's regulations. (Executive agreements were described above.[32]) The Supreme Court ruled against the conservation groups on the merits.[33]

But most relevant to our purposes, the Court rather summarily concluded that the political question doctrine did not bar adjudication of the dispute. Justice White's majority opinion iterated *Baker*'s admonition that "not every matter touching on politics is a political question . . . and more specifically . . . 'it is error to suppose that every case or controversy which touches foreign relations lies beyond judicial cognizance.'"[34] With scant reference to the *Baker* criteria, Justice White simply wrote that "courts have the authority to construe treaties and executive agreements,"[35] which was the task at hand, and "we cannot shirk this responsibility merely because our decision may have significant political overtones."[36] Justice Marshall wrote a dissenting opinion, joined by Justices Blackmun, Brennan, and Rehnquist, arguing that the executive agreement could not evade the duty to impose sanctions on Japan. The dissent thus tacitly agreed that the dispute did not raise a political question and was justiciable.[37] Justice Rehnquist's inclusion in this dissent is perhaps surprising. He is, of course, not infrequently at loggerheads with this particular contingent of colleagues. Furthermore, one might have expected Justice Rehnquist to view the case as nonjusticiable, given his broad view of the political question doctrine in *Goldwater*. Perhaps, however, Justice Rehnquist could distinguish *Japan Whaling* from *Goldwater* in that it was commenced by a private litigant and it involved less of a direct clash between the political branches; those distinguishing features may recommend justiciability.

Political Questions, Human Rights, and Terrorism

In light of *Baker*, *Goldwater*, and *Japan Whaling*, what role should the political question doctrine play in the human rights and terrorism context? A good argument can be made that the doctrine is entirely irrelevant to most human rights and terrorism cases. Alternatively, a less extreme argument ably shows that the *Baker* criteria, with some embellishment from *Goldwater* and *Japan Whaling*, do not counsel judicial restraint in most human rights and terrorism cases. Both arguments are particularly compelling when nonstate actors are the defendants in a given case.

Take *Tel-Oren v. Libyan Arab Republic*[38] as an example. As has been described, the case concerned PLO terrorism and torture primarily committed against Israelis between Haifa and Tel Aviv; the PLO was the sole defendant when the case reached the Court of Appeals.[39] Although all three judges on the panel agreed to dismiss the case, only Judge Robb's concurring opinion reasoned that the case was nonjusticiable under the political question doctrine. Judge Robb stressed the political character of human rights and terrorism cases. He indicated that the president and the Congress, not the judiciary, should respond to international torturers and terrorists, who "are frequently pawns . . . in international politics."[40] He warned that "*ad hoc* intervention by courts into international affairs may very well rebound to the decisive disadvantage of the nation."[41] In general, he suggested that the judicial vindication of international political and human rights is ill-advised.[42] Judge Robb referred to several of *Baker*'s criteria and concluded that "[w]e ought not to parlay a two hundred years-old statue [i.e., the Alien Tort Statute] into so sensitive an area of foreign policy. . . . Every consideration that informs the sound application of the political question doctrine militates against this result."[43]

Contrary to Judge Robb's opinion, however, it is dubious whether the political question doctrine has any relevance to *Tel-Oren*. As Judge Edwards, writing separately, correctly perceived: "Nonjusticiability based upon 'political question' is *at best a limited* doctrine, and it is *wholly inapposite* to this case."[44] To begin, according to the Supreme Court, the doctrine may preclude the review of political questions, but not political cases; and the vindication of political rights do not necessarily raise political questions. Judge Robb did not adhere to that guidance when he focused on *Tel-Oren* as a political case involving political rights. Of course, by their very nature, terrorism and human rights cases both have political overtones. They often involve offenses aimed at advancing the defendant's political perspective, usually to the detriment of the plaintiff's political agendum and in violation of the plaintiff's political and human rights. If the rights at issue in *Tel-Oren* are nonjusticiable, then so are those involved in virtually every case of torture, genocide, apartheid, summary execution, hijacking, hostage taking, and crimes against internationally protected persons. That conclusion might suit Judge Robb, who broadly favored judicial passivity in cases having international ramifications; in fact, he expressly spoke against the watershed case of *Filartiga v. Pena-Irala*[45] and its "modern mission"[46] of judicially enforceable human rights. But that conclusion contradicts the axiom, expressed in *Baker* and emphasized by *Japan Whaling*, that not every case touching foreign relations is nonjusticiable.[47] It is also worth repeating (perhaps like a mantra) that the doctrine is one of political questions, not political cases.

More specifically, what political question does a case such as *Tel-Oren* raise? It hardly involved the type of issues that the three Supreme Court cases presented. *Tel-Oren* neither involved a challenge to a state legislature (*Baker*) nor a conflict between the political branches (*Goldwater*) nor a confrontation with the executive branch (*Japan Whaling*). Instead, individuals commenced *Tel-Oren* and they did not sue any United

States governmental institution. *Tel-Oren* was simply a suit involving the PLO and civilians that PLO terrorists had maimed or murdered. In a word, the case did not raise a political question; it did not raise the horizontal separation-of-powers concerns that underlie the political question doctrine. Rather, it involved the preliminary question of whether the requirements of a jurisdictional statute (the Alien Tort Statute) were satisfied. However that question was decided, it was not a political question under the Supreme Court's guidelines. And however much it was disputed, the question did not involve the political branches. The bulk of human rights and terrorism cases simply do not confront courts with a challenge against one political branch, much less a conflict between two branches.

Even Justice Rehnquist's expansive political question perspective in *Goldwater* contained a caveat when a private party commences a lawsuit. In contrast to Congress being the complainant, private plaintiffs are unable to protect their rights and interests in nonjudicial political settings.[48] Justice Rehnquist tacitly confirmed this point by his vote in *Japan Whaling*.[49] As Professor Scharpf's noted commentary explains, "even in the field of foreign affairs," "the Court is limiting . . . the political question by a normative qualification: where important individual rights are at stake, the doctrine will not be applied."[50] The Supreme Court's exercise of authority over those rights is "so central to its function that it is willing to pay a very high price in order to avoid a general delegation of this task to the political . . . authorities."[51]

Despite these considerations, courts have often held that the political question doctrine is relevant when a private party sues the United States government in an international case. For instance, in certain cases against the government concerning the Vietnam War and, more recently, the Nicaraguan conflict, lower federal courts have held the actions to be nonjusticiable.[52] Those cases were viewed to involve intimately the United States' overt and covert military policies — that aspect of the political branches' foreign affairs authority accorded the greatest judicial deference. It could well be argued, nevertheless, that such cases have been wrongly decided. By deeming those cases to be nonjusticiable, the courts have forfeited an important opportunity to adjudicate, if not remedy, the United States government's alleged international law violations. This result gives the poor impression that the federal government cannot be called to account for violating international law. Relatedly, the federal courts' narrow acceptance of civil resistance has reinforced that impression. Professor Francis Boyle has offered important and even novel litigation advice about defending nonviolent civil resistance under international and constitutional law.[53] Benefits might ensue from giving government protesters and civil resisters their successful day in court. In any event, however, litigation involving those individuals is not really dispositive of a case such as *Tel-Oren*. The litigation over both the United States' military operations and civil resistance has not usually involved a direct violation of individual rights, in distinction to *Tel-Oren* and to most other human rights and terrorism cases. In addition, *Tel-Oren* was not commenced against the United States, and the merits of the case were not intertwined with any federal military decisions. So especially when private victims sue a defendant other than the United States, the presumption remains that the political question doctrine is simply inapposite.

Judge Robb's use of the doctrine, moreover, seems to misconceive the separation-of-powers concept. The separation of powers does not contemplate "a complete division of authority between the three branches";[54] the "separate powers were not intended to operate with absolute independence."[55] Instead, the separation of powers includes a structural syntax by which each branch independently shares authority; this sometimes results in one branch even checking and balancing the others. Under Montesquieu's influence, the Constitution's framers decided that "checks and balances were the foundation of a structure of government that would protect liberty" and so they "provided for a Judicial Branch equally independent" of the executive and legislative branches.[56] The federal judiciary, in this way, does not emasculate its role, grounded in *Marbury v. Madison*, "to say what the law is."[57] The separatism of the federal departments thus impliedly may counsel activism as well as restraint. So the relationship among the federal departments — independent but also interdependent — is more complex than Judge Robb suggests. Hence, as a rule, the horizontally arranged separation of powers simply commands the federal judiciary to be mindful of its coordinate branches' authority. But only in exceptional situations directly involving the political branches does the political question doctrine recommend that a court abstain from exercising jurisdiction.

Under Judge Robb's opinion, however, the exception is the rule in international matters. By misconceiving the separation of powers, he eviscerates any judicial role in human rights and terrorism cases. Because the president and the Congress possess more international authority than the judiciary, Judge Robb suggests that the federal courts must possess none. But the federal courts hold important authority over cases that arise under international law or involve foreign actors. Federal courts should not avoid exercising that authority under the political question cop-out, particularly when the defendant is other than the United States. That human rights and terrorism cases have political and foreign relations overtones, again, does not, standing alone, make the political question doctrine relevant. Judge Robb's posture in *Tel-Oren*, therefore, violates *Baker*'s teachings, ultimately misconceptualizing the judicial function in international cases under separation-of-powers concerns.

Let us now briefly pursue an alternative analysis. Assume, solely for analytical purposes, that the political question doctrine is somehow not inapposite to a specific human rights or terrorism case, such as *Tel-Oren*.[58] This assumption would require that *Tel-Oren* and the question that it presented — i.e., how the Alien Tort Statute applies in the human rights and terrorism context — must be analyzed under *Baker*'s multiple criteria.[59] But even upon applying *Baker*'s criteria, it seems that Judge Robb was incorrect to have viewed *Tel-Oren* as nonjusticiable. First, the statute's applicability to human rights and terrorism cases is hardly a question that has been constitutionally committed to the president or the Congress. To the contrary, the statute itself directs the judiciary to govern certain disputes involving law of nations or treaty violations.[60] Second, judicially discoverable and manageable standards exist for determining whether alien tort jurisdiction should encompass PLO torture and terrorism. *Tel-Oren* primarily involved statutory interpretation, the mainstay of the judiciary's daily work, and treaty interpretation, which is also clearly within the judiciary's functional province.[61] *Japan Whaling* indicated that the judiciary "cannot shirk this responsibility" of statutory and treaty construction "merely because [a] decision may have significant political overtones."[62] The judiciary very ably can apply terrorism and human rights norms that recent treaties have defined and codified with sufficient clarity. Third, *Tel-Oren* was not impossible to adjudicate without an initial policy decision by a political branch. By enacting the Alien Tort Statute into law and by recodifying that statute periodically, the Congress and the president had initially and previously decided that the judiciary should adjudicate certain cases that implicate international law. Moreover, in myriad ways, the political branches have articulated a national policy against terrorism and human rights violations. Fourth, exercising judicial authority in *Tel-Oren* would not have shown disrespect to the political branches. *Tel-Oren* did not involve the United States as a litigant; it did not directly involve the United States' military policy regarding the PLO; and if it implicated the nation's foreign policy, a judgment against the PLO would probably have been very consistent with the Reagan administration's PLO policy in 1984. In addition, judicial respect for the other branches should not be exaggerated to skew the separation-of-powers concept or to eviscerate the judiciary's international authority. Fifth, adjudicating *Tel-Oren* would not have violated the separation of powers by undermining or questioning any previous political decisions. Sixth, exercising judicial authority in *Tel-Oren* would not have created a national embarrassment from having multifarious pronouncements on a question by the different branches of government. If anything, the court would have spoken in unison with its coordinate branches by reaching *Tel-Oren*'s merits and rendering a judgment against the terrorists.[63] Such a judgment, again, would have been congruent with the Reagan administration's stance against the PLO and international outlaws.

Just as *Baker*'s criteria should illustrate that *Tel-Oren* was justiciable, they would demonstrate the justiciability of most human rights and terrorism cases. Assuming *arguendo* that the political question doctrine is relevant, *Baker*'s criteria might not render each and every human rights or terrorism case to be justiciable. Again, particular political question concerns may arise in cases against the United States government.[64] And someone might argue that those concerns also exist when a nation-state is sued in a human rights or terrorism case. But even putting aside for now the serious problems with that argument, we may now note that federal courts rarely get to the issue of whether to exercise their authority over a nation-state. The judiciary often lacks authority altogether because the Foreign Sovereign Immunities Act of 1976 does not confer jurisdiction over nation-states in most human rights and terrorism cases.[65] So apart from cases against the United States and foreign governments, the *Baker* criteria should not normally limit adjudication in our context.

In short, two arguments have been pressed: the political question doctrine is usually irrelevant to human rights and terrorism cases; but even upon applying the *Baker* criteria, the majority of those cases remain justiciable. The horizontal separation of powers should not counsel judicial passivity simply due to the cases' international and political implications. Indeed, the judiciary is a particularly appropriate institution to exercise authority over disputes involving humanitarian norms. The judiciary is above the fray of international controversies; its nonpolitical nature helps to ensure that federal courts will function as a just and neutral body in those disputes. Compared with the president and the Congress, the judiciary may be criticized much less for being politically, nationally, and geopolitically biased when handling complaints brought by the victims of terrorism and human rights offenses. Judicial activism may even benefit the executive and legislative departments. If the judiciary independently supervises human rights and terrorism cases, the political branches may avoid involvement in such disputes, thus precluding whatever international criticism might ensue from their involvement. For all of these reasons, Judge Robb's reliance on the political question doctrine in *Tel-Oren* was misplaced. As Judge Edwards concluded: "To the extent that Judge Robb's reliance on political question principles arises from his concern about court intervention in foreign affairs, the Act of State Doctrine delineates the bounds of proper judicial restraint."[66] We turn, then, to the act-of-state doctrine.

Act-of-State Doctrine

Under the act-of-state doctrine, United States courts refrain from examining the legitimacy of certain foreign sovereign acts that were committed within the sovereign's own territory.[67] The doctrine may be viewed as a "special" choice-of-law rule.[68] Rather than apply ordinary choice-of-law principles to determine which of conflicting norms governs the sovereign's behavior, the court simply assumes the legitimacy of that behavior under the sovereign's domestic law. This assumption then supersedes any conflicting substantive norm or policy relevant to the issue at hand. The act-of-state doctrine bears obvious similarities to the sovereign immunity doctrine.[69] Act of state is also dissimilar, however, in the following ways: it relates to the exercise of judicial authority, not to the possession of authority; it may cause a court to abstain from examining a single sovereign act, but not necessarily to dismiss a case in its entirety; it may be raised by a nation-state or a nonstate actor whose behavior was allegedly committed under the color of sovereign authority; and it is primarily regulated by federal common law, not by statute.[70]

The Supreme Court's classic act-of-state pronouncement occurred in 1897, in *Underhill v. Hernandez:*[71] "Every sovereign State is bound to respect the independence of every other sovereign State, and the courts of one country will not sit in judgment on the acts of the government of another done within its own territory. Redress of grievances by reason of such acts must be obtained through the means open to be availed of by sovereign powers as between themselves."[72] *Underhill* prescribed a large dose of judicial restraint: Courts should not exercise their authority over any sovereign territorial acts. The political branches, instead, should govern controverted issues of sovereign behavior.

In the last few decades, however, the Supreme Court has redefined *Underhill*'s act-of-state perspective. The most radical doctrinal changes came from what was also the most newsworthy of the modern cases, *Banco Nacional de Cuba v. Sabbatino.*[73] Rendered in 1964, *Sabbatino* considered whether the act-of-state doctrine precluded judicial review of Cuba's expropriation of property without just compensation. With international tensions mounting, the United States had reduced the import quota for Cuban sugar, and the Castro government retaliated by nationalizing certain companies in Cuba in which United States citizens held interests. Cuba's shipping agent transported sugar previously owned by one such company to a commodities broker in New York. A dispute ensued about whether the proceeds from the sale were payable to Cuba or to the prior owners of the sugar. In seeking those funds, Cuba claimed that its expropriation was justified as a domestic sovereign act and beyond judicial purview under the act-of-state doctrine. Conversely, the prior owners' receiver claimed that Cuba did not have good title to the commodity because the expropriation violated international law; the receiver argued that the act-of-state doctrine should not insulate international law offenses from the exercise of judicial authority and review.

The *Sabbatino* opinion, which Justice Harlan authored, departed from *Underhill* in two significant ways. The Supreme Court first revised its view of the act-of-state doctrine's foundation. Although *Underhill* had stressed that the doctrine is predicated upon notions of sovereign independence and reciprocal sovereign respect, *Sabbatino* countered that the doctrine is not "compelled either by the inherent nature of sovereign authority . . . or by some principle of international law."[74] Post-*Sabbatino* decisions have posited the same perspective.[75] Therefore, "[w]hile historic notions of sovereign authority do bear upon the wisdom of employing the act of state doctrine, they do not dictate its existence."[76] International comity only subsidiarily supports the doctrine. According to *Sabbatino*, constitutional considerations primarily engender the act-of-state doctrine, even though the Constitution does not expressly mandate the doctrine.[77] The doctrine particularly "arises out of the basic relationships between branches of government in a system of separation of powers. It concerns the competency of dissimilar institutions to make and implement particular kinds of decisions in the area of international relations."[78] As with the political question doctrine, the act-of-state doctrine horizontally defines the appropriate scope of authority that the judiciary should exercise in relation to its coordinate branches. The act-of-state doctrine, however, has a more narrow range and purpose than the political question doctrine does: It is relevant only when the judiciary is called upon to examine foreign sovereign acts; it is used only to avoid judicial interference with the political branches' foreign relations. At the same time, the act-of-state doctrine "does not irrevocably remove from the judiciary the capacity to review the validity of foreign acts of state."[79] Quoting from *Baker*, the *Sabbatino* Court concluded that "it cannot . . . be thought that 'every case or controversy which touches foreign relations lies beyond judicial cognizance.'"[80]

From these passages, the second distinction between *Sabbatino* and *Underhill* begins to emerge. *Underhill* suggested that the act-of-state doctrine completely precludes judicial examination of all sovereign acts. Under *Sabbatino*, however, the doctrine is not absolute and inflexible, but counsels judicial restraint only on certain issues and in certain circumstances. *Sabbatino*'s formulation is wedded more properly to the separation of powers than *Underhill*'s formulation is. As we have emphasized, the federal judiciary possesses important authority over disputes potentially implicating foreign relations, even though the political branches have greater international authority. Federal judges should not languish under superficial references to the act-of-state doctrine whenever a case has international ramifications. Rather they should carefully and comprehensively assess whether such ramifications truly require the bold step of judicial passivity under the horizontal separation of powers. Compared with *Underhill, Sabbatino* more appropriately balanced the judiciary's joint responsibilities of providing justice to private litigants in international cases and not impinging upon the political branches' foreign policy initiatives.

The *Sabbatino* Court offered a matrix for determining whether the act-of-state doctrine permits judicial review of particular sovereign behavior:

It should be apparent that the greater the degree of codification or consensus concerning a particular area of international law, the more appropriate it is for the judiciary to render decisions regarding it, since the courts can then focus on the application of an agreed principle to circumstances of fact rather than on the sensitive task of establishing a principle not inconsistent with the national interest or with international justice. It is also evident that some aspects of international law touch much more sharply on national nerves than do others; the less important the implications of an issue are for our foreign relations, the weaker the justification for exclusivity in the political branches. The balance of relevant considerations may also be shifted if the government which perpetrated the challenged act of state is no longer in existence, . . . for the political interest of this country may, as a result, be measurably altered.[81]

That matrix is essentially divisible into three criteria, to be applied on a case-by-case and an issue-by-issue basis: the degree of international codification or consensus (if any) on an issue; the nature and significance of an issue under the nation's current foreign relations; and whether the government that authorized the act is extant or has been supplanted. Those criteria "reflect the proper distribution of functions between the judicial and political branches of Government on matters bearing upon foreign affairs."[82] Applying its new guidelines to the specific case at hand, the *Sabbatino* Court held that the judiciary should not examine the validity of Castro's nationalization of sugar. This holding largely derived from the lack of international consensus at the time, particularly between the United States and Soviet blocs, concerning the legality of nationalization: "There are few if any issues in international law today on which opinion seems so divided as the limitations on a State's power to expropriate."[83]

Although its analytical framework represented progress, *Sabbatino* did not provide an elixir. Congress statutorily reversed *Sabbatino*'s specific holding on nationalizations.[84] And when the executive department offers a suggestion about whether to apply the doctrine in a specific case, the executive's input may supersede any use of *Sabbatino*'s framework, even though *Sabbatino*'s second criterion may actually support that practice.[85] Similarly, certain new exceptions to the doctrine may preempt the "*Sabbatino* analysis" in special contexts[86] — although one or more of *Sabbatino*'s criteria may also support those exceptions. Finally, no Supreme Court case or doctrine escapes criticism by some members of the bench or the bar or by legal academics — perhaps the harshest of all.[87] *Sabbatino*, nevertheless, has remained the linchpin in the judiciary's analysis of many or most act-of-state issues. As such, its matrix may illuminate the doctrine's application in the human rights and terrorism context.

Acts of State, Human Rights, and Terrorism

In contrast to the political question doctrine, the act-of-state doctrine truly requires examination in many human rights and terrorism cases. It is obviously pertinent when the defendant is a nation-state that lacks jurisdictional immunity in a specific case. Since nation-states often have sovereign immunity in the human rights and terrorism context,[88] however, the doctrine has more practical relevance when the defendant is a nonstate actor who (or which) claims to have behaved under the color of nation-state authority. Nonstate defendants — the Argentine general who supervised scores of human rights violations, the Paraguayan police official who committed torture, and the Nazi war criminal[89] — cannot invoke sovereign immunity. Each of those individuals, however, can raise the act-of-state defense. In human rights and terrorism cases, therefore, this defense is inapposite only regarding defendants who have behaved without any sovereign support.[90]

That the doctrine is frequently relevant does not mean, of course, that it necessarily renders human rights and terrorism litigation to be nonjusticiable. Quite the contrary is true. Under the *Sabbatino* matrix, the federal courts should normally exercise their authority over the cases in this context. We proceed, then, to a *Sabbatino* analysis of human rights and terrorism cases. It should be stressed, however, that this analysis generally assumes the following: that the federal court has authority over the defendant (nation-state or nonstate) under a jurisdictional statute; that the defendant's behavior was committed as a sovereign act or under sovereign authority;[91] and that the offense was committed within the relevant sovereign's territory.

Under the first *Sabbatino* criterion, federal courts must consider whether a sufficiently codified norm governs the defendant's behavior, whether a sufficient consensus prohibits that behavior. Although such a codification and consensus may not have existed in 1964 regarding nationalization, the same cannot be said currently about fundamental human rights violations or hijacking or terrorism. *Filartiga v. Pena-Irala*, which concerned international torture, highlighted this point. The Second Circuit viewed *Filartiga* as "diametrically opposed to the conflicted state of law that confronted the *Sabbatino* Court."[92] "Indeed," *Filartiga* continued, "there are few, if any, issues in international law today on which opinion seems to be united as the limitations on a state's power to torture persons held in its custody."[93]

A similar global consensus prohibits, for example, genocide, war crimes, apartheid, hijacking, hostage taking, and crimes against internationally protected persons. Such universal norms have been codified and crystallized through a plethora of resolutions, declarations, conventions, customs, judicial decisions, and the writings of publicists. Even assuming that each of those sources does not independently condemn the offenses at hand, they cumulatively prohibit those acts with more than sufficient clarity and consensus. Drawing upon such sources, the *Restatement (Third) of Foreign Relations Law* (*Restatement*) identifies each of those offenses as a violation of customary law.[94] The *Restatement*, moreover, suggests that "[a] claim arising out of an alleged violation of fundamental human rights . . . would . . . probably not be defeated by the act of state doctrine, since the accepted international law of human rights is well established and contemplates external scrutiny of such acts."[95] Likewise, under a few other decisions that we have already discussed, *Sabbatino*'s first criterion impliedly did not counsel judicial abstention regarding either the human rights violations committed during Argentina's "dirty war"[96] or the mistreatment and probable murder of a Swedish diplomat.[97] This precedent establishes that human rights and terrorism cases alike can satisfy *Sabbatino*'s initial criterion.

The high degree of codification and consensus on human rights and terrorism norms permits federal courts, under *Sabbatino*, "to focus on the *application* of an agreed principle . . . rather than on the sensitive task of *establishing* a principle not inconsistent with the national interest or with international justice."[98] When federal courts exercise authority over these particular norms, they perform a function for which they are especially well suited. In this way, the judiciary also works prudently and with the proper respect that is due to both the political branches and other nation-states. The horizontal separation-of-powers concerns are satisfied because the federal courts are simply applying certain norms that the president and the Congress have helped to establish. To the extent that international comity subsidiarily underlies the act-of-state doctrine, it, too, is satisfied when federal courts adjudicate norms that are universal in nature and not idiosyncratic to the United States.[99] One might argue that antiterrorism norms do not satisfy *Sabbatino*'s first criterion as well as human rights norms do. But as many legal sources condemn terrorism as condemn human rights violations. Especially given the extensive treaty law at hand, terrorism is subject to the same international codification and consensus as human rights violations are.

Under *Sabbatino*'s second criterion, federal courts should consider the significance and implications of a particular issue for the United States' foreign relations. This criterion actually relates to the first. The more that an issue is resolvable by norms that are well codified and well accepted, the less likely it is that the issue will have serious or negative foreign policy implications. When adjudicating strongly accepted norms, federal courts do not myopically force the United States' value judgments upon foreign sovereign behavior. The judiciary, instead, construes and applies norms that the foreign sovereign itself has normally fostered and promulgated. Such adjudications may hoist the foreign sovereign upon its own normative petard, but they are relatively unlikely to cause foreign policy rifts between that sovereign and the political branches.

This factor certainly supports the justiciability of both human rights and terrorism cases. The vast majority of nation-states have subscribed to the treaty and customary norms that regulate human rights and terrorism. International organizations themselves have adopted the major conventions. The General Assembly has adopted the Genocide, Torture, Apartheid, Hostage, and Internationally Protected Persons conventions, and the International Civil Aviation Organization has adopted the Montreal and Hague conventions.[100] Such widespread support — concerning human rights and terrorist offenses alike—should limit adverse international reaction to the United States' adjudication of these offenses. Indeed, adjudicating human rights and terrorism cases may very positively enhance the United States' foreign relations. The relevant treaties and the corresponding customary law, after all, authorize, and sometimes obligate, the use of domestic judicial machinery in responding to terrorist and human rights offenses.[101] By adjudicating those acts in civil or criminal litigation, the United States can satisfy its legal commitments and hold itself out as a true champion of humanitarian and pacifistic values. Taking such a stance should improve, not impinge upon, the United States' international status and relations. Hence judicial authority may be orchestrated in horizontal concert with the political branches' position and responsibilities regarding human rights and terrorism.

It would be naive, of course, to suggest that the domestic adjudication of human rights and terrorism cases will never upset or anger a foreign sovereign. And while the norms that regulate these cases are widely subscribed, certain nation-states might object to a United States court's application and interpretation of those norms, perhaps particularly in the terrorism arena. The possibility of triggering a foreign sovereign's ire, however, should not normally recommend judicial restraint under *Sabbatino's* second criterion. This criterion focuses more upon how an issue generally relates to the federal government's foreign policy and less upon how a particular nation-state may react to that issue's adjudication. This focus is logical because, according to *Sabbatino*, the separation of powers and not international comity primarily motivate the act-of-state doctrine. Again, the federal government's foreign policy agenda generally supports the adjudication of human rights and terrorism issues. Furthermore, a nation-state predisposed to protest these lawsuits may bark loudly only when the country itself is a defendant. The FSIA reduces the likelihood of that scenario, however, because it excludes judicial authority over nation-states in most cases in this context; if a federal court is without jurisdiction in a case against a nation-state, it never has to reach the question of whether to exercise its authority under the act-of-state doctrine. On the other hand, when a nonstate actor, such as a government official, is the defendant and raises the act-of-state defense, his or her nation-state may actually choose not to protest the offense's adjudication—thus diminishing potential foreign policy rifts for the United States. In lieu of claiming the sovereign prerogative to sponsor human rights violations or terrorism, the nation-state might try to distance itself from the defendant and from those offenses.[102]

Although we have stressed the significant role that the judiciary can and should play in international cases, nothing stops the executive from communicating its view about whether judicial authority should be exercised in a specific case that ostensibly has foreign relations implications of a significant magnitude. That communication can come in the form of an amicus brief that either the federal court invites or that the State or Justice Departments initiate themselves. The Constitution does not expressly command the courts to elicit or to heed the executive's suggestions regarding justiciability. Nevertheless, pursuant to the separation of powers, some Supreme Court precedent suggests that the executive branch's lead should be followed regarding the act-of-state doctrine. A plurality of justices in a post-*Sabbatino* opinion agreed that "[i]t would be wholly illogical to insist that [act of state], fashioned because of fear that adjudication would interfere with the conduct of foreign relations, be applied in the face of an assurance from that branch of the Federal Government which conducts foreign relations that [interference] would not obtain."[103] Conversely, federal courts will probably apply the act-of-state doctrine and not exercise authority in those relatively rare instances when the executive directly indicates the need for the doctrine. In at least two cases specifically in the human rights and terrorism context, courts have already sought and followed the executive's advice about the propriety of judicial authority; the executive branch suggested that the court in one case should assume authority, but that in the other it should not.[104]

Executive branch recommendations against justiciability, however, should be particularly kept within reasonable limits. A presumption against the act-of-state defense should exist, so that the judiciary can consistently apply the international rule of law in human rights and terrorism cases. This presumption is appropriate, since foreign relations are normally served, not hurt, by the adjudication of these cases. Accordingly, executive amicus briefs that favor the act-of-state defense should be sparingly used as a separation-of-powers safety valve in relatively rare cases. For example, if the executive branch is strenuously negotiating with a nation-state for the release of American hostages and that nation-state is involved in a pending terrorism case, an executive suggestion of judicial inaction in the case may be warranted. But such a situation should be the exception, not the rule. The overriding separation-of-powers goal is to be sensitive to the political branches' international authority, while preserving judicial independence in most human rights and terrorism cases.

Finally, applying the third *Sabbatino* criterion is straightforward. When a new government has supplanted the foreign regime that sponsored the offenses at issue in a case, the act-of-state doctrine has less force than otherwise. The United States' relations with the new government are less likely to be harmed by an adverse judgment concerning the acts of a predecessor regime; this is in contrast to adjudicating the acts that a current foreign sovereign itself committed or supported. Within the *Sabbatino* matrix, this criterion has proved to be the least significant. This factor, nevertheless, might push the scales even further against the act-of-state defense in certain human rights and terrorism cases. For example, this criterion may arguably be persuasive in litigation involving offenses committed by deposed officials from the prior governments of Argentina and the Philippines.[105]

In summary, the act-of-state doctrine must be considered whenever a human rights or terrorist offense is allegedly committed under the color of sovereign authority. Upon applying the *Sabbatino* analysis, however, it is apparent that the doctrine should not render most cases in this context to be nonjusticiable. Perhaps unequaled in any other area of public international law, human rights and terrorism norms are subject to an overwhelming codification and consensus. The clarity of and agreement on these norms goes far in satisfying *Sabbatino*'s two primary criteria. Applying those norms — and thus examining sovereign behavior — is usually consistent with the proper judicial function in international cases and is appropriate in relation to the political branches. In those relatively rare cases in which adjudication may possibly interfere with foreign relations, the act-of-state doctrine remains available to the judiciary, especially upon the executive's suggestion. Normally, however, the important adjudication of heinous human rights and terrorism offenses should override the act-of-state defense.

Forum non Conveniens

Forum non conveniens is the final judicial abstention doctrine to consider. Since it is predicated primarily upon pragmatic concerns rather than on the constitutional allocation of authority, we will examine it only briefly. Under *forum non conveniens,* a court may decide not to exercise its authority when an alternative tribunal can capably adjudicate the lawsuit and would provide a more convenient forum for trying the lawsuit. For instance, in a federal civil action involving extraterritorial human rights violations or terrorism, the defendant may move for the case's dismissal under *forum non conveniens,* claiming that the case should instead be adjudicated in the nation-state where the offense occurred (i.e., the "situs nation-state"). In comparing the convenience of the federal and foreign tribunals, courts consider the following factors: "access to sources of proof; availability of . . . witnesses; . . . and all other practical problems that make trial of a case easy, expeditious and inexpensive. There may also be a question as to the enforceability of a judgment if one is obtained. *The court will weigh advantages and obstacles to fair trial.*"[106]

At first blush, those factors may seem to indicate that *forum non conveniens* would push many human rights and terrorism cases out of federal court and into a tribunal in the situs nation-state. In many or most cases, however, that conclusion may be wrong. "At the outset of any *forum non conveniens* inquiry," the Supreme Court recently stressed, "the court must determine whether there exists an alternative forum" that can appropriately manage the lawsuit.[107] That predicate may be lacking, for instance, when "the remedy offered by the other forum is clearly unsatisfactory."[108] Put another way, a clear prerequisite to *forum non conveniens* is "an alternative forum that will take jurisdiction of the case and where the plaintiff can get the relief he would get in federal court."[109] Many human rights and terrorism cases simply cannot meet this requirement. If the plaintiff was victimized in a nation-state of ongoing, and often unredressed, human rights violations or terrorism, a tribunal in the situs will probably not mete out justice in the case. Some nation-states may be unwilling and others unable to provide a sufficient remedy to the victims; it is exceedingly doubtful that most such foreign tribunals will offer relief comparable to that available in federal court.

So in the absence of a feasible alternative tribunal, federal judges need not even apply the convenience factors mentioned above. After all, those factors are subsumed by an evaluation of the "advantages and obstacles to fair trial."[110]

Filartiga offers an example. Before bringing their lawsuit in federal court, the plaintiffs had commenced a legal proceeding in Paraguay against the torturer. As a result of that proceeding, the plaintiffs' Paraguayan attorney was arrested, shackled by the same torturer to the walls of police headquarters, threatened with death, and subsequently disbarred without just cause.[111] The Paraguayan proceeding, perhaps needless to say, quickly came to a halt. Accordingly, later, when the defendant raised *forum non conveniens* in the federal action, the doctrine did not merit much consideration and was rejected out of hand.[112] Quite obviously, the Paraguayan judicial system could not be counted on to provide justice in a second proceeding if it had not done so in the first. In some sense, *Filartiga* befits the Supreme Court's directive that *forum non conveniens* is inappropriate "where the alternative forum does not permit litigation of the subject matter of the dispute."[113]

In addition to *Filartiga*, federal courts have contemplated the foreign nation-state's current political climate under the *forum non conveniens* analysis. For instance, in one corporate case, the situs, Ecuador, was controlled by a military government that possessed veto power over judicial decisions.[114] The federal court rejected the *forum non conveniens* defense, despite the case's greater connections with the foreign situs, because the "status and powers of the judiciary [in the situs were] 'uncertain.'"[115] Hence the presence of humanitarian violations, military force, or violence within the foreign situs may recommend against the defendant's use of *forum non conveniens*.

Of course, in some cases, the prerequisite of a feasible and capable alternative tribunal may be satisfied. Numerous foreign tribunals are very capable of justly adjudicating human rights and terrorism cases. When such a foreign tribunal is available, the *forum non conveniens* doctrine must be seriously considered. We may borrow an example from another context—in particular, the horrid 1984 industrial disaster in Bhopal, India. Scores of lawsuits were brought in United States federal courts on behalf of those injured or killed by the lethal gas released at Union Carbide's chemical plant. In a consolidated proceeding, the Second Circuit Court of Appeals decided that the cases should be tried in India rather than in the United States.[116] The court found that the prerequisite to the *forum non conveniens* defense was present: "despite some of the Indian system's disadvantages, it afforded an adequate alternative forum for the enforcement of plaintiffs' claims."[117]

But even when that prerequisite is established in a human rights or terrorism case, the *forum non conveniens* defense will not necessarily render the case to be nonjusticiable. The opposite conclusion may sometimes be reached, for several reasons. First, a presumption exists that "the plaintiff's choice of forum should rarely be disturbed,"[118] although that presumption is strongest when the plaintiff is a United States citizen.[119] Second, it is important to the *forum non conveniens* doctrine that the plaintiff did not choose an inconvenient forum for the specific purpose of vexing, harassing, or oppressing the defendant.[120] That consideration would certainly not bar the justiciability of most or all human rights or terrorism cases. Such litigation is commenced in the United States often because the plaintiffs have fled to this country and the defendants can be served with federal process. There is simply no evidence that any of the recent human rights or terrorism cases have been brought in federal court to vex, harass, or oppress the defendants. Third, a federal court in these cases may provide a relatively convenient forum because the plaintiffs and, usually, the defendants are present or have some presence within the United States. Since at least certain key witnesses and items of proof will already be in the United States, the convenience factors may actually favor a federal forum over a forum in the situs nation-state. Fourth, if at least ideally the same body of international law would govern a case either in federal court or in foreign court, there is less of a reason for the case to be dismissed in federal court to proceed elsewhere. The same international law should emit the same juridical results in both the federal and foreign tribunals. Fifth and finally, the judgments that federal judges render against defendants in human rights and terrorism cases are admittedly not easy to enforce, especially when the defendant is a nonstate actor. If enforcement-of-judgment difficulties, however, are permitted to prevent victims from pursuing their meritorious and significant claims, then federal judicial authority will effectively be controlled and foreclosed by the ability of international outlaws to run from United States judgments and from the rule of law inself.[121]

Whether a federal or foreign tribunal issues a judgment against a terrorist or human rights offender, enforcing the judgment will probably be difficult. It thus makes sense to encourage federal courts to render whatever judgment is appropriate in a given case and only later let plaintiffs worry about enforcing the judgment in the United States or abroad. In sum, the pragmatic considerations of *forum non conveniens* may often recommend that federal courts exercise their authority in human rights and terrorism cases. The significance of these cases, under jurisprudential, political, and legal dimensions, should tilt the balance in favor of federal judicial activism in this context.

Conclusion

When statutory jurisdiction exists in human rights and terrorism cases, federal judges should consider further the constitutional relationship between the judiciary and its coordinate branches to determine the propriety of exercising their authority. The political question and act-of-state doctrines express horizontal separation-of-powers concerns. The political question doctrine is inapposite or, at a minimum, uncompelling in most human rights and terrorism cases. The act-of-state doctrine is relevant, but it also does not recommend judicial abstention in most cases, largely due to the universal nature of human rights and terrorism norms. In a rare case, these doctrines may recommend that the judiciary put aside its not insignificant authority in international litigation. But such cases are very much the exception, not the rule. Finally, *forum non conveniens* likewise does not recommend judicial abstention in most human rights and terrorism cases. By adjudicating these cases, although ever mindful of the political branches' international authority, the judiciary can constitutionally perform an important function in redressing some of the world's most egregious offenses.

CHAPTER 6

Legislative Prescriptions: Twenty-first Century Epilogue

As the United States moves into the twenty-first century, federal jurisdiction over human rights and terrorism cases will become increasingly important. The international protection of individual lives and physical integrity will continue to evolve from rhetoric to reality. As we will soon further demonstrate in part two, the world community has agreed that fundamental rights must not be breached in any setting; it condemns human rights violations and terrorist activities committed anywhere in the world. On an expanding basis, the world legal order invites the external scrutiny of international offenses, even when the offender and the victim are of the same nationality and when a nation-state sponsors offenses against its own nationals.

As this global evolution continues, it is likely that domestic courts will particularly be called upon to redress international offenses, in both the criminal and civil settings. Recall that the Covenant on Civil and Political Rights ("Covenant") and the Torture Convention expressly oblige domestic courts to provide civil remedies to individuals injured by the offenses that the instruments prohibit.[1] For parties to those instruments — and for nonparties under customary law — nation-states are not only permitted, but obligated to assume jurisdiction over those offenses.[2] Moreover, as we will see, under the universality principle of jurisdiction, domestic courts may also be compelled to assume authority over certain heinous offenses with which they have no connection.[3] Under customary law, the universality principle originally permitted all nation-states to assume jurisdiction over piratical offenses occurring on the high seas, whether or not the forum nation-state had any nexus with the pirates or their victims. But today, the Geneva, Hague, Montreal, Torture, Apar-

theid, Hostage, and Internationally Protected Persons conventions all encompass the concept of universal jurisdiction.[4] Those treaties obligate
each party's judiciary to address any offender in the forum nation-state's
custody, even when an extraterritorial offense does not in any way involve the forum or its nationals. That obligation applies to both civil and
criminal cases, under current learning.[5] An international judicial forum,
of course, might someday be established to remedy the modern offenses;
the trial at Nuremberg provides a precedent for such an endeavor, particularly in the criminal context.[6] But repeated calls for an international
criminal court have thus far gone unheeded,[7] and the modern treaties
explicitly identify the parties' own domestic judiciaries as the essential
civil apparatus for vindicating human rights violations and terrorism.
The parties to those conventions — and nonparties under custom and general principles of law — will thus be obligated to respond judicially to the
victims of egregious offenses. Before long, civil litigation such as *Filartiga v. Pena-Irala*,[8] involving a foreign torture incident between foreigners, may not at all seem an unusual case to be commenced in a federal
court. Perhaps similarly, other domestic (and even regional) adjudicative
bodies around the world may be faced with *Filartiga*-like litigation on
an evermore frequent basis.[9] Accordingly, as the internationalization of
human rights and terrorism norms grows during the coming century, so
will the solicitation of domestic judicial responses to the violations of
those norms.

The United States, therefore, should ensure that its judiciary possesses
and exercises authority over human rights and terrorism cases. By so doing, the nation will meet its international obligation to offer civil redress
to human rights and terrorism victims. It will also, in this way, meet its
universal jurisdictional obligations to remedy heinous offenses occurring
anywhere in the world; that commitment primarily stems from treaties
to which the United States is a party. Just as the nation had a responsibility to provide civil remedies for offenses against ambassadors in the
eighteenth century — as evidenced by the Marbois and Van Berckel sce-
narios[10] — it today has a similar responsibility regarding the modern offenses. In the eighteenth century, satisfying that commitment was critical
to the nation's infant status in the world community. Today, satisfying
that commitment is critical to the nation's status as a global front-runner
in combating human rights violations and terrorism. Although the United

States' position in the world will be very different in the twenty-first century than it was in the eighteenth, it surely retains its legal obligation to redress international offenses judicially, and its enhanced global position makes that obligation all the more compelling.

In part one we demonstrated why, under vertical federalism, the federal courts rather than the state courts should have jurisdiction to fulfill the nation's obligations in human rights and terrorism cases. In part one we also showed that the federal courts should exercise jurisdiction in these cases, consistently with horizontal separation-of-powers considerations. The alien tort and federal question statutes, as currently written, would normally seem to provide federal jurisdiction over cases involving nonstate defendants.[11] And the judicial abstention doctrines, under current Supreme Court precedent, would normally seem to recommend the exercise of jurisdiction over those cases.[12] Confusion and disagreement, however, continue to surround both the jurisdictional statutes and the judicial abstention doctrines in the circuit and district courts. It is thus prescient to conclude part one by offering a model piece of legislation ("model revision").[13] We will create an entirely new jurisdictional statute relevant to cases against nonstate terrorists and human rights offenders. This statute will leave no doubt in any federal judge's mind that civil jurisdiction exists and should be exercised over nonstate defendants. Although we have argued that such judicial authority already exists under the current law, the model revision will clarify, confirm, and concretize that authority. The model revision will thus ensure that federal courts play an active role in future human rights and terrorism litigation.

As part one has also shown, it is often difficult to establish jurisdiction over nation-state defendants in human rights and terrorism cases under the Foreign Sovereign Immunities Act of 1976 (FSIA). That conclusion was largely based upon a statutory interpretation of the FSIA.[14] Granted, litigation involving nation-states may raise particular considerations of international comity and foreign relations that are not present when nonstate actors are sued. We will, nevertheless, also offer a model revision to the FSIA. We will create an entirely new exception to sovereign immunity under the FSIA, affording judicial authority when nation-states sponsor or support human rights violations or terrorism. The model revision also establishes a presumption that that authority should usually be exercised. For those commentators and the few judges who already interpret the FSIA to confer human rights and terrorism jurisdiction over nation-state defendants,[15] the model revision may simply illuminate or confirm their viewpoint. For all others, the model revision will signify a substantial increase of FSIA authority. This legislative prescription, as with the prescription concerning nonstate defendants, is well supported by the federalism and separation-of-powers considerations that we have discussed throughout part one. The domestic authority that the model revisions encompass is also legitimate under international jurisdictional principles and is justified within the world legal order, as part two will illuminate.

Jurisdiction over Nonstate Defendants

Either the alien tort or federal question statutes (28 U.S.C. sections 1350 and 1331) might be revised to provide, with greater clarity, federal jurisdiction over the modern human rights and terrorism cases. Section 1350 or 1331 could be amended specifically to address the problems that judges and litigators have had in applying the statutes in our context.[16] Given the checkered past of these statutes, however, it may be advisable simply to create an entirely new statute for cases involving nonstate defendants — a jurisdictional *tabula rasa*.

The new legislation, let us call it "28 U.S.C. section 1390," should provide the following:

1390. Action for human rights violations or terrorist offenses.

(a) The district courts shall have original jurisdiction over any civil action brought by a citizen or an alien against any defendant other than a foreign state who or which has committed within or outside the United States an international law violation listed in subsection (b). Such actions shall be deemed to arise under federal law; this subsection shall provide a cause of action where one does not otherwise exist. This subsection shall not affect plaintiffs' ability to allege jurisdiction under any other section of this chapter; this subsection shall not preclude jurisdiction in actions against a foreign state under section 1330 of this chapter.

(b) The international law violations referred to in subsection (a) are limited to:

(1) genocide;

(2) torture;

(3) summary execution;

(4) causing the disappearance of individuals;

(5) slavery, slave trading, and apartheid;

(6) prolonged arbitrary detention;

(7) war crimes;

(8) piracy, hijacking of vessels and aircraft, and violent acts committed against vessels and aircraft;

(9) hostage taking; and

(10) crimes against internationally protected persons.

District courts shall define the acts listed in subsection (b) consistently with treaties and international customary law.

(c) All defendants shall be deemed legally capable of committing the acts listed in subsection (b). The defenses of superior orders and political question shall not be available; the act-of-state defense shall not be available, unless the executive branch determines that the United States foreign policy interests require application of the act-of-state doctrine, and a suggestion to that effect is filed with the court. A presumption shall exist against the *forum non conveniens* defense, and a case shall not be dismissed under this defense, unless the court imposes conditions assuring that the case will proceed against the defendant in the alternate tribunal and will be adjudicated sufficiently and fairly.

The crux of model section 1390 is absolutely to provide what sections 1350 and 1331 have sometimes not provided: a federal forum for human rights and terrorism cases. Since the United States may not only be encouraged, but obliged under international law to provide such a forum, the federal courts should possess and exercise the jurisdiction that the model revision recommends. Of course, section 1390's justifications, scope, and goals essentially derive from our earlier discussions and critiques of the existing law. Federalism and separation-of-powers considerations ably support the model revision. While our prior discussions might fully serve to support and explain section 1390, an examination of each subsection may still be warranted.

Subsection (a)

Subsection (a) sweepingly ensures that federal jurisdiction exists when any individual — citizen or alien — suffers certain international law offenses at the hands of any nonstate defendant — citizen, alien, or political or terrorist organization. The vertical federalist control over international law and foreign affairs dictates this omnibus provision of district court authority. This authority may be especially significant in cases involving aliens, since the judiciary's response to these cases may specifically influence the United States' relations with an alien's nation-state.[17] But providing federal jurisdiction is actually important in any case that concerns a violation of international law, even cases involving only United States citizens. International law is federal law, and every case involving that law may have some foreign relations implications. Hence subsection (a) predicates federal jurisdiction upon the occurrence of an international offense, rather than on the litigants' nationalities. It intentionally avoids limiting jurisdiction by alienage, diversity, and amount-in-controversy requirements,[18] although it does not bar plaintiffs from invoking other jurisdictional provisions, if available. The goal is simply to afford the broadest possible basis of federal authority over federal law and federal interests. This is consistent with the very purpose of the arising-under clause in article III of the Constitution: to provide relatively uniform, objective, and effective adjudication of cases that somehow involve federal components.[19] Federal courts continue to be viewed as better able to perform that task than the decentralized state tribunals are.[20]

In cases where aliens sue aliens or foreign organizations, article III's alienage clause does not support jurisdiction under model subsection (a).[21] Similarly, when citizens from the same state oppose each other, article III's diversity clause does not support jurisdiction under subsection (a).[22] In both of those instances, however, article III's arising-under clause offers ample constitutional support for federal jurisdiction. Recall that when plaintiffs invoke any jurisdictional statute other than section 1331, there is arising-under authority whenever a federal question is merely an "original ingredient" in the case.[23] The original-ingredient test would obviously be met in every section 1390 case. By the statute's very terms, each case would necessarily present the question of whether international law has been violated; that international question is an explicit requisite for jurisdiction under section 1390. It is not perfectly logical that the Constitution's arising-under clause more expansively supports federal jurisdiction under section 1390 than under 1331.[24] But the Supreme Court has repeatedly read the arising-under clause broadly in nonsection 1331 cases,[25] and section 1390 can certainly take advantage of that fact.

In addition to raising federal international questions, section 1390 cases raise federal statutory questions. Specifically recall our discussion of *Verlinden B. V. v. Central Bank of Nigeria*,[26] an FSIA case in which the arising-under clause rather than the alienage clause supported federal jurisdiction.[27] Even though the Netherlands contract law would govern the merits of this suit between foreign actors, the case arose under federal law because, at "the threshold of every [FSIA] action," the district courts "must apply the detailed federal standards set forth in the [FSIA]."[28] *Verlinden* surely supports arising-under jurisdiction in section 1390 cases, since the district courts would have to apply the several detailed parts of section 1390 in every human rights or terrorism case. In other words, since applying the FSIA's standards raises federal statutory questions, so does the application of section 1390's standards. Arising-under authority was also justifiable in *Verlinden* due to the "sensitive issues concerning the foreign relations of the United States, and the primacy of federal concerns is evident."[29] That justification would likewise support arising-under authority in section 1390 cases, since by their very nature human rights and terrorism cases raise foreign relations concerns for the United States. The nation has an international commitment to entertain those cases, and the way in which its courts handle this litigation may obviously have foreign relations implications.[30] Again, the goal of article III's arising-under clause is to keep cases involving federal law and national issues in federal court. Section 1390 would further that goal in the human rights and terrorism context. Under *Verlinden*, once jurisdiction is constitutional in a section 1390 case — due to the initial presence of both international and federal statutory questions — it remains constitutional, even if nonfederal rules of decision are eventually applied on the merits.

Subsection (a) recognizes a federal cause of action for the international law violations listed in subsection (b). The issue of whether individuals have a private cause of action for these offenses has been subject to much judicial disagreement. We have argued that a federal cause of action is not actually necessary in section 1350 cases;[31] and we have argued that human rights and terrorism victims usually do have a federal cause of action under the various genuses of section 1331 jurisdiction.[32] Nevertheless, by explicitly providing a federal cause of action, in case one is deemed not otherwise to exist, section 1390 specifically allows plaintiffs to avoid the treacherous cause-of-action hurdle. Congress is constitutionally able to recognize a private cause of action for international law violations,[33] just as it can recognize a cause of action for any federal law violation. Subsection (a)'s phraseology — providing that these actions "shall be deemed to arise under federal law" — is actually similar to that used in other recently enacted jurisdictional statutes.[34] Those statutes, as with section 1390, draw upon article III's expansive arising-under component. By expressly providing a federal cause of action, section 1390 will help to ensure that human rights and terrorism cases are heard in federal court rather than in state court. That objective comports with the Constitution's vertical federalism.

Lastly, subsection (a) confirms that federal jurisdiction is available irrespective of where an offense occurs. The United States obviously has an important interest in human rights violations or terrorist acts that occur on its soil. The United States may also have a significant concern with foreign offenses that are somehow directed toward its citizens or its other national interests and assets. Whenever the nation has a sufficient connection with an offense occurring either within or without the country, federal jurisdiction is eminently reasonable.[35] But even when the United States is not directly connected with a heinous foreign offense — as in *Filartiga* — its extraterritorial jurisdiction is proper. This conclusion draws support from our examination of alien tort jurisdiction over extraterritorial offenses, under statutory and precedential analyses and under the transitory-tort doctrine.[36] Because federal law is at issue, and due to the foreign relations implications at stake, extraterritorial tort cases involving breaches of treaty and international custom belong in federal court. Moreover, all domestic courts possess universal jurisdiction to redress subsection (b)'s limited category of ghastly offenses, despite any national or territorial link with those acts.[37] Universal jurisdiction has a deep heritage in international and American jurisprudence; its early applications to extraterritorial acts of piracy, slave trading, and war crimes will be documented below.[38] As already mentioned and as will be discussed further, the United States today may be obligated to exercise universal jurisdiction over those and the more modern human rights and terrorist offenses under treaty and customary law; this is so even when foreigners commit those acts extraterritorially against other foreigners.[39] Furthermore, on a policy level, federal court jurisdiction must encompass extraterritorial offenses, if the judiciary's international authority is to fulfill its deep potential. It is extremely difficult to bring international outlaws to justice, and domestic courts should be encouraged to assume universal jurisdiction over all such defendants when found in the forum nation-state's territory. Hence in light of both the nation's international commitments and federalism concerns, subsection (a) correctly advances federal universal jurisdiction over heinous extraterritorial offenses.

Subsection (b)

Subsection (b) identifies the international law violations that are subject to federal jurisdiction under section 1390. Federal judges have expressed uncertainty and confusion about which international offenses fall within their authority under sections 1350 and 1331.[40] By specifically listing several human rights violations and terrorist activities, and by providing some definitional guidance as to those offenses, subsection (b) should help to erase any doubt about the international offenses that plaintiffs can allege in federal court. Nothing per se would stop future plaintiffs from alleging additional international offenses under sections 1350 and 1331. And in a sense, section 1390 has a narrower scope than sections 1350 and 1331, since only section 1390 limits jurisdiction to particular international law violations. In practice, however, section 1390 should significantly expand the number of human rights and terrorism cases that federal courts adjudicate. By enacting section 1390, Congress may expressly and elaborately inform the courts of the cases that it thinks the judiciary should hear. As a result, the courts may be more inclined to assume jurisdiction under section 1390's extensive directives than under the tersely phrased alien tort and federal question statutes. Both international and vertical federalism concerns, again, dictate an active role for the federal judiciary in human rights and terrorism cases. That role may be furthered by subsection (b)'s specification of offenses that are particularly susceptible to federal court treatment.

Several considerations have guided the selection of offenses included in subsection (b). Most importantly, multilateral treaties, with widespread subscription, have prohibited each of the offenses listed. By treaty for the parties, and by custom and general principles of international law for nonparties, all nation-states are bound to observe, implement, and promote these fundamental norms. There should be no doubt that international law proscribes the human rights and terrorist offenses at hand. Much of part one has been spent making that very point. We have extensively documented how the Covenant and the Geneva, Torture, Apartheid, Genocide, Hague, Montreal, Hostage, and Internationally Protected Persons conventions sanction the private enforcement of the norms found in those instruments.[41] In part two we will further document how those conventions, along with other legal sources, compel all nation-states to assume civil jurisdiction over the offenses listed in subsection (b).[42] Treaties have extensively defined these offenses; international custom also helps to define those acts; and subsection (b) specifically advises federal courts to use those definitions in human rights and terrorism litigation. Federal judges should, therefore, be quite capable of redressing subsection (b)'s well-proscribed and well-defined offenses. In a word, international law bars these offenses and encourages their reparation in federal courts. Particularly given the fact that certain treaties explicitly condemn hijacking and terrorism, those offenses are surely as deserving as human rights violations to be included in subsection (b). We have previously discussed, moreover, the parallelism between human rights violations and terrorism.

The Supreme Court's formulation of the act-of-state doctrine, in *Banco Nacional de Cuba v. Sabbatino*,[43] also supports the selection of the offenses found in subsection (b). (Although *Sabbatino* is relevant to subsection (b), the act-of-state defense itself is addressed in subsection (c).) Under the first prong of what we have called the "*Sabbatino* matrix," domestic courts should adjudicate international norms on which a high degree of codification and consensus exists.[44] That prong certainly supports federal jurisdiction over the human rights violations as well as the terrorist offenses contained in subsection (b). When faced with those particular offenses, federal judges do not need to read the plaintiffs' complaints with red-white-and-blue blinders. Rather than myopically involving just United States norms, those complaints involve quintessentially supranational norms, thus inviting extraterritorial adjudication. When these highly codified and subscribed treaty norms are at issue, federal court activism is relatively unlikely to offend other nation-states. The judiciary, after all, is applying norms that the global community has created and promoted with great consensus. That consensus exists regarding terrorism and human rights violations both. Rather than troubling other nation-states, the federal adjudication of subsection (b)'s offenses should demonstrate that the United States is fulfilling its international obligations to all other nation-states by addressing offenses that strike at the heart of global order. Federal jurisdiction over human rights and terrorism should thus enhance rather than hurt the United States' foreign relations. This conclusion actually supports jurisdiction under both the first and second prongs of the *Sabbatino* matrix, since the latter recommends federal adjudication when it is in the best interests of the nation's foreign relations.[45] Given *Sabbatino*'s support, subsection (b)'s treaty-based offenses are quite suitable for judicial attention.

In short, subsection (b) serves the purpose of identifying those norms that deserve the attention of federal judges, rather than state judges. This subsection includes the principal offenses that were recognized and were on the minds of lawmakers when the Alien Tort Statute was passed in the eighteenth century.[46] Those offenses — including piracy and violations of ambassadorial rights — are now covered by treaty and they continue to merit federal redress. Subsection (b) further encompasses the present century's human rights and terrorism offenses that require federal court review. The United States recognizes the norms against all of these offenses under federal law by treaty or custom.[47] As such, these norms should always be subject to federal jurisdiction when violated, particularly given the foreign relations implications at stake. Vertical federalism demands no less. Just as the first Judiciary Act sought federal control over international offenses in the eighteenth century, the modern Judiciary Act should have the same aspiration in the twenty-first century. Although our goal is to identify the current international offenses that are susceptible to adjudication, one could argue that subsection (b)'s offenses should be expanded in the future. For example, it might eventually be argued that the claims of indigenous populations might raise justiciable controversies befitting the human rights paradigm. Those claims are certainly important, as leading commentators have discussed.[48] Such claims, however, are not presently subject to the same type of well-defined and universal norms that regulate subsection (b)'s offenses. For now, subsection (b) provides an accurate list of offenses particularly deserving federal court adjudication.

Subsection (c)

Subsection (c) addresses various defenses that are often raised in human rights and terrorism cases. Current statutory law offers virtually no guidance about how courts should evaluate those defenses, especially in our context. Federal judges have inconsistently ruled on those defenses, and subsection (c) may thus fill an unfortunate lacuna in the law. At least two of the relevant defenses — the act-of-state and political question doctrines — hinge on the judiciary's deference to its coordinate branches. It may thus be particularly helpful if the Congress and the president, by writing and signing section 1390, expressly indicate their position about whether the act-of-state and political question doctrines should permit the adjudication of human rights and terrorism cases. Buttressed by our earlier discussions, we may now explain why neither those nor any other defenses should normally bar the exercise of jurisdiction in section 1390 cases.

According to subsection (c), nonstate actors (e.g., government officials, soldiers, terrorist groups) cannot legitimately claim either that they lack the legal personality to commit international offenses or that their acts are justifiable because committed pursuant to a superior's orders. Both defenses, logically, must be unavailable if judicial authority over human rights violations and terrorism is to amount to anything. Nonstate actors are capable of committing and do commit international offenses. They are the subjects of international law at least insofar as fundamental rights and responsibilites are concerned.[49] The key to understanding legal personality, again, is not to fixate superficially upon a defendant's name or label, but to consider whether the defendant has committed an act that international law prohibits and which has international ramifications. Most of the human rights and terrorism treaties explicitly apply to both nation-state and nonstate actors; in addition, the type of nonstate actor who or which committed the act is usually irrelevant to the treaties' application. Under our earlier contextual analyses, when nonstate defendants act in public and global settings, they are capable of violating human rights and terrorism norms, whether or not their offenses are sovereign-sponsored.[50] For example, the PLO, nonstate terrorists in *Tel-Oren v. Libyan Arab Republic*,[51] actually did commit offenses in Israel that international law prohibits. It should be needless to say that terrorists are legally capable of committing terrorism and human rights violations, even without sovereign support or guidance.

In those specific instances when the nonstate defendant is an individual who did act under a sovereign directive, the superior-orders defense should not avail under subsection (c). This conclusion essentially derives from the modern conception of legal personality. If the superior-orders defense were to be accepted, then only nation-states would be held responsible for these international law violations — which contradicts the current idea that nonstate actors possess rights and responsibilities when fundamental norms are at stake.[52] Rejecting this defense is especially appropriate due to the blatant immorality and heinousness of the offenses addressed in section 1390. Both precedent and multilateral treaties explicitly reject the superior-orders defense,[53] and subsection (c) is on firm ground by making this defense unavailable.

Subsection (c) next bars a defense based on the political question doctrine. While always of questionable validity and utility,[54] the doctrine is completely inapposite to human rights and terrorism cases brought against nonstate defendants. The doctrine is premised upon separation-of-powers concerns specifically relevant when a branch of the United States government is a party to a lawsuit.[55] Since section 1390 does not encompass suits against the United States, the political question doctrine is irrelevant. As we have extensively described, the doctrine is one of political questions, not political cases; the mere political nature of human rights and terrorism cases should not cause judicial inaction under horizontal separation-of-powers concerns.[56] That these cases involve individual plaintiffs alleging violations of fundamental rights further supports justiciability. Moreover, even under *Baker v. Carr*'s criteria,[57] human rights and terrorism cases appear justiciable, as we have also described.[58] For all of these reasons, subsection (c) denies the political question defense, expressly acknowledging that the federal courts should exercise their authority in cases against nonstate defendants.

In addition, subsection (c) advises federal judges not to dismiss a case under the act-of-state doctrine unless the executive branch recommends that the nation's foreign policy interests require dismissal. A presumption against the act-of-state defense is appropriate under the *Sabbatino* matrix.[59] Judges should normally exercise jurisdiction over the human rights and terrorist offenses at hand because, again, an extremely high degree of codification and consensus prohibits both sets of those offenses under treaty and custom. Given that international accord, adjudicating those offenses will not normally harm the United States' relations with other nation-states. Under *Sabbatino*, no other set of international norms deserves domestic adjudication as much as the well-subscribed norms found in section 1390. The *Restatement (Third) of Foreign Relations Law* suggests an exception to the act-of-state doctrine when fundamental rights are violated,[60] recognizing that the horizontal separation of powers should not usually bar human rights and terrorism litigation.

Subsection (c), nevertheless, encompasses a "separation-of-powers safety value," considered above,[61] permitting the executive branch to intervene in those rare cases when adjudication may negatively influence foreign relations. This statutory conception draws somewhat upon the (second) "Hickenlooper Amendment" of 1964.[62] While making the act-of-state doctrine presumptively inapplicable to nationalization cases, the Hickenlooper Amendment allows the president to recommend that the doctrine be applied in specific nationalization cases, when required by "the foreign policy interests of the United States."[63] Even if the Constitution does not mandate that the judiciary defer to the executive branch in the nationalization or the human rights and terrorism contexts, courts usually should and do heed the executive's advice about the act-of-state doctrine. By specifically allowing the executive to intervene in cases having particularly sensitive foreign relations overtones, subsection (c) satisfies horizontal separation-of-powers concerns. This result helps to delineate the proper role of federal courts in human rights and terrorism cases vis-à-vis the political branches, under the act-of-state doctrine.

Finally, subsection (c) also creates a presumption against the *forum non conveniens* defense. This presumption is especially appropriate due to both the lack of alternative judicial fora[64] and the extreme importance of human rights and terrorism cases. The defendant thus has the burden of proving that a foreign tribunal will fairly and more conveniently adjudicate the case; this burden should include a demonstration that the plaintiff can receive the same remedy in the foreign tribunal that is permitted in the federal tribunal. In addition, courts should never dismiss without imposing the following type of conditions, which sometimes can be enforced by holding a defendant's assets in escrow: the defendant will submit to the jurisdiction of the foreign court; the defendant will fully abide by whatever judgment and monetary damages the foreign court orders; and if the case does not proceed properly in the foreign court, the defendant will resubmit to the federal district court's authority.[65] Subsection (c), therefore, presumptively allows human rights and terrorism victims to institute their cases in federal court, while helping to safeguard the victims' procedural rights in those occasional instances when a case is conditionally dismissed under the *forum non conveniens* defense.

Jurisdiction over Nation-State Defendants

We will now offer a statutory model concerning human rights and terrorism jurisdiction over nation-state defendants. To ensure that such federal jurisdiction is available and normally exercised, two new additions to the FSIA are in order.[66] Initially, section 1605(a) should be revised to include an explicit "human rights and terrorism exception" to jurisdictional immunity. This first model revison — which we will label "28 U.S.C. section 1605(a)(7)" — should provide as follows:

1605. General exceptions to the jurisdictional immunity of a foreign state.

(a) A foreign state shall not be immune from the jurisdiction of courts of the United States or of the States in any case. . . .

(7) in which the foreign state, as a matter of sovereign policy, has allegedly practiced, encouraged, or condoned the following offenses, wherever and against whomever committed, and as defined consistently with treaties and international customary law: genocide, torture, summary execution, causing the disappearance of individuals, slavery, slave trading, apartheid, prolonged arbitrary detention, war crimes, piracy, hijacking of vessels and aircraft, violent acts committed against vessels and aircraft, hostage taking, and crimes against internationally protected persons. Such actions shall be deemed to arise under federal law; this subsection shall provide a cause of action where one does not otherwise exist.[67]

Furthermore, a new provision should be added to the FSIA concerning the judicial abstention doctrines. The FSIA presently offers virtually no guidance about whether and how courts should apply those doctrines if sovereign immunity is unavailable. Congress should probably revise the FSIA to illuminate how those doctrines (especially the act-of-state doctrine) affect the exercise of FSIA jurisdiction in all relevant contexts —

tort, property, and commercial. Nevertheless, our legislative prescription —
let us call it "28 U.S.C. section 1612"—concerns the justiciability of only
human rights and terrorism cases:

> 1612. Judicial abstention doctrines in human rights and terrorism cases.
> When a foreign state is not entitled to immunity under subsection 1605(a)(7)
> of this chapter, the political question and *forum non conveniens* defenses shall
> be deemed inapplicable; the act-of-state defense shall not be available, unless
> the executive branch determines that the United States foreign policy interests
> require application of the act-of-state doctrine, and a suggestion to that effect
> is filed with the court.

Our FSIA revisions, sections 1605(a)(7) and 1612, together parallel our
model revision concerning nonstate defendants, section 1390. The model
revisions have some stylistic differences. Sections 1605(a)(7) and 1612 follow the organizational and lexical format of the FSIA, while section 1390
follows the format of provisions such as sections 1331 and 1350. On a
substantive level, however, our two sets of revisions largely overlap. Of
course, we could alternatively propose one statute that provides human
rights and terrorism jurisdiction over both nation-state and nonstate defendants. We have not selected that alternative here, however, because
Congress has chosen to keep jurisdiction over nation-states statutorily
separate from jurisdiction over nonstate actors. Congress probably in-
tends that the FSIA should continue to encompass all of the jurisdiction
permitted over nation-states. Hence, despite the intersection of model sections 1605(a)(7), 1612, and 1390, we have adhered to the statutory division
between federal jurisdiction over nation-state and nonstate defendants.

We turn, then, to the substance of our FSIA model revisions. A
reasonable person could assert plausible arguments against both sections
1605(a)(7) and 1612. Even if one agrees that judicial authority should
exist and be exercised over nonstate defendants in human rights and terrorism cases, one might argue against extending such jurisdiction over
nation-state defendants. The argument would probably refer to the special deference that is owed to nation-states; to the demise or deteriora-
tion of the United States' relations with those nation-states successfully
hauled before a federal court; and to the available and purportedly more
appropriate responses that the political branches might make to sovereign-
sponsored international law violations. All of those considerations are

surely important. And Congress might actually be more inclined to adopt our model revision concerning nonstate defendants than our model FSIA revisions. Congress only conceived of the FSIA fairly recently and it specifically intended the immunity exceptions to be limited in scope; recall, for instance, that the tort exception applies only to a limited number of torts that must occur on the United States' soil.[68]

It is maintained, however, that the proposed FSIA amendments are sound and should be adopted. Our goal is to ensure federal jurisdiction over fundamental norms that the world legal order obligates all nation-states to observe and enforce.[69] It is even arguable that the United States *must* assume jurisdiction over these norms, irrespective of whether the defendant is a nonstate or nation-state actor. Following the prosecution of crimes against humanity after the Second World War, international law has devoted attention to the behavior of nation-states within their own boundaries and even in relation to their own nationals.[70] The continuing work of the International Law Commission (ILC), for example, has focused upon sovereign responsibility for violations of universal human rights and terrorism norms.[71] As we will discuss below, the ILC's norms apply whenever a sovereign sponsors a violation of those norms.[72] Providing federal jurisdiction when a nation-state commits these offenses is thus consistent with the burgeoning internationalization of humanitarian norms. In most cases involving violations of fundamental rights, external scrutiny of sovereign acts is legitimate under international law and laudable.

According to the FSIA, the goal of the restrictive sovereign immunity theory is to "serve the interests of justice and . . . protect the rights of both foreign states and litigants in United States courts."[73] Adding an immunity exception for human rights violations and terrorism meshes with the FSIA's goal. Those offenses, like no other, cry out for justice and effective redress. The balance between sovereign deference and individual interests should normally favor the latter when violence or humanitarian offenses are at issue. Increasingly archaic notions of sovereign immunity should give way to the growing respect for individual rights and integrity. Since the FSIA provides authority over certain commercial and property claims,[74] it should certainly provide jurisdiction over claims involving horrid and monstrous acts. Extending federal jurisdiction to human rights and terrorism cases may possibly be construed as disrespectful to foreign sovereigns, but so may the extension of jurisdiction in commercial and property cases. After all, in commercial cases, a federal court may hold that a sovereign has broken its contractual promise, that the sovereign is not good to its bargain; and in property and nationalization cases, a federal court may hold that a sovereign has unlawfully confiscated or stolen private property. So it cannot be said that only human rights and terrorism cases may trouble foreign sovereigns; other FSIA cases may have the same result. Even if the FSIA's initial motivation was to reduce sovereign immunity particularly in the commercial context, it contains various noncommercial immunity exceptions, and Congress should add one more immunity exception to govern the most important international genre of cases in our time. Hence, although one might initially dispute the extension of human rights and terrorism jurisdiction over nation-state defendants, both modern international law and the FSIA's purpose support our model sections 1605(a)(7) and 1612. The following description of those two sections may further justify our aspiration to revise the FSIA.

Section 1605(a)(7)

Section 1605(a)(7) explicitly and comprehensively provides what the current FSIA, at best, only vaguely provides: jurisdiction when nation-states practice, encourage, or condone human rights and terrorist offenses. Under vertical federalism, that authority belongs in federal court.[75] Since our analytical starting point is that domestic jurisdiction is appropriate over nation-states in the human rights and terrorism context, section 1605(a)(7) helps to guarantee that federal courts hear these actions. Section 1605(a)(7) may help the United States to satisfy its international commitment to enforce the relevant offenses, and that result may benefit the nation as a whole.

Article III of the Constitution clearly supports this grant of federal authority. When aliens sue their own or other foreign governments under section 1605(a)(7), alienage jurisdiction does not exist, but the arising-under clause provides constitutional authority. Such cases necessarily involve questions of both international law and, under *Verlinden*, questions of federal statutory law.[76] When United States citizens sue foreign governments under section 1605(a)(7), a type of "diversity jurisdiction" exists, as does arising-under jurisdiction. The foreign relations implications of all section 1605(a)(7) cases also support the federal courts' arising-under jurisdiction, according to *Verlinden*. By providing a private cause of action for human rights violations and terrorism, in case one does not otherwise exist, section 1605(a)(7) acknowledges that these FSIA cases arise under federal law. This acknowledgment, as in model section 1390, may also reduce confusion about whether plaintiffs have a cause of action to bring to federal court.

The human rights violations and terrorist acts found in section 1605(a)(7) are the same as those found in section 1390. Similar reasoning supports the inclusion of these offenses in both model revisions. These offenses, again, have been subject to virtually universal condemnation under treaty and custom. Given their equally well-codified and well-defined status, and given the fact that innocent individuals may often be victimized, section 1605(a)(7) does not distinguish between human rights violations and terrorism. Hierarchically superior to other international norms, the norms protecting all of these basic individual rights may not legally be violated by any nation-state.[77] As we will soon extensively discuss, the Nuremberg precedent, the ILC's efforts, multilateral conventions, the universality principle, and other legal developments have together created this elite set of norms.[78] As a result, every nation-state should redress violations of those norms, even when another sovereign breaches those norms against its own citizens and in its own territory. For this reason, section 1605(a)(7) affords jurisdiction irrespective of wherever and against whomever the offenses occur. The first two prongs of the *Sabbatino* matrix also support the selection of the offenses in section 1605(a)(7). The codification and consensus prohibiting the relevant offenses justifies federal court jurisdiction under national and international systemic considerations.

Section 1612

Assuming that section 1605(a)(7) establishes federal jurisdiction in a specific case, section 1612 posits that courts should normally exercise that jurisdiction. In the absence of current statutory guidance, section 1612 recommends justiciability under three doctrines: the political question, act-of-state, and *forum non conveniens* doctrines. To begin, section 1612 rejects the political question defense in cases against nation-state defendants. One might argue that the political question doctrine takes on special considerations when nation-states are sued. But in actuality, whether a nonstate actor or a foreign nation-state is the defendant, nary a human rights or terrorism case will present a "political question"— at least as that term is conceptualized by the doctrine of the same name. The doctrine's separation-of-powers concerns remain inapposite unless one or more branches of the federal government are themselves directly involved in a specific case or conflict.[79] The mere political aura of human rights and terrorism cases, again, does not trigger the political question doctrine under Supreme Court precedent. Hence section 1612 disallows nation-states from raising this defense, just as model section 1390 disallows nonstate actors from raising the defense.

While the *forum non conveniens* doctrine may be conditionally available under model section 1390, it is unavailable in cases against nation-states under section 1612. The vast majority of nation-states maintain a relatively substantial diplomatic presence, often including lawyers, in Washington, D.C., and New York. So it cannot realistically be claimed that nation-state defendants will be very inconvenienced or disadvantaged when sued in federal court. Most human rights and terrorism cases against nation-states will thus usually involve both a plaintiff and a defendant "present" in the United States. Compared with foreign nonstate defendants, foreign nation-states surely have greater resources to litigate a case in a United States court. The only alternative forum having greater contacts with the case may be a court within the defendant nation-state's territory. Since the plaintiff may generally receive more objective and fairer treatment in federal court than in the defendant's home court, nation-states particularly should be precluded from raising *forum non conveniens*. Our overall goal is to ensure justice in this important set of human rights and terrorism cases, and that goal may be best served by simply rejecting the *forum non conveniens* defense when nation-states are sued. Federal courts usually defer to the plaintiff's selection of a judicial forum, and that selection should not be disturbed under section 1612.

Finally, the act-of-state doctrine is presumptively unavailable under section 1612. Even when the defendant is a nation-state, that doctrine should be avoided, given the overwhelming codification and consensus against both the human rights and terrorist offenses at hand, and given the political branches' commitment to prevent and redress those offenses.

The separation-of-powers and international comity considerations underlying the *Sabbatino* matrix should not usually bar adjudication when nation-states sponsor human rights violations or terrorism. Nevertheless, section 1612, like section 1390, provides an executive branch safety valve, allowing judicial abstention in those cases that may especially impinge upon the United States' foreign relations. Perhaps that safety valve will be opened and should be opened more often when nation-states themselves (rather than nonstate actors) defend human rights and terrorism cases. *Sabbatino's* second criterion — which focuses on a case's implications for foreign relations — may support such executive intervention. Again, even if not constitutionally obligated to do so, courts should normally follow the executive's suggestions about the act-of-state defense. But the main point is that that defense should not even be entertained unless the executive so suggests. Section 1612's act-of-state concept parallels section 1390 in drawing upon the Hickenlooper Amendment. That legislation was passed due to the Congress's strong sentiment that when nation-states nationalize property without paying just compensation, they should not be able to shield their illegal behavior in United States courts under the act-of-state defense.[80] A *fortiori*, a greater impulse should counsel against the act-of-state doctrine in most human rights and terrorism cases. Just as the Congress once took a bold step in the nationalization context, it should do the same today in the humanitarian context by adopting model section 1612 in conjunction with model section 1605(a)(7).

Conclusion

This chapter has offered legislative prescriptions to ensure that the federal judiciary possesses and utilizes authority over human rights and terrorism cases. The model respecting nonstate defendants essentially confirms our interpretations of, and aspirations for, the existing statutes and doctrines — although it surely clarifies and elaborates upon the existing law. The FSIA model significantly expands judicial authority over nation-states. Both models are justified by the vertical federalism and horizontal separation-of-powers ideas interwoven throughout part one. Therefore, both models help to define the federal judiciary's proper institutional role within the United States legal system. The importance

of fulfilling that role will multiply as the globe's human rights and terrorism norms continue to expand, quantitatively and qualitatively, during the coming century. Part two will justify our prescriptions particularly in light of world legal order considerations. Our model statutes,
then, ultimately seek to define the proper status of federal courts in
relation to the international as well as to the domestic legal orders.

II

Domestic Jurisdiction
in the World Legal Order

[A]n essential distinction should be drawn between the obligations of a [nation-] State towards the international community as a whole, and those arising vis-à-vis another [nation-]State. . . . [T]he former are the concern of all [nation-] States. In view of the importance of the rights involved, all [nation-]States can be held to have a legal interest in their protection; they are obligations erga omnes. Such obligations derive, for example, . . . from the outlawing of . . . aggression, and of genocide, as also from the principles and rules concerning the basic rights of the human person, including protection from slavery and racial discrimination.
International Court of Justice, *Concerning the Barcelona Traction, Light & Power Co. (Belg. v. Spain),* 1970 I.C.J. 4, 33

[T]he torturer has become—like the pirate and slave trader before him—hostis humani generis, an enemy of all mankind.
Judge Kaufman, *Filartiga v. Pena-Irala,*
630 F.2d 876, 890 (2d Cir. 1980)

[When] exercising jurisdiction under the universality principle, . . . neither the nationality of the accused or the victim(s), nor the location of the crime is significant. The underlying assumption is that the crimes are offenses against the law of nations or against humanity and that the prosecuting nation is acting for all nations.
Judge Lively, *Demjanjuk v. Petrovsky,* 776 F.2d 571, 582–83
(6th Cir. 1985), cert. denied, 475 U.S. 1016 (1986)

[T]he term "paradigm" . . . stands for the entire constellation of beliefs, values, techniques, and so on shared by the members of a given community. [It alternatively] denotes one sort of element in that constellation, . . . which, employed as models or examples, can replace explicit rules as a basis for the solution of the remaining puzzles. . . .

In much the same way, [political and] scientific revolutions are inaugurated by a growing sense . . . that an existing paradigm has ceased to function adequately in the exploration of an aspect of nature to which that paradigm itself had previously led the way.
T. Kuhn, *The Structure of Scientific Revolutions* 175, 92 (2d ed. 1970)

CHAPTER 7

Federal Courts as Global Actors

We continue to define "jurisdiction" as the systemic distribution of legitimate authority among institutional actors. In part two, however, the system under examination is not the United States legal order, but the world legal order. By "world legal order," we refer to the international legal system that regulates foreign relations and enforces the rights and obligations that international law recognizes. Our inquiry will thus focus upon the legitimate authority of a domestic court, particularly the federal judiciary, as an actor within the international legal system. In other words, assuming that federal jurisdiction over human rights and terrorism cases is justified by federalism and separation-of-powers concerns, we will question whether it is also justified by world legal order concerns.

That question is relevant due to the very nature of *Filartiga v. Pena-Irala*[1] and its progeny. The modern cases present truly international disputes, sometimes of worldwide interest and import. They often involve foreign litigants, extraterritorial offenses, and violations of foreign and international law. Another nation-state has usually had greater links with these cases than has the United States; in fact, the United States has usually not had any direct link with the offenses at issue.[2] So human rights and terrorism litigation hardly involves mere local problems and mere municipal law. Instead, the litigation essentially raises inquiries about the federal courts' "international jurisdiction," that is, inquiries about the relationship between the federal courts and both foreign courts and the world legal order itself. For instance, when should federal courts champion human rights and terrorism complaints with which they do not have a connection? When should federal courts defer to the authority of other national courts? And ultimately, what is the proper role of federal courts in the world legal order? Part two addresses all of these inquiries. In so doing, it considers the federal courts' legitimate authority and appropriate status vis-à-vis the world legal order, not the United States domestic order.

The implication of our endeavor is that when faced with human rights or terrorism cases, federal judges should not confine themselves to domestic jurisdictional questions. Rather, they should extend their jurisdictional inquiry to the international system and its rules. In these cases, federal judges are being asked to act as an agent of both the domestic and the international legal orders and, therefore, they should fully consider their institutional role in both systems.

We will begin part two, in this chapter, by identifying the legal principles for thinking about a domestic court's international jurisdiction and by further describing the relevance of those principles. Hence we will initially conceptualize federal jurisdiction in the international system, just as part one initially conceptualized federal jurisdiction in the national system. In the subsequent chapter, we will examine the universality principle of jurisdiction. That principle justifies domestic jurisdiction in most of the cases in our genre and it thus demands comprehensive discussion. Finally, part two will conclude by considering how recent structural or paradigmatic changes in the world legal order itself may further justify federal universal jurisdiction in human rights and terrorism cases. Part two's ultimate goal, in a sense, is to demonstrate that the legislative prescriptions offered in the prior chapter are proper under international law and world legal order concerns.

Domestic Jurisdiction under International Law Principles

Public international law has established principles for determining when domestic courts have international authority over offenses that also affect the interests of another nation-state. Those jurisdictional principles, of course, are inapposite when purely domestic offenses are at issue. For example, on Wall Street, a stockbroker, a New Yorker, illegally churns the account of a client, a Californian. If that hypothetical case gave rise to federal criminal or civil proceedings, United States domestic law (constitutional, conflicts, statutory, common law) and national systemic considerations (federalism, separation of powers) would entirely dictate the availability of judicial authority.[3] By contrast, when an offense involves one or more international components, jurisdiction should depend upon both domestic and international law. Those components are present when the litigants are aliens, foreign organizations, or nation-states or when the litigation concerns behavior occurring outside of the United States. Hence when another nation-state or the world legal order itself has an interest in the offense being litigated, federal judges should evaluate their authority under both domestic norms and international law's jurisdictional principles. As suggested just above, judges may otherwise act parochially and in ignorance of one of the two systems that they represent in international cases — the world legal order.

Under most of the international principles, domestic jurisdiction is predicated upon the connections existing between a sovereign and the particular offense. The nation-state where the action is brought (i.e., the "forum nation-state" or "forum sovereign") normally lacks authority unless it possesses certain links with the offense. In summary form, public international law's primary jurisdictional bases include the following: the territoriality principle, providing authority when an offense is committed within the forum nation-state; the nationality principle, providing authority when the offender is the forum nation-state's national; the passive-personality principle, providing authority when the victim is the forum nation-state's national; the protective principle, providing authority when an extraterritorial act threatens the forum nation-state's security or a basic governmental function; and the universality principle, providing authority when the offense is particularly heinous, universally condemned, and threatens the international legal order.[4] Our focus is, of course, on how those principles regulate adjudicative authority. But the principles more comprehensively govern a nation-state's authority to create law that is applicable to specific actors, events, or things ("legislative jurisdiction"); a nation-state's authority to subject specific actors or things to its adjudicative and administrative processes ("adjudicatory jurisdiction"); and a nation-state's authority to compel specific actors to comply with its law and to remedy noncompliance ("enforcement jurisdiction").[5]

Under the jurisdictional principles, save universality, the forum nation-state has international authority only when an offense directly involves its territory, citizens, or security. The forum sovereign may also compare its links with an offense against those of other interested nation-states:

Under international law, the jurisdiction of a state depends on the interest that state, in view of its nature and purposes, may reasonably have in exercising the particular jurisdiction asserted and on the need to reconcile that interest with the interest of other states in exercising jurisdiction. The nature and significance of the interests of a state in exercising jurisdiction depend on the relation of the transaction, occurrence, or event, and of the person to be affected, to the state's proper concerns.[6]

The jurisdictional principles, then, are the vehicles by which to assess a domestic court's authority over international cases. They conceptualize federal jurisdiction vis-à-vis the world legal order, comparable to how the jurisdictional statutes and the judicial abstention doctrines conceptualize federal court authority vis-à-vis the United States legal order. Since the two legal orders are systemically separable,[7] it is logical that each has its own jurisdictional apparatus, structuring authority in a way that serves each system's purpose and contours.

Under the conventional seventeenth-century wisdom and ideals, the world legal order is primarily nonhierarchical and horizontal. Without a supranational monarchical body to govern most matters, all nation-states have been sovereign and juridically equal to one another. We will eventually consider how post–World War II developments have somewhat revised and centralized the international order systemically or paradigmatically.[8] But for our present discussion, if the jurisdictional principles are to restrict a sovereign's authority over international cases, the sovereign must normally impose those restrictions upon itself voluntarily. When the international principles do not support jurisdiction, sovereigns should, and usually do, decline authority even over litigants in their custody or control. A sovereign may be motivated by respect for other nation-states and the expectation of reciprocal behavior by other sovereigns. For the decentralized sovereign system to avoid discord, it must generally rely upon nation-states' independent adherence to the territoriality, nationality, passive-personality, protective, and universality principles. Without those bases, jurisdiction amounts to momentary assertions of naked power.

A nation-state may thus not legally assert legislative, adjudicatory, or enforcement jurisdiction over every person and thing in its control — even when that jurisdiction is legitimate under domestic law. Instead, in every international case, the legality of domestic authority also depends upon international law's jurisdictional principles. Those principles are to foster cooperative foreign relations. As the *Restatement (Third) of Foreign Relations (Restatement)* advises: "International law deals with the propriety of the exercises of jurisdiction by a [nation-]state, and the resolution of conflicts of jurisdiction between [nation-]states."[9]

A conflict may occur when two (or more) nation-states each have a jurisdictional interest in a particular case and each wants to exercise that jurisdiction. One hypothetical example would be the intention of two nation-states to prosecute for a theft — one country (X) being the thief's nation-state of nationality, the other (Y) being the locus of the offense and the victim's nation-state of nationality. In such instances, as suggested above, each nation-state might evaluate its interest against that of the other.[10] The forum nation-state having custody of the defendant (X, for example) might permit the second sovereign to adjudicate the offense, assuming that the latter (Y) has greater links with the offense and is capable of fair litigation.[11] Such reasonable deference — displaying horizontal respect for another sovereign's authority over its people or the events in its territory — may enhance foreign relations and the world legal order's stability.

That foreign relations goal is not usually served, however, when the forum nation-state declines to exercise jurisdiction specifically under the universality principle. Universal jurisdiction supposes that a limited array of egregious offenses, including certain human rights violations and terrorist acts, are subject to every nation-state's authority, irrespective of both the offense's location and the victim's and the offender's nationalities. Every sovereign represents the world legal order when adjudicating universal offenses, and the assumption of that jurisdiction is sometimes obligatory. Regarding at least the universal offenses, the world legal order may be more vertical and centralized, as we will discuss;[12] the legal order endeavors to permit relatively little sovereign discretion concerning the observance of these norms. In contrast to the other jurisdictional bases, the universality principle may operate uniquely within the international legal system. Under the *Restatement,* the universality principle does not require the forum sovereign to reconcile its interest (or noninterest) in an offense with that of other sovereigns.[13] That fact may have special relevance in civil human rights and terrorism cases. Those civil cases, unlike criminal proceedings, do not involve the possibility of extradition. So when the universality principle underlies a case, the forum sovereign should not defer to the interests of another nation-state, unless the *forum non conveniens* doctrine (discussed in chapter 5) requires the case's conditional transfer to the second sovereign. The subsequent chapters will more fully examine universal jurisdiction and its broader world legal order implications.

Domestic Jurisdiction in the Civil Context

We may consider here whether the several jurisdictional principles of public international law apply equally to civil and criminal litigation. Those principles were traditionally said to regulate only criminal cases.[14] Apparently, since nation-states themselves commence only criminal cases, those cases raise special foreign relations concerns. Only criminal cases purportedly raise the international systemic concerns that the jurisdictional principles help to regulate.[15] On the other hand, in civil cases, restrictions on international jurisdiction were supposedly left "to the states themselves for determination, each in accordance with its own internal law."[16] Under each nation-state's domestic law, only comity notions and conflict-of-law rules (i.e., "private international law") supposedly governed domestic jurisdiction in civil cases that contained international components.

In both theory and practice, however, the purported schism between criminal and civil jurisdiction has eroded. First of all, as recently recognized, the traditional dichotomy between criminal and civil cases may always have been false, or at least overstated. As a leading scholar suggests: "The jurisdiction of the courts in civil matters is . . . more effectively determined and circumscribed by international rules of jurisdiction than many observers recognize or admit."[17] In actuality, the jurisdictional principles, comity notions, and conflict rules all somewhat involve identifying the forum sovereign's interests in the dispute and comparing such interests against the contacts of other sovereigns.[18] That is to say, those various approaches all essentially involve an analysis of sovereign interests and possible deference to the sovereign having the greatest interests in a case. Given the theoretical overlapping of those jurisdictional approaches, a significant disparity may never have really existed between how domestic authority was conceptualized in civil and criminal transnational cases. The jurisdictional principles, comity notions, and conflict rules may really be as different flasks are to similar wines. In the final analysis, "both the public and private international systems coordinate human behavior, and . . . thus the values that inform both systems must necessarily be the same."[19]

Whatever distinction has existed between criminal and civil jurisdiction has been further eroded by the ever-growing intersection between public and private international law. That intersection encompasses legal actors — with nonstate actors increasingly possessing rights and duties under public international law and, conversely, with nation-states increasingly engaging in private international business transactions.[20] In other words, the demarcation between public and private actors and between sovereign and nonsovereign actors has become fuzzy. The intersection of public and private international law also stems from an overlapping of normative devices — with multilateral treaties being used increasingly today to govern not just public and criminal issues, but also private commercial and corporate transactions.[21] With the coalescing of both public and private actors and norms, there may be little reason to distinguish conceptually between domestic jurisdiction in the criminal and civil contexts. This conclusion suggests that public international law's jurisdictional principles should apply to both criminal and civil litigation. As the *Restatement* succinctly provides: "The principles governing jurisdiction . . . apply to criminal as well as to civil regulation."[22] And specifically concerning the universality principle: "[J]urisdiction on the basis of universal interests has been exercised in the form of criminal law, but international law does not preclude the application of non-criminal law on this basis, for example, by providing a remedy in tort or restitution for [the] victims."[23] Recent human rights and terrorism precedent has also specifically extended the universality principle to the civil context.[24]

Applying the jurisdictional principles to a civil case is especially appropriate when the claim derives from the very same set of rules that would apply if a criminal case were commenced against the defendant. Disputes involving the United States' antitrust and securities laws provide good examples. When a foreign business's extraterritorial behavior intentionally has illegal effects in this country, the federal judiciary should be just as mindful of world legal order concerns when applying the antitrust or securities laws in either civil or criminal cases. Irrespective of whether a case takes the form of a civil or criminal proceeding, a foreign sovereign may have the same reaction — be it a positive, negative, or non-committal reaction — to the extension of federal jurisdiction over one of its national corporations.[25] The jurisdictional principles, again, try to regulate conflicts over domestic authority. So it puts form over substance to think that federal jurisdiction will elicit different foreign reactions depending upon whether the same regulations are applied in a civil or criminal setting. If the jurisdictional principles are theorized as placing *limitations* upon domestic international authority, they should equally restrict legislative and adjudicative competences over identical values and norms in civil and criminal cases.[26]

Conversely, if the principles are theorized as *authorizing* domestic international authority, the extension of jurisdiction should be equally important to the forum nation-state in both the criminal and civil contexts.[27] This is true when a significant sovereign policy underlies the norms at issue, such as the important economic and market policies underlying the federal antitrust and securities laws. Those policies can be furthered if the jurisdictional principles authorize their extension in civil as well as criminal proceedings. The British scholar D. W. Bowett agrees: "[W]hat matters is not whether the jurisdiction is civil or criminal, but rather whether the jurisdiction is a manifestation of [nation-] State policy, designed to confer on the [nation-]State control over activities or resources to the extent necessary to pursue that policy."[28] In fact, in civil antitrust and securities cases that have international components, it is not unusual for federal judges to assess and support their authority under the jurisdictional principles.[29] Indeed, judges today do not usually distinguish between applying the jurisdictional principles in civil and criminal antitrust and securities cases.

From the foregoing discussion, it should be clear that international law's jurisdictional principles are applicable to civil litigation involving human rights violations and terrorism. The *Restatement* squarely supports this conclusion,[30] as does the growing intersection between public-criminal and private-civil international law. As with antitrust and securities cases, the very same substantive norms may govern human rights and terrorism cases whether commenced by a federal prosecutor or by an individual plaintiff. "Indeed," as Professor Brownlie writes, "as civil jurisdiction is ultimately reinforced by procedures of enforcement involving criminal sanctions, there is in principle no great difference between the problems created by assertion of civil and criminal jurisdiction over aliens."[31] Human rights and terrorism litigation certainly involves significant issues of national and international public policy, and the jurisdictional principles should thus especially guide judicial authority in both the civil and criminal contexts. In certain civil human rights and terrorism cases, federal judges have already made explicit and implicit references to public international law's jurisdictional principles.[32] This is appropriate whether the defendant in a civil case is a nonstate actor or a nation-state.[33]

Assuming, then, that the jurisdictional principles govern civil litigation, we may now specifically apply those principles to human rights and terrorism cases. Our goal is to determine the federal judiciary's international authority over those cases. Our "final task," as articulated by Myres McDougal and his colleagues, "is that of appraising the impact of the claim to competence and the counterclaim to immunity or lack of jurisdiction upon the common interests of the community."[34]

Domestic Jurisdiction in Human Rights and Terrorism Cases

The specific facts of each human rights and terrorism case will essentially determine whether the jurisdictional principles support federal court authority. We begin with the territoriality principle. When a human rights violation or terrorist act occurs in the United States, the territoriality principle clearly supports federal jurisdiction. Such an offense is of obvious federal concern, thus triggering the nation's authority. The territoriality principle, for example, supported federal jurisdiction over terrorist acts committed in California and Washington, D.C., in, respectively, *Liu v. Republic of China*[35] and *de Letelier v. Republic of Chile*.[36]

A variation of the territoriality principle is the "objective territorial" principle, supporting jurisdiction when an extraterritorial act has intentional effects or intentionally causes injuries within the forum nation-state.[37] Within our context, objective territorial jurisdiction would exist, to hypothesize one example, if a terrorist just inside the Mexican border fired a rifle and killed a person standing in Texas. The objective territorial principle might conceivably support federal jurisdiction over a human rights offense committed outside of the United States but causing injuries within the United States. For instance, if a heinous offense victimized a United States tourist abroad, objective territorial jurisdiction would arguably exist over a claim by the tourist's parents if, as a result, they suffered emotional distress within the United States.[38] Arguably, objective territorial jurisdiction might even exist over the tourist's own claim, to the extent that his or her physical or mental injuries seriously worsened once back in the United States. Regarding either the parents' or the tourist's claim, however, it would be questionable whether the defendant intended to cause injuries within the United States. Admittedly, there is not much precedent for this type of use of the objective territorial principle.

In addition to the territoriality principle and its variations, the federal judiciary possesses authority vis-à-vis the world legal order when a United States citizen either commits or is victimized by terrorism or a human rights violation. The nationality and passive-personality principles, respectively, are applicable to those situations. Only recently, however, has the world community accorded the passive-personality principle the same status and weight as that of the nationality principle. The United States and other nation-states had previously been somewhat slow to recognize that the forum sovereign has as strong an interest when its citizen is victimized by an egregious offense as when its citizen commits such an offense.[39] In any event, when the nationality or passive-personality principles support federal jurisdiction in a human rights or terrorism case, the location of the offense is irrelevant. So in the example given just above, involving the United States citizen victimized abroad, the passive-personality principle would support federal jurisdiction over the tourist's claim. The passive-personality principle, if stretched, might conceivably apply to the claim of the tourist's parents, assuming that they had a cause of action. The nationality principle would not support federal jurisdiction over either the tourist's or the parents' claim, however, unless the offender-defendant happened to be a United States citizen.

The territoriality, objective territorial, nationality, and passive-personality principles may support federal jurisdiction in specific human rights and terrorism cases in which the United States has a direct connection. Most of the modern litigation, however, has postured alien against alien and has involved entirely extraterritorial offenses. Those jurisdictional principles, therefore, have not been of much force in *Filartiga v. Pena-Irala*[40] and its progeny. So this leads us to examine the protective and the universality principles.

Protective jurisdiction has traditionally been attached to offenses such as espionage against the forum sovereign, counterfeiting the forum sovereign's currency, and falsifying the forum sovereign's official records.[41] Under recent treaties and federal statutes, however, the protective principle has emerged to provide strong and expanding domestic authority over terrorist offenses. Such offenses include the taking of American hostages and crimes against internationally protected persons who are United States citizens, although the passive-personality principle might also support federal jurisdiction in those situations. Various federal judges, lawmakers, and commentators have advocated this extension of protective jurisdiction, due to the national security interests that terrorism so blatantly strikes.[42] Compared with the objective territorial principle, the protective principle has the advantage of not requiring that any tangible effects be directly felt within the continental United States. Protective jurisdiction may thus extend to a civil case involving entirely extraterritorial terrorist acts — for example, a suit brought by a United States diplomat injured by terrorism at an American embassy abroad. Such jurisdiction will less likely apply to an extraterritorial human rights offense, unless the offense somehow threatens the nation's security or governmental functions.

The protective principle's new application to terrorism is a noteworthy development, but this principle, too, has not supported federal jurisdiction in most of the recent civil cases. Those cases have simply not concerned offenses directed at the United States or its citizens. This fact has rendered the protective principle irrelevant to most cases, as it has the passive-personality principle.

One might argue that protective jurisdiction should exist when terrorism is directed against a United States ally and the ally's injured national (or a representative) sues the terrorist in federal court. After all, terrorism is often committed against nation-states that symbolize or represent a particular ideological or geopolitical perspective. A terrorist attack upon Great Britain, for instance, may be portrayed as an assault also against the United States or even against all members of NATO or the Western bloc. Particularly given the joint efforts of nation-states to redress terrorism and given the difficulties of bringing terrorists to justice, it may be politically prudent and legally sound to expand protective jurisdiction to terrorism directed against either the forum nation-state or that nation's allies. Under this view of the protective principle, federal civil authority would be permissible when a national of either the United States or an ally is hurt or killed by terrorism committed anywhere in the world. Protective jurisdiction, in this way, would have been relevant to *Tel-Oren v. Libyan Arab Republic.*[43] That case primarily involved citizens of Israel, surely an ally of the United States, suing the PLO in federal court for terrorism committed in Israel.

This expanded vision of the protective principle, however, is only recommendatory in nature. There is a lack of precedent for it. So when aliens sue aliens in federal court for extraterritorial terrorism and other humanitarian offenses, the protective principle may currently be as unavailing as the territoriality, objective territorial, nationality, and passive-personality principles.

Hence the plaintiffs in most human rights and terrorism cases may need to rely upon the universality principle. Fortunately for such plaintiffs, federal universal jurisdiction should normally exist over those heinous offenses, irrespective of both the litigants' nationalities and the location of the act. A full examination of the very relevant universality principle awaits us in the next chapter.

Conclusion

Part two extends our jurisdictional inquiry from the United States legal system to the international legal system. An appreciation and assessment of federal court authority vis-à-vis the world legal order is very appropriate, given the truly international character of the modern human rights and terrorism cases. Public international law's jurisdictional principles offer the proper vehicles for identifying the federal judiciary's proper role as a global actor in civil litigation. Since most of that litigation has involved foreign actors and extraterritorial behavior, however, the territoriality, objective territorial, nationality, passive-personality, and even protective principles have been of limited significance. Unless the United States has a direct connection with a human rights or terrorist offense, only the universality principle can support federal jurisdiction in this genre of civil cases.

CHAPTER 8

Universal Jurisdiction

The universality principle, as mentioned, provides every nation-state with jurisdiction over a limited category of offenses generally recognized as of universal concern.[1] Such domestic authority exists regardless of the situs of the offense and the nationalities of the offender and the offended. While the other jurisdictional bases demand direct connections between the forum sovereign and the offense, the universality principle assumes that every sovereign has an interest in exercising jurisdiction to combat egregious offenses that have been universally condemned. Piracy and slave trading are the prototypal offenses over which every nation-state's authority exists; pirates and slave traders have long been considered the enemies of all humanity.

Recently, however, the category of universal offenses has expanded significantly. Following the Second World War, the Allies drew some support from the universality principle in asserting jurisdiction over war crimes, crimes against peace, and crimes against humanity. In the postwar decades, nation-states have recognized that universal jurisdiction also extends to hostage taking, crimes against internationally protected persons, hijacking, sabotage of aircraft, torture, genocide, apartheid, and other offenses. That jurisdictional expansion has derived from multilateral conventions, customary international law, other legal and doctrinal developments, and changes in the world legal order itself. Moreover, while the universality principle was earlier thought to govern only criminal jurisdiction, the modern principle is also relevant to civil cases, as was demonstrated earlier.[2] Whether the older or newer offenses are at issue, and whether in the criminal or civil context, universal jurisdiction should today be liberally assumed. The universality principle does not require the forum sovereign to balance its interest in a case with those of other sovereigns. Hence when it exists, universal jurisdiction should normally be exercised whether a nonstate or sovereign actor is the defendant.[3]

Admittedly, universal jurisdiction is in a gestational period. But various institutional actors within the United States have already relied upon the universality principle, explicitly or implicitly, in responding to the new offenses. A judicial trend is evident, for instance, in the Second Circuit's statement in *Filartiga v. Pena-Irala*,[4] involving an entirely Paraguayan torture incident: "[T]he torturer has become—like the pirate and slave trader before him—*hostis humani generis*, an enemy of all mankind."[5] Similarly, the federal district court in *United States v. Layton*,[6] which involved terrorism committed in Guyana, observed that "nations have begun to extend [universal] jurisdiction to . . . crimes considered in the modern era to be as great a threat to the well-being of the international community as piracy."[7] The Sixth Circuit, too, recently recognized universal jurisdiction over war crimes in *Demjanjuk v. Petrovsky*,[8] involving the extradition of Ivan the Terrible to Israel. A final judicial example comes from *United States v. Yunis*,[9] concerning a Lebanese citizen's hijacking of a Jordanian aircraft in the Middle East; the district court assumed authority over "aircraft piracy and hostage taking" because these acts "fit within the category of heinous crimes for purposes of asserting universal jurisdiction."[10] In addition, congresspersons have increasingly cited the universality principle, particularly regarding domestic jurisdiction over terrorism under new legislation.[11] The *Restatement (Third) of Foreign Relations Law (Restatement)* has also underscored the recent expansion of universal jurisdiction.[12]

The universality principle's new prominence, and its particular significance in human rights and terrorism cases, makes it worthy of comprehensive analysis. Our discussion will generally correspond to three evolutionary stages: universal jurisdiction over piracy and slave trading beginning, respectively, in the sixteenth and nineteenth centuries; universal jurisdiction over war crimes, crimes against peace, and crimes against humanity following the Second World War; and finally, universal jurisdiction currently over human rights violations and terrorism. Universal jurisdiction over pirates, slave traders, and war criminals is often taken for granted, although a misunderstanding of such domestic authority is not uncommon. The two initial discussions, therefore, seek to clarify the earlier applications of universal jurisdiction and to define their modern relevance. After having laid that analytical foundation, the third discussion, regarding the modern offenses, will occupy most of our time. As will be demonstrated, federal courts today often have the right, if not the obligation, to exercise their domestic authority over the globe's terrorists and human rights offenders. As will be very evident from the legal sources at hand, universal jurisdiction equally applies to both human rights violations and terrorism. The universality principle legitimizes that authority vis-à-vis the world legal order, without any nexus between the United States and the offense.

Universal Jurisdiction over Piracy and Slave Trading

Piracy

Piracy is the oldest offense that invokes universal jurisdiction. Even "[b]efore International Law in the modern sense of the term was in existence, a pirate was already considered an outlaw, a *'hostis humani generis.'*"[13] For roughly five centuries, every nation-state has had legislative, adjudicatory, and enforcement jurisdiction over all piratical acts on the high seas, even when neither the pirates nor their victims are nationals of the forum nation-state.[14] There are two theories of how international law regulates piracy: the first characterizes piracy as an offense under the law of nations itself (an offense *jure gentium*), which is thus redressable by all nation-states under universal jurisdiction; the second regards piracy as a domestic offense, which international law defines solely to determine the acts that every sovereign has universal jurisdiction to redress under its law.[15] Protracted debate has surrounded the two theories. But at least for our purposes, the difference between those views appears "a matter of tweedledum and tweedledee," as Professor McDougal and his associates have put it.[16] Since both theories subject piracy to universal jurisdiction, the same essential result is achieved. Whatever distinction exists between those theories is particularly irrelevant in the United States.[17]

We should thus turn to the rationales for subjecting piracy to the universality principle. Under international law, piracy is committed only aboard vessels on the high seas or a place outside of any nation-state's jurisdiction.[18] During the seventeenth century, support emerged for the principle of the "freedom of the high seas."[19] Under this principle, every sovereign was accorded an equal right to the high seas, thus undermining the idea that one nation-state could be sovereign over entire seas. Contrary to some common rhetoric, however, the freedom-of-the-high-seas principle does not provide the correct rationale for universal jurisdiction over piracy. Expanding only rights of navigation and exploration, the principle does not permit sovereigns to capture all pirates or to redress all piratical offenses. It does not envision the high seas as "a condominium with all states exercising concurrent jurisdiction over all vessels and persons on the high seas."[20] Under the "floating-territorial" jurisdictional basis, domestic authority over nonpiratical acts on the high seas is normally limited to the nation-state of the vessel's registration.[21] For example, when one Canadian national steals from another Canadian on board a Canadian-flag vessel on the high seas, only Canadian authorities have jurisdiction to board the vessel; only Canada has civil and criminal jurisdiction to redress the offense. Although other nation-states would probably not contest that jurisdiction, Canada's authority would be based upon the floating-territorial, passive-personality, or nationality bases. But the universality principle would not support Canada's or any other sovereign's jurisdiction over such nonpiratical offenses. Just as the freedom-of-the-high-seas principle does not justify universal jurisdiction over a nonpiratical act such as stealing, it does not justify universal jurisdiction over piracy. Hence piracy's mere occurrence on the high seas does not alone subject the offense to universal jurisdiction.

Instead, the authority of all nation-states over all pirates is an exception to the general rule limiting each sovereign's jurisdiction on the high seas to its own vessels and nationals. One rationale for this exception is that by engaging in piracy, individuals and their vessels become denationalized. As an outlaw entirely outside of any sovereign's law, "[t]he pirate has in fact no national character."[22] Even if a pirate vessel flies a nation-state's flag, it is a vessel over "which no national authority reigns,"[23] and "the protection of the national flag is forfeited."[24] Both the pirate and the vessel are considered "stateless."[25] Because no nation-state has any greater connection to these stateless pirates and their vessels than any other, every sovereign has universal jurisdiction over the pirates.

Specific pirate vessels that have never registered in any nation-state might accurately be labeled as stateless. The idea that all pirates and their vessels are stateless is, however, "a misleading hyperbole."[26] As correctly indicated by the Harvard Law School's *Research on Piracy*, under Professor Manley O. Hudson's direction:

[A] state does not lose its claim of allegiance or any of its ordinary legislative, executive or judicial jurisdiction against its national because he has committed piracy on the high sea. . . . Likewise if the pirate ship had a national character before it was engaged in piracy, its participation in piracy does not withdraw it from the ordinary jurisdiction . . . of its flag state. . . . The ordinary jurisdiction, because of the piracy, no longer excludes the common jurisdiction [of all nation-states] on the high sea, but it may still exist and be otherwise unaffected.[27]

Like other international criminals, pirates can retain their nationality and still be subject to universal jurisdiction. The law of the sovereign that confers nationality upon a ship or pirate will determine whether that nationality is lost or retained as a result of the offense.[28]

A more accurate rationale for not limiting jurisdiction over pirates to their nation-state of nationality relies upon the fundamental nature of piratical offenses. Piracy may comprise particularly heinous and wicked acts of violence or depredation,[29] which are often committed indiscriminately against many nation-states' vessels and nationals. As Justice Story recognized, pirates are the enemies of all people, subjecting their offenses to the redress of all sovereigns, due to the threatening acts that they commit: "A pirate is deemed, and properly deemed, *hostis humani generis*. But why is he so deemed? Because he commits hostilities upon the subjects and property of any or all nations without any regard to right or duty."[30] Piratical attacks, particularly when viewed cumulatively, may disrupt important commerce and navigation on the high seas. Such lawlessness was especially harmful to the world at a time when sovereign intercourse primarily occurred by way of the high seas, thus making piracy the concern of all nation-states. Allowing any nation-state to capture and punish pirates, who can quickly flee across the seas, was basically "a matter of sea-policing."[31] Under the most convincing rationale, therefore, piracy's fundamental nature and consequences explain why it has historically been subject to universal jurisdiction.

What, then, is the current legal status and relevance of universal jurisdiction over piracy? While universal jurisdiction over piracy originally arose under customary law, nation-states eventually recognized this jurisdiction under treaty law. Currently, the 1982 United Nations Convention on the Law of the Sea provides: "On the high seas, or in any other place outside the jurisdiction of any State, *every State* may seize a pirate ship or aircraft, or a ship or aircraft taken by piracy and under the control of pirates, and arrest the persons and seize the property on board. The courts of the State which carried out the seizure may decide upon the penalties to be imposed."[32] That provision is identical to its counterpart in the 1958 Convention on the High Seas.[33] Parties to the 1982 Convention have the right, but not the obligation, to assume jurisdiction over piratical acts with which they have no connection. Nonparties to the 1982 Convention, including the United States, are still entitled to universal jurisdiction over piracy under customary international law. The 1958 and 1982 conventions codified the customary universal jurisdiction over piracy. Since the United States had exercised customary universal jurisdiction over piracy many times prior to 1958, and since the United States was a party to the 1958 Convention, it is eminently reasonable to assume that the United States today accepts the principle of universal jurisdiction over piracy. The United States, moreover, has accepted most provisions in the 1982 Convention as statements of binding customary law.[34] Hence federal courts possess customary universal piracy jurisdiction, which today pertains to both criminal and civil proceedings.[35]

Under the 1982 Convention (and almost verbatim in the 1958 Convention), piracy is defined to include any illegal act of violence, detention, or depredation, *"committed for private ends* by the crew or the passengers of a private ship or a private aircraft, and directed on the high seas, against another ship or aircraft."[36] That definition is problematic due to its requirement that the offense must be committed for a private end. Pirates still occasionally attack vessels for private gain;[37] in such instances, domestic courts possess universal jurisdiction over the offenders. But outlaws on the high seas today are more often terrorists and hijackers who act for political reasons. In the 1985 hijacking of the *Achille Lauro*, for example, the hijackers' immediate objective was the release of certain Palestinian terrorists imprisoned in Israel.[38] Clearly, the hijackers did not commit an act of violence or detention for private ends, as the definition of piracy requires. Because such behavior does not constitute piracy, nation-states could not legally claim universal jurisdiction over the offenders as pirates. In an *Achille Lauro*-type scenario, universal jurisdiction may exist for offenses other than piracy, such as hostage taking.[39] Universal jurisdiction specifically over piracy, however, will not reach today's politically motivated actors on the high seas.[40] The 1982 Convention should have broadened piracy's definition to include the *Achille Lauro* offenses, as other critics have also observed.[41]

The concept of universal jurisdiction over piracy has had enduring value, however, by supporting the universality principle's expansion to more current offenses. As we shall see, this normative expansion is appropriate, particularly given our understanding of the correct justification for universal jurisdiction over piracy. Before turning to the modern offenses, we will briefly consider how the universality principle first extended to encompass slave trading.

Slave Trading

Certain nineteenth-century treaties extended the universality principle to slave trading. Bearing a link with universal jurisdiction over piracy, the treaties particularly applied to slave traders found on vessels on the high seas.[42] Under several treaties that Great Britain initiated, the parties' naval vessels were permitted to "search, detain, or send in for trial suspected merchant vessels belonging to the contracting states."[43] Each treaty described particular methods by which a party's navy could detain a vessel flying another party's flag and, if necessary, take the crew into custody.[44] The treaties also established means of judicially redressing slave trading, once the offenders were captured. Some treaties, for example, created "mixed tribunals," in which the slave traders were prosecuted in courts that the parties jointly created and administered.[45] These tribunals may be the precursors to the international military tribunals that the Allies jointly established to redress war crimes following the Second World War. Other treaties bound each party individually "to employ all the means at its disposal for putting an end to [the slave] trade and for punishing those who engage in it."[46] Acting under such authority, "British naval vessels seized slave traders on the high seas during the nineteenth century and punished them as if they were pirates."[47]

Whether their offenses were redressed in international or domestic tribunals, slave traders were subjected to a common or universal jurisdiction due to the heinous nature of their behavior.[48] Although slave trading, in contrast to piracy, did not threaten interstate commerce and navigation on the high seas, some nation-states viewed it as an act especially worthy of condemnation and international response. As with piracy under customary law, the British-initiated treaties represented an early consensus that jurisdiction over slave traders was permissible, even absent any direct connection between the capturing sovereign and the slave trading. A few treaties even declared that slave traffic constituted piracy.[49] Under treaty law, therefore, the parties could bring the slave-trading citizens of other parties to justice.[50]

Although slave trading, very fortunately, is no longer prevalent, universal jurisdiction continues to be available over this offense. Slave trading is currently subject to the universality principle under the 1982 United Nations Convention on the Law of the Sea;[51] newer conventions aimed at abolishing slavery and protecting individual liberty;[52] and modern customary law.[53] Universal jurisdiction under the first of those sources is naturally limited to offenders found transporting slaves on the high seas, similar to the nineteenth-century treaties. Universal jurisdiction under the latter sources exists whenever the forum sovereign has custody of slave traders. The current universality principle supports federal court jurisdiction over slave traders in either civil or criminal cases.[54]

Universal Jurisdiction over War Crimes

Overview of the Relevant Tribunals and Offenses

Following the Second World War, universal jurisdiction reached several offenses other than piracy and slave trading. This expansion of the universality principle began in the postwar trials of individuals who had committed various war crimes. These cases premised jurisdiction, in part, on the universality principle, as "the courts of one State frequently tried and punished war crimes committed outside of the State by foreign nationals."[55] Again, under the modern view of universal jurisdiction, that precedent is pertinent today to both criminal and civil actions.[56]

Various tribunals prosecuted individuals associated with the Axis powers. Major German war criminals were tried at Nuremberg by the International Military Tribunal (IMT), which the United States, Great Britain, France, and the Soviet Union together established and administered.

The Allies created the IMT through the London Agreement, to which they annexed the Charter of the International Military Tribunal (IMT Charter).[57] Nineteen other nation-states also assented to the London Agreement. While the IMT dealt with the major criminals, whose offenses had "no particular geographical localisation,"[58] the trials of other individuals took place in fora separately administered by one of the Allies in the territorial zone that it was occupying ("zonal tribunals"). For instance, the United States tried Germans in Nuremberg, which was in the American-occupied zone, after the IMT had concluded its trial there. Such zonal tribunals were conducted pursuant to Control Council Law No. 10 ("C.C. Law No. 10").[59] Still other trials took place in military and domestic tribunals around the world. Some individuals faced trial by the nation-states in which they had committed their crimes, but others were tried by whatever nation-state had captured them.[60] War crimes trials have even occurred years after the Nazi atrocities. Two prominent examples are Israel's trial of Adolph Eichmann in 1961 and its recent trial of John Demjanjuk, both for crimes committed before Israel was a nation-state.[61] Finally, war crimes trials also occurred in the Far East. At the International Military Tribunal for the Far East, for example, twenty-eight Japanese were tried for offenses against Allied troops and for offenses committed in various territories.[62]

The defendants in the various postwar trials were charged with many different offenses. As categorized by the IMT's Charter and C.C. Law No. 10, however, the three primary offenses were crimes against peace (i.e., waging aggressive war); war crimes (i.e., murdering or mistreating prisoners of war and civilians in occupied territory); and crimes against humanity (i.e., murdering or mistreating civilians, including religious and ethnic persecutions, even when a nation-state committed those acts against its own nationals and within its own territory).[63] To some extent, other tribunals also adopted these categorical approaches to the Nazi offenses.

No specific precedent existed prior to the Second World War for subjecting those offenses to the universality principle. The legitimacy of extending universal jurisdiction over the Axis defendants, therefore, may logically depend upon the strength of the analogy between their offenses and piracy. Like piracy, the Axis's offenses involved "violent and predatory action,"[64] which descended to the level of bestiality. According to one commentator, because the universality principle applies to piracy, it must *a fortiori* apply to the more heinous offenses that the Axis powers committed.[65] While piracy was often committed indiscriminately against the nationals of all nation-states, the Nazi offenses "imperiled civilization."[66] The Axis's offenses, like piracy, thus became offenses of international concern. Moreover, war crimes and crimes against humanity are particularly analogous to piracy in that they are typically committed in locations where they will not be prevented or punished easily; this parallel supported the necessity of extending universal jurisdiction to the Axis's offenses.[67]

Although the connections between piracy and war crimes are significant, a few distinctions between the offenses should be considered. The first distinction concerns the location of the offenses: pirates act on the high seas, while war criminals primarily act in the sovereign territory of particular nation-states. This is not a significant distinction, however. Under the floating-territorial principle, a vessel on the high seas is usually subjected to the exclusive jurisdiction of its nation-state of registration; it is only because piratical acts trigger an exception to that nation-state's exclusive jurisdiction that the universality principle permits any sovereign to seize the pirates and to redress their offenses. So universal jurisdiction over both war crimes and piracy actually depends upon an exception to territorial sovereignty. The locations of these offenses — whether committed on a particular sovereign's land or on a vessel registered with a particular sovereign — are thus not significantly different. The very nature of both offenses justifies universal jurisdiction, wherever they occur. A second distinction between piracy and war crimes is that the former has a private purpose, while the latter has a sovereign or public purpose, however grossly misguided. The war crimes tribunals did not address this distinction. Due possibly to the egregious nature of the Axis's offenses, the tribunals' judges might simply have felt compelled to invoke the universality principle without regard to the disparate purposes behind war crimes and piracy. Hence, while the Axis's offenses substantially paralleled piracy, the distinction between the purposes of those offenses is significant. The Allies' partial reliance on the universality principle thus represents a marked expansion of universal jurisdiction. This development heralds the universality principle's recent extension to publicly motivated terrorist acts and human rights offenses, as we will discuss below.

The Allies' Reliance on the Universality Principle

The postwar tribunals asserted that their authority was "not an arbitrary exercise of power on the part of the victorious Nations,"[68] but supported by international law's jurisdictional principles. As indicated in a recent opinion, *Demjanjuk v. Petrovsky,* "it is generally agreed that the establishment of these tribunals and their proceedings were based on universal jurisdiction."[69] Despite this agreement, however, reliance on the universality principle was not always so obvious. It is difficult to discern whether the tribunals in certain cases expressly relied upon the universality principle; extensive discussions of universal jurisdiction do not abound. Of course, some judgments refer to bases of jurisdiction other than the universality principle.[70] The forum sovereigns did not always need to raise the universality principle; they could cite to other jurisdictional principles when they had a specific connection with an offense. Furthermore, due to the occupation of Germany, the IMT's and the zonal tribunals' jurisdiction arguably arose from the Allies' assumption of whatever jurisdiction Germany would have had over the war criminals, although that argument has been criticized.[71] Hence some war crimes cases did not expressly rely upon the universality principle, and some cases did not need to rely upon that principle, although most modern lawyers have come to view all of the war crimes cases as epitomizing the universality principle.

With these qualifications in mind, let us focus on explicit and implicit references to universal jurisdiction found in the postwar tribunals' judgments and related documents. The IMT's judgment, unfortunately, includes only one, somewhat vague reference to the universality principle: "The Signatory Powers created this Tribunal, defined the law it was to administer, and made regulations for the proper conduct of the Trial. In doing so, *they have done together what any one of them might have done singly;* for it is not to be doubted that *any nation* has the right to set up special courts to administer law."[72] According to one commentator, this passage "could conceivably have meant a claim to the exercise of a universal jurisdiction, if emphasis were placed on the words 'any nation.'"[73] That is, the universality principle may be inferred from the idea that any single nation-state would have had jurisdiction over the Axis's offenses, regardless of whether the sovereign had any direct connection with the specific offenses at issue. This reading draws some support from a memorandum of the secretary general of the United Nations.[74]

The proceedings of the zonal tribunals and other courts, however, contain more explicit references to the universality principle. A prominent example is *In re List*,[75] decided by the United States tribunal in Nuremberg. The defendant German officers had commanded the execution of hundreds of thousands of civilians in Greece, Yugoslavia, and Albania; the grossly high number of executions was based on varying ratios of about twenty-five to one hundred civilians murdered for each German soldier killed or wounded. *List* is also known as the "Hostage Case," since the civilians were taken hostage in order to be summarily executed. The tribunal convicted most of the defendants for war crimes and crimes against humanity under C.C. Law No. 10.

In discussing its jurisdiction over such offenses, the zonal tribunal indicated that the defendants had committed international crimes. The tribunal explained that "[a]n international crime is . . . an act *universally recognized* as criminal, which is considered a grave matter of international concern and for some valid reason cannot be left within the exclusive jurisdiction of the state that would have control over it under ordinary circumstances."[76] Surrendering these international offenders to the Nazis for prosecution would have been the "equivalent [of] a passport to freedom."[77] Any nation-state that captures a war criminal may either "surrender the alleged criminal to the state where the offense was committed, or . . . retain the alleged criminal for trial under its own legal processes."[78] The United States chose the latter alternative in *List* by relying upon the universality principle. The United States did not have any direct connections with the extermination of the hostages, regarding either the location of the offenses or the nationalities of the defendants or their victims. Nevertheless, the United States claimed jurisdiction because the defendants had committed offenses that were, in the tribunal's words, "universally recognized" under existing customary and treaty law.[79] The defendants were thus subject to the authority of any sovereign that had custody over them.

Other cases from zonal and military tribunals also refer to the universality principle.[80] In the *Almelo Trial* of 1945,[81] German defendants, facing a British military court sitting in the Netherlands, were charged with having committed two war crimes in Almelo, Holland: executing a British airman without a trial and killing a Dutch civilian who had been living in hiding. For the former offense, Great Britain based jurisdiction on the victim's membership in the British armed forces. For the latter offense, Britain had to base jurisdiction on other grounds. One such ground was universal jurisdiction, under which "every independent state has in International Law jurisdiction to punish pirates and war criminals in its custody regardless of the nationality of the victim or the place where the offense was committed."[82]

In the *Zyklon B Case* of 1946,[83] a British military court in Hamburg assumed jurisdiction over a case involving three German industrialists charged with having knowingly supplied poison gas used for the extermination of Allied nationals. Although British citizens were not among the victims of these specific offenses, several grounds were identified to support Great Britain's jurisdiction under international law. First, as postulated, Great Britain could base its jurisdiction on the territoriality and particularly the nationality principles because the Allies had assumed supreme authority in Germany and thus had "the right to try German nationals for crimes of any kind wherever committed."[84] Alternatively, through an expansion of the passive-personality principle, Great Britain asserted a jurisdictional interest in redressing offenses committed against the nationals of its allies. Finally, jurisdictional support derived from the universality principle, under which every nation-state has jurisdiction to punish war criminals.[85]

Sitting in Wiesbaden in 1945, the United States Military Commission convicted several Germans in the *Hadamar Trial.*[86] This case involved claims that the defendants and their underlings had executed by lethal injection nearly five hundred Polish and Russian civilians at a sanatorium in Hadamar, Germany. As in the *Zyklon B Case,* the tribunal here supported its jurisdiction on the territoriality, nationality, passive-personality, and universality principles. In asserting the universality principle, the United States Military Commission claimed jurisdiction irrespective of the nationalities of the defendants and their victims and regardless "of the place where the offence was committed, particularly where, for some reason, the criminal would otherwise go unpunished."[87]

Finally, another United States Military Commission, sitting in Shanghai in 1947, assumed jurisdiction over *In re Eisentrager.*[88] The defendants were all German nationals who, following the surrender to the

Allies, continued military efforts against the United States by assisting the Japanese in China. The defendants argued that because they were residing in China, they were subject only to Chinese law and jurisdiction. Relying partly on the universality principle and citing the transnational nature of the offenses at hand, the tribunal rejected the defendants' jurisdictional argument:

A war crime . . . is not a crime against the law or criminal code of any individual nation, but a crime against the *jus gentium*. The laws and usages of war are of universal application, and do not depend for their existence upon national laws and frontiers. Arguments to the effect that only a sovereign of the *locus criminis* has jurisdiction and that only the *lex loci* can be applied, are therefore without any foundation.[89]

List, the *Almelo Trial*, the *Zyklon B Case*, the *Hadamar Trial*, and *Eisentrager* provide some of the postwar cases' most explicit references to the universality principle. These cases have certainly helped to extend universal jurisdiction from piracy and slave trading to the publicly motivated offenses associated with the Axis nation-states. In addition, according to some commentators, any other cases in which the forum sovereign assumed jurisdiction without direct connections to the offense "must also be regarded as instances of the adoption of the universality principle *in practice.*"[90] In other words, numerous fora presumably relied upon the universality principle to redress war crimes when they could not rely on any other jurisdictional ground.

The Eichmann Courts' Reliance on the Universality Principle

Another important judicial precedent is many years removed from most postwar trials. In *Attorney General of Israel v. Eichmann*,[91] Israel kidnapped Adolph Eichmann in Argentina and prosecuted him in Jerusalem in 1961. As chief of the Gestapo's Jewish Section, Eichmann had primary responsibility over the persecution, deportation, and extermination of hundreds of thousands of Jews and others in Germany and certain occupied territories. One of Eichmann's responsibilities was supervising the "'final solution' of the Jewish question."[92] Under Israel's Nazis and Nazi Collaborators (Punishment) Act, Eichmann was charged with "crimes against the Jewish people, crimes against humanity, and war crimes." Following diplomatic and UN Security Council debate over the kidnapping, Israel tried Eichmann. The District Court of Jerusalem convicted Eichmann and sentenced him to death, and the Supreme Court of Israel affirmed.[93]

The district court opined that Israel's jurisdiction over Eichmann "conforms to the best traditions of the law of nations."[94] Under international law, Israel based its jurisdiction "on a dual foundation: the universal character of the crimes in question and their specific character as intended to exterminate the Jewish people."[95] The court further explained:

The State of Israel's "right to punish" the accused derives . . . from two cumulative sources: a universal source (pertaining to the whole of mankind) which vests the right to prosecute and punish crimes of this order in every State within the family of nations; and a specific or national source, which gives the victim nation the right to try any who assault their existence.[96]

The first jurisdictional source draws upon the universality principle, and the second upon the protective and passive-personality principles. Perhaps of all of the war crimes cases, the *Eichmann* judgments most elaborately refer to the universality principle. Both the district and Supreme Court opinions describe the precedent of universal jurisdiction over piracy, analogize piratical acts to the Nazi atrocities, and draw support for the universality principle from the Allies' war crimes cases. The district court concluded that the universality principle justified Israel's redress of Eichmann's offenses: "The jurisdiction to try crimes under international law is *universal*."[97] The Supreme Court similarly concluded:

[T]here is full justification for applying here the principle of universal jurisdiction since the international character of "crimes against humanity" . . . dealt with in this case is no longer in doubt. . . . [T]he basic reason for which international law recognizes the right of each State to exercise such jurisdiction in piracy offences — notwithstanding the fact that its own sovereignty does not extend to the scene of the commission of the offence . . . and the offender is a national of another State or is stateless — applies with even greater force to the above-mentioned crimes.[98]

Not only do all the crimes attributed to the appellant bear an international character, but their harmful and murderous effects were so embracing and widespread as to shake the international community to its very foundations. The State of Israel therefore was entitled, pursuant to the principle of universal juris-

diction and in the capacity of a guardian of international law and an agent for
its enforcement, to try the appellant. That being the case, no importance attaches to the fact that the State of Israel did not exist when the offences were
committed.[99]

While the *Eichmann* judgments persuasively demonstrate the legitimacy of universal jurisdiction over war crimes and crimes against humanity, a few particular aspects of the case merit examination. First, Israel's
abduction of Eichmann may be briefly considered. Argentina did not
authorize Israel's apprehension of Eichmann; Israel's action thus violated Argentina's territorial sovereignty, as Israel eventually conceded.[100]
Although every nation-state has universal jurisdiction over pirates, slave
traders, and war criminals, the universality principle did not permit Israel to transgress Argentina's sovereignty over its land. However atrocious Eichmann's offenses, Israel could not legitimize its violation of
Argentina's sovereignty by the universality principle or any other jurisdictional principle of international law. Returning Eichmann to Argentina
might have been the proper remedy for the illegal abduction, but Argentina eventually waived its right to protest Israel's jurisdiction over Eichmann.[101] Of course, Argentina's claim concerning the violation of its
territorial sovereignty was distinct from whatever claim Eichmann had
concerning his kidnapping.[102]

Second, the *Eichmann* case is different from the previous Nazi trials
because the nation-state of Israel did not exist when Eichmann committed his offenses. As just indicated, Israel based its jurisdiction on the universality, passive-personality, and protective principles. Because Eichmann's victims were not Israelis when Eichmann acted, and because
Eichmann never threatened Israel's security, Israel's reliance on the passive-personality and protective principles expanded those jurisdictional
bases. While the validity of that jurisdictional expansion has been
debated,[103] the fact that Israel was not a nation-state when Eichmann
acted was without effect on Israel's jurisdiction under the universality
principle. The basic premise of universal jurisdiction holds that every
nation-state has an interest in judicially redressing particular offenses of
international concern. Logically, that sovereign interest is not limited to
nation-states that existed when the international offenses occurred. Acts
such as piracy, war crimes, and crimes against humanity disrupt the international legal order itself, and their consequences are not wholly erad-

icated until the offender is brought to justice. When any nation-state provides judicial redress against universal offenders, all others benefit. Given
the universality principle's purpose of redressing a special category of offenses, Israel's universal jurisdiction was valid despite Israel's lack of existence when Eichmann acted, as the Supreme Court of Israel recognized.[104]

Universal Jurisdiction over
Human Rights Violations and Terrorism

Following the war crimes cases, the expansion of universal jurisdiction over human rights violations and terrorism has stemmed from the
growing world consensus condemning such offenses. Terrorists, hijackers, and human rights offenders are comparable to pirates, slave traders,
and war criminals because their behavior is particularly reprehensible
and it often indiscriminately endangers human lives and property interests. Terrorism and human rights violations are thus the concern of the
world's legal system, rather than the sole province of individual nation-
states. Like piracy, terrorism and hijacking may adversely affect international commerce and transportation. Like war crimes, the modern offenses may upset and destabilize the international legal order. Terrorism,
hijacking, and human rights violations may be more analogous to war
crimes than to piracy, however, because they usually promote nonprivate
goals and may even be sovereign-sponsored. In this way, the modern
universality principle continues the significant jurisdictional expansion
that the war crimes cases engendered over publicly motivated offenses.
The universality principle today invites the external review of a growing
array of humanitarian violations, although the forum sovereign has no
direct connection whatsoever with the offense. As with crimes against
humanity, the modern offenses may trigger universal jurisdiction even
when a nation-state or a government official harms that sovereign's own
citizens within that sovereign's own territory.

Multilateral Conventions

The universality principle currently draws support from various sources.
But we begin with several multilateral treaties examined earlier regard-
ing other legal issues: the Geneva, Torture, Apartheid, Hague, Montreal,
Hostage, and Internationally Protected Persons conventions.[105]

Of these postwar instruments, the Geneva Conventions particularly address offenses that had previously invoked universal jurisdiction under customary practice. The four Geneva Conventions each protect specific classes of persons during an armed conflict between parties to the Conventions; the Conventions also apply during "all cases of partial or total occupation of the territory of a [party]."[106] Each Geneva Convention identifies certain offenses as being "grave breaches" of the instruments; these include "willful killing, torture or inhumane treatment, including biological experiments" or "willfully causing great suffering or serious injury to body or health."[107] Although the Geneva Conventions do not explicitly refer to the terms *war crimes* or *crimes against humanity*, the Conventions' grave breaches partly overlap with the definitions of war crimes and crimes against humanity in the IMT Charter and C.C. Law No. 10. The Geneva Conventions provide that "[e]ach [party] shall be under the *obligation* to search for persons alleged to have committed, or to have ordered to be committed, . . . grave breaches, and shall bring such persons, *regardless of their nationality*, before its own courts."[108] Hence every party is obligated to exercise jurisdiction over those who commit grave breaches of the Geneva Conventions, even if it has no connection to, and is not engaged in, the armed conflict or occupation during which the offense occurs. The only exception to this obligation is that a party may extradite such offenders to another party.

The Torture, Hague, Montreal, Hostage, and Internationally Protected Persons conventions all contain the following provision, with insignificant variation: "The State Party in the territory of which the alleged offender is found shall, *if it does not extradite him, be obliged, without exception whatsoever and whether or not the offense was committed in its territory*, to submit the case to its competent authorities for the purpose of prosecution, through proceedings in accordance with the laws of that State."[109] Hence these conventions, similar to the Geneva Conventions, create a jurisdictional obligation to redress torture, hijacking, and certain terrorist activities; again, the parties may alternatively extradite the offenders. The Apartheid Convention has a similar provision, although the assumption of domestic jurisdiction over the perpetrators of apartheid appears to be permissive, not obligatory, even when a party fails to extradite an offender.[110]

The Geneva, Torture, Apartheid, Hague, Montreal, Hostage, and Internationally Protected Persons conventions have all been viewed as recognizing universal jurisdiction over the offenses at issue. Each treaty grants domestic jurisdiction over offenses committed extraterritorially and without regard to the nationalities of either the offenders or their victims.[111] Each treaty thus effectively establishes universal domestic authority, even when federal and other domestic courts have no links with the modern offenses. Despite their penal "extradite-or-prosecute" language, each treaty should support universal jurisdiction in civil cases, such as *Filartiga*, as well as in criminal cases. Just as the conventions justify federal jurisdiction over private causes of action vis-à-vis the national system,[112] they justify federal jurisdiction over private human rights and terrorism actions vis-à-vis the world legal order. As the federal district court announced in *Von Dardel v. Union of Soviet Socialist Republics*,[113] a recent civil action involving the alleged summary execution of an internationally protected person: "The concept of universal violations is not limited to criminal jurisdiction, but extends to the enforcement of civil law as well."[114]

Nevertheless, regarding either the civil or criminal context, universal jurisdiction under the multilateral conventions requires full examination. Our analysis will be organized under three questions. The answers that we reach may have different applications in different federal cases — partly depending upon whether the United States is a party to the specific convention that is relevant to the case. (Recall that the United States is a party to the Geneva Conventions and to all of the terrorism and hijacking treaties, but not to the Apartheid and Torture conventions, although the Senate is presently considering the Torture Convention.) The analysis will also depend upon whether other interested sovereigns are parties to the relevant convention. Our analysis will not, however, distinguish between human rights violations and terrorism. The human rights and terrorism treaties contain the same extradite-or-prosecute language. To the extent that that language helps to support modern universal jurisdiction, it equally accomplishes that result regarding human rights and terrorism cases alike. Hence even if one tries to distinguish human rights norms from terrorism norms on political or other grounds, the treaties themselves treat those norms similarly. As a matter of positive law, universal jurisdiction should provide federal judicial authority over both human rights and terrorist offenses.

1. May the parties legitimately confer jurisdiction on themselves by agreement over the nationals of other parties? As part of their sovereign ability to adopt treaties, parties may agree to regulate, at least among themselves, domestic jurisdiction over extraterritorial offenses. A party's jurisdiction over another party's national is legitimate if the modern conventions represent the world community's recognition of universal jurisdiction or, alternatively, if the conventions merely represent agreements by the parties that they will not object to any party's exercise of jurisdiction under the treaty.[115] Even if customary law had not previously subjected a particular offense to universal jurisdiction, a group of nation-states could obligate themselves to redress that offense, when committed by a party's national. Parties may agree to regulate both criminal and civil jurisdiction among themselves — perhaps even without reference to the universality principle or any other jurisdictional basis. A party's jurisdiction over another party's national might, quite simply, spring from the agreement itself.

Under the modern conventions, one party could not legitimately protest the exercise of jurisdiction over its citizen by a second party, although it could request its citizen's extradition in the criminal context. In fact, if the second party failed to prosecute or extradite the offender, it would violate its treaty obligation; with the exception of the Apartheid Convention, the parties *must* prosecute or extradite offenders in their custody.[116] Logically, this obligation should also *compel* the parties to assume universal jurisdiction in civil cases when the defendant has violated the modern treaties. The obligatory nature of the universality principle represents a transformation; recall that universal jurisdiction over piracy, for example, was only permissive. This development reflects the parties' increased commitment to respond collectively and obligatorily to particular offenses of international concern.

Connecting this analysis specifically to the United States judiciary, we reach the following conclusion: At a minimum, the federal courts legitimately possess universal jurisdiction over the nationals of other parties to the Geneva, Hague, Montreal, Hostage, and Internationally Protected Persons conventions. Since the United States is a party to those specific treaties, it arguably must exercise its universal jurisdiction in civil cases, at least when federal court authority is also legitimate within the United States legal system.

*2. Does a nonparty have a legitimate basis for protest when a party
assumes jurisdiction over the nonparty's national?* Many nonparties might
choose not to protest legal proceedings against their nationals for hijacking, war crimes, hostage taking, torture, apartheid, and crimes against
internationally protected persons. Rather than complain to the forum
sovereign or to an international body, a nonparty might try to distance
itself from the defendant and the alleged offense, given the general condemnation of these particular acts.[117] Nevertheless, in some instances, a
nonparty might still object to jurisdiction being extended pursuant to a
treaty that it has never explicitly accepted. The treaties are not expressly
limited, by their terms, to offenses committed by only the nationals of
parties. But a presumption may still exist that their jurisdictional norms
are without effect on nonparties and their nationals.[118] Under this presumption, the analysis of a jurisdictional protest has two components:
whether a treaty is affiliated with customary norms that bind nonparties; and whether a nonparty can effectively object to the force of those
customary norms.

First, as we have already discussed, a treaty may bind nonparties
through the codification, crystallization, or creation of customary norms.
The Geneva Conventions may have codified preexisting customary universal jurisdiction over war crimes. The Torture Convention perhaps partially represents a crystallization of the IMT's and zonal tribunals' universal jurisdiction over crimes against humanity; perhaps the hijacking and
terrorism conventions similarly crystallize customary universal jurisdiction
over crimes against peace. To some extent, the Apartheid Convention
arguably has codified or crystallized customary universal jurisdiction
over slave trading. Of course, these treaties have also expanded universal
jurisdiction over offenses that are more broadly conceived than under
prior customary practice. A treaty, however, may create or generate new
customary norms obligating nonparties. Recall the International Court
of Justice's important pronouncement that certain norms, "which, while
only conventional or contractual in . . . origin, [have] since passed into
the general *corpus* of international law, . . . so as to have become binding even for countries which have never, and do not, become parties to
[a] [c]onvention."[119] The Geneva, Hague, Montreal, Torture, Apartheid,
Hostage, and Internationally Protected Persons conventions are precisely
the type of well-subscribed treaties, having global implications, that

may generate norms binding upon nonparties. Naturally, the older, particularly well accepted treaties — such as the Geneva, Hague, and Montreal conventions — are especially capable of norm generation. But to the extent that any of the treaties have codified, crystallized, or created binding jurisdictional customary rules, a nonparty might be precluded from challenging a party's jurisdiction over its national.

Second, however, there is the persistent objector doctrine. Even assuming that a convention encompasses a customary norm of universal jurisdiction, a specific nonparty might have persistently objected to that jurisdictional norm or to the treaty in general. While a persistent objector's jurisdictional protest would at least be meritorious,[120] the success of that protest is far from assured. Recent commentators have questioned the legitimacy and efficacy of a nation-state's persistent objection to fundamental (or *jus cogens*) norms.[121] They suggest that fundamental norms are binding on all nation-states, and thus even objecting sovereigns may not effectively ignore them. This suggestion would overrule the objecting sovereign's rejection of such a norm, even when the norm specifically targeted the persistent objector, as with the Apartheid Convention and South Africa.[122] And this suggestion would surely weaken a nonparty's protest to universal jurisdiction over hijacking, terrorism, war crimes, apartheid, and torture. The dubiousness of a persistent objector's legal ability to violate a fundamental norm might also render dubious its legal ability to protest a party's jurisdictional enforcement of a fundamental norm. The international condemnation of certain heinous acts may implicitly justify universal jurisdiction over those offenses, thus preempting challenges to such jurisdiction. The International Court of Justice's famous dictum in the *Barcelona Traction* case may support this point, because it indicates that all nation-states have a legal interest and obligation in protecting against such offenses — "they are obligations *erga omnes*."[123] *Barcelona Traction* will be explored further below, as will the general idea that fundamental norms bind all nation-states.[124]

For now, linking this analysis to the United States, we may conclude: Since the United States is a party to the hijacking, terrorism, and war crimes conventions, and since those conventions may represent customary law binding upon nonparties, the federal courts possess universal jurisdiction when a nonparty's national commits at least those offenses. This domestic jurisdiction may well be legitimate even when the defendant's nation-state has persistently objected to the treaty at hand. Finally, the United States statutes that implement the hijacking and terrorism conventions are not expressly limited in application to the nationals of parties.[125]

3. *How do the multilateral conventions affect the obligations and rights of nonparties to exercise universal jurisdiction over the offenses at issue?* This question dovetails with the second. It examines the legal ability of nonparties to *assume*, instead of protest, universal jurisdiction. Again, presumptively, treaties regulate the behavior of only the parties.[126] As just discussed, however, these conventions may codify, crystallize, or create jurisdictional norms binding on nonparties under customary law. The human rights, hijacking, and terrorism conventions were ostensibly intended to have a broad appeal and purpose; the drafters evidently aspired toward universal jurisdiction for all sovereigns.[127] Therefore, corresponding with the second question's analytical path, the modern conventions may obligate nonparties to assume universal jurisdiction. Parties and nonparties alike may be obligated to prosecute or extradite offenders in their custody in the criminal context. Parties and nonparties may be similarly obliged to exercise jurisdiction over extraterritorial offenses between aliens in the civil context. These obligations may strengthen the longer that a specific convention has been established and the more that it is accepted. When a nonparty has not persistently objected to such customary law, its jurisdictional obligations may be particularly clear.

As a result, the United States may be obliged to assume universal jurisdiction not only under the treaties that it has ratified, but also under the Apartheid and Torture conventions (although the nation might especially balk at having a customary law obligation to extradite criminals[128]). The nation's customary jurisdictional duty may particularly emanate from the Torture Convention, which President Reagan sent to the Senate for its advice and consent.[129] The nation has surely not persistently objected to whatever custom that the Torture Convention has generated for nonparties. So even before the United States becomes a party to the Torture Convention, it may obligatorily possess universal jurisdiction over extraterritorial torture committed by and against aliens. Apparently, the nation has also not specifically objected to the Apartheid Convention's jurisdictional norms. Although one might thus argue that the federal courts must exercise universal jurisdiction over acts of apartheid, the executive department's general lack of commitment toward the Apartheid Convention may dilute that argument. But possibly, especially as support for both treaties continues to grow, international law may preclude nonparties from persistently objecting to the obligation to exercise universal jurisdiction.[130] If that is the case, then the United States could not legally object to its obligatory assumption of universal jurisdiction over torture or apartheid.

We may pursue, however, an alternative analysis. It might be maintained that nonparties have a right, but not an obligation, to exercise universal jurisdiction over the modern offenses. Under this view, a nonparty's universal jurisdiction is not directly based on the conventions, but stems from general principles of international law. More specifically, as Professor Schachter posits: "[T]he adoption of a general multilateral treaty *through the processes of international organization*" indicates that "the community of states recognize that universal jurisdiction exists for the crime in question."[131] By sponsoring the treaties, international organizations have engendered or recognized the general principle that all nation-states possess universal jurisdiction over international offenses. If domestic jurisdiction springs from that general principle, rather than from a treaty-based obligation, then universal jurisdiction is permissible, but not mandatory, for nonparties.

Just as with piracy, the universality principle today removes the barrier normally prohibiting domestic jurisdiction over offenses with which a sovereign has no direct connection. Due to the global concern with certain humanitarian offenses, the world community permits every sovereign to redress those offenses. The UN General Assembly has adopted the Apartheid, Torture, Hostage, and Internationally Protected Persons conventions;[132] through the process of that adoption, the world community has demonstrated its legal permission that all nation-states may exercise universal jurisdiction over those offenses. In fact, the Security Council in 1985 unanimously adopted a resolution condemning hostage taking and specifically appealing to all nation-states to become parties to the terrorism and hijacking conventions.[133] The International Civil Aviation Organization (ICAO) has adopted the Hague and Montreal conventions;[134] that organizational process similarly evinces the general principle that all domestic courts may redress hijacking and the sabotage of aircraft. So while parties are obligated — under treaty law — to redress the modern offenses, nonparties have the right — under general principles deriving from the international organizations' adoption of the treaties — to redress those offenses. This view gains force from the fact that the international organizations adopted or approved each of these treaties by consensus or with few dissenting votes. The *travaux preparatoires* of each convention, moreover, indicate that the jurisdictional provisions were drafted with some reliance upon the universality principle.[135] This is significant because the universality principle has traditionally created a common jurisdiction for all nation-states, and that was apparently the intention of the drafters of the modern treaties. By adopting treaties which, on their face and in their purpose, encompass universal jurisdiction, the UN and the ICAO have impliedly recognized the general principle that all sovereigns may redress hijacking, terrorism, and humanitarian offenses.

The nonparties' jurisdictional right may draw support from sources other than the processes of international organization. Granted, actual nonparty exertions of universal jurisdiction have been sparse heretofore. Under certain, relatively new doctrinal developments, however, the world community may implicitly recognize every sovereign's universal jurisdiction over the modern offenses. These developments involve international criminal law, the *erga omnes* doctrine (i.e., certain obligations flow to all sovereigns), and the *jus cogens* doctrine (i.e., certain norms compel all sovereigns). We will consider general international criminal law here, but will discuss *erga omnes* and *jus cogens* more specifically below (in this and particularly the next chapter[136]).

Both the atrocities of the Second World War and the Nuremberg precedent precipitated the growth of international criminal law. This evolution has taken various forms, including the promulgation of the very treaties that we have been discussing; certain General Assembly measures; and several International Law Commission (ILC) efforts. By resolution in 1946, the General Assembly affirmed the international law principles contained in the IMT Charter and Judgment.[137] Those principles include the recognition of *nonstate* liability for war crimes, crimes against peace, and crimes against humanity, correctly characterized as offenses *jure gentium*. The General Assembly also directed a committee (eventually the ILC) to formulate an International Criminal Code that is "a general codification of offences against the peace and security of mankind,"[138] pursuant to the IMT's Charter and Judgment. The resulting Draft Code of Offences identifies various acts as "crimes under international law for which the responsible individuals shall be punished," including terrorism and the offenses that the IMT addressed.[139] As with proposals for an international criminal court, however, the General Assembly has not yet adopted the Draft Code or subsequent legislative efforts.[140]

The ILC has also addressed the criminal responsibility of nation-states. Under the ILC's Draft Convention on State Responsibility, an international crime (in contrast to a delict) is "[a]n internationally wrongful act which results from the breach by a State of an international obligation so essential for the protection of fundamental interests of the international community that its breach is recognized as a crime by that community as a whole."[141] Such sovereign offenses include aggression, which would subsume sovereign-sponsored terrorism. The offenses also include widespread violations of essential human rights, such as slavery, genocide, and apartheid.[142] Nation-states may thus be liable for roughly the same offenses for which nonstate actors are liable. The Draft Convention has not received formal approval, however, and some dispute continues over the ILC's distinction between international crimes and delicts.

These various efforts have characterized terrorism, hijacking, and basic humanitarian offenses as international crimes. This characterization may help to invoke the universality principle. As the *Restatement* commentary indicates: "An international crime is presumably subject to [the] universal jurisdiction" of all nation-states.[143] Of course, an international tribunal may also be provided with jurisdiction over international offenses; and granted, a distinction may be drawn between substantive criminal law and the conferral of domestic jurisdiction over violations of that substantive law. Nevertheless, the condemnation of hijacking, terrorism, apartheid, war crimes, and torture as international offenses impliedly supports each sovereign's right to subject those offenses to the universal jurisdiction of its domestic courts. Although some sources of international criminal law have not yet been formally approved, the growing codification and consensus regarding those norms suggests the legal order's permission for all sovereigns to remedy egregious extraterritorial offenses, wherever and by whomever committed. Under modern jurisdictional concepts, such domestic authority should be available in either criminal or civil cases. The exercise of universal jurisdiction in civil actions obviously serves the values that underlie the burgeoning international criminal law.

In conclusion, nonparties to the Geneva, Apartheid, Torture, Hague, Montreal, Hostage, and Internationally Protected Persons conventions have the right — if not the obligation — to assume universal jurisdiction over the offenses at hand. Though a nonparty to the Torture and Apartheid conventions, the United States may at least be entitled to exercise universal jurisdiction over torture and apartheid. This jurisdictional right draws support from the international organizations' adoption of those conventions, giving rise to general principles of international law. It also stems from the overall development of international criminal law. As the law continues to grow, so will the right of nonparties to remedy the modern offenses. The strengthening of that jurisdictional right, in turn, will help to counter any challenge to a party's or nonparty's exercise of universal jurisdiction. The *erga omnes* and *jus cogens* doctrines have also elevated human rights and terrorism norms to the apex of international law's normative pyramid, as will be explained.[144] The lofty status of these norms helps to sanctify the universal entitlement of all sovereigns to redress today's *hostis humani generis*.

Universal Jurisdiction over Other Modern Offenses

In the modern period, we have thus far focused upon offenses that are addressed by multilateral conventions containing extradite-or-prosecute language. We may now consider modern universal jurisdiction over other offenses that are not addressed by such treaties. We initially confront genocide and then additional offenses.

Genocide. Although not synonymous, the term *genocide* is conceptually derivative of the crimes against humanity that the IMT and zonal tribunals addressed. Those tribunals partly relied on the universality principle to redress crimes against humanity and other offenses.[145] By resolving to accept the IMT's legal principles in 1946,[146] the UN may thus have codified the universal jurisdictional right of all nation-states to redress crimes against humanity and genocide. Also in 1946, the General Assembly passed a resolution[147] declaring genocide to be an international crime and instructing the Economic and Social Council to draft the Genocide Convention.[148] The General Assembly adopted the Convention, which entered into force in 1951. While the Geneva Conventions address certain grave breaches committed during armed conflict and occupation, genocide may be "committed in time of peace or in time of war."[149] The Convention defines genocide as the commission of particular acts "with intent to destroy, in whole or in part, a national, ethnical, racial or religious group."[150]

The multilateral conventions discussed just above typically obligate the parties to prosecute or extradite offenders in their custody, even if they lack any direct link with the offense. The Genocide Convention, however, does not obligate the parties to prosecute all offenders in their custody, nor does it explicitly address the right to prosecute such offenders. Under article 6 of the Genocide Convention, "[p]ersons charged with genocide . . . shall be tried by a competent tribunal of the State in the territory of which the act was committed, or by such international penal tribunal as may have jurisdiction."[151] Hence article 6 obligates the parties to exercise domestic jurisdiction pursuant to the territoriality principle and also refers to prosecution by an international body.

Because the territoriality principle is the only basis of domestic jurisdiction that article 6 mentions, some debate has ensued over whether genocide is subject to the parties' universal jurisdiction. Some have argued that territoriality is the exclusive jurisdictional basis.[152] Others, however, have argued that article 6 only enumerates one possible basis of domestic jurisdiction, and that "genocide remains a crime giving rise to a universal jurisdiction under *customary international law*."[153]

The latter view is correct. Granted, the Genocide Convention does not oblige the parties to penalize all offenders in their custody, and the *travaux preparatoires* indicate that the parties decided not to include such an obligation in the Convention.[154] Nevertheless, that the parties have imposed a *duty* to remedy genocide under the territoriality principle does not necessarily mean that they have deprived themselves of the customary law *right* to exercise universal jurisdiction over genocide. Nothing suggests that the parties intended such a deprivation of their customary law rights. As the district court in *Eichmann* aptly put it: "[T]he reference in Article 6 to territorial jurisdiction is not exhaustive. Every sovereign State may exercise its existing powers within the limits of *customary international law*."[155] The customary law right to exercise universal jurisdiction over genocide preceded the Genocide Convention, as the precedent of the war crimes trials indicates. It is anomalous to argue that General Assembly resolutions affirming the Nuremberg principles, declaring genocide to be an international offense, and creating a convention to outlaw genocide have deprived the parties of their customary law right to universal jurisdiction over genocide. That argument also leads to the dubious conclusion that nonparties have more expansive jurisdictional authority — the customary universal jurisdiction over genocide — than do parties to the Genocide Convention. Moreover, after the Genocide Convention entered into force, the Eichmann judgments, the recent *Demjanjuk* opinion, and the *Restatement* have all recognized the customary law right of every nation-state to redress genocide.[156]

Universal jurisdiction over genocide under customary law can coexist with territoriality jurisdiction under treaty law; the former relates to a jurisdictional right, the latter to a jurisdictional obligation. Every nation-state has the right to exercise universal jurisdiction over genocidal acts under customary law, regardless of both the location of the genocide and the nationalities of the offenders and their victims. This jurisdictional right logically appertains to civil and criminal cases both. The parties to the Genocide Convention have simply obligated themselves to redress offenses specifically committed within their territory. Now that the United States has become a party to the Convention, it is obliged to redress genocidal acts occurring in its territory, although such offenses are unlikely. The United States also retains its jurisdictional right, under customary law, to redress genocide in federal courts, even when the nation has no links with the particular act and actors.

Additional Offenses. Apart from genocide, universal jurisdiction may exist over other offenses that are fundamentally detrimental to the world community. The universality principle may extend, for instance, over behavior that the Covenant prohibits.[157] Three examples of such offenses are summary execution, prolonged arbitrary detention, and murder or causing the disappearance of individuals. The Covenant does not contain any extradite-or-prosecute language, and the support for universal jurisdiction over these additional offenses may not be as strong as it is for genocide. But the Covenant expressly recognizes the necessity of providing domestic judicial remedies to individual victims.[158] In addition, these three offenses partly overlap with those at issue in the war crimes tribunals. Since the tribunals partly relied upon the universality principle,[159] that precedent supports customary universal jurisdiction over summary execution, prolonged arbitrary detention, and murder or causing the disappearance of individuals. Further support stems from the fact that the prohibitions of those three offenses are obligations *erga omnes* and *jus cogens* norms. Arguably, every nation-state has universal jurisdiction over violations of those obligations and norms, when basic individual rights are violated.[160] International criminal law may buttress universal jurisdiction over summary execution, prolonged arbitrary detention, and murder or causing the disappearance of individuals in either the criminal or civil context.[161] Therefore, a strong case may be made for federal universal jurisdiction over those three offenses.

If the universality principle is extended to additional human rights violations, it should also extend to terrorist acts other than those addressed by the Hostage, Hague, Montreal, and Internationally Protected Persons conventions. The world legal order has condemned all forms of terror as a means of political or social coercion. This condemnation includes all violence having international ramifications, from the bombing of public and private buildings to the killing of customs officials. As with human rights norms, the illegality of terrorism is evinced by the war crimes trials (specifically, the punishment of crimes against peace); international criminal law; and the *erga omnes* and *jus cogens* doctrines. Since the prohibition against terrorism is a quintessentially fundamental norm, the world legal order may implicitly permit every nation-state to redress all types of terrorism. Whether or not the forum sovereign is directly connected with the offense, it acts on behalf of all other sovereigns by exercising domestic judicial authority over terrorists. As with piracy, it is extremely difficult to bring terrorists to criminal and civil justice; the necessity of universal jurisdiction over terrorists helps to justify that jurisdiction. Indeed, as Professor Dinstein has concluded, "[t]he terrorist has replaced the pirate as the *hostis humani generis par excellence.*"[162] At a time when nation-states are coming together to redress terrorism, each sovereign logically possesses domestic authority to penalize whatever terrorists are in its custody. Under this analysis, the United States federal judiciary has universal jurisdiction over all terrorist offenses. This conclusion will obviously strengthen through the subsequent exercise of universal jurisdiction.

Conclusion

The universality principle justifies, and sometimes mandates, federal court jurisdiction over civil cases involving human rights violations and terrorism. This authority is legitimate vis-à-vis the world legal order, irrespective of the offense's situs and the plaintiff's and defendant's identities and nationalities. Although the modern universal jurisdiction is largely bottomed on multilateral conventions, it also stems from the earlier universal jurisdiction over pirates, slave traders, and war criminals. The universality principle's expansion is consistent with various legal efforts to curtail and redress terrorist activities and violations of fundamental rights. Universal crimes, obligations *erga omnes*, and *jus cogens* norms may be viewed as doctrinal siblings, sharing the common lineage of a modern world legal order concerned with global peace and human dignity. As the counterterrorism and human rights agenda continues to grow, so will, and should, the assumption of universal jurisdiction in the future. At the same time, it must be ensured that the defendant's procedural rights are also respected in federal and other domestic courts.[163]

CHAPTER 9

The Human Rights Paradigm

By theorizing "jurisdiction" as the systemic distribution of authority, we necessarily make assumptions about the nature and structure of the system being examined. In other words, it is impossible to define an institution's legitimate and appropriate authority within a legal order without first presuming some vision of the legal order itself. This is true of the United States legal system, in which the federal judiciary's proper role in any context depends, in large part, upon the system's constructs of vertical federalism and horizontal separation of powers. Regarding the international legal system, the starting point for analysis generally presumes a highly decentralized and horizontal order of juridically equal sovereigns, supreme over the individuals and events in their separate territories. Under this supposition, nation-states must voluntarily adhere to the jurisdictional principles and reciprocally consider the jurisdictional interests of other sovereigns in an offense. Adjudicative laissez-faire is normally the ideal when a tribunal has no connection with an international case, lest one sovereign step on the toes of another sovereign or its citizens. Universal jurisdiction over human rights and terrorism cases, accordingly, may seem a rather extraordinary exception to the domestic authority that the world legal order normally permits. Our discussion of the universality principle thus was largely devoted to justifying such extraterritorial jurisdiction within the decentralized world legal order.[1] Since the global order, as traditionally conceived, predominantly consists of sovereign actors, we have also had to justify how nonstate actors possess international rights and duties. Although the modern multilateral conventions simplified our analyses, we were still primarily working within the sovereign-dominated framework that international lawyers presume as their analytical starting point.

But perhaps that starting point is flawed, or at least not as systemically hospitable to human rights and terrorism cases as it should be. Perhaps it is time to reconceptualize the world legal order itself to account more accurately for the enormous growth of modern humanitarian law. It now may be meaningful to speak of the "human rights paradigm," by which the decentralized statist structure has partly yielded to a more hierarchical and an individualistic structure. Under this paradigmatic revision of the legal system, the recent growth of universal jurisdiction does not merely represent a legal or doctrinal expansion. It, instead, more pervasively, is a constituent in the structural transformation of the world legal order. Within the human rights paradigm, when an individual claims that a foreign actor has violated his or her fundamental rights on foreign soil, external judicial review of the offense should seem ordinary. The modern paradigm may thus obligate federal and other domestic courts to assume civil jurisdiction over human rights and terrorism cases with which they have no direct connection.

To pursue this thesis, we may first find it helpful to examine briefly the nation-state system, dating from the seventeenth century. Our purpose is to understand the system that is being revised and, moreover, to see how that system itself transformed a previous legal order. As Neustadt's and May's recent and provocative text, *Thinking in Time*, suggests, "use of history can stimulate imagination: Seeing the past can help one envision alternative futures."[2]

The Westphalian System

Within the medieval order, the pope, under the notion of a Christian commonwealth, vertically governed Europe.[3] Such "papal central guidance was coordinated with feudal loyalties to family, church, guild and prince."[4] The pope was eventually faced with secular confrontation, notably Philip IV's attempt to tax the French clergy in 1302 without Rome's permission. This conflict caused pope Boniface VIII to issue the bull *Unam Sanctam*, which defined the "plentitude of Papal power over all the Christian community, including France and her king."[5] The bull famously continued: "At the time of the flood there was, indeed, one ark of Noah, prefiguring one Church; it . . . had one steersman and commander, namely Noah, and we read that outside of it all things existing on earth were destroyed."[6] And "spiritual power exceeds any earthly power in dignity and nobility, as spiritual things excel temporal ones."[7] Although both the spiritual and feudal domains were under God's heavens, the papacy viewed itself as superior to the king on earth.

Philip, nevertheless, disavowed the bull. This is particularly significant because he ruled "over one of the earliest political units to achieve statehood in the modern sense."[8] By defying the pope's centralized rule, Philip helped to spawn the nation-state as the basic, if not the only, organizing unit of the world legal order. In fact, as of the thirteenth century, at least England and France displayed the attributes of a modern territorial sovereign. The historian Joseph Strayer writes: "By 1300 it was evident that the dominant political form in Western Europe was going to be the sovereign state. . . . Loyalty to the state was stronger than any other loyalty."[9] He continues, however, that "the sovereign state of 1300 . . . was still not very strong. . . . It took four to five centuries for European states to overcome their weaknesses, . . . to bring lukewarm loyalty up to the white heat of nationalism."[10]

It may be untenable to select a single date or event that signifies the world legal order's shift to decentralized nation-state control. By most accounts, however, the Peace of Westphalia, in 1648, formally represents the beginning of the nation-state system.[11] The Treaty of Westphalia (incorporating the Treaties of Munster and Osnabruch) expressly marked the end of the Thirty Years War. The war, most specifically, was started when Duke John William died without heir in 1609, which caused a conflict over succession. But it was, more generally, a conflict between the forces supporting the globe's vertical control (the pope, the emperor, roughly the status quo) against those supporting its horizontal control (non-Catholic denominations, emerging nation-states). This was not only a war between armed forces. As Professor Gross describes, preceding 1648, "powerful intellectual, political, and social forces were at work which opposed . . . the aspirations and the remaining realities of the unified control of Pope and Emperor. In particular the Reformation and the Renaissance, . . . each in its own field, attacked the supreme authority claimed by the Pope and the Emperor."[12] The Thirty Years War, then, was a conflict over the very structure of world government. And in the end, the spiritual and feudal hierarchies could not restrain in battle or philosophy the Calvinists and Lutherans, the growing middle class, or the burgeoning nation-states. The Hapsburg empire was defeated, and the pre-Reformation secular and sectarian arrangement would not be centrally reconstituted.

The Treaty of Westphalia basically recognized a new arrangement of decentralized sovereign world order. This constitutive instrument acknowledged the territorial sovereignty of European nation-states; it established dispute resolution mechanisms; and it separated church and state, but allowed each sovereign to oversee religious matters within its territory.[13] Under Westphalian dogma, the international legal system is exclusively composed of nation-states, sovereign over their territory, citizens, and natural resources. Within this arrangement, national "governments are *sovereign* and *equal* by juridical fiat, rather than by virtue of some higher authority within the world order system."[14] The Westphalian Treaty drew upon the work of philosophers and legal commentators, prominently including Hugo Grotius's seminal 1625 treatise, which postulated sovereign absolutism, although resting on natural law.[15] Of course, the treaty was not without ambiguity or pretext. In some instances, sovereign authority was less than absolute, and in others, there was a commingling, conscious or not, of old and new world ideals.[16] The document was also not without dispute. Its arduous negotiation took nearly four years, and even once completed, the parties had to repudiate a papal bull that condemned the instrument.[17] Nevertheless, the treaty's creation remains the quintessential "juridical event" that gave rise to the sovereign-state system: "The Peace of Westphalia, for better or worse, marks the end of an epoch and the opening of another. It represents the majestic portal which leads old into the new world."[18]

Thinking in Paradigms

The essence of what we have just described may be contemplated in terms of a "paradigm"— the Westphalian paradigm. Thomas Kuhn, a natural, turned social, scientist has helped to illuminate the notion of paradigms. In an important and controversial work, Kuhn examined the structure of scientific revolutions. He observed that, within a given scientific community, practitioners share "law, theory, application, and instrumentation together . . . provid[ing] models from which spring particular coherent traditions of scientific research."[19] "Copernican astronomy" is but one example of such a model. Kuhn has criticized historiography for its fixation with science as an incremental accumulation of knowledge, with practitioners only "mopping up" or implementing the "normal science" of past scientific achievements.[20] That explanation does not contemplate the occasional and significant scientific revolutions, "those noncumulative developmental episodes in which an older paradigm is replaced in whole or in part by an incompatible new one."[21] An example here is the revolutionary replacement of Copernican for Ptolemaic astronomy.[22] But Kuhn advises that, both before and after such revolutions, even natural scientists' assumptions are not without some relativity, subjectivity, and even irrationality.[23]

The term *paradigm* is central to Kuhn's theory. In his original work, Kuhn somewhat vaguely and variously employed that term. In subsequent writings, however, he has reduced the confusion by identifying two basic usages. The term, in its first sense, is "global, embracing all the shared commitments of a scientific group"[24] and structurally encompassing "universally recognized scientific achievements . . . for a community of practitioners."[25] While the term first "stands for the *entire constellation* of beliefs, values, techniques, and so on shared by . . . a given community," the second usage denotes "*one sort of element* in that constellation, the concrete puzzle-solutions which, employed as models or examples, can replace explicit rules as a basis for the solution of remaining puzzles of normal science."[26] The second sense resembles the term's more common or layperson's usage, more like the dictionary definition; it "isolates a particularly important sort of commitment" of a scientific group "and is thus a subset of the first" sense.[27] "Disciplinary matrix"—"the common possession of the practitioners of a professional discipline . . . composed of ordered elements of various sorts"[28]—is a synonym for paradigm's first definition. "Exemplar"—a problem-solving example that practitioners share[29]—is a synonym for its second definition.

A scientific revolution occurs when an existing paradigm cannot accommodate novel and illuminating discoveries and phenomena. New ideas may initially be suppressed; they may later be grappled with as "anomalies" within a disciplinary matrix or an exemplar.[30] A true crisis of faith occurs, however, once the new knowledge becomes too significant and too inexplicable as accumulated knowledge under the preconceived system—that is, when new ideas substantially oppose, rather than supplement or expand, old theories. During the crisis, intellectual divisiveness may be the norm. "Transition" or "preparadigm periods" may see practitioners "split into a number of competing schools, each claiming competence for the same subject matter but approaching it in quite different ways."[31] But eventually, according to Kuhn, paradigmatic crises lead to the development of new theories, under which the discoveries are not anomalies, but may actually be postulates or tautologies.[32] The culmination of this revolutionary process is a systemic makeover — a "paradigm shift" — with new paradigm replacing old.[33] This conceptualization of a paradigm shift may remind one of Hannah Arendt's description of modern political revolutions (especially when a disciplinary matrix, rather than an exemplar, shifts). Revolutions, she wrote, do not signify "restoration," but "that an entirely new story, a story never known or told before, is about to unfold."[34] And revolutionaries "are agents in a process which spells the definite end of an old order and brings about the birth of a new world."[35] In either science or politics, it is sometimes not the rules that change, but the game.

International Paradigms

Under Kuhn's approach, the Westphalian system represents the seventeenth-century paradigm of international relations, as Richard Falk has suggested.[36] Decentralized and secular tendencies were initially quieted and repelled; the conflict with Philip IV later exemplified the incongruency between those tendencies and papal authority. Eventually, however, the forces for decentralization could not be explained away as anomalous insurgents. Instead, the phenomena of nation-state sovereignty led to a major crisis, the Thirty Years War, culminating in the Westphalian Treaty and a paradigmatic shift to decentralized sovereign authority. This systemic shift befits the broader, global concept of a paradigm, designating a revolution against the old world's disciplinary matrix. One should always be cautious about digging up a theory or an approach from one area of learning and planting it in another. But even if international law's paradigm is not as explicit or concrete as that which guides natural scientists, the Westphalian perspective can reasonably be viewed in terms of a model or paradigm — as "giving juridical expression to [the] political reality" of sovereign governance.[37]

This, of course, leads us to the preliminary question for which we have been preparing: If the sovereign system is cognizable as the West-phalian paradigm, how have the post–Second World War developments affected that paradigm? Put another way, has the landslide of support for humanitarian norms engendered another new disciplinary matrix — a post-Westphalian matrix — or at least a modern exemplar for human rights and terrorism cases? Of course, such inquiries are impossible to answer with absolute certainty and conviction, for they contemplate no less than the legal order's very structure. Moreover, any structural trans-formation is presently ongoing, and the process is probably incomplete. But despite the tentative nature of present information, we may gener-ally observe several trends quite suggestive of a paradigm shift. Perhaps it is time to ring out the Westphalian paradigm and ring in the human rights paradigm.

We begin by noting the significant parallel between the arrival of the two systems. As with the Westphalian arrangement, the human rights paradigm has not developed overnight. The ambitious creation of the League of Nations, following the First World War, surely prefigured the movement to increased central guidance that has followed the Second. The experiment with the League may be loosely analogous to Philip IV's momentary "sovereign victory" over Rome,[38] both, in their time, precur-sors of world order revision. But following both experiences, another major conflict was necessary to introduce a true paradigm shift — the Thirty Years War in the seventeenth century, and World War II in the twentieth century — though neither conflict automatically changed all aspects of world order. Like the seventeenth-century conflict, World War II was marked by longevity, especially if seen as somewhat deriva-tive of World War I. Both the Thirty Years War and the Second World War complexly implicated many issues and ideas. At bottom, however, the Second World War was a confrontation over nationalistic aggression and the sovereign treatment of human beings. Just as the Thirty Years War demonstrated the fallacies of papal-dominated governance, the Sec-ond World War magnified the inadequacies of horizontal and sovereign-dominated governance. While the League of Nations had resolved minor global conflicts, it was incapable of adequately responding to major Axis aggression, such as Italy's invasion of Ethiopia, or to the Nazi atrocities. The League was all but formally defunct during the war.[39] In 1945 only military might ended the bloodiest war in history, with Germany's and Japan's surrender.

Post–Second World War II legal instruments and institutions began to constitute a new world regime, akin to the Westphalian Treaty's accomplishment. Apart from the documents of surrender, the first new instruments, the Charter of the International Military Tribunal (IMT Charter) and Control Council Law No. 10 (C.C. Law No. 10),[40] were intended to redress the globe's most reprehensible offenders. Those instruments forged important achievements: the creation of transnational judicial fora, in contrast to having allowed Germany perfunctorily to prosecute its own war criminals after World War I;[41] the acknowledgment of individual responsibility for international law violations, culminating in the IMT's sobering realization that offenses "against international law are committed by men, not by abstract [sovereign] entities";[42] and the recognition of both military aggression and a sovereign's mistreatment of its own citizens as international offenses.[43] Such developments were not without some controversy and criticism, but neither was the completion of Westphalian peace. The IMT Charter and C.C. Law No. 10, therefore, essentially admitted the failed premise of horizontal order — absolute sovereignty. Absent adequate centralized or external checks, internal atrocities bled into extraterritorial aggression. If omnipotent nation-states had been the legal system's "exclusive subjects," the cliché was now threadbare.

Beyond the tribunals' charters have come other waves of important instruments that diminish sovereign absolutism and aggrandize individualism. These documents include the new legal order's "constitution"— the United Nations Charter — and the "international bill of rights"— the Universal Declaration of Human Rights and the two International Covenants.[44] Also included are the other treaties that we have studied: the Genocide, Torture, Geneva, Apartheid, Hague, Montreal, Hostage, and Internationally Protected Persons conventions.[45] Given the commitments and values that these instruments have together established, their influence on present global order is not without some comparison to the Westphalian Treaty's influence on seventeenth-century order.

We are not suggesting that a perfect match exists between the evolutions of the two legal orders. The systems are obviously far too complex to have developed on a structural tit-for-tat. The point, instead, is that general and significant parallels can be drawn between the systemic development of both periods, from early conflict and dispute resolution, to major armed confrontation, to postwar accords attempting peace and security. Of course, on a substantive level, virtually every change in the modern system represents a reversal of the Westphalian system. Every movement toward vertical order and sovereign relativity brings the globe closer to a type of pre-Westphalian central control. The peace of the Second World War, like that of the Thirty Years War, may well represent the end of one epoch and the opening of yet another.[46]

The human rights and antiterrorism movement distinctly and characteristically reflects a shift in the relevant disciplinary matrix. The post–World War II developments cannot reasonably be viewed incrementally to supplement or implement the Westphalian logic. In Kuhn's terms, rather than "mopping up" the "normal science" of horizontal order, legal practitioners have created instruments that are anathema to rigid decentralization. Truly revised beliefs, values, commitments, generalizations, and techniques are before us. The establishment of international pacifistic and humanitarian organizations is revolutionary when viewed against the Westphalian arrangement. Creating norms to govern a sovereign's territorial behavior is similarly revolutionary. Although we may take the postwar developments somewhat for granted, they simply cannot be squared with the science of decentralized and exclusive sovereign governance. These developments have not restored the world legal order to the preconflict status quo, but have dramatically changed the order, unfolding a new story of global issues and relations.[47] In addition, the humanitarian movement is culturally mirrored in society, in popular music, film, and literature.[48] Modern scholarship, from various walks of academia, also reflects the movement and the changed global perspective. Specifically in international law scholarship, commentators have even helped to transform the disciplinary matrix; the postwar's greatest scholars, Myres McDougal being the first to come to mind, have played a very influential role, just as commentators did in the Westphalian era.

Of course, one cannot deny that nation-states remain the primary global actors. Some might even say that the world is neither predominantly plane nor predominantly pyramidal; rather, it is primarily structured under the bipolarization of Western versus Eastern blocs. And one also cannot pretend that human rights and terrorism norms are consistently followed; a mere glance at the morning newspaper shatters that pretension. At the same time, it cannot be reasonably contested that sovereignty's primacy and strength has been significantly diminished at least in the context of human rights and terrorism. How, then, do we justify, on the one hand, the continued dominance of nation-states (in singular or bloc form) with, on the other hand, the centralized attention to individual rights? First, no disciplinary matrix logically controls or explains all phenomena. Recall Kuhn's suggestion that even a natural scientist's system contains some irrationality and relativity; recall, too, that even the Westphalian peace contained some ambiguity, some mixture of old and new world ideas.[49] Second, if the human rights paradigm is unfolding, the globe is witnessing only the transition toward that paradigm shift. The true fruition of the Westphalian arrangement, after all, took centuries. Since even established paradigms contain some ambiguity, the transition period between systems especially can present a mixture of values: "Dual loyalty to the past and to that which is still to come injects an element of incoherence in . . . international law activity during any period of transition from one world order system to another."[50] Third, since, as Kuhn advises, a new paradigm may replace an old paradigm in whole or in part,[51] the human rights paradigm may only partly replace the Westphalian paradigm. This idea does not undercut the concept of a paradigm as a vehicle of understanding. For within any complex area, there can logically be more than one disciplinary matrix. Just as the natural or social sciences, in their different disciplines, contain several matrices, so can public international law. For the time being, the horizontal sovereign system may be the analytical starting point, for example, concerning the topic of domestic farm production. But the existence of that model does not preclude an individualistic and more centralized paradigm where humanitarian rights are at issue. Even if a completely vertical world order never comes, and even if the new paradigm currently contains more limited implications than the Westphalian paradigm, there exists a new gestalt of human rights and terrorism. One might conclude that the humanitarian disciplinary matrix has shifted or is about to shift.

It also is possible to view the human rights paradigm not as a disciplinary matrix, but as an "exemplar." The use of that term — which, again, refers to shared examples for problem solving — is perhaps especially appropriate, since we have focused on human rights and terrorism in the

context of cases or legal proceedings. After all, litigation essentially involves solving problems between parties; it requires models that practitioners (judges and counsel) share for resolving disputes. The post–World
War II developments, however, have changed the basic premises and
ground rules that govern international cases in our genre. Practitioners
must now confront new substantive human rights and terrorism norms;
new rules of individual rights and of nonstate and nation-state responsibility; and the overriding and novel idea that every government may
be concerned with humanitarian violations wherever occurring. Those
precepts simply do not mesh with the Westphalian mode of problem solving. It is not that Nuremberg and the postwar treaties have augmented
the old rules of international litigation, but that they have revised the
old rules so radically that a new paradigm or exemplar is necessary.
Scholars have demonstrated how federal courts have already applied
those rules in different contexts of rights abuses; this phenomena began
in the years just following the Second World War.[52]

The modern exemplar may today provide a model for disputes involving only a handful of human rights violations and terrorist offenses. As
nation-states, however, add more individual rights to the international
agendum, the "human rights exemplar" will grow as a problem-solving
tool. For example, that exemplar may eventually help to solve cases brought
by the victims of illegal chemical warfare, although no such litigation has
yet been commenced. The exemplar's value for resolving puzzles may increase, too, whenever nonhumanitarian issues and matters are transferred
from horizontal sovereign authority to vertical global concern. In sum, as
Kuhn suggests, the modes by which a community solves problems is at least
as important and informative as the results of problem solving—something
like, the "medium is the message."[53] And at least in the modern human
rights and terrorism cases, the Westphalian paradigm, as a litigation-
exemplar, is surely outmoded. Particularly as the new exemplar becomes
crystallized, and as more issues become internationalized, the human
rights paradigm may be increasingly valuable in various contexts.

Federal Courts and the Modern Paradigm

Let us assume, then, that the developments of the last five decades
have had some paradigmatic implications. Rather than signifying merely

discrete and singular events, the postwar developments represent broad and fundamental changes in the world legal order's governance of humanitarian concerns. With that assumption, we are left with our ultimate inquiry: What is the proper jurisdictional role of domestic courts, particularly the federal judiciary, in the new human rights paradigm? In other words, since an institution's jurisdiction depends upon the legal system in which it operates, what impact does the system's evolving centralization and increased individualistic perspective have on federal court authority over human rights and terrorism cases? Our answer may again be organized into two parts, according to Kuhn's dual conceptions of "paradigm."

Initially, if the human rights movement has engendered a new disciplinary matrix, federal jurisdiction is especially appropriate over humanitarian violations. This is true even absent any direct connection between the forum sovereign and the human rights or terrorist offense. Under the new matrix, such offenses are the concern of all nation-states and thus subject to every sovereign's authority. Based on postwar precedent and treaties, that matrix essentially recognizes individuals as the "subjects" of basic human rights; it recognizes domestic institutions as potential guardians of those rights. The universality principle — providing civil jurisdiction in an action such as *Filartiga v. Pena-Irala,* the Paraguayan torture case[54] — is symptomatic of that paradigm shift. If federal authority is legitimate vis-à-vis the world legal order under treaty and customary universal jurisdiction, it is, *a fortiori,* legitimate if a centralized matrix has developed. The universality principle is the specific vehicle that justifies federal jurisdiction over *Filartiga* and much of its progeny. But that newly expanded principle is really part and parcel of the overall structural revision of global humanitarian guidance.

Domestic courts should help to bridge the gap between the waning Westphalian matrix and the human rights matrix. The federal judiciary may even facilitate this transition by implementing the new legal order's fundamental norms and postulates. Since individuals may not bring any claims before the International Court of Justice,[55] the assumption of domestic jurisdiction over human rights and terrorism cases is especially necessary. While domestic courts are horizontally arranged in relation to the world legal order, they may appropriately enforce norms that are emitted by centralized institutions, such as the UN and the International Civil Aviation Organization. The absence of a truly global civil tribunal[56] does not foreclose federal court jurisdiction over human rights and terrorism claims; it suggests only that, institutionally, the world has not yet fully provided human rights and antiterrorism enforcement machinery. In the meantime, federal courts may legitimately act as "double agents" of both the United States legal system and the world legal order. This suggestion draws some theoretical support from the work of the renowned French academic Georges Scelle, who described the notion of *dedoublement fonctionnel* ("functional doubling").[57] From this notion, we can suggest that federal courts should function as international tribunals, at least when fundamental humanitarian norms are at issue. Such a relatively limited functional doubling does not stretch federal courts beyond their "institutional elasticity" or beyond their most "manifest mandate".[58] In fact, the modern treaties and general world order trends may even obligate federal courts to represent the international system.

The assumption of this role is also supported by the ever-emerging presence of regional humanitarian institutions, including the European Commission and Court of Human Rights,[59] the Inter-American Court of Human Rights,[60] and the African Commission on Human Rights.[61] These bodies do not necessarily function uniformly with each other. For example, their adjudicative and enforcement jurisdiction differs somewhat, and each places somewhat different limitations on individuals' ability to commence a claim. Although an in-depth examination of these bodies is beyond our immediate topic, the regional institutions generally represent a diminution of sovereign control over violations of individual rights and, concomitantly, increased external control over those offenses. The domestic adjudication of *Filartiga*-like cases dovetails with the transregional attention to humanitarian issues and concerns. These domestic and regional efforts, when taken together, represent institutional patterns befitting and advancing the human rights paradigm. And somewhat circuitously, it is that paradigm that justifies domestic and regional jurisdiction over extraterritorial human rights violations and terrorism. Hence the federal adjudication of the modern cases helps to crystallize the new disciplinary matrix, and that matrix helps to justify federal jurisdiction over *Filartiga* and its progeny. Replaced in Kuhnian terms: "A paradigm is what members of a scientific community . . . share. Conversely, it is their possession of a common paradigm that constitutes a scientific community of a group of otherwise disparate men."[62]

Next we may contemplate federal jurisdiction under the assumption that the human rights paradigm represents only a new exemplar rather than a new disciplinary matrix. As discussed above, lawsuits are quite analogous to exemplars, since they essentially involve modes for solving problems between the litigants. In any litigation model, a threshold issue is whether the forum has jurisdiction. Various postwar developments signify that federal jurisdiction is proper vis-à-vis the world legal order in the exemplar of human rights and terrorism cases.

These modern developments naturally include the extension of the universality principle and the general growth of international criminal law.[63] In addition, the recent expansion of the *erga omnes* and *jus cogens* doctrines has likewise had paradigmatic implications for federal jurisdiction in the new exemplar. We have previously made only brief references to these doctrines. In 1970 the International Court of Justice illuminated the concept of obligations *erga omnes*, literally obligations "flowing to all," in its renowned dictum in *Barcelona Traction*.[64] As the court explained, in contrast to a nation-state's obligations "arising vis-à-vis another state," obligations *erga omnes* "are the concern of all States. In view of the importance of the rights involved, all States can be held to have a legal interest in their protection."[65] Those obligations stem from both "general international law" and "international instruments of a universal or quasi-universal character."[66] For example, they today "derive from the outlawing of acts of aggression, and of genocide, as also from the principles and rules concerning the basic rights of the human person, including protection from slavery and racial discrimination."[67] Somewhat similarly, *jus cogens* literally means "compelling law." The *jus cogens* doctrine refers to certain peremptory norms "accepted and recognized by the international community of States as a whole . . . from which no derogation is permitted."[68] Treaties conflicting with such norms are void. As presently expanded, *jus cogens* norms overlap with the examples of *erga omnes* obligations mentioned in *Barcelona Traction*.[69] Apart from their specific functional applications, the universality principle and the *erga omnes* and *jus cogens* doctrines have together helped to give hierarchical order to international norms. Just as some constitutional rights are deemed more fundamental than others,[70] some international rights are more fundamentally significant to the world legal order.[71] The individual rights that we have discussed commonly appear on the lists of rights that the universality principle and the *erga omnes* and *jus cogens* doctrines protect. As such, these rights exist at the top of international law's normative hierarchy, and all global actors need to be vigilant in guarding and enforcing them.

The elevated position of those norms has significant implications for the new exemplar, going far to legitimize federal jurisdiction over human rights and terrorism cases. When federal judges assume authority over those cases, they correctly pay juridical credence to the most fundamental international norms. Prolific codification and sustained consensus condemning human rights violations and terrorism dictates domestic court jurisdiction in these critical areas.[72] As we have argued, a parallel consensus governs human rights and terrorism norms. The compulsory nature of the *erga omnes* and *jus cogens* doctrines may suggest that domestic jurisdiction over human rights and terrorism claims is not just legitimate, but obligatory. Because each nation-state has an obligation to all others to follow the human rights and antiterrorism norms, the federal courts should meet and further these obligations by adjudicating violations of those norms. Indeed, commentators have suggested that the *Barcelona Traction* dictum may sanction a type of *actio popularis*, enabling every nation-state to vindicate the universal rights common to all individuals.[73]

Under this vision, the emergence of universal jurisdiction does not exist in an intellectual vacuum, but dovetails with the expansion of the *jus cogens* and *erga omnes* doctrines. These developments together, if not separately, have paradigmatic or structural significance. They together herald the propriety of federal court jurisdiction in the exemplar of human rights and terrorism cases. When judges and lawyers begin to approach the puzzle of these cases, the post–World War II developments signify that federal courts ordinarily possess authority in relation to the international legal system. Even if those developments have not invoked a new disciplinary matrix, they have at least created new jurisdictional ground rules for the exemplar of human rights and terrorism.

Finally, at both the jurisdictional level and on the merits, the strident debate over *Filartiga* and its progeny indicates the evolution of a new exemplar. In law, as in science,[74] transition or preparadigm periods should be expected to evoke intellectual turmoil among practitioners. The very system in which judges and lawyers have been trained to operate, after all, is changing. Some practitioners adapt better, or at least differently, than do others, depending partly on their own jurisprudential and political perspectives. Establishing major revisions of the modes by which lawyers approach international cases does not come easily. This fact could not be better punctuated than by the antagonism that Judges Bork and Edwards (and to a lesser extent, Robb) openly displayed in *Tel-Oren v. Libyan Arab Republic*,[75] concerning PLO terrorism in Israel. Judge Bork was quite on point when he concluded that the bench could only agree on their disagreeability: "[I]t is impossible to say even what the law of this circuit is. Though we agree on nothing else, I am sure that my colleagues join me in finding that regrettable."[76] Of course, judges and lawyers often disagree; their legal education teaches them to disagree. But it is the *extent* or the *nature* of the debate in *Tel-Oren* and other human rights and terrorism cases that illustrates a true crisis of faith in the Westphalian exemplar. The practitioners are often wholly at odds over the most basic aspects of these cases—including jurisdiction, substantive norms, legal personality, and sovereign responsibility.[77]

Perhaps what best illuminates the new exemplar's arrival is that the debate over *Filartiga* and *Tel-Oren* sometimes seems to be fundamentally misguided. For instance, when one is mindful of the post–World War II developments, the Borkian restrictive fixation with explicit causes of action, or with individuals as mere objects, seems not merely wrong, but fundamentally flawed or misplaced. The same could even be said of Judge Edwards's view that nonstate terrorists are legally incapable of committing terrorism or torture.[78] Such viewpoints were perhaps postulates of the Westphalian exemplar, but they are anomalies in the human rights exemplar. As Professor Falk once described: "[T]hose who persist in carrying on their inquiries within the old paradigm end up with trivial results, because either they work on irrelevant problems or they work on relevant problems within an inappropriate procedure."[79] As much as the *Filartiga* opinion is synchronized with the human rights exemplar, other opinions, notably Judge Bork's in *Tel-Oren*, is so out of sync that it appears parochial and trivial. And yet it is this very discord, as Kuhn teaches, that exemplifies the introduction of a new exemplar. As the coming decades unfold, it will become increasingly evident that *Filartiga* provides the correct exemplar for adjudicating the modern human rights and terrorism cases. *Filartiga*'s wisdom will become more and more apparent.

Conclusion

Although the universality principle justifies federal jurisdiction in most human rights and terrorism cases, other legal trends and doctrines also legitimize that authority in relation to the world legal order. The human rights and antiterrorism agenda may have global paradigmatic implications, when the war crimes cases, the postwar instruments, and the expanded *jus cogens* and *erga omnes* doctrines are grouped together. Rather than being singular or unique, those legal developments represent a shift in the disciplinary matrix of human rights and terrorism; they, alternatively, at least represent a shift in the lawyer's exemplar for solving human rights and terrorism cases. Those systemic developments equally pertain to human rights and terrorism cases, which, again, deserve similar treatment under positive and nonpositive law. Given these paradigmatic views of the human rights movement, federal court jurisdiction in *Filartiga* and most of its progeny is especially appropriate. The movement has significantly diminished the Westphalian paradigm's exaltation of sovereignty over basic individual rights. It is, therefore, the revised legal order itself — the vertical shift toward an individualistic perspective — that justifies federal authority in the modern cases. The human rights paradigm offers the ultimate jurisdictional support to *Filartiga*.

CONCLUSION

A few brief concluding words should suffice, since each chapter has ended with its own conclusion. In fact, we pulled together the themes of part one by offering a legislative prescription, hoping to ensure that federal statutory jurisdiction always exists, and is usually exercised, over human rights and terrorism cases. Federalism concerns, separation-of-powers considerations, and the national government's commitment to redress international offenses all dictated the terms of our proposed legislation. Part two demonstrated that federal court authority over those offenses is legitimate not just vis-à-vis the United States legal order, but also vis-à-vis the world legal order. From our discussions of the universality principle and the modern international paradigm, it is clear that the federal courts should assume civil jurisdiction over the following extraterritorial offenses, irrespective of the nationalities or identities of the plaintiffs and defendants: genocide; torture; summary execution; causing the disappearance of individuals; slavery; slave trading; apartheid; prolonged arbitrary detention; war crimes; piracy; hijacking of aircraft; violence committed against vessels and aircraft; hostage taking; crimes against internationally protected persons; and all other terrorist activities. When individuals anywhere in the world are victimized by those offenses, federal courts should represent both the domestic and international legal orders in civil litigation. The federal courts' systemic authority, under the vertical and horizontal conceptions that we have outlined throughout this book, permit and even demand that the courts play such a role in this compelling area of international litigation.

Although the past decade has witnessed dozens of human rights and terrorism actions, *Filartiga v. Pena-Irala*[1] triggered this disputed, but vibrant, genre of civil cases. In a sense, perhaps the *Filartiga* case and controversy should have been expected. Just as, according to de Tocqueville, "[s]carcely any question arises in the United States which does not become, sooner or later, a subject of judicial debate,"[2] important international questions are also ripe for judicial decision and disagreement. Human rights and terrorism norms have been debated, and yet advanced, since the Second World War. It is thus logical that individual litigants have now begun to test the global and federal legal orders' commitment to humanitarian norms. It is fitting that this civil litigation has been commenced in the courts of the nation that proudly holds itself out to be the international champion of democratic, civil, and human rights. In a different context, Justice Stevens recently commented: "Freedom of access to the courts is a cherished value in our democratic society. Incremental changes in settled rules of law often result from litigation."[3] It is providing such judicial access to the victims of international offenses that has been the underlying thesis of this book. Hopefully, if the *Filartiga*-line of cases is followed, rather than the perspective of *Tel-Oren v. Libyan Arab Republic*,[4] then humanitarian norms can be fulfilled in federal courts, even if only incrementally. We have, therefore, tried to explain why the watershed case of *Filartiga* was correctly decided some ten years ago; why the past decade's litigation should have more consistently followed *Filartiga*'s teachings; and why the judicial decisions of this and future decades should endeavor to satisfy *Filartiga*'s promise.

NOTES

Introduction

1. *Filartiga v. Pena-lrala*, 630 F.2d 876 (2d Cir. 1980).

2. *Id.* at 878.

3. The international law and jurisdictional holding was made by the Second Circuit in *id.*, while the money judgment was rendered upon remand to the district court in 577 F. Supp. 860 (E.D.N.Y. 1984).

4. The cases concerning Argentina include *Forti v. Suarez-Mason*, 672 F. Supp. 1531 (N.D. Cal. 1987), *modified by* 694 F. Supp. 707 (N.D. Cal. 1988), and *Siderman de Blake v. Republic of Argentina*, No. CV–82–1772 (C.D. Cal. Sept. 28, 1984) (available on LEXIS, Genfed library, Courts file), *vacated and dismissed*, order (C.D. Cal. Mar. 7, 1985). The war crimes case is *Handel v. Artukovic*, 601 F. Supp. 1421 (C.D. Cal. 1985). For a compilation of the Marcos cases, see Recent Developments, "Alien Tort Claims Act—Act of State Doctrine—Act of State Doctrine Requires Dismissal of Human Rights Claims Brought Against Former Philippine President Residing in the United States," 27 *Va. J. Int'l L.* 433, 433 n.1 (1987).

Although the present book focuses upon civil litigation, the topic of the United States' criminal responses to international offenses, particularly terrorism, has been well examined in, *e.g.*, George, "Federal Anti-Terrorist Legislation," in *Legal Responses to International Terrorism* 25 (M. C. Bassiouni ed. 1988).

5. These cases, respectively, are *Persinger v. Islamic Republic of Iran*, 729 F.2d 835 (D.C. Cir.), *cert. denied*, 469 U.S. 881 (1984), and *Von Dardel v. Union of Soviet Socialist Republics*, 623 F. Supp. 246 (D.D.C. 1985).

6. *Tel-Oren v. Libyan Arab Republic*, 726 F.2d 774 (D.C. Cir. 1984) (per curiam), *cert. denied*, 470 U.S. 1003 (1985).

7. *Tel-Oren*, 726 F.2d at 823 (Bork, J., concurring).

8. *Id.* at 775 (Edwards, J., concurring).

9. *Id.* at 827 (Robb, J., concurring).

10. See Randall, "Special U.S. Civil Jurisdiction," in M. C. Bassiouni, *supra*

note 4, at 89, 110–12; Randall, "Further Inquiries into the Alien Tort Statute and a Recommendation," 18 *N.Y.U.J. Int'l L. & Pol.* 473, 511–12 (1986).

11. This definition draws upon R. Falk, *The Role of Domestic Courts in the International Legal Order* 21 (1964); see chapter 2 for an elaboration of that term. *See also Restatement (Third) of Foreign Relations Law* § 401, *et seq.* For domestic lawyers, a rough equivalent of this conceptualization of jurisdiction is the term *subject matter jurisdiction.*

12. International Covenant on Civil and Political Rights, Dec. 16, 1966, art. 4, G.A. Res. 2200A, 21 U.N. GAOR Supp. at 53, U.N. Doc. A/6316 (1966) [hereinafter Covenant].

13. Geneva Convention for the Amelioration of the Condition of the Wounded and Sick in Armed Forces in the Field, Aug. 12, 1949, 6 U.S.T. 3114, T.I.A.S. No. 3362, 75 U.N.T.S. 31 [hereinafter Geneva Convention I]; Geneva Convention for the Amelioration of the Condition of Wounded, Sick and Shipwrecked Members of the Armed Forces at Sea, Aug. 12, 1949, 6 U.S.T. 3217, T.I.A.S. No. 3363, 75 U.N.T.S. 85 [hereinafter Geneva Convention II]; Geneva Convention Relative to the Treatment of Prisoners of War, Aug. 12, 1949, 6 U.S.T. 3316, T.I.A.S. No. 3364, 75 U.N.T.S. 135 [hereinafter Geneva Convention III]; Geneva Convention Relative to the Protection of Civilian Persons in Time of War, Aug. 12, 1949, 6 U.S.T. 3516, T.I.A.S. No. 3365, 75 U.N.T.S. 287 [hereinafter Geneva Convention IV]. These four instruments are collectively referred to as the Geneva Conventions or the Geneva Conventions of 1949.

14. Convention on the Prevention and Punishment of the Crime of Genocide, Dec. 9, 1948, 78 U.N.T.S. 277 (entered into force Jan. 12, 1951) [hereinafter Genocide Convention].

15. Convention on the Suppression and Punishment of Apartheid, *adopted* Nov. 30, 1973, 1015 U.N.T.S. 243 [hereinafter Apartheid Convention], *adopted by* G.A. 3068, 28 U.N. GAOR Supp. (No. 30) at 75, U.N. Doc. A/Res/3068 (1973), *reprinted in* 13 I.L.M. 50 (1974).

16. Convention Against Torture and Other Cruel, Inhuman or Degrading Treatment or Punishment, 23 I.L.M. 1027 (1984) (draft) and 24 I.L.M. 535 (1985) (final with minor revisions) [hereinafter Torture Convention]. *See* "Message to the Senate Transmitting the Convention Against Torture and Other Inhuman Treatment or Punishment," 24 *Weekly Comp. Pres. Doc.* 642 (May 20, 1988).

17. This topic is discussed in chapter 3.

18. Convention for the Suppression of Unlawful Seizure of Aircraft, Dec. 16, 1970, 22 U.S.T. 1641, T.I.A.S. No. 7192, 860 U.N.T.S. 105 (entered into force Oct. 14, 1971) [hereinafter Hague Convention], *reprinted in* 10 I.L.M. 133 (1971)

19. Convention for the Suppression of Unlawful Acts Against the Safety of Civil Aviation, Sept. 23, 1971, 24 U.S.T. 565, T.I.A.S. No. 7570, 974 U.N.T.S. 177 (entered into force Jan. 26, 1973) [hereinafter Montreal Convention], *reprinted in* 10 I.L.M. 1151 (1971). The Hague and Montreal Conventions will together be

called the "hijacking conventions (or treaties)." The term *terrorism* often will be used to include the offenses that the hijacking conventions prohibit.

20. International Convention Against the Taking of Hostages, Dec. 4, 1979, 18 I.L.M. 1456 [hereinafter Hostage Convention], *adopted by* G.A. Res. 34/146, 34 U.N. GAOR Supp. (No. 39), U.N. Doc. A/C.6/34L.23 (1979).

21. Convention on the Prevention and Punishment of Crimes Against Internationally Protected Persons, Including Diplomatic Agents, Dec. 14, 1973, 28 U.S.T. 1975, T.I.A.S. No. 8532, 1035 U.N.T.S. 167 [hereinafter Internationally Protected Persons Convention], *adopted by* G.A. Res. 3166, 27 U.N. GAOR Supp. (No. 10), U.N. Doc. A/Res/3166 (1974), *reprinted in* 13 I.L.M. 41 (1974). This and the Hostage Convention sometimes together will be called the "terrorism conventions (or treaties)."

22. This topic is discussed in chapter 3.

23. *See generally* R. Falk, *Revolutionaries and Functionaries* (1988).

24. This topic is discussed in chapter 4.

25. This topic is discussed in chapter 8.

26. *See, e.g.,* G.A. Res. A/40/61, U.N. Doc. 86–00872(1986); S.C. Res. 579, U.N. SCOR (2637 mtg), U.N. Doc. 85–38352 (1985), *reprinted in* 25 I.L.M. 243 (1986).

27. International Law Association, Report of the Sixty-First Conference 314 (1984). This report is discussed in J. Murphy, *State Support of International Terrorism* 19–20, 34–36 (1989).

28. *See generally* Paust, "The Link Between Human Rights and Terrorism and Its Implications for the Law of State Responsibility," 11 *Hastings Int'l & Compar. L. Rev.* 41 (1987).

1. Foreign Relations as Shared Federal Relations

1. See *infra* notes 30–31 and accompanying text regarding the national government's very limited judicial authority under the Articles of Confederation.

2. Articles of Confederation, art. IX, 1 Stat. 6 (1781).

3. Articles of Confederation, art. VI, 1 Stat. 5 (1781).

4. *See generally* L. Henkin, *Foreign Affairs and the Constitution* 33 (2d ed. 1975); Dickinson, "The Law of Nations as Part of the National Law of the United States," 101 *U. Pa. L. Rev.* 26, 34–46 (1952).

5. J. Madison, *Journal of Constitutional Convention* 60 (E. Scott ed. 1893). Edmund Randolph expressed virtually identical sentiments; *see id.* at 19.

6. *See* I *The Records of the Federal Convention of 1787* 30 (M. Farrand ed. 1937) (resolution that "a national government ought to be established consisting of a supreme legislative, judiciary and executive"). Of course, as between the Federalists and Anti-Federalists, and as between representatives of large and small states, there was debate over the exact scope of proper national authority.

7. The Federalist No. 38, at 43 (J. Jay) (C. Rossiter ed. 1961).

8. M. Farrand, *supra* note 6, at 316.

9. The president has the authority to appoint ambassadors and other public ministers and consuls, with the Senate's advice and consent, U.S. Const. art. II, § 2, cl. 2, and may receive foreign ambassadors and other public ministers, U.S. Const. art. II, § 3. These provisions impliedly empower the president to establish embassies and consulates in foreign nations. Such authority thus is not afforded the states, which, under the Tenth Amendment, have only the powers not delegated to the federal government.

10. C. Warren, *The Making of the Constitution* 382 (1928) (correspondence to Lord Carrington). Actually, Jefferson considered himself neither a Federalist nor an Anti-Federalist nor a member of any political party. *See Anti-Federalists Versus Federalists* 121–23 ("If I could not go to heaven but with a [political] party, I would not go there at all") (J. Lewis ed. 1967) (correspondence to Francis Hopkinson).

11. Articles of Confederation, art. XIII, 1 Stat. 8 (1781).

12. Virginian Edmund Randolph proposed to the Convention that the national legislature be empowered "to negative all laws passed by the several States, contravening . . . the articles of Union; and to call forth the force of the Union agst. any member of the Union failing to fulfill its duty under the articles," M. Farrand, *supra* note 6, at 21.

13. *See generally* Henkin, "International Law as Law in the United States," 82 Mich. L. Rev. 1555, 1555–61 (1984). The constitutional and federal nature of nontreaty international law sources is discussed in chapters 2 and 3.

14. See chapters 2 and 3 regarding the sources of international law.

15. *See, e.g., Martin v. Hunter's Lessee,* 1 Wheat. 304 (1816) (Supreme Court has authority to review and correct the decision of the Virginia Court of Appeals that a land claim based on a Virginia statute, as construed, should prevail over a competing land claim protected under two U.S.–Great Britain treaties). We will shortly discuss the constitutional basis of such appellate jurisdiction.

16. *United States v. Belmont,* 301 U.S. 324, 331 (1937). Under the Litvinov Assignment, an executive agreement between the United States and the Soviet Union, the Soviet government assigned its rights to funds that a private New York banker held for a private Russian corporation. *Belmont* decided that the federal government was permitted to collect the assigned funds, despite the defense that the Soviet Union had illegally confiscated the funds and that enforcing the assignment would violate New York State public policy.

17. The Federalist, *supra* note 7, No. 42, at 264 (J. Madison).

18. Apart from the clauses specifically relating to foreign affairs, other clauses, such as the taxing and spending provision (clause 1), may also be used to support Congress's foreign policy decisions. For example, Congress may appropriate funds to support the United Nations or NATO or to construct an embassy in a foreign nation.

19. *McCulloch v. Maryland,* 4 Wheat. 316, 407 (1819).

20. *See generally* L. Henkin, *supra* note 4, at 68, 74–79.

21. Two-thirds of the senators present must concur in the president's making of a treaty, art. II, § 2, cl. 2. Ratification, a concept that the Constitution does not expressly mention, occurs, in practice, only when the Senate transmits its advice and consent to the president (sometimes with conditions or reservations attached), and the president then decides whether to ratify the treaty. Ratification thus essentially involves the president's second acquiescence to a treaty. *See generally* L. Henkin, R. Pugh, O. Schachter & H. Smit, *International Law* 182–83 (2d ed. 1987).

22. Some executive agreements have received the approval of both Houses of Congress, whereas other agreements have been approved by neither. *See generally* L. Henkin, *supra* note 4, at 173–87; Lissitzyn, "The Legal Status of Executive Agreements on Air Transportation," 17 *J. Air L. & Commerce* 436, 438–44 (1950). Of those executive agreements receiving congressional approval, some were even created at Congress's behest. The Supreme Court has placed its imprimatur upon executive agreements, *see, e.g., United States v. Pink,* 315 U.S. 203 (1942); *United States v. Belmont,* 301 U.S. 324 (1937); *B. Altman & Co. v. United States,* 224 U.S. 583 (1912), but has not clarified the permissible scope of those agreements. Instead, restrictions on executive agreements have generally come from presidents' self-imposed limitations as well as from legislation, such as the Case Act, 1 U.S.C. § 112(b) (Supp. II 1978), requiring the president to transmit written and oral agreements, once concluded, to Congress.

23. *See, e.g.,* Bilateral Agreement between the Republic of Afghanistan and the Islamic Republic of Pakistan on the Principles of Mutual Relations, in Particular on Non-Interference and Non-Intervention, as supported by the U.S. and U.S.S.R., 88 Dept. St. Bull. 2135, at 56–60 (Apr. 14, 1988) (agreement concerning, *inter alia,* self-determination, nonintervention, prohibiting assistance to terrorist groups, and preventing terrorism); Memorandum of Understanding on Hijacking of Aircraft and Vessels and other Offenses, 24 U.S.T., T.I.A.S. No. 7579 737 (Feb. 15, 1973) (U.S., Cuba, Czechoslovakia, and Switzerland hijacking agreement).

24. *See Restatement (Third) of Foreign Relations Law* § 102 [hereinafter *Restatement*]; *see also* Statute of the International Court of Justice, art. 38 (1) (b), 59 Stat. 1055, 1060.

25. Regarding certain practices, the president may even expressly articulate the nation's *opinio juris.* For example, while the United States will not sign the 1982 United Nations Convention on the Law of the Sea, President Reagan indicated that the nation will abide by specific provisions of the treaty as a matter of customary law; *See* U.S. Oceans Policy, 83 Dept. St. Bull. No. 2075, at 70–71 (1983). The president referred to those specific provisions as encompassing "traditional uses of the oceans." *See also Restatement, supra* note 24, at Introductory Note to Part V. The Convention, not yet in force, is *reprinted in* The Law of the Sea, U.N. Doc. A/Conf. 62/122, U.N. Sales No. E. 83.V.5 (1983). The president may also indicate that the United States will no longer follow a particular

custom; an example of this perhaps was President Reagan's declaration that the nation would cease adhering to the practices outlined in the unratified SALT II treaty. *See generally* Gordon, "Reagan Declares U.S. is Dismantling Two Nuclear Subs," *N.Y. Times,* May 28, 1986, at A1, col. 6.

26. *See generally Restatement, supra* note 24, at § 702 (customary law of human rights). See chapter 3 for a discussion of the customary law of human rights and terrorism.

27. The president's authority has been aggrandized through a combination of constitutional implication, political infighting, and the day-to-day practice of acting as the United States' chief representative to other nations. For instance, although the Constitution is silent about which branch of government may recognize foreign governments and which branch may terminate a treaty, the executive department has assumed both powers. Regarding recognition, *see generally* Galloway, *Recognizing Foreign Governments: The Practice of the United States* (1978). President Carter's unilateral termination of the Mutual Defense Treaty of 1954 with the Republic of China (Taiwan), when switching recognition to the People's Republic of China, brought both the recognition and the treaty termination issues, particularly the latter, to the center of debate. See chapter 5 for a discussion of that situation's adjudication. The Supreme Court, however, has not decided whether the president may constitutionally terminate treaties unilaterally. *See generally* Reisman & McDougal, "Who Can Terminate Mutual Defense Treaties," *Nat'l L. J.,* May 21, 1979, at 19; *Nat'l L. J.,* May 28, 1979, at 17. The executive's authority to engage the nation in wars undeclared by Congress is another much-debated subject. *See generally* Ely, "Suppose Congress Wanted a War Powers Act that Worked," 88 *Colum. L. Rev.* 1379 (1988); Van Alstyne, "Congress, the President, and the Power to Declare War," 121 *U. Pa. L. Rev.* 1 (1972); Note, "Congress, the President, and the Power to Commit Forces to Combat," 81 *Harv. L. Rev.* 1771 (1968).

28. *Youngstown Sheet & Tube Co. v. Sawyer,* 343 U.S. 579, 635 (1952) (Jackson, J., concurring).

29. *Id.* (Jackson, J., concurring).

30. Articles of Confederation, art. IX, 1 Stat. 6 (1781).

31. *See* Frank, "Historical Bases of the Federal Judicial System," 13 *L. & Contemp. Probs* 3, 7–9 (1948).

32. The Federalist, *supra* note 7, No. 3, at 43.

33. See chapter 2 for a discussion of the older term *law of nations* in comparison to the newer term *international law.*

34. 4 W. Blackstone, *Commentaries* *68.

35. *See generally id.* at *67, *70–71 (law of nations violations punishable as common law crimes). See chapter 2 regarding the provision of private or civil remedies for those offenses.

36. Violations of "safe-conducts" involved "committing acts of hostilities against such as are in amity, league, or truce with us, who are here under a general

implied safe-conduct; these are breaches of public faith, without the preservation of which there can be no intercourse or commerce between one nation and another," W. Blackstone, *supra* note 32, at *68.

37. 21 *J. Cont. Cong.* 1136–37 (1781). *See* Casto, "The Federal Courts' Protective Jurisdiction over Torts Committed in Violation of the Law of Nations," 18 *Conn. L. Rev.* 467, 490–91 (1986).

38. 21 *J. Cont. Cong.* 1136–37 (1781).

39. *Id.*

40. See Casto, Correspondence, 83 *Am. J. Int'l L.* 901, 902–3(1989), regarding Connecticut's enactment of a statute in response to the 1781 resolution.

41. Accounts of the Marbois affair are contained in Casto, *supra* note 37, at 491–94; Randall, "Federal Jurisdiction over International Law Claims: Inquiries into the Alien Tort Statute," 18 *N.Y.U. J Int.'l L. & Pol.* 1, 24–26 (1985); Rosenthal, "The Marbois–Longchamps Affair," 63 *Pa. Mag. Hist. & Biog.* 294 (1939).

42. Rosenthal, *supra* note 41, at 296.

43. 28 *J. Cont. Cong.* 314 (1785).

44. *See De Longchamps,* 1 U.S. (1 Dall) 111 (1784).

45. Accounts of the Van Berckel incident are contained in Letter from P. J. Van Berckel to John Jay (Dec. 18, 1787), *reprinted in* 3 *The Diplomatic Correspondence of the United States of America from the Signing of the Definitive Treaty of Peace 10th September, 1783, to the Adoption of the Constitution, March 4, 1789* 496–97 (1837) [hereinafter *Diplomatic Correspondence];* Casto, *supra* note 37, at 494.

46. *Diplomatic Correspondence, supra* note 43, at 497.

47. 34 *J. Cont. Cong.* 109, 111 (1788).

48. *Id.*

49. The Grand Jury charge in the case may be found in *Daily Advertiser,* May 10, 1788, at 2, col. 4 & 3, col. 1 (law of nations is part of England's common law and "expressly adopted by our Constitution"). A description of the case's disposition is in J. Goebel, I *History of the Supreme Court of the United States* 310–11 (1971).

50. Recall that the 1781 resolution also recommended the need for both criminal and civil jurisdiction in such instances. *See supra* notes 37–40 and accompanying text.

51. A nation violates its responsibility under international law when it injures an alien, and such injuries include denying an alien justice. *See* L. Henkin, R. Pugh, O. Schachter & H. Smit, *supra* note 21, at 1041 (2d ed. 1987) (injury by a nation may be caused by a "failure by the [nation] to provide redress for an injury inflicted on the alien by some private person — for example, a failure of the [nation] to provide judicial remedies to an alien on whom physical or economic injury has been inflicted by a resident of the [nation]").

52. The Federalist, *supra* note 7, No. 80, at 476 (A. Hamilton).

53. *See id.* at 476–77.

54. Id. at 477.

55. *See supra* notes 13–15 and accompanying text.

56. The nonexclusivity of federal jurisdiction in relation to the Alien Tort Statute is discussed in chapter 2.

57. *See id.*

58. *See supra* notes 52–54 and accompanying text.

59. A civil action involving the Van Berckel incident would be supported by both the alienage and the federal question clauses of article III and their statutory counterparts in 28 U.S.C. §§ 1332(a) (2), 1350, and 1331. In a civil action concerning the Marbois affair, jurisdiction, under those constitutional clauses, could be predicated statutorily on 28 U.S.C. §§ 1350 or 1331, but not on § 1332(a)(2) due to the presence of both French plaintiffs and defendants. These issues are discussed in chapters 2 and 3.

2. From Constitutional to Statutory Authority

1. This conceptualization of jurisdiction draws upon Falk, *The Role of Domestic Courts in the International Legal Order* 21–24 (1964), which was influenced by Professor McDougal's writings, such as, M. McDougal & Associates, *Studies in World Public Order* (1960). Falk and McDougal focus more on an institution's jurisdiction within the international legal system than in the United States' legal system.

2. See chapter 1.

3. See chapter 1.

4. The Federalist No. 80, at 475 (A. Hamilton) (C. Rossiter ed. 1961).

5. *Id.* at 476 (emphasis added).

6. Ex Parte McCardle, 7 Wall. 506, 514 (1869).

7. Halpern, "'Exorbitant Jurisdiction' and the Brussels Convention: Toward a Theory of Restraint," 9 *Yale J. World Pub. Ord.* 369, 369(1983).

8. In *A Theory of Justice* (1971), Professor John Rawls utilizes the notion of "reflective equilibrium" in his study of moral philosophy. Individuals may reassess and revise the principles that they identified in the "original position," so that "the best account of a person's sense of justice is . . . the one which matches his [original] judgments in reflective equilibrium," *id.* at 48.

9. These particular provisions are among the most important bases of federal jurisdiction, and some of those provisions have been especially important to human rights and terrorism cases. Nevertheless, it is not suggested that these jurisdictional statutes are the only provisions that are conceivably relevant to human rights and terrorism cases.

10. These prescriptions are set out in chapter 6.

11. 28 U.S.C. § 1332(a)(1) & (2) (1982), *as amended by* Judicial Improve-

ments and Access to Justice Act, Pub. L. No. 100–702, 102 Stat. 4646 (1988) (increasing amount-in-controversy requisite from $10,000 to $50,000).

12. See chapter 1.

13. Judiciary Act of 1789, ch. 20, § 11, 1 Stat. 73, 88 (1789). See P. Bator, D. Meltzer, P. Mishkin & D. Shapiro, *Hart and Wechsler's The Federal Courts and the Federal System* 1656–58 (3d ed. 1988) regarding the statutory development of diversity and alienage jurisdiction.

14. The Supreme Court has articulated this rationale in, *e.g.*, *Guaranty Trust Co. v. York*, 326 U.S. 99, 111 (1945); *Erie R. R. v. Tompkins*, 304 U.S. 64, 74 (1938); *Bank of the United States v. Deveaux*, 9 U.S. (5 Cranch) 61, 87 (1809). Valuable examinations of diversity jurisdiction's origins are provided by Frank, "Historical Bases of the Federal Judicial System," 13 *L. & Contemp. Probs* 3 (1948); Friendly, "The Historic Basis of the Diversity Jurisdiction," 41 *Harv. L. Rev.* 483 (1928); Moore & Weckstein, "Diversity Jurisdiction: Past, Present, and Future," 43 *Tex. L. Rev.* 1 (1965).

15. Discussion of the relative abilities and virtues of federal and state courts remains of contemporary interest. Neuborne, "The Myth of Parity," 90 *Harv. L. Rev.* 1105 (1977), powerfully argues that federal courts are superior to state courts. *But see* Solime & Walker, "Constitutional Litigation in Federal and State Courts: An Empirical Analysis of Judicial Parity," 10 *Hastings Const. L. Q.* 213 (1983).

16. ALI, *Study of the Division Between State and Federal Courts* 99–108 (1969), provides a thoroughgoing study of the criticisms of diversity jurisdiction.

Diversity jurisdiction demands "complete diversity." Article III confers judicial power to controversies "between Citizens of different States" (§ 2, clause 1), and its statutory counterpart is interpreted to require diversity of citizenship between *every* plaintiff and *every* defendant in a multiparty action; *see Strawbridge v. Curtis*, 7 U.S. (3 Cranch) 267 (1806). If citizens of the same state are on both sides of the lawsuit, the underlying reason for diversity jurisdiction is thought to disappear.

17. In a given case, of course, more than one statutory provision may support the district court's jurisdiction.

18. Several provisions of the Judiciary Act of 1789 linked federal jurisdiction (at the trial or appellate level) with the presence of aliens in a lawsuit. Some of those provisions specifically concerned aliens who were foreign dignitaries, while others concerned all aliens; *see* Randall, "Federal Jurisdiction over International Law Claims: Inquiries into the Alien Tort Statute," 18 *N.Y.U. J. Int'l L. & Pol.* 1, 15–19 (1985). The current counterparts to such provisions include, for example, 28 U.S.C. § 1350 (1982) (the alien tort statute) and 28 U.S.C. § 1251 (1982) (Supreme Court's original, nonexclusive jurisdiction over cases to which ambassadors and certain other foreign dignitaries are parties).

19. See chapter 1.

20. Alienage and diversity jurisdiction have, since the Judiciary Act of 1789, contained an amount-in-controversy requirement. That requirement limits fed-

eral jurisdiction, a result that the Anti-Federalists surely welcomed. See *infra* note 45 and accompanying text regarding the Federalist/Anti-Federalist compromise over federal jurisdiction generally. In addition, the original amount in controversy required for alienage jurisdiction, $500, was conceivably created to block claims that British merchants made against Americans following the War of Independence. Many of the merchants' claims fell below $500 and they had no recourse but to seek recovery in hostile state courts. See *infra* notes 46–51 and accompanying text.

21. *Hodgson and Thompson v. Bowerbank*, 9 U.S. (5 Cranch) 303 (1809).

22. Art. III, § 2, cl. 1 (emphasis added). For new attention to *Hodgson*, see Mahoney, "A Historical Note on *Hodgson v. Bowerbank*," 49 *U. Chi. L. Rev.* 725 (1982); *see also infra* note 23.

23. Some controversy has arisen over whether *Hodgson* constitutionally invalidated the alienage provision in the Judiciary Act of 1789 as being inconsistent with article III. Alternatively, *Hodgson* might not have constitutionally invalidated the jurisdictional provision, but simply confined it, through statutory construction, to confer authority in controversies between an alien and a citizen. *See* Mahoney, *supra* note 22. The disagreement over those alternatives partly relates to whether the *Dred Scott* decision (of 1857) or *Hodgson* involved the first federal law that the Supreme Court held to be unconstitutional subsequent to *Marbury v. Madison*.

Hodgson's rule also disallows § 1332(a)(2) jurisdiction in cases between aliens in which citizens are additional parties to the action. *See, e.g., Lavan Petroleum Co., v. Underwriters at Lloyds*, 334 F. Supp. 1069 (S.D.N.Y. 1971). An examination of 28 U.S.C. § 1332(a)(3), concerning jurisdiction in cases between citizens in which aliens are additional parties, is contained in Note, "Federal Jurisdiction over Suits Between Diverse United States Citizens with Aliens Joined to Both Sides of the Controversy under 28 U.S.C. § 1332(a)(3)," 38 *Rutgers L. Rev.* 71 (1985).

24. *See Verlinden B.V. v. Central Bank of Nigeria*, 461 U.S. 480, 493 (1983).

25. This example loosely draws upon *Persinger v. Islamic Republic of Iran*, 729 F.2d 835 (D.C. Cir. 1984), in which a marine, a former hostage in Tehran, and his parents sued Iran for injuries related to the marine's seizure and detention. Since a nation-state was sued, the Foreign Sovereign Immunities Act of 1976 was the relevant statute, rather than alienage jurisdiction, applicable in a case against the individual captors. Iran is not a party to the Hostage Convention. See chapter 4 for a discussion of *Persinger*.

26. This example is hypothetical. The plaintiff, naturally, would have to establish a sufficient link between the United States citizens and violations of the Geneva Conventions; the first and third Geneva Conventions would be most relevant.

27. *Filartiga v. Pena-Irala*, 630 F.2d at 876 (2d Cir. 1980).

28. This example is hypothetical, but springs to mind from recent accounts of China's continued violations of Tibetans' human rights. *See, e.g.*, Gargan,

"Beijing Accused of Human Rights Abuses in Tibet," *N.Y. Times*, July 31, 1988, at A15, col. 1.

29. 630 F.2d at 876. See introduction regarding the facts in the *Filartiga* case.

30. 28 U.S.C. § 1350 (1982), titled the Alien Tort Claims Act, is popularly called the Alien Tort Statute.

31. The following discussion of *Filartiga* and of § 1350 will sometimes draw upon Randall, "Further Inquiries into the Alien Tort Statute and a Recommendation," 18 *N.Y.U. J. Int'l L. & Pol.* 473 (1986), and Randall, *supra* note 18. The N.Y.U. Journal has consented to the use of these essays.

32. *Filartiga*, 630 F.2d at 878.

33. This numerical conclusion derives from a LEXIS search of opinions prior to June 30, 1980 (when *Filartiga* was decided), that consider the Alien Tort Statute as a basis of federal jurisdiction. Of course, plaintiffs might have tried to invoke the statute in additional cases. LEXIS does not report all cases; and even of the reported cases, the judge's opinion must expressly mention the statute for LEXIS to discover the case in its search.

34. *IIT v. Vencap, Ltd.*, 519 F.2d 1001, 1015 (2d Cir. 1975) (Friendly, J.).

35. This number is based upon a post-*Filartiga* LEXIS search, with the same qualifications as mentioned in *supra* note 33.

36. *Filartiga*, 630 F.2d at 890.

37. *See generally* Burley, "The Alien Tort Statute and the Judiciary Act of 1789: A Badge of Honor," 83 *Am. J. Int'l L.* 461 (1989); Casto, "The Federal Courts' Protective Jurisdiction over Torts Committed in Violation of the Law of Nations," 18 *Conn. L. Rev.* 467, 488–98 (1986); Randall, *supra* note 18, at 11–31 (1985).

38. See chapter 1 for descriptions of those situations.

39. A Bill to Establish the Judicial Courts of the United States (no date), *reprinted in Early American Imprints* No. 45657 (Readex Microprint). *See* Casto *supra* note 37, at 496–98.

40. *See supra* note 39 and accompanying text.

41. Judiciary Act of 1789, ch. 20, § 13, 1 Stat. 73, 80–81 (1789).

42. The Supreme Court could not constitutionally be granted jurisdiction in such an action because article III does not provide the Court with original jurisdiction over cases involving aliens other than dignitaries. While such an action (involving a nondignitary) would involve federal law (i.e., the international law against piracy, as incorporated into federal law), the Supreme Court has only appellate, not original, jurisdiction over cases arising under federal law.

43. Judiciary Act of 1789, ch. 20, § 9, 1 Stat. 73, 77 (1789).

44. *See supra* note 39 and accompanying text.

45. Warren, "New Light on the History of the Federal Judiciary Act of 1789," 37 *Harv. L. Rev.* 49, 53 (1923).

46. *See generally* I *American State Papers, Foreign Relations* 193–200 (1793). Such British complaints were reciprocated by various postwar charges that Ameri-

cans made against Britons. *See generally id.* at 201–37; S. Bemis, *Jay's Treaty* 135–38 (2d ed. 1962).

47. Definitive Treaty of Peace, Sept. 3, 1783, United States–Great Britain, 8 Stat. 80, T.S. No. 104, *reprinted in* II *Treaties and Other International Acts of the United States of America* 151, art. IV, at 154 (H. Miller ed. 1931).

48. The state courts generally followed state laws that undoubtedly impeded the progress of such British claims. *See generally* S. Bemis, *supra* note 46, at 133–37. Disputes over these claims and other postwar problems were eventually addressed by the Treaty of Amity, Commerce, and Navigation, Nov. 19, 1794, United States–Great Britain, 8 Stat. 116, T.S. No. 105, *reprinted in* II *Treaties and Other International Acts of the United States of America* 245 (H. Miller ed. 1931). That treaty is known as "Jay's Treaty," John Jay having been its chief negotiator for the United States. The seminal study of the treaty is S. Bemis, *supra.*

49. *See generally* Dickinson, "The Law of Nations as Part of the National Law of the United States," 101 *U. Pa. L. Rev.* 26, 26–28, 33 (1952).

50. *See* S. Bemis, *supra* note 46, at 140 n.18, 436.

51. *See* Casto, *supra* note 37, at 497–98; *see also* Randall, *supra* note 18, at 28–31.

52. Art. III, § 2, cl. 1.

53. This is because article III's alienage provision does not confer jurisdiction where an alien sues an alien; *see supra* notes 21–28 and accompanying text.

54. See the explanation in chapter 1 that the supremacy clause in article VI and the arising-under clause in article III encompasses the law of nations and treaties.

55. Blum & Steinhardt, "Federal Jurisdiction over International Human Rights Claims: The Alien Torts Claims Act after Filartiga v. Pena-Irala," 22 *Harv. J. Int'l L. J.* 53, 98 (1981) (emphasis in original). Those commentators, however, concede that that argument may not necessarily be dispositive, *id.* at 98 n.193. Judge Henry Friendly also raised doubts about the statute's constitutionality, in *IIT v. Vencap, Ltd.*, 519 F.2d 1001, 1015 (2d Cir. 1975).

56. See chapter 3, which focuses upon the Constitution's arising-under clause to illuminate the statutory arising-under provision, 28 U.S.C. § 1331. As will be discussed, article III's arising-under language is normally read more broadly to support jurisdictional statutes other than § 1331 (such as § 1350) than it is to support jurisdiction in § 1331 cases. The problem with Blum and Steinhardt's argument, *see supra* note 55 and accompanying text, may be that they confusedly applied the more narrow § 1331 arising-under standard to § 1350, rather than the normally expansive article III arising-under standard.

57. *Osborn v. Bank of the United States*, 22 U.S. (9 Wheat.) 737, 824 (1824).

58. *Filartiga*, 630 F.2d at 889 n.25. On remand, the district court actually applied Paraguayan law in part; *see* 577 F. Supp. 860 (E.D.N.Y. 1984).

59. *Verlinden*, 461 U.S. 480 (1983).

60. The FSIA governs federal court jurisdiction over nation-states and their

agencies and instrumentalities. See chapter 4 regarding the FSIA. See chapter 3 regarding *Verlinden*.

61. *Verlinden*, 461 U.S. at 493–94.

62. *Id.* at 493.

63. One might argue that the foreign relations implications of FSIA cases are distinguishable from, and greater than, those of alien tort cases because the former involve foreign sovereign defendants, while the latter involve nonsovereign defendants. That distinction, although of some weight, is, however, somewhat simplistic. Rather than just focusing upon the defendant's identity in a given case, substantial attention should also be paid to the case's broader foreign relations ramifications. A case's substantive issues and overall federal context may have important international effects even when a nonstate actor is sued. In any event, § 1350's constitutionality in alien-versus-alien suits primarily rests upon the presence of a federal/international law question, with foreign relations considerations a subsidiary justification for federal (rather than state) court jurisdiction.

64. *Tel-Oren v. Libyan Arab Republic*, 726 F.2d 774 (D.C. Cir. 1984) (per curiam), *cert. denied*, 470 U.S. 1003 (1985). *Tel-Oren* is mentioned in the introduction.

65. *Tel-Oren*, 726 F.2d at 776 (Edwards, J., concurring).

66. *Tel-Oren*, 517 F. Supp. 542 (D.D.C. 1981). In addition to the PLO and Libya, the defendants initially were the Palestine Information Office, the National Association of Arab Americans, and the Palestine Congress of North America.

67. *See Tel-Oren*, 726 F.2d at 798 (Bork, J., concurring). The "state" in "statist" refers here to a nation-state.

68. *Id.* at 817 (Bork, J., concurring), *quoting* I L. Oppenheim, *International Law: A Treatise* 19 (H. Lauterpacht 8th ed. 1955); *see also* Brownlie, "The Place of the Individual in International Law," 50 *Va. L. Rev.* 435, 435–40 (1964).

69. *Tel-Oren*, 726 F.2d at 817 (Bork, J., concurring).

70. *Id.* (Bork, J., concurring).

71. *See id.* at 812–16 (Bork, J., concurring).

72. *Dreyfus v. Von Finck*, 534 F.2d 24 (2d Cir.), *cert. denied*, 429 U.S. 835 (1976).

73. The *Dreyfus* court also held that the plaintiff was without a private cause of action under the law of nations and various treaties for the original confiscation of plaintiff's property when he was paid an amount well below actual value; the same basic holding applied concerning the defendants' subsequent repudiation of a settlement that was to provide additional compensation to plaintiff; *see Dreyfus*, 534 F.2d at 29–31. *See infra* notes 131–40 regarding the establishment of a cause of action in alien tort cases.

74. *Id.* at 30–31, *quoting* von Redlich, *The Law of Nations* 5 (2d ed. 1937).

75. *See Tel-Oren*, 726 F.2d at 775 (Edwards, J., concurring).

76. *Id.* at 791 (Edwards, J., concurring) (emphasis added).

77. *Id.* (Edwards, J., concurring).

78. *Id.* at 792 (Edwards, J., concurring).

79. *Id.* at 794–95 (Edwards, J., concurring).

80. *See id.* at 795 (Edwards, J., concurring). Judge Edwards might prefer the term *nonofficial torture*, rather than the term *nonsovereign torture*, to refer to torture that is not sovereign-sponsored. We will use the latter term, however, for reasons to become apparent in *infra* notes 104–9 and accompanying text.

According to Judge Edwards, terrorism is simply not a law of nations violation; *see id.* at 795–96 (Edwards, J., concurring). Hence whereas torture, according to Judge Edwards, cannot be committed in a nonsovereign capacity, terrorism is simply not an international law violation because of the global disagreement about the meaning and legitimacy of terrorism. See chapter 6 for disagreement with this view of terrorism.

81. Lissitzyn, "Territorial Entities Other than Independent States in the Law of Treaties," 125 *Recueil des Cours* 5, 15 (1968) (footnote omitted) (emphasis in original).

82. Take the United States' legal system as just one example, illustrating the relativity of individuals' and other nonstate actors' legal personalities. Individuals obviously do not possess the authority to regulate interstate commerce, for instance, which is within Congress's jurisdiction under art. I, § 8, cl. 3 of the Constitution; so in this regard, individuals may be said to be objects of the legal system, without "standing" in connection with the commerce power. If, however, Congress uses that power in a way that allegedly violates a Bill of Rights provision (the due process clause, for example), then the affected individual is considered a legal subject, normally with standing to challenge the government's action. While the domestic legal order is distinct from the international legal order, the point remains that actors in both orders possess relative rights and responsibilities. Individuals and other nonstate actors are neither wholly the subjects nor wholly the objects of either legal order.

83. *See Tel-Oren*, 726 F.2d at 817 (Bork, J., concurring); *supra* note 71 and accompanying text.

84. Judge Edwards also suggested this problem with Judge Bork's approach; *see* 726 F.2d at 790 (Edwards, J., concurring).

85. *Filartiga*, 630 F.2d at 884.

86. *Forti v. Suarez-Mason*, 672 F. Supp. 1531 (N.D. Cal. 1987), *modified by* 694 F. Supp. 707 (N.D. Cal. 1988) (permitting jurisdiction additionally over the tort of "causing the disappearance" of individuals). *See generally* Note, "Remedying Foreign Repression Through U.S. Courts: Forti v. Suarez-Mason and the Recognition of Torture, Summary Execution, Prolonged Arbitrary Detention and Causing Disappearance as Cognizable Claims under the Alien Tort Claims Act," 20 *N.Y.U. J. Int'l L. & Pol.* 405 (1988).

87. Argentina's dirty war and state of siege date from President Peron's, and later a military junta's, action against purportedly subversive civilians from the

mid-1970s to early 1980s. That action involved multitudinous and heinous human rights abuses, including those against the plaintiffs in *Forti*.

88. *Forti*, 672 F. Supp. at 1540.

89. *Id.* (citations omitted).

90. Covenant on Civil and Political Rights, 21 U.N. GAOR Supp. at 53 [hereinafter Covenant]. See introduction for a full citation to, and brief description of, the Covenant. Even though the United States is not a party to the Covenant, it is bound by the substance of those provisions by customary international law and other legal sources; see chapter 3.

91. H. Lauterpacht, *International Law and Human Rights* 10–11 (1968).

92. *Id.* at 11. That conclusion perhaps befits Lauterpacht's "monist" view of international law. But "dualism" might also offer theoretical support to that conclusion, since domestic lawmakers are free to adopt international law rules. Discussions of monism and dualism are contained, *e.g.*, in I. Brownlie, *Principles of Public International Law* 33–35, 58–59 (3d ed. 1979); Ginsburgs, "The Validity of Treaties in the Municipal Law of the 'Socialist' States," 59 *Am. J. Int'l. L.* 523 (1965).

93. *Fernandez v. Wilkinson*, 505 F. Supp. 787 (D. Kan. 1980), *aff'd on other grounds, Rodriguez-Fernandez v. Wilkinson*, 654 F.2d 1382 (10th Cir. 1981).

94. *Lareau v. Manson*, 507 F. Supp. 1177 (D. Conn. 1980), *aff'd in part and modified in part*, 651 F.2d 96 (2d Cir. 1981).

95. *Fernandez*, 505 F. Supp. at 795.

96. *Id.* at 798. This decision was affirmed on federal statutory law grounds; *see* 654 F.2d at 1382.

97. *See Lareau*, 507 F. Supp. at 1187 n.9. The use of the Standard Minimum Rules by federal courts is mentioned in *id.* See Christenson, "Using Human Rights Law to Inform Due Process and Equal Protection Analyses," 52 *U. Cin. L. Rev.* 3 (1983), and Lockwood, "The United Nations Charter and United States Civil Rights Litigation: 1946–1955," 69 *Iowa L. Rev.* 901 (1984), regarding the more general and increasingly frequent use of international norms to inform constitutional standards.

98. *Lareau*, 507 F. Supp. at 1187 n.9. The circuit court on appeal also looked to the Standard Minimum Rules; *see* 651 F.2d at 106–7.

99. *Respublica v. De Longchamps*, 1 U.S. (1 Dall.) 111, 116–17 (Pa. Sup. Ct. 1784) (emphasis added).

100. Just two examples of famous, early piracy cases that the Supreme Court decided are *United States v. Brig Malek Adhel*, 43 U.S. (2 How.) 210 (1844), and *United States v. Smith*, 18 U.S. (5 Wheat.) 153 (1820).

101. See chapter 8 regarding the statelessness of pirates and the hyperbole involved in that characterization.

102. *See, e.g., de Letelier v. Republic of Chile*, 488 F. Supp. 665 (D.D.C.) (jurisdiction upheld), 502 F. Supp. 259 (D.D.C. 1980) (judgment for plaintiff); *United States v. Layton*, 509 F. Supp. 212 (N.D. Cal.), *appeal dismissed*, 645 F.2d 681 (9th Cir.), *cert. denied*, 452 U.S. 972 (1981).

103. The fact that the PLO may be politically motivated, while pirates act for private or pecuniary reasons, does not distort the analogy here; see chapter 8.

104. The PLO committed both torture and terrorism in *Tel-Oren*. Judge Edwards opined that terrorism is not an international law violation, *see supra* note 80; his discussion of the international law violations that nonstate actors may commit was thus limited to nonsovereign torture.

105. Covenant, at art. 5, 21 U.N. GAOR Supp. at 53 (emphasis added). Judge Edwards's discussion of nonsovereign torture did not refer to the Covenant; *see Tel-Oren*, 726 F.2d at 794–95 (Edwards, J., concurring). See chapter 3 regarding how the Covenant (and the Torture Convention) may subject the United States, a nonparty to each of those instruments, to customary obligations.

106. Torture Convention (emphasis added). The Convention defines torture as "any act by which severe pain or suffering, whether physical or mental, is intentionally inflicted on a person for such purposes as obtaining from him or a third person information or a confession, punishing him for an act he or a third person has committed or is suspected of having committed, or intimidating or coercing him or a third person, or for any reason based on discrimination of any kind, when such pain or suffering is inflicted by or at the instigation of or with the consent or acquiescence of a public official or other person acting in an official capacity. It does not include pain or suffering arising only from, inherent in or incidental to lawful sanctions," art. I, U.N. GAOR Supp. (No. 51) at 197. See introduction, note 16, for a full citation to the Torture Convention.

107. *Tel-Oren*, 726 F.2d at 795 (Edwards, J., concurring). Judge Edwards referred to the Torture Convention, although it then was not in final form. As indicated in the introduction, the Convention has now entered into force, and President Reagan transmitted it to the Senate for advice and consent on May 29, 1988.

108. "Terrorism" is sometimes also conceptualized as involving certain violent acts that have international repercussions; *see, e.g.*, Note, "Terrorism as a Tort in Violation of the Law of Nations," 6 *Fordham Int'l L. J.* 236, 241 (1982).

109. "International Military Tribunal (Nuremberg), Judgment and Sentences," 41 *Am. J. Int'l L.* 172, 221 (1947).

110. *See supra* notes 91–98 and accompanying text regarding the domestic law recognition of legal rights.

111. See chapters 3 and 6; *see also infra* note 125 and accompanying text.

112. *Tel-Oren*, 726 F.2d at 790 (Edwards, J., concurring). With regard to the Alien Tort Statute's requirements, Judge Edwards strongly disagreed with Judge Bork, whom he is criticizing in the quoted passage.

113. Immigration and Nationality Act, 8 U.S.C. § 1101 (a)(3)(e) (1982).

114. *See, e.g., Trans-Continental Inv. Corp., S.A. v. Bank of the Commonwealth*, 500 F. Supp. 565, 569–70 (D.C. Cal. 1980); *Valanga v. Metropolitan Life Ins. Co.*, 259 F. Supp. 324, 327–28 (E.D. Pa. 1966); Hassan, "Panacea or Mirage? Domestic Enforcement of International Human Rights Law: Recent Cases," 4 *Hous. J. Int'l L.* 13 (1981); Note, *supra* note 108; Comment, "Torture as a Tort

in Violation of International Law: Filartiga v. Pena-Irala," 33 *Stan. L. Rev.* 353 (1981).

115. Judge Edwards considered this alternative interpretation in *Tel-Oren*, 726 F.2d at 782–88. He saw validity, however, in both the majority and alternative approaches. Judicial support for the alternative formulation also comes from *Adra v. Clift*, 195 F. Supp. 857 (D. Md. 1961), which upheld jurisdiction under the Alien Tort Statute where the Lebanese ambassador to Iran sued his former wife, an Arab national living in the United States, and her new husband. Allegedly against a Lebanese court decree, the wife had withheld the plaintiff's daughter from the plaintiff, concealing the daughter's name and nationality through falsification of a passport. The court found that, under Maryland tort law, "[t]he unlawful taking or withholding of a minor child from the custody of the parent or parents entitled to such custody is a tort," *Adra*, 195 F. Supp. at 862. The wife *additionally* violated the law of nations through passport falsification and by international travel under concealed identity.

116. "A 'tort' is simply the Norman word for a 'wrong,' but 'torts' have typically been distinguished from crimes and from 'wrongs' identified with contractual relations. Tort law, then, is concerned with civil wrongs not arising from contracts," G. White, *Tort Law in America* xi (1980). Regarding eighteenth-century torts and their overlapping with current torts, *see* 3 W. Blackstone, *Commentaries* *103, *27. The torts of assault, battery, nuisance, trespass to real property, and false imprisonment, for example, "acquired their distinctive names centuries ago and were freely illustrated in our legal literature at an early period," Winfield & Goodhart, "Trepass and Negligence," 49 *L. Q. Rev.* 359–60 (1933).

117. The Alien Tort Statute is jurisdictional in nature; as will be discussed shortly, it neither provides a cause of action nor requires one under federal law. Hence, once jurisdiction attaches, the case may be likened to a tort case, and choice-of-law considerations dictate the law to be applied on the merits. While the case continues to involve international components, the same body of choice of law presumptively regulates tort cases involving either international or domestic interstate elements. Choice-of-law doctrines vary, but at least the *lex loci* approach generally dictates that the law of situs of the tort should be applied to substantive issues. (The forum's law regulates procedural issues.) If, however, the situs's substantive law conflicts with the forum's strongly held public policy, or if it would lead to a truly unjust decision, the forum may reject the situs's law in whole or in part; *see generally* R. Weintraub, *Commentary on the Conflict of Laws* 58–61 (1971).

118. *Abiodun v. Martin Oil Serv., Inc.*, 475 F.2d 142, 145 (7th Cir.), *cert. denied*, 414 U.S. 866 (1973).

119. *Lopes v. Reederi Richard Schroeder*, 225 F. Supp. 292, 296 (E.D. Pa. 1963).

120. *United States v. Smith*, 18 U.S. (5 Wheat.) 153, 160–61 (1820). *See generally* Jay, "The Status of the Law of Nations in Early American Law," 42 *Vand. L. Rev.* 819 (1989).

121. *See Filartiga*, 630 F.2d at 881–84; *Forti*, 672 F. Supp. at 1542. See chapter 3 regarding the relationship between the law of nations (particularly custom) and written instruments (e.g., treaties, resolutions, declarations).

122. *See Tel-Oren*, 726 F.2d at 813–16 (Bork, J., concurring); *see also supra* note 71 and accompanying text.

123. *United States v. La Jeune Eugenie*, 26 F. Cas. 832, 846 (D. Mass. 1821) (No. 15, 551).

124. *Filartiga*, 630 F.2d at 881, citing *The Paquete Habana*, 175 U.S. 677 (1900), and *Ware v. Hylton*, 3 U.S. (3 Dall.) 198 (1796).

125. *See, e.g., Restatement (Third) of Foreign Relations Law* at § 404. See chapters 3 and 6 for an elaboration upon those offenses.

126. *Forti*, 672 F. Supp. at 1540 n.6 (emphasis added).

127. *But see* 26 Op. Att'y Gen. 250 (1907) (opining that Mexican citizens were tortiously injured by a United States company's diversion of Rio Grande boundary between United States and Mexico as governed by bilateral convention).

128. See chapter 3.

129. *See id.* regarding how even treaties that are primarily criminal or regulatory in character may themselves implicitly give rise to private causes of action, perhaps without recourse to the law of nations or customary law, at least under the first genus of § 1331 jurisdiction.

130. *See, e.g., Filartiga*, 630 F.2d at 880–85; *Forti*, 672 F. Supp. at 1541–43, 694 F. Supp. at 710–11.

131. *Davis v. Passman*, 442 U.S. 228, 237 (1979).

132. *Id.* at 240 n.18.

133. 26 Op. Att'y Gen. 250, 252 (1907).

134. 1 Op. Att'y Gen. 57, 59 (1795).

135. *See, e.g., Filartiga*, 630 F.2d at 880–89; *Forti*, 672 F. Supp. at 1539–40.

136. *Jaffee v. Boyles*, 616 F. Supp. 1371 (W.D.N.Y. 1985).

137. *Id.* at 1378. Similar reasoning is found in *Dreyfus*, 534 F.2d at 24, and in *Tel-Oren*, 726 F.2d at 801 (Bork, J., concurring). Commentators' discussions of § 1350 and causes of action are found, *e.g.*, in Casto, *supra* note 37, at 478–80; D'Amato, "What Does Tel-Oren Tell Lawyers?" 79 *Am. J. Int'l L.* 92 (1985); Randall, *supra* note 31, at 477–95.

138. See chapter 3; *see also Tel-Oren*, 726 F.2d at 779 n.4 (Edwards, J., concurring).

139. The presence of an international law violation supports the constitutionality of § 1350 cases, even though plaintiff's cause of action may arise under nonfederal tort law. *See supra* notes 53–63 and accompanying text.

140. Regarding the national interest involved in § 1332 cases, *see* supra notes 14–16, 18–20, and accompanying text.

141. See *supra* note 134 and accompanying text.

142. *E.g., Filartiga*, 630 F.2d at 885–86; *Forti*, 672 F. Supp. at 1540, n.6. *See generally* Blum & Steinhardt, *supra* note 55, at 63–64.

143. See chapter 5.
144. See chapter 8.

3. Federal Questions, Human Rights, and Terrorism

1. 28 U.S.C. § 1331 (1982). This chapter's examination of arising-under jurisdiction draws upon Randall, "Federal Questions and the Human Rights Paradigm," 73 *Minn. L. Rev.* 349 (1988) (to which the author holds the copyright).

2. This conclusion relates to the prior discussion that both the supremacy clause and article III's arising-under clause encompass treaty as well as non-treaty international law sources; see chapter 1.

3. *See* art. VI, cl. 2; The Federalist No. 80, at 476 (A. Hamilton) (C. Rossiter ed. 1961) ("The mere necessity of uniformity in the interpretation of the national laws" demands that the federal judiciary possess authority over cases arising under federal law).

4. *Osborn v. Bank of the United States*, 22 U.S. (9 Wheat.) 738 (1824).

5. *Bank of the United States v. Planters' Bank*, 22 U.S. (9 Wheat.) 904 (1824).

6. *Osborn*, 22 U.S. at 817.

7. *Osborn* concerned the constitutionality of Ohio's tax on the federal bank, whereas *Planters' Bank* involved the bank's suit on a promissory note.

8. *Osborn*, 22 (9 Wheat.) at 824; *see also id.* at 822 ("If it be a sufficient foundation for jurisdiction, that the title or right set up by the party, may be defeated by one construction of the constitution or law of the United States, and sustained by the opposite construction, . . . then all the other questions must be incidental to this, which gives the jurisdiction").

9. Judiciary Act of March 3, 1975, ch. 137, 18 Stat. 470.

10. The 1875 Judiciary Act did limit federal question jurisdiction with an amount-in-controversy requirement; it also directed dismissal or remand if a suit did "not really and substantially involve a dispute or controversy properly within [the court's] jurisdiction." Congress, however, subsequently omitted both of those limitations on statutory federal question jurisdiction.

11. According to the bill's drafter, prior jurisdictional legislation "did not confer the whole [judicial] power which the Constitution conferred. . . . [But t]his bill does. . . . This bill gives precisely the power which the Constitution confers — nothing more, nothing less," 2 Cong. Rec. 4986 (1874) (remarks of Sen. Carpenter). These comments concern the Judiciary Act of 1875 in its entirety (not just the federal question provision) and they apparently constitute the full evidence of Congress's intention concerning the bill's arising-under component. *See also Franchise Tax Bd. v. Laborers Vacation Trust*, 463 U.S. 1, 8 n.8 (1983); Forrester, "Federal Question Jurisdiction and § 5," 18 *Tulane L. Rev.* 263, 276–78 (1943); Fraser, "Some Problems in Federal Question Jurisdiction," 49 *Mich. L. Rev.* 73, 74–75 (1950).

12. *Verlinden B.V. v. Central Bank of Nigeria* 461 U.S. 480 (1983).

13. *Id.* at 492.

14. *Id.* at 494 (emphasis added).

15. *Id.* at 495.

16. The federal district courts have original jurisdiction under 28 U.S.C. § 1330(a) over foreign nations and their agencies and instrumentalities in cases befitting one of the FSIA's limited exceptions to sovereign immunity; see chapter 4. The plaintiff in *Verlinden* claimed that both the waiver and commercial activity exceptions to immunity applied.

17. See the discussion of this topic in chapter 2.

18. *Verlinden*, 461 U.S. at 493–94.

19. Attempts by notable commentaries to define what statutory federal question jurisdiction does or should require include Cohen, "The Broken Compass: The Requirement that a Case Arise 'Directly' under Federal Law," 115 *U. Pa. L. Rev.* 890 (1967); Chadbourn & Levin, "Original Jurisdiction of Federal Questions," 90 *U. Pa. L. Rev.* 639, 649 (1942); Mishkin, "The Federal 'Question' in the District Courts," 53 *Colum. L. Rev.* 157 (1953); Wechsler, "Federal Jurisdiction and the Revision of the Judicial Code," 13 *L. & Contemp. Probs* 216, 223–34 (1948); Note, "The Outer Limits of 'Arising Under,'" 54 *N.Y.U. L. Rev.* 978 (1979).

20. *Romero v. International Terminal Operating Co.*, 358 U.S. 354, 379 (1958) (footnote omitted).

21. *See* Note, *supra* note 19, at 988–95 (criticizing as "mythical" the difference between the statutory and constitutional language and concluding that the only defensible limitation on *Osborn* is the judicial requirement that § 1331 cases must indicate a substantial reliance on a federal proposition).

22. A noted commentary strenuously argues that the statutory arising-under provision deserves a different analysis than the constitutional arising-under provision because the former confers only original lower court jurisdiction, whereas the latter encompasses both original and appellate jurisdiction; Mishkin, *supra* note 19 at 163–76. According to Professor Mishkin, the Constitution's arising-under clause must be broad enough to comprehend cases that during litigation present a crucial federal issue. The Supreme Court must be permitted to have the final say, in such instances, under its appellate jurisdiction, *id.* at 163. But since "it may often be difficult to determine the presence and materiality of a federal question until some point long after the litigation has started," the inclusion within original lower court jurisdiction of "all cases which might conceivably turn finally upon an issue of national law would create an impossible situation," *id.*

Professor Mishkin's argument reduces to the following: Since arising-under jurisdiction may be applied in different contexts, a different interpretation is required for each application. His analytical distinction between the original and appellate applications of arising-under jurisdiction is flawed, however, because it does not acknowledge that one doctrinal approach may be used to analyze arising-under jurisdiction in different contexts. As perfectly put, "[i]t is not the meaning of 'arising under' that varies but the posture of the case," Note, *supra* note 19, at 989–90.

23. *Franchise Tax Bd. v. Laborers Vacation Trust*, 463 U.S. 1, 8 (1982).

24. Although the author hopes to offer an original approach by which to analyze the federal question caselaw, the idea of organizing the federal question caselaw into certain categories or genuses derives support from *Merrell Dow Pharmaceuticals v. Thompson*, 106 S.Ct. 3229, 3232–35 (1986); *Franchise Tax Bd.*, 463 U.S. 1, 27–28 (1982); *Republic of Philippines v. Marcos*, 806 F.2d 344, 352–54 (1986); *Verlinden*, 647 F.2d 320, 325–26 (2d Cir. 1981), *rev'd on other grounds*, 461 U.S. 480 (1983); *T. B. Harms Company v. Eliscu*, 339 F.2d 823, 825–28 (2d Cir. 1964), *cert. denied*, 381 U.S. 915 (1965).

Whether warranted or not, one rule remains constant in each genus: the well-pleaded complaint rule, which contrary to *Osborn* requires that the presence of a federal question must be determined only from the plaintiff's complaint, bill, or declaration and not from the defendant's answer or the anticipated defenses. *See, e.g.*, *Franchise Tax Bd.*, 463 U.S. at 9–10; *Gully v. First Nat'l Bank*, 299 U.S. 109, 113 (1936); *Taylor v. Anderson*, 234 U.S. 74, 75–76 (1914).

25. Not referring here per se to a jurisprudential term of art, "positive law" encompasses the legal sources that the United States' legislative and executive branches have enunciated or recognized. Those sources are ordinarily expressed in writing, although certain legal practices, including international custom, also constitute positive law. While the first two genuses both identify causes of action under federal law, the second genus generally requires greater judicial creation and cognition of the cause of action. Causes of action under the second genus thus often arise less directly under the positive federal law. However, specifically when federal judges recognize the Covenant's and the Torture Convention's express causes of action as a matter of customary law under the first genus and as a matter of custom and federal common law under the second genus, there is not really much difference between the sources of law applied in the first two genuses. Admittedly, some of the genuses sometimes overlap. *See infra* notes 37–39, 47–56, 101–4, and accompanying text.

26. *American Well Works Company v. Layne and Bowler Company*, 241 U.S. 257 (1916).

27. *Id.* at 260 (emphasis added). Although the Court has separated the concepts of "jurisdiction" and "cause of action" in other instances (*see, e.g.*, *Bell v. Hood*, 327 U.S. 678, 682 (1946)), Justice Holmes indicated here that the former depends on the latter. In *Davis v. Passman*, 442 U.S. 228 (1979), the Court also seems to separate the concept of jurisdiction from the concept of cause of action; *see generally Davis*, 442 U.S. at 236–45. *Davis*, however, will be used shortly for its definitions of "cause of action."

28. *United States v. Memphis Cotton Oil Co.*, 288 U.S. 62, 67 (1933).

29. *U.S. v. Dickinson*, 331 U.S. 745, 748 (1947).

30. *Davis*, 442 U.S. 228 (1979).

31. *Id.* at 238 (emphasis added). "Right" here apparently refers to a benefit or the entitlement to be free from a certain injury.

32. *Id.* at 240 n.18 (emphasis added). *See generally* D'Amato, "What Does Tel-Oren Tell Lawyers?" 79 *Am. J. Int'l L.* 92 (1985).

33. *Davis,* 442 U.S. at 242 (emphasis added).

34. *Id.* Otherwise, "such rights are to become merely precatory," *id.*

35. *Cort v. Ash,* 422 U.S. 66, 78 (1975) (emphasis added). *Cort* is one of the most significant of the many recent cases in which the Supreme Court has considered whether to infer a private cause of action from federal statutes that are primarily criminal or regulatory in nature. Such cases include *Daily Income Fund, Inc. v. Fox,* 464 U.S. 523, 534–41 (1984); *California v. Sierra Club,* 451 U.S. 287, 292–98 (1981); *Transamerica Mortgage Advisors, Inc. v. Lewis,* 444 U.S. 11, 14–19 (1979); *Touche Ross & Co. v. Redington,* 442 U.S. 560, 568–78 (1979); *Cannon v. University of Chicago,* 441 U.S. 677, 683–709 (1979); *Johnson v. Railway Express Agency,* 421 U.S. 454, 459–61 (1975); *J. I. Case Superintendent of Insurance v. Bankers Life & Cas. Co.,* 404 U.S. 6, 13 N.9 (1971); *J. I. Case Co. v. Borak,* 377 U.S. 426 (1964). The quest to determine congressional intent subsumes the *Cort* criteria. For criticism of those criteria, see *Cannon,* 441 U.S. at 730 (Powell, J., dissenting), which suggests that the Supreme Court has actually streamlined and has grown somewhat less committed to the *Cort* criteria.

36. *Thompson v. Thompson,* 108 S. Ct. 513, 516, 98 L. Ed. 512, 520 (1988).

37. Preliminary to identifying such rights, we must put aside the Oppenheim-Bork argument that individuals are without the legal personality to possess virtually any modern international rights; see chapter 2 for a discussion of this issue. We proceed, instead, on the assumption (blatantly correct, if not tautological) that individuals may possess the rights that individuals possess.

38. See introduction, notes 12 and 16, for the full citations to these instruments.

39. *See* Torture Convention, at arts. 12–14, 23 I.L.M. at 1030–31; Covenant, at art. 2(3).

40. *See generally Restatement (Third) of Foreign Relations* § 111 reporters' note 5 [hereinafter *Restatement*].

41. *See id.* at § 111; *see also* Riesenfeld, Editorial Comment, "The Doctrine of Self-Executing Treaties and Community Law: A Pioneer Decision by the Court of Justice of the European Community," 67 *Am. J. Int'l L.* 504 (1973); Riesenfeld, Editorial Comment, "The Doctrine of Self-Executing Treaties and GATT: A Notable German Judgment," 65 *Am. J. Int'l L.* 548, 550 (1971); Riesenfeld, Editorial Comment, "The Doctrine of Self-Executing Treaties and United States v. Postal: Win at Any Price?" 74 *Am. J. Int'l L.* 892 (1980).

42. *See* L. Henkin, R. Pugh, O. Schachter & H. Smit, *International Law* 202 (2d ed. 1987).

43. Strictly speaking, the fact that the Fifth Amendment is a constitutional

norm does not make it easier to classify as self-executing than an international norm would be. In any event, the overlapping of constitutional norms and human rights and terrorism norms, *see infra* notes 58–59 and accompanying text, may mean that both types of norms should be liberally viewed to be self-executing and thus to provide a cause of action and jurisdiction.

44. Schachter, "The Obligation to Implement the Covenant in Domestic Law," in *International Bill of Rights* 311, 327 (L. Henkin ed. 1981).

45. *See* Covenant, at art. 2(2); Torture Convention, at arts 4, 5, 23 I.L.M. at 1028.

46. The conclusion that the Covenant and the Torture Convention are self-executing really overlaps with our earlier conclusion that those instruments satisfy the arising-under requirement. The self-executing treaty concept boils down to whether an instrument creates an enforceable private cause of action or whether it creates merely hortatory expectations and unfulfilled sovereign obligations. According to one federal judge: "[A]n individual has access to courts for enforcement of a treaty's provisions *only when it is self-executing, . . . when it expressly or impliedly provides a private right of action,*" *Tel-Oren*, 726 F.2d at 808 (Bork, J., concurring) (emphasis added). Since this judge makes the arising-under and self-executing concepts both dependant upon whether plaintiff has a cause of action, each concept makes consideration of the other somewhat redundant. When a federal human right exists, a plaintiff has a cause of action under *Davis's* first definition. In turn, the presence of that cause of action makes plaintiff's claim both self-executing and properly subject to arising-under jurisdiction. *See generally* D'Amato, *supra* note 32.

47. See introduction, note 16 and accompanying text. Although the Torture Convention appears self-executing, if the Senate conditioned its advice and consent upon a contrary interpretation, the Convention might have to be implemented through additional legislation. The pending torture legislation, see *supra* notes 125, 127, and accompanying text, specifically providing district court jurisdiction over torture cases, would help in this regard.

48. *Restatement, supra* note 40, at § 702 (specifically regarding sovereign-sponsored offenses). Also prohibited under § 702 are consistent patterns of gross violations of human rights recognized under international law.

49. *See generally id.,* at pt. 7 introductory note and § 702 comments a and c (describing customary human rights norms as binding on the United States and noting reliance on the Universal Declaration). The several comments and reporters' notes to § 702 more fully describe the customary law of human rights.

50. *Filartiga v. Pena-Irala*, 630 F.2d 876, 883 (2d Cir. 1980) (quoting 34 U.N. ESCOR, Supp. [No. 8] 15, U.N. Doc. E/cn.4/1/610 [1962]). See chapter 2 for a discussion of *Filartiga*.

51. *Filartiga*, 630 F.2d at 880–85.

52. (*W. Ger. v. Den.; W. Ger. v. Neth.*) (1969) 1969 I.C.J. 3, 39, 42 (Judgment of Feb. 20) [hereinafter *Continental Shelf Cases*].

53. *Continental Shelf Cases*, 1969 I.C.J. at 42. Although the case specifically concerned the delimitation of the continental shelf under a treaty on that subject, the opinion's language suggests an approach to the treaty-custom relationship applicable in any context. *See also Restatement, supra* note 40, at § 102, reporters' note 2.

54. Vienna Convention on the Law of Treaties, May 23, 1969, art. 38, 1969 U.N. Jurid. Y.B. 140, 150, U.N. Doc. A/CONF.39/27, 8 I.L.M. 679, 694 (1969) (emphasis added).

55. Whether a treaty has generated custom binding upon nonobjecting nonparties depends, in part, on the length of time that the treaty has been in force and whether the treaty has gained widespread representative participation; *Continental Shelf Cases*, 1969 I.C.J. at 42. The *Restatement, supra* note 40, at § 102 (3), provides that treaties may lead to the creation of custom when "agreements are intended for adherence by states generally and are in fact widely accepted." Of course, to apply such standards to the Covenant and to the Torture and Apartheid conventions would involve substantial empirical research. In this chapter we have reasonably assumed, however, that the very fundamental norms that those instruments contain are binding on the United States and are norms to which the nation is committed. That assumption draws support from the *Restatement, supra* note 40, at §§ 702, 703, and from the overlapping between the norms at hand and those that the United States' Bill of Rights encompasses; *see infra* notes 58–59 and accompanying text.

56. *Restatement, supra* note 40, at § 703 comment c.

57. *Davis,* 442 U.S. at 240 n.18.

58. *See generally Reid v. Covert,* 354 U.S. 1, 16–17 (1957); L.Henkin, *Foreign Affairs and the Constitution* 137–40 (1972).

59. *Davis,* 442 U.S. at 242. Although *Davis* advised that the presumption of a private remedy is especially proper when a specific issue is not committed explicitly to the executive or congressional branches, *see supra* note 33 and accompanying text, in chapter 5 we will demonstrate the propriety of federal judicial responses to human rights and terrorism cases and how such responses are actually consistent with the political branches' condemnation of international offenses.

60. In part, that article obligates parties: "(a) To ensure that any person whose rights or freedoms . . . are violated shall have an *effective remedy,* notwithstanding that the violation has been committed by persons acting in an official capacity; (b) To ensure that any person claiming such a remedy shall have his right thereto determined by competent judicial, administrative or legislative authorities, . . . and to develop the possibilities of *judicial remedy*" (emphasis added).

61. Torture Convention, at art. 12, 23 I.L.M. at 1030.

62. *Id.* at art. 14, 23 I.L.M. at 1030; *see also id.* at art. 13, 23 I.L.M. at 1030.

63. *See supra* note 56 and accompanying text. See *supra* notes 48–56 and

accompanying text regarding the United States' customary law obligations associated with the Covenant and the Torture Convention.

64. See introduction, notes 13–15, 18–21, for full citations to those instruments. Since the United States is not a party to the Apartheid Convention, that instrument would not only have to give rise to an implied cause of action, but that cause of action would have to be recognized under federal customary law, for § 1331 jurisdiction to exist over acts of apartheid.

65. *Cort*, 422 U.S. at 78 (emphasis in original).

66. *See generally* cases in *supra* note 35.

67. This concept is discussed in chapter 2.

68. *Cort's* remedy criteria do not require federal law to imply that any particular form of relief (e.g., money damages) is appropriate. The issue of whether plaintiff has an implied remedy and a private cause of action "is analytically distinct and prior to the question of what relief, if any, a litigant may be entitled to receive," *Davis*, 442 U.S. at 239. Hence "remedy" only refers to the implied propriety of invoking federal judicial power to enforce plaintiff's implied rights. Of course, if jurisdiction is successfully invoked, issues related to the case's merits and to the plaintiff's relief remain.

69. For example, the caselaw indicates that the word "treaty" in § 1331 should be read liberally to include various types of international agreements, since such agreements "could have a significant bearing on this country's international relations and thus should be heard in federal court," *Hyosung (America), Inc. v. Japan Air Lines Co., Ltd.*, 624 F. Supp. 727, 730 (S.D.N.Y. 1985); *see also Weinberger v. Rossi*, 456 U.S. 25, 29–30 (1982); *B. Altman & Co. v. United States*, 224 U.S. 583, 601 (1912). From this precedent, it is logical to suggest that a treaty's substantive provisions likewise should be liberally interpreted to serve federalism concerns.

70. *See* Randall, "Further Inquiries into the Alien Tort Statute and a Recommendation," 18 *N.Y.U. J. Int'l L. & Pol.* 473, 488–92 (1986).

71. See chapter 1.

72. *Von Dardel v. Union of Soviet Socialist Republics*, 623 F. Supp. 246 (D.D.C. 1985).

73. *de Letelier v. Republic of Chile*, 488 F. Supp. 665 (D.D.C.) (jurisdiction upheld), 502 F. Supp. 259 (D.D.C. 1980) (judgment for plaintiffs).

74. *Von Dardel*, 623 F. Supp. at 249.

75. Jurisdiction was available under 28 U.S.C. §§ 1330(a), 1331, and 1350 (*Von Dardel*, 623 F. Supp. at 250), although the court focused on the FSIA and Alien Tort Statute. Although we discuss *Von Dardel* regarding the implication of private causes of action, new Supreme Court precedent suggests that only the FSIA, and not § 1331 or other jurisdiction provisions, are relevant regarding nation-state defendants; see chapter 4. This new precedent, however, does not disturb the present discussion.

76. *Von Dardel*, 623 F. Supp. at 254 (emphasis added); *see also id.* at 259

(when the well-being of a diplomat was violated under the English (and then American) common law, a private cause of action was recognized and this "right to sue has recently been reaffirmed by Congress").

77. *de Letelier*, 502 F. Supp. at 260 n.1. Jurisdiction over Argentina was upheld under the FSIA; 488 F. Supp. at 665. Jurisdiction over the nonstate defendants was upheld under § 1331 and 1350, *inter alia*, as is summarily indicated in *de Letelier*, 502 F. Supp. at 266. de Letelier's representatives were joined by other plaintiffs in commencing the action.

78. *Chumney v. Nixon*, 615 F.2d 389 (6th Cir. 1980).

79. *See* 18 U.S.C. § 113 (1982) (assault defined); 49 U.S.C. § 1472(k)(1) (1982) (assault prohibited in United States' special aircraft jurisdiction).

80. *Chumney*, 615 F.2d at 394.

81. *Id. But see In re Mexico City Aircrash of October 31, 1979*, 708 F.2d 400, 404–8 (9th Cir. 1983) (suggesting that *Chumney* contradicts the majority view).

82. *Chumney*, 615 F. 2d at 395.

83. See chapter 2 for a discussion of *Filartiga*.

84. *Filartiga*, 630 F.2d at 887 n.22. The court rejected the contention that only directly self-executing instruments are binding in federal courts, *see id.* at 883. Even if a treaty does not, standing alone, confer a cause of action binding in a United States court, it may be "evidence of an emerging norm of customary international law," *id.* at 880 n.7, and may help create expectations about the protection of individual rights, *id.* at 883.

85. *Tel-Oren*, 726 F.2d at 781 (only first emphasis added); see chapter 2 regarding *Tel-Oren*. Judge Edwards's suggestion, made in the Alien Tort Statute context, may provide less support for § 1331 jurisdiction over human rights claims than the *Filartiga* dictum does. While the *Filartiga* court apparently viewed §§ 1331 and 1350 as coterminous, Judge Edwards distinguished the two provisions, indicating that only § 1331 requires a private cause of action under international law, *see id.* at 779 n.4.

86. *See Tel-Oren*, 726 F.2d at 781 (Edwards, J., concurring) (referring to the offenses that *Restatement* § 702 identified). At the same time, Judge Edwards did not believe that either explicit or implicit private remedies exist for nonofficial torture; see chapter 2.

87. *Cort*, 422 U.S. at 78.

88. P. Bator, P. Mishkin, D. Shapiro & H. Wechsler, *Hart and Wechsler's The Federal Courts and the Federal System* 863 (3d ed. 1973) (hereinafter *Federal Courts*). For the purposes of this genus, we adopt *Davis's* second and more demanding cause-of-action definition.

89. *Erie R.R. v. Tompkins*, 304 U.S. 64 (1938).

90. *Id.* at 78 (emphasis added).

91. *Hinderlider v. La Plata River Co.*, 304 U.S. 92 (1938).

92. Friendly, "In Praise of Erie — and of the New Federal Common Law," 39 *N.Y.U. L. Rev.* 383, 405 (1964) (emphasis added).

93. *Romero v. International Terminal Operating Co.*, 358 U.S. 354, 393 (1958) (Brennan, J., dissenting in part and concurring in part).

94. See chapter 1 for a discussion of this conclusion.

95. *Banco Nacional de Cuba v. Sabbatino*, 376 U.S. 398 (1964).

96. *Sabbatino*, 376 U.S. at 426. See chapter 5 for a further discussion of *Sabbatino*.

97. *Sabbatino*, 376 U.S. at 425.

98. *Id.* at 424.

99. Friendly, *supra* note 92, at 408 n.119.

100. Hill, "The Law-Making Power of the Federal Courts: Constitutional Preemption," 67 *Colum. L. Rev.* 1024, 1031 (1967).

101. *Textile Workers Union of America v. Lincoln Mills of Alabama*, 353 U.S. 448, 457 (1957).

102. See *supra* notes 48–55 and accompanying text.

103. The *Filartiga* court, which primarily found jurisdiction under the Alien Tort Statute (see chapter 2), referred to a possible federal common law basis of the plaintiffs' claim, 630 F.2d at 885–87; in *dictum*, the court suggested that § 1331 might also support jurisdiction over plaintiffs' claim, *see supra* notes 83–84 and accompanying text.

104. *Forti v. Suarez-Mason*, 672 F. Supp. 1531, 1543–44 (N.D. Cal. 1987). *Forti* also rested jurisdiction upon 28 U.S.C. § 1350; see chapter 2.

105. *Lincoln Mills*, 353 U.S. at 457.

106. *Marbury v. Madison*, 1 U.S. (Cranch) 137, 163 (1803).

107. See generally *Restatement*, *supra* note 40, at § 703 comment c.

108. *Federal Courts*, *supra* note 88, at 533 (discussing relation of state and federal law).

109. Wechsler, *supra* note 19, at 224 (emphasis added).

110. *Id.* at 225.

111. The amalgam of article I and article III support is discussed in Mishkin, *supra* note 19, at 188–93; Wechsler, *supra* note 19, at 224–25; and Note, "The Theory of Protective Jurisdiction," 57 *N.Y.U. L. Rev.* 933, 947–59 (1982). The article I support includes the necessary-and-proper clause, art. I, § 8, cl. 18, by which Congress implicitly may delegate its authority to the judiciary through jurisdictional grants. Article III supports protective jurisdiction because federal jurisdictional statutes are laws of the United States, and cases involving those statutes thus arise under federal law for article III purposes, *see* Mishkin, *supra* note 19, at 188–93; Wechsler, *supra* note 19, at 225. Arguably, through the adoption and utilization of nonfederal rules of decisions, federal judges may "federalize" those rules (that is, transform nonfederal law to federal); the causes of action that those rules supply thus arise under federal law for article III purposes.

112. Mishkin, *supra* note 19, at 192.

113. *Id.*

114. *E.g.*, Galligan, "Article III and the 'Related to' Bankruptcy Jurisdic-

tion: A Case Study in Protective Jurisdiction," 11 *U. Puget Sound L. Rev.* 1 (1987); Brown, "Beyond Pennhurst — Protective Jurisdiction, The Eleventh Amendment, and the Power of Congress to Enlarge Federal Jurisdiction in Response to the Burger Court," 71 *Va. L. Rev.* 343 (1985); Note, *supra* note 111.

115. *See supra* notes 4–8 and accompanying text.

116. *Lincoln Mills*, 353 U.S. at 459 (1957) (Burton, J., concurring). See Brown, *supra* note 114, at 370–75 for a succinct discussion of Supreme Court opinions at least impliedly supporting some form of protective jurisdiction. *See generally Mesa v. California*, 109 S.Ct. 959, 968–69 (1989) (discussing the fact that the Supreme Court has not previously, and did not in the instant case, explicitly find the need to adopt the protective jurisdiction theory).

117. *Id.* at 460 (Frankfurter, J., dissenting). *See generally* Note, "Over-Protective Jurisdiction?: A State Sovereignty Theory of Federal Questions," 102 *Harv. L. Rev.* 1948 (1989) (criticizing overly expansive views of protective jurisdiction).

118. *See* Note, "Rules of Decision in Nondiversity Suits," 69 *Yale L. J.* 1428, 1450–51 (1960).

119. In other words, we assume that in general the protective jurisdiction theory is constitutionally sound, for the reasons already fully explicated in Professors Mishkin's and Wechsler's work and the sources cited in *supra* note 114. Readers who reject that assumption — and thus agree with Justice Frankfurter's dissenting opinion in *Textile Mills, see supra* note 117 and accompanying text — might as well go directly to the fourth genus; the remaining readers will witness the extension of Mishkin's and Wechsler's theories specifically to human rights and terrorism cases. For related discussions of protective jurisdiction in the context of the Alien Tort Statute, see Casto, "The Federal Courts' Protective Jurisdiction over Torts Committed in Violation of the Law of Nations," 18 *Conn. L. Rev.* 467, 512–25 (1986); Note, *supra* note 111, at 1018–24.

120. *See supra* notes 12–22 and accompanying text.

121. See chapter 1. For a related argument that jurisdiction in *Verlinden, see supra* notes 12–18 and accompanying text, was constitutional under the protective jurisdiction theory, see Note, *supra* note 111, at 1003–14. The Supreme Court, however, did not specifically rule on the theory's application in *Verlinden*, finding that *Osborn* simply supported jurisdiction; *see Verlinden*, 461 U.S. at 491 n.17.

122. Mishkin, *supra* note 19, at 192.

123. See chapter 8 for a discussion of those federal laws and treaties.

124. Omnibus Diplomatic Security and Antiterrorism Act, Pub. L. No. 99–399, 100 Stat. 853 (codified in scattered titles and sections as described in 22 U.S.C. § 4801 (Supp. IV 1986)).

125. Torture Victim Protection Act, S. 824, 100th Cong., 1st Sess. (1987); H.R. 1417, 100th Cong. 1st Sess. (1987).

126. *See*, respectively, titles XII (18 U.S.C. § 2331 (Supp. IV 1986)) and VIII (37 U.S.C. § 1013 (Supp. IV 1986)) of the Act.

127. If enacted, that statute would become 28 U.S.C. § 1367 and would provide a new basis of district court original jurisdiction in civil cases.

128. *Franchise Tax Bd.*, 463 U.S. 1 (1982).

129. *Id.* at 9. *Merrell Dow Pharmaceuticals v. Thompson*, 478 U.S. 804, 817 (1986), ostensibly confirmed the validity of this approach.

130. *Franchise Tax Bd.*, 463 U.S. at 13.

131. *Smith v. Kansas City Title & Trust Co.*, 255 U.S. 180 (1921).

132. *Id.* at 199.

133. The *Osborn* and *Smith* opinions agree that arising-under jurisdiction may be legitimate when just a federal question, not a federal cause of action, exists. But since *Smith* involved the *general* federal question statute, whereas *Osborn* involved a more *specific* federal question jurisdictional grant, the Supreme Court's conclusion is dubious that the former (i.e., § 1331) requires a federal element greater than the latter; *see supra* notes 12–22 and accompanying text. Perhaps the point, again, is simply that *Smith* and the fourth genus are inconsistent with any genus that requires a federal cause of action under § 1331.

134. *Republic of Philippines v. Marcos*, 806 F.2d 344 (2d Cir. 1986), *cert. denied*, 107 S. Ct. 2178 (1987).

135. *Marcos*, 806 F.2d at 354.

136. *Id.* at 344, *quoting Merrell Dow*, 478 U.S. at 810.

137. *Marcos*, 806 F.2d at 354.

138. *See supra* notes 16–18 and accompanying text about *Verlinden*. The comparison between *Verlinden* and *Marcos* is this author's; *Marcos* did not itself rely expressly upon *Verlinden*.

139. *Verlinden*, 461 U.S. at 493.

140. *Marcos*, 806 F.2d at 354 (citation omitted).

141. *Forti*, 672 F. Supp. 1531 (N.D. Cal. 1987), *modified by* 694 F. Supp. 707 (N.D. Cal. 1988).

142. *Forti*, 672 F. Supp. at 1544.

4. Judicial Authority over Nation-State Offenders

1. Foreign Sovereign Immunities Act, 28 U.S.C. §§ 1330, 1332(a)(1)–(3), 1391(f), 1441(d), 1602–11 (1982).

2. Circuit court decisions reaching this conclusin (prior to *Amerada Hess*) include *Frovola v. Union of Soviet Socialist Republics*, 761 F.2d 370, 372 (7th Cir. 1985); *McKeel v. Islamic Republic of Iran*, 722 F.2d 582, 586–87 (9th Cir. 1983), *cert. denied*, 469 U.S. 880 (1984); *Goar v. Compania Peruana de Vapores*, 688 F.2d 417, 421 (5th Cir. 1982); *Houston v. Murmansk Shipping Co.*, 667 F.2d 1151, 1153 (4th Cir. 1982); *Rex v. Compania Peruana de Vapores, S.A.*, 660 F.2d 61 (3d Cir. 1981), *cert. denied*, 102 S.Ct. 1971 (1982); *Williams v. Shipping Corp. of India*, 653 F.2d 875, 880–81 (4th Cir. 1981), *cert. denied*, 455 U.S. 982 (1982); *Ruggiero v. Compania Peruana de Vapores*, 639 F.2d 872, 875–78 (2d Cir. 1981).

See generally Leigh, "Judicial Decisions (Amerada Hess)," 82 *Am. J. Int'l L.* 126 (1988); Comment, "*Amerada Hess Shipping Corp. v. Argentine Republic:* An Alien Tort Statute Exception to Foreign Sovereign Immunity," 72 *Minn. L. Rev.* 829, 843–51 (1988). A few decisions that upheld jurisdiction under the FSIA, however, indicated that jurisdiction might additionally be available under other bases of jurisdiction; *see, e.g., Von Dardel v. Union of Soviet Socialist Republics,* 623 F. Supp. 246 (D.D.C. 1985) (upholding jurisdiction under §§ 1331 and 1350 in addition to the FSIA), as discussed in chapters 2 and 3.

   3. *Amerada Hess Shipping Corporation v. Argentine Republic,* 830 F.2d 421 (2d Cir. 1987), *rev'd,* 109 S.Ct.683 (1989).

   4. *Id.* at 425. See chapter 2 regarding the Alien Tort Statute.

   5. *Amerada Hess,* 830 F.2d at 423.

   6. *Id.* at 427.

   7. *Id.* at 431 (Kearse, J., dissenting).

   8. *Argentine Republic v. Amerada Hess Shipping Corp.,* 109 S.Ct. 683 (1989). The majority not only held that the FSIA is jurisdictionally exclusive, but that none of the FSIA's exceptions to immunity applied in the case.

   9. Although Justice Blackmun concurred in that holding, he opined that the majority opinion should not have reached the issue of whether the FSIA itself provided jurisdiction in the case, *see supra* note 8, an issue that the court of appeals had not reached and had reserved; *id.* at 692–93 (Blackmun, J., concurring in part, joined by Marshall, J.).

   10. *Id.* at 688. That conclusion was also prefigured by *Verlinden B. V. v. Central Bank of Nigeria,* 461 U.S. 480, 489, 491 n.16 (1983) (dictum) ("Congress clearly intended [FSIA] to govern all actions against foreign sovereigns").

   11. *Amerada Hess,* 109 S.Ct. at 688–89. The Court also disagreed that "Congress' failure in the FSIA to enact an express *pro tanto* repealer of the Alien Tort Statute" meant that § 1350 survived the FSIA as a jurisdictional vehicle over nation-states, *id.* at 689.

   12. By holding the FSIA to be the sole jurisdictional vehicle over nation-states, the Court necessarily implies that not just § 1350, but every other jurisdictional statute (including § 1331), is irrelevant when nation-states are sued. Chief Justice Rehnquist almost expressly said as much in *id.* at 689.

   13. *The Schooner Exchange v. McFadden,* 11 U.S. (7 Cranch) 116 (1812).

   14. *Id.* at 137. Although this opinion is often labeled the "absolute view" of sovereign immunity, Chief Justice Marshall recognized that "a prince, by acquiring private property in a foreign country, . . . may possibly be considered as so far laying down the prince, and assuming the character of a private individual," *id.* at 145.

   15. Background on the sovereign immunity doctrine's evolution is provided in Von Mehren, "The Foreign Sovereign Immunities Act of 1976," 17 *Colum. J. Transnat'l L.* 33 (1978); Note, "The Foreign Sovereign Immunities Act of 1976: Giving the Plaintiff His Day in Court," 46 *Fordham L. Rev.* 543 (1977); Note, "Sovereign Immunity," 18 *Harv. Int'l L. J.* 429 (1977).

16. See chapter 2 regarding international legal personality.

17. See § 1602 of the FSIA regarding the statute's intent. See commentaries cited in *supra* note 15 for general discussions of the FSIA.

18. See chapter 2 regarding alienage jurisdiction.

19. *Verlinden*, 461 U.S. 480 (1983). See chapter 3 regarding this case.

20. *Id.* at 493.

21. Six exceptions to immunity are contained in § 1605: a waiver exception (§ 1605(a)(1)); a commercial-activity exception (§ 1605(a) (2)); a property exception (§ 1605(a)(3)); an immovable-property exception (§ 1605(a)(4)); a tort exception (§ 1605(a)(5)); and an exception in certain arbitration contexts (§ 1605(a)(6)). In addition, § 1605(b) concerns nonimmunity in certain admiralty settings, and § 1607 excludes immunity when a nation-state is sued on a counterclaim, within certain limitations.

22. The district courts have jurisdiction over nation-states to the extent that liability is permitted under § 1606.

23. 28 U.S.C. § 1605(a)(5) (1982).

24. *de Letelier v. Republic of Chile*, 488 F. Supp. 655, 668–73 (D.D.C.) (jurisdiction upheld), 502 F. Supp. 259 (D.D.C. 1980) (judgment for plaintiffs).

25. *See Liu v. Republic of China*, 642 F. Supp. 297, 303–5 (N.D. Cal. 1986). Even when the defendant's tort occurs in the United States, § 1605(a) (5) provides two exceptions to the tort exception to immunity. Under § 1605(a)(5)(A), the tort exception is inapplicable to claims "based upon the exercise or performance or the failure to exercise or perform a discretionary function regardless of whether the discretion be abused." A "discretionary function" has been defined as including the "'planning level' of governmental activity," as opposed to the "'operational level'" of implementing governmental plans and policy; *Olsen by Sheldon v. Government of Mexico*, 729 F.2d 641, 647 (9th Cir.), *quoting Thompson v. United States*, 592 F.2d 1104, 1111 (9th Cir. 1979) (from the context of the Federal Tort Claims Act), *cert. denied*, 469 U.S. 917 (1984). *de Letelier*, however, rejected the argument that the discretionary-function exception to the tort exception applied to the ambassador's assassination because the offense "is clearly contrary to the precepts of humanity as recognized in both national and international law," *de Letelier*, 488 F. Supp. at 673. Similarly, *Liu* held that § 1605(a) 5)(A) is unavailable when a sovereign's policy allegedly includes killing United States citizens, *Liu*, 642 F. Supp. at 304–5. A second exception to the tort exception is found in § 1605(a)(5)(B), making the tort exception inapplicable to claims "arising out of malicious prosecution, abuse of process, libel, slander, misrepresentation, deceit, or interference with contract rights." § 1605(a)(5)(B) was not relevant to either *de Letelier* or *Liu*.

26. The examples in text are extrapolated, respectively, from *Siderman de Blake v. Republic of Argentina*, No. CV-82-1772 (C.D. Cal. Sept. 28, 1984) (available on LEXIS, Genfed library, Courts file), *vacated and dismissed* (C.D. Cal. Mar. 7, 1985) (FSIA grounds for dismissal), and *Tel-Oren v. Libyan Arab*

Republic, 726 F.2d 774 (D.C. Cir. 1984) (per curiam) (FSIA grounds for dismissing complaint against Libya), *cert. denied*, 740 U.S. 1003 (1985).

27. *Amerada Hess*, 109 S.Ct. at 683; *see supra* notes 3–12 and accompanying text.

28. *Martin v. Republic of South Africa*, 836 F.2d 91 (2d Cir. 1987).

29. *Id.* at 93–96. The circuit court opinion discusses only the commercial-activity exception and does not give any indication about whether the plaintiff raised the tort exception at any stage of the litigation. It may reasonably be surmised that § 1605(a)(5)'s territorial limitation either caused plaintiff not to raise that provision or caused the district court to reject easily that provision's relevance. The district court's opinion in the case is unpublished.

30. *Persinger v. Islamic Republic of Iran*, 729 F.2d 835 (D.C. Cir. 1984).

31. *Id.* at 838–42.

32. More fully, 28 U.S.C. § 1603(c) (1982) defines the United States to include "all territory and waters, continental or insular, subject to the jurisdiction of the United States."

33. See *supra* note 23 and accompanying text.

34. *Persinger*, 729 F.2d at 842 (emphasis added).

35. *See id.* at 845 (Edwards, J., dissenting in part and concurring in part). This point relates to the United States' international jurisdiction under the "objective territorial" principle (or the "effects doctrine"); see chapter 7 for a discussion of this topic.

36. *See generally Persinger*, 729 F.2d at 842–43 (marshalling support from precedent and legislative history for such a ruling).

37. 28 U.S.C. § 1605(a)(1) (1982).

38. Paust, "Draft Brief Concerning Claims to Foreign Sovereign Immunity and Human Rights: Nonimmunity for Violations of International Law under the FSIA," 8 *Houston J. Int'l L.* 49, 65–67 (1985); *see also* Belsky, Merva, & Roht-Arriaza, "Implied Waiver under the FSIA: A Proposed Exception to Immunity for Violations of Peremptory Norms of International Law," 77 *Cal. L. Rev.* 365 (1989).

39. Although this argument is drawn particularly from Professor Paust's fine work, *supra* note 38, it has been cast here in terms that especially overlap with, and relate to, the discussion in chapter 3 of treaty rights and remedies. Professor Paust also more broadly argues that, by simply being bound by international law, a nation-state necessarily waives its immunity when it violates that law. That broader argument is not addressed here because it actually overlaps with, and is thus considered by, our subsequent discussion of whether sovereign immunity is per se unavailable when the defendant violates international law; *see infra* notes 51–55 and accompanying text.

40. *Von Dardel v. Union of Soviet Socialist Republics*, 623 F. Supp. 246 (D.D.C. 1985).

41. *Von Dardel* sustained jurisdiction under §§ 1331 and 1350 and the FSIA,

see chapters 2 and 3, although, following *Amerada Hess*, the FSIA is the only jurisdictional vehicle available over the Soviet Union.

42. *Von Dardel*, 623 F. Supp. at 255 (footnote omitted).

43. *Id.* at 255–56.

44. *Id.* at 256. The court's decision also drew support from 28 U.S.C. § 1604 (1982), which makes sovereign immunity "[s]ubject to existing international agreements to which the United States is a party at the time of the enactment of" the FSIA. Under the court's interpretation, the claim of sovereign immunity was subject to the Internationally Protected Persons Convention and the Vienna Convention on Diplomatic Immunity. If the Soviet Union violated those treaties, it could not claim the FSIA's protection because the statute is *subject to* (or inferior to) the norms of those treaties; *Von Dardel*, 623 F. Supp. at 254–55. This § 1604 argument overlaps with the waiver exception argument. *See generally* Paust, *supra* note 38, at 61–65; Comment, "The Foreign Sovereign Immunities Act and International Human Rights Agreements: How They Coexist," 17 *U.S.F.L. Rev.* 71 (1982). *But see Frovola v. Union of Soviet Socialist Republics*, 761 F.2d 370, 373–76 (7th Cir. 1985) (rejecting the § 1604 argument).

45. *Frovola*, 761 F.2d 370 (7th Cir. 1985).

46. After the lawsuit had been filed, the Soviet Union permitted the plaintiff's husband to emigrate to the United States, at which point the plaintiff withdrew her request for injunctive relief, but maintained her claim for damages, *id.* at 371.

47. *Id.* at 378.

48. This discussion of *Von Dardel* focuses on the Internationally Protected Persons Convention, rather than on the Vienna Convention on Diplomatic Immunity, because the former was extensively discussed in chapter 3. The former also provides a private right and remedy more readily than the latter does.

49. See chapter 3 for further information on causes of action in relation to these conventions. Those treaties may provide a private cause of action in various ways; this depends upon the terms of each instrument, whether an instrument is in force in the United States, and the theory under which one evaluates the existence of a private cause of action. Again, some treaties may expressly provide a private cause of action, while others may do so impliedly, see *id.*

50. *Frovola*, 761 F.2d at 377–78, amply identifies such precedent. Even though the distinction between the legal personalities of nonstate actors and nation-states should not be exaggerated, see chapters 2 and 9, federal judges often act with particular restraint when the latter are involved in a case.

51. Paust, *supra* note 38, at 59 (emphasis added).

52. See chapter 5 regarding the act-of-state doctrine, which sometimes applies when nonstate actors as well as nation-states are sued.

53. *Compare Von Dardel*, 623 F. Supp. at 253–54 (immunity under FSIA does not extend to "clear violations of universally recognized principles of international law," including offenses against diplomats) *and de Letelier*, 488 F. Supp.

at 673 (discretionary-function exception to tort exception to sovereign immunity, § 1605(a)(5)(A), does not apply to the assassination of the former Chilean ambassador, which "is clearly contrary to the precepts of humanity as recognized in both national and international law") *with Berkovitz v. Islamic Republic of Iran*, 735 F.2d 329, 331 (9th Cir.), *cert. denied*, 469 U.S. 1035 (1984) (rejecting argument that "unfriendly nature of political assassination," even coupled with animosity between United States and Iran, provides exception to sovereign immunity) *and Frovola*, 558 F. Supp. at 363 n.3 (N.D. Ill. 1983) (rejecting argument that where emigration of plaintiff's spouse is denied, Soviet Union's jurisdictional immunity is impliedly waived "from the fact that the Soviet Union violated international law"), *aff'd*, 761 F.2d 370, (7th Cir. 1985).

54. *E.g., Frovola*, 761 F.2d at 370.

55. *See supra* note 53.

56. *See* 28 U.S.C. § 1602.

5. The Separation of Powers in Human Rights and Terrorism Cases

1. See the discussion of this topic in chapter 2.

2. See chapter 1.

3. *Baker v. Carr*, 369 U.S. 186, 210 (1962).

4. C. Wright, *Law of Federal Courts* 74 (4th ed. 1983).

5. *See Colegrove v. Green*, 328 U.S. 549 (1946). Some partial reliance on the doctrine was displayed in *Gilligan v. Morgan*, 413 U.S. 1 (1973); *see also Goldwater v. Carter*, 444 U.S. 996 (1979) (Rehnquist, J., plurality opinion concurring in judgment), discussed in *infra* notes 22–29 and accompanying text. A recent, swift, and potent rejection of the political question defense occurred in the important case of *INS v. Chadha*, 462 U.S. 919, 942–43 (1983).

6. McGowan, "Congressmen in Court: The New Plaintiffs," 15 *Ga. L. Rev.* 241, 256 (1981).

7. Henkin, "Is There a 'Political Question' Doctrine?" 85 *Yale L. J.* 597, 597 (1976).

8. *Id.* at 601. *See generally* Champlin & Schwarz, "Political Question Doctrine and Allocation of the Foreign Affairs Power," 13 *Hofstra L. Rev.* 215 (1985). *But see* Mulhern, "In Defense of the Political Question Doctrine," 137 *U. Pa. L. Rev.* 97 (1988).

9. *See generally infra* notes 38–66 and accompanying text.

10. *Baker*, 369 U.S. at 186.

11. *Id.* at 208–10, 226–37. As discussed therein, the federal judiciary's relationship with its coordinate federal branches, not with the states, gives rise to political question considerations.

12. *Id.* at 210.

13. *Id.* at 217.

14. *Id.* at 209.

15. *Id.* at 217.

16. This is discussed in chapter 1.

17. *Baker,* 369 U.S. at 211.

18. *Id.* at 211–12.

19. *See id.* at 212–13.

20. See chapter 1. The subjects on the list of nonjusticiable topics (in the text) are especially within the president's domain.

21. See chapter 1.

22. *Goldwater,* 444 U.S. at 996 (1979).

23. *Goldwater,* 617 F.2d 697 (D.C. Cir. 1979).

24. *Goldwater,* 444 U.S. at 996. Four Supreme Court Justices — Chief Justice Burger and Justices Rehnquist, Stewart, and Stevens — voted to dismiss and vacate under the political question doctrine; Justice Powell agreed with the result to dismiss and vacate, but on ripeness, not political question, grounds; Justice Marshall concurred in the result only; Justices White and Blackmun would have set the case for plenary consideration, rather than the expedited review that the case received; and Justice Brennan would have affirmed the circuit court's judgment in the president's favor.

25. *Id.* at 1002 (Rehnquist, J., concurring in judgment).

26. *Id. at* 1004 (Rehnquist, J., concurring in judgment) (footnote omitted).

27. *Id.* at 999 (Powell, J., concurring in judgment).

28. *See id.* at 998–1002 (Powell, J., concurring in the judgment).

29. *Id.* at 1006 (Brennan, J., dissenting).

30. *Japan Whaling Association v. American Cetacean Society,* 478 U.S. 221 (1986).

31. *See id.* at 225–26.

32. See chapter 1.

33. *See Japan Whaling,* 478 U.S. at 231–41.

34. *Id.* at 229–30.

35. *Id.* at 230.

36. *Id.*

37. *See id.* at 241–50 (Marshall, J., dissenting). Although the dissent did not discuss the political question doctrine, it obviously did not view the case as raising a political question, since it would have held for the conservation groups upon reaching the merits.

38. *Tel-Oren v. Libyan Arab Republic,* 726 F.2d 774 (D.C. Cir. 1984) (per curiam), *cert. denied,* 470 U.S. 1003 (1985).

39. See introduction and chapter 2 for additional information.

40. *Tel-Oren,* 726 F.2d at 826 n.5 (Robb, J., concurring).

41. *Id.* (Robb, J., concurring).

42. *Id.* at 826–27 (Robb, J., concurring).

43. *Id.* at 827 (Robb, J., concurring).

44. *Id.* at 796 (Edwards, J., concurring) (some emphasis added).

45. *Filartiga v. Pena-Irala*, 630 F.2d 876 (2d Cir. 1980). See chapter 2 regarding *Filartiga*.

46. *See Tel-Oren*, 726 F.2d at 827 (Robb, J., concurring).

47. *See supra* notes 17–19, 30–37 and accompanying text.

48. *See supra* note 26 and accompanying text.

49. *See supra* note 37 and accompanying text.

50. Scharpf, "Judicial Review and the Political Question: A Functional Analysis," 75 *Yale L. J.* 517, 584 (1966).

51. *Id. See generally* Lobel, "The Limits of Constitutional Power: Conflicts Between Foreign Policy and International Law," 71 *Va. L. Rev.* 1071, 1153–66 (1985).

52. *See generally* Cole, "Challenging Covert War: The Politics of the Political Question Doctrine," 26 *Harv. Int'l L. J.* 155 (1985); Tigar, "Judicial Power, The 'Political Question Doctrine,' and Foreign Relations," 17 *U.C.L.A. L. Rev.* 1135 (1970); Recent Developments, "Constitutional Law: Political Question Doctrine and Conduct of Foreign Policy," 25 *Harv. Int'l L.J.* 433 (1984).

53. See F. Boyle, *Defending Civil Resistance under International Law* (1987). *See generally The Law of Dissent and Riots* (M. C. Bassiouni ed. 1971); *Civil Disobedience in America* (D. Weber ed. 1978).

54. *Nixon v. Administrator of Gen. Servs.*, 433 U.S. 425, 443 (1977).

55. *U.S. v. Nixon*, 418 U.S. 683, 707 (1974).

56. *Bowsher v. Synar*, 478 U.S. 714, 722 (1986) (particularly referring to Madison's reliance on Montesquieu in The Federalist No. 47).

57. *Marbury v. Madison*, 5 U.S. (1 Cranch) 137, 177 (1803).

58. *Tel-Oren* offers a valuable example because Judges Robb and Edwards specifically debated the political question doctrine at length. Judge Bork also referred to the doctrine, but rested his concurrence in the dismissal on other grounds, partly due to the "murky and unsettled" contours of the political question doctrine; *Tel-Oren*, 726 F.2d at 803 n.8 (Bork, J., concurring). Judge Edwards critically argued, however, that Judges Robb's and Bork's ultimate positions were one and the same; *see id.* at 790 (Edwards, J., concurring).

59. See *supra* note 15 and accompanying text for *Baker's* criteria.

60. *See Tel-Oren*, 726 F.2d at 797 (Edwards, J., concurring). See chapter 2 regarding the Alien Tort Statute.

61. *See generally supra* notes 19–20 and accompanying text.

62. *Japan Whaling*, 478 U.S. at 230; *see also supra* notes 34–36 and accompanying text.

63. *See Goldwater*, 444 U.S. at 1001 (Powell, J., concurring in judgment) (arguing that if the case were ripe for review, its "final disposition of the question presented . . . would eliminate, rather than create, multiple constitutional interpretations"). *See supra* note 28 and accompanying text.

The Supreme Court, while considering whether to grant a petition for certiorari in *Tel-Oren*, invited the solicitor general to file briefs in the case "expressing the views of the United States," 469 U.S. 811 (1984). The solicitor general subsequently filed a brief that argued against certiorari, and the Supreme Court denied the petition. The solicitor general's position was predicated upon the divergent positions taken by the D.C. Circuit panel: "[F]urther review of the judgment below, without the benefit of a majority opinion, would be imprudent and premature," Brief for the United States as Amicus Curiae at 9, *Tel-Oren*, 726 F.2d at 774, *reprinted in* 24 I.L.M. 427, 432 (1985). Hence the solicitor general's position neither relates directly to the separation-of-powers concerns nor contradicts the author's discussion of the political question doctrine. In fact, the solicitor general's brief expressly suggested that the political question issue "is not properly presented" for review or discussion "because a majority of the [appellate] panel voted to affirm the dismissal on other grounds," Brief, 24 I.L.M. at 431 n.8.

64. *See supra* notes 52–53 and accompanying text.

65. See chapter 4 regarding sovereign immunity. See chapter 6 regarding why the political question doctrine does not apply even when nation-state defendants lack immunity; the doctrine should be relevant only when the federal government is a party to a lawsuit.

66. *Tel-Oren*, 726 F.2d at 797 n.30 (Edwards, J., concurring). Judge Edwards was referring generically to the relevance of the act-of-state doctrine in most human rights and terrorism cases — in contrast to the complete irrelevance of the political question doctrine. The act-of-state doctrine was not relevant to the specific case of *Tel-Oren, see infra* note 90 and accompanying text.

67. *See generally* Bazyler, "Abolishing the Act of State Doctrine," 134 *U. Penn. L. Rev.* 325 (1986); Chow, "Rethinking the Act of State Doctrine: An Analysis in Terms of Jurisdiction to Prescribe," 62 *Wash. L. Rev.* 397 (1987).

68. See Henkin, "Act of State Today: Recollections in Tranquility," 6 *Colum. J. Transnat'l L.* 175, 178–82 (1967).

69. See chapter 4 regarding sovereign immunity.

70. *But see infra* note 84 regarding the statutory treatment of the act-of-state doctrine in the limited context of nationalization.

71. *Underhill v. Hernandez*, 168 U.S. 250 (1897).

72. *Id.* at 252. Professor Bazyler has referred to *Underhill's* act-of-state discussion as being dictum. *See* Bazyler, *supra* note 67, at 331–33. *Underhill*, nevertheless, as Bazyler acknowledges, has been repeatedly viewed as representing the "traditional" or "classic" statement of the doctrine.

73. *Banco Nacional de Cuba v. Sabbatino*, 376 U.S. 398 (1964). *Sabbatino* was the first of a triptych of relatively recent Supreme Court cases involving the act-of-state doctrine, with the other cases being *Alfred Dunhill of London, Inc. v. Republic of Cuba*, 425 U.S. 682 (1976), and *First Nat'l City Bank v. Banco Nacional de Cuba*, 406 U.S. 759 (1972).

74. *Sabbatino*, 376 U.S. at 421.

75. *See* post-*Sabbatino* cases cited in *supra* note 73.

76. *Sabbatino*, 376 U.S. at 421.

77. *Id.* at 423.

78. *Id.*

79. *Id.*

80. *Id., quoting Baker*, 369 U.S. at 211.

81. *Sabbatino*, 376 U.S. at 428.

82. *Id.* at 427–28.

83. *Id.* at 428 (footnote omitted).

84. The (second) "Hickenlooper Amendment," 22 U.S.C. § 2370(e)(2) (1982) (also called the "*Sabbatino* Amendment"), as judicially interpreted, directs courts not to apply the act-of-state doctrine specifically when a nationalization violates international law and the expropriated property ends up in the United States, unless the president specifically advises that the doctrine should be applied. Chapter 6 offers additional information on the Hickenlooper Amendment. With the exception of the nationalization context, however, this legislation did not affect *Sabbatino's* analytical matrix, which courts have subsequently used in various contexts, including human rights and terrorism cases; *see, e.g., infra* notes 92–93, 96–97, and accompanying text.

85. *See infra* notes 103–4 and accompanying text. Federal judges may sometimes request the executive department's input. *Id.* Executive-judicial communications regarding the act-of-state doctrine may also be pursuant to a statute. *See supra* note 84.

86. *See* Bazyler, *supra* note 67, at 368–74. It has even been suggested that there may be a per se "human rights exception" to the act-of-state doctrine, *see, e.g., id.*, at 373–74, although that exception, if one exists, may simply be rationalized as supported by the *Sabbatino* criteria; *see infra* notes 88–105 and accompanying text.

87. *See, e.g.*, Bazyler, *supra* note 67; Chow, *supra* note 67; Davis, "Domestic Development of International Law: A Proposal for an International Concept of the Act of State Doctrine," 20 *Tex. Int'l L. J.* 341 (1985); Note, "Judicial Balancing of Foreign Policy Considerations: Comity and Errors Under the Act of State Doctrine," 35 *Stan. L. Rev.* 327 (1983).

88. See chapter 4.

89. These three examples are drawn from, respectively, *Forti v. Suarez-Mason*, 672 F. Supp. 1531 (N.D. Cal. 1987), *modified by*, 694 F. Supp. 707 (N.D. Cal. 1988); *Filartiga*, 630 F.2d at 876; and *Handel v. Artukovic*, 601 F. Supp. 1421 (C.D. Cal. 1985).

90. It is for this reason that the act-of-state doctrine was inapplicable in *Tel-Oren*. Under the assumption that the PLO acted without sovereign support, Judge Edwards, for instance, indicated that the doctrine simply does not apply "to acts by *non-recognized entities* committed in the territory of a recognized state," *Tel-Oren*, 726 F.2d at 790 (Edwards, J., concurring) (emphasis added). At the same time, nonstate actors can violate international law; see chapter 2.

91. This second and significant assumption was ostensibly found lacking in, *e.g., Dunhill,* 425 U.S. at 694 (repudiation of debt); *Filartiga,* 630 F.2d at 889 (torture); and *Forti,* 672 F. Supp. at 1546 (human rights violations). As these cases should suggest, it is not always easy to determine whether the defendant's behavior was sovereign-sponsored. For instance, in *Filartiga,* the police official and his act of torture had international ramifications and violated the law of nations; see chapter 2. But the act-of-state doctrine was arguably inapplicable because the defendant's behavior violated "the Constitution and laws of . . . Paraguay, and wholly [was] unratified by the nation's government," *Filartiga,* 630 F.2d at 889. Even though the defendant's offense may not have been an act of state, the *Filartiga* court thought it necessary to suggest that the *Sabbatino* matrix supported justiciability in the case at hand, *see infra* notes 92–93 and accompanying text.

92. *Filartiga,* 630 F.2d at 881.

93. *Id. Filartiga's* act-of-state point here may be dictum, *see supra* note 91.

94. *Restatement (Third) of Foreign Relations Law* § 702 [hereinafter *Restatement*]. *See generally* Paust, "Federal Jurisdiction over Extraterritorial Acts of Terrorism and Nonimmunity for Foreign Violators of International Law under the FSIA and the Act of State Doctrine," 23 *Va. J. Int'l L.* 191 (1983).

95. *Restatement, supra* note 94, at § 443 comment c.

96. *See Forti,* 672 F. Supp. at 1544–47, which is discussed in chapter 2. The *Forti* court stressed the heinous and condemnable nature of the defendant's violation of "fundamental human rights," *id.* at 1546, which is implicitly linked with *Sabbatino's* first criterion. Although the court referred to *Sabbatino's* analysis, it did not, however, actually rely upon that analysis because it was uncertain that the defendant's acts were committed under the color of state authority or ratified by the *de facto* military government in Argentina, *id.* at 1546; *see also supra* note 91. The defendant's behavior, nevertheless, constituted an international law violation.

97. *See Von Dardel v. Union of Soviet Socialist Republics,* 623 F. Supp. 246, 253–54, (D.D.C. 1985), which is discussed in chapters 3 and 4.

98. *Sabbatino,* 376 U.S. at 428 (emphasis added).

99. *See Filartiga,* 630 F.2d at 881; R. Falk, *The Role of Domestic Courts in the International Legal Order* 9–10 (1964).

100. This fact is indicated by the citations to these instruments in the introduction. The four Geneva Conventions, although not United Nations instruments, also have been subscribed to by the vast majority of nation-states, as indicated by the citations to these instruments in the introduction.

101. See chapters 3 and 8.

102. In a sense, this point relates to the issue of whether a nonstate actor's behavior in a case is actually sovereign-linked or sovereign-sponsored, *see supra* note 91 and accompanying text.

103. *First Nat'l City Bank,* 406 U.S. at 769–70 (1972). This point generally

relates to the validity of the "Bernstein exception," by which the act-of-state defense is rejected when the executive processes a letter to the judiciary, suggesting that the doctrine is not necessary in a specific case. Only a plurality of the Supreme Court has approved of this exception, *see* Bazyler, *supra* note 67, at 368–70.

104. This occurred in *Tel-Oren*, in which the Supreme Court did not grant certiorari, ostensibly following the solicitor general's advice in this regard, *see supra* note 63. This also occurred in *Filartiga*, in which, at the Second Circuit's request, the Departments of State and Justice filed a joint amicus memorandum recommending that jurisdiction be sustained; jurisdiction subsequently was sustained.

Professor Falk has strongly counselled against virtually any judicial deference to ad hoc executive branch suggestions under the act-of-state doctrine; *see* R. Falk, *supra* note 99, at 10–13. But his view seems unreasonably extreme and absolutist. Falk's perspective may have been motivated by the fact that he focused almost entirely on federal courts in relation to the world legal order, but insufficiently in relation to the political branches.

105. *See generally Forti*, 672 F. Supp. at 1531, concerning the Argentina scenario. *See generally* Recent Development, "Alien Torts Claims Act — Act of State Doctrine — Act of State Doctrine Requires Dismissal of Human Rights Claims Brought Against Former Philippine President Residing in the United States," 27 *Va. J. Int'l L.* 433 (1987), regarding the Philippines scenario.

106. *Gulf Oil Corp. v. Gilbert*, 330 U.S. 501, 508 (emphasis added); *see also Koster v. (American) Lumbermens Mutual Casualty Co.*, 330 U.S. 518 (1947). *See generally* Stein, "Forum Non Conveniens, and the Redundancy of Court-Access Doctrine," 133 *U. Penn. L. Rev.* 781, 812–22 (1985). It may be noted that 28 U.S.C. § 1404 is relevant when a case is to be transferred from one federal district court to another federal district court on convenience grounds.

107. *Piper Aircraft Co. v. Reyno*, 454 U.S. 235, 254 n.22 (1981) (citation omitted).

108. *Id.*

109. *Phoenix Canada Oil Co. Ltd. v. Texaco, Inc.*, 78 F.R.D. 445, 455 (D. Del. 1978), *quoting* C. Wright, *Law of Federal Courts* 186 n.23 (3d ed. 1976); *see also Restatement (Second) of Conflict of Law* § 84 comment c (1971) ("the action will not be dismissed unless a suitable alternative forum is available to the plaintiff").

110. See *supra* note 106 and accompanying text.

111. *See Filartiga*, 630 F.2d at 878.

112. Upon remand from the Second Circuit, the district court briefly considered and rejected the *forum non conveniens* defense. The district court's particular rationale for rejecting the defense was that the defendant had defaulted in the case, *see Filartiga*, 577 F. Supp. 860, 862 (E.D.N.Y. 1984).

113. *Piper Aircraft*, 454 U.S. at 254 n.22.

114. *Phoenix Canada Oil*, 78 F.R.D. at 455–56.

115. *Id.* at 456 (footnote omitted). In *Gibbon v. American University of Beirut*, No. 83 Civ. 1183 (S.D.N.Y. Sept. 27, 1983) (available on LEXIS, Genfed library, Courts file), also not a human rights or terrorism case, the court indicated that terrorist activities within a foreign city (Beirut) may possibly influence a federal court against dismissing in favor of a foreign tribunal, although *forum non conveniens* ultimately did not cause dismissal in that case.

116. *In re Union Carbide Corp. Gas Plant Disaster*, 809 F.2d 195 (2d Cir. 1987).

117. *Id.* at 198. Some conditions were placed on that dismissal. *See generally* Galanter, "Legal Torpor: Why So Little Has Happened in India after the Bhopol Tragedy," 20 *Tex. Int'l L. J.* 273 (1985); Recent Developments, "Jurisdiction: Foreign Plaintiffs, Forum Non Conveniens, and Litigation Against Multinational Corporations," 28 *Harv. Int'l L. J.* 202 (1987); Judicial Decisions, "Forum Non Conveniens — Conditional Dismissal of Tort Claim by Foreign Plaintiffs," 80 *Am. J. Int'l L.* 964 (1986).

118. *Gulf Oil*, 330 U.S. at 508.

119. *Piper Aircraft*, 454 U.S. at 255–56.

120. *Gulf Oil*, 330 U.S. at 508.

121. See Randall, "Special U.S. Civil Jurisdiction," in *Legal Responses to International Terrorism* 89, 109 (M. C. Bassiouni ed. 1988).

6. Legislative Prescriptions

1. See the discussion of this point in chapter 3.

2. That jurisdictional obligation is discussed in *id.*

3. See the discussion of this point in chapter 8.

4. See *id.* The treaties establish the obligation to prosecute those who commit the relevant offenses, despite any link between the forum and the offense, unless the forum extradites the offender. That responsibility is permissive, not obligatory, under the Apartheid Convention, *id.* Universal jurisdiction over genocide exists under customary law, *id.*

5. See the discussion of this issue in chapters 7 and 8.

6. See the discussion of the war crimes trials in chapter 8.

7. This point is also mentioned in chapters 8 and 9.

8. *Filartiga v. Pena-Irala*, 630 F.2d 876 (2d Cir. 1980). See chapter 2 regarding this case.

9. See chapter 9 for a discussion of this topic.

10. These cases are discussed in chapter 1.

11. See chapters 2 and 3 for discussions of these statutes.

12. See chapter 5 regarding these doctrines.

13. This attempt to create a new jurisdictional statute regarding nonstate defendants draws somewhat upon the author's earlier suggestions for revising 28 U.S.C. § 1350. See Randall, "Further Inquiries into the Alien Tort Statute and a Recommendation," 18 *N.Y.U. J. Int'l L. & Pol.* 473, 511–32. See *id.* for references

to other suggestions and proposals by commentators and lawmakers for revising § 1350. The Torture Victim Protection Act, S. 824, 100th Cong., 1st Sess. (1987); H.R. 1417, 100th Cong., 1st Sess. (1987), which has been pending in Congress for several years, would provide a new federal jurisdictional grant over claims involving torture or extrajudicial killings.

14. See chapter 4 for the discussion of the FSIA.

15. That interpretation is mentioned in *id.*

16. See chapters 2 and 3 for the discussion of these problems.

17. These foreign relations implications are discussed in chapters 1 and 2.

18. See chapter 2 regarding how those requirements may undermine the federal judiciary's authority over international cases.

19. Art. III, § 2, cl. 1. See chapter 1 for an analysis of the arising-under clause.

20. This point is made in chapter 2.

21. Art. III, § 2, cl. 1. See chapter 2 for an analysis of alienage jurisdiction.

22. Art. III, § 2, cl. 1. See chapter 2 for an analysis of diversity jurisdiction.

23. *Osborn v. Bank of the United States*, 22 U.S. (9 Wheat) 738, 822, 824 (1824). See chapter 3 regarding this case.

24. See chapter 3 for a discussion of this issue.

25. These cases are discussed in chapter 3.

26. *Verlinden B.V. v. Central Bank of Nigeria*, 461 U.S. 480 (1983). This case is discussed in chapters 3 and 4.

27. Alienage jurisdiction did not exist because a foreign corporation was suing an instrumentality of a foreign nation-state, as discussed in chapters 2 and 3.

28. *Verlinden*, 461 U.S. at 494.

29. *Id.* at 493.

30. Although FSIA cases involve nation-state defendants and § 1390 cases will involve nonstate defendants, the latter will still raise foreign relations implications due to the very nature of human rights and terrorism cases, see chapter 3.

31. This point is made in chapter 2.

32. This point is made in chapter 3. The fourth genus of § 1331 jurisdiction does not require a federal cause of action, but only a federal question, and human rights and terrorism cases can usually meet that requisite easily, see *id.*

33. Congress is empowered to "define and punish Piracies and Felonies committed on the high seas, and Offenses against the Law of Nations," art. I, § 8, cl. 10. See chapters 2 and 3 regarding Congress's domestic authority to implement international norms in both the civil and criminal settings. See chapter 1 regarding the full expanse of Congress's express and implied international authority.

34. *See generally* C. Wright, A. Miller & E. Cooper, 13B *Federal Practice and Procedure* §§ 3568–3585 (2d ed. 1984) [hereinafter *Federal Practice*].

35. This conclusion is supported by both domestic and international jurisdictional concerns. See chapter 7 regarding domestic jurisdiction under international law.

36. This analysis of extraterritorial jurisdiction is contained in chapter 2.

37. Extraterritorial universal jurisdiction is examined in chapter 8.

38. See *id.*

39. This jurisdictional obligation is analyzed in *id.*

40. See the discussion of this problem in chapters 2 and 3.

41. See chapter 3 for this documentation of private causes of action.

42. See chapters 8 and 9 for this documentation of compulsory domestic civil jurisdiction.

43. *Banco Nacional de Cuba v. Sabbatino*, 376 U.S. 398 (1964).

44. See chapter 5 for the discussion of the "*Sabbatino* matrix."

45. See *id.* The third prong of the *Sabbatino* matrix, the least important, is not relevant to our present discussion, see *id.*

46. These early offenses are examined in chapters 1 and 2.

47. See chapter 3 regarding the United States' recognition of those norms. See chapter 1 regarding the fact that international law is part of federal law.

48. *See generally* Current Developments, "Revision of ILO Convention No. 107," 81 *Am. J. Int'l L.* 756 (1987); Nettheim, "Indigenous Rights, Human Rights and Australia," 61 *Australian L. J.* 291 (1987); "Are Indigenous Populations Entitled to International Juridical Personality," 1985 *Am. Soc. Int'l L. Proc.* 189 (R. Falk, presiding).

49. This statement reiterates points about legal personality made in chapter 2.

50. See *id.*

51. *Tel-Oren v. Libyan Arab Republic*, 726 F.2d 774 (D.C. Cir. 1984) (per curiam), *cert. denied*, 470 U.S. 1003 (1985).

52. Although we have not previously discussed the superior-orders defense, it somewhat overlaps with our examination of the legal personality of nonstate actors and the capacity of those actors to violate international law, see chapter 2.

53. *See, e.g.,* treaties discussed in chapters 3 and 8. *See generally* L. Green, *Superior Orders in National and International Law* (1976); D'Amato, "Superior Orders vs. Command Responsibility," 80 *Am. J. Int'l L.* 604 (1986); Paust, "My Lai and Vietnam: Norms, Myths, and Leader Responsibility," 57 *Military L. Rev.* 99, 170–75, (1972); Levie, "Some Comments on Professor D'Amato's Paradox," 80 *Am. J. Int'l L.* 608 (1986).

54. See chapter 5 for the analysis of the political question doctrine.

55. See *id.*

56. See *id.* regarding the limited nature of this doctrine.

57. *Baker v. Carr*, 369 U.S. 186, 217 (1962).

58. See chapter 5.

59. See *id; supra* notes 43–45 and accompanying text.

60. *Restatement (Third) of Foreign Relations Law* § 443 comment c.

61. See chapter 5 regarding this "safety valve" under caselaw, rather than statutory law.

62. 22 U.S.C. § 2370(e)(2)(1982) (also called the "*Sabbatino* Amendment").

63. *Id. See generally* L. Henkin, R. Pugh, H. Smit & O. Schachter, *International Law* 178–80 (2d ed. 1987). Although the Hickenlooper Amendment reversed *Sabbatino*'s result specifically in the nationalization context, it did not influence the application of *Sabbatino*'s three-prong analysis in other contexts; see chapter 5.

64. See chapter 5 for the discussion of *forum non conveniens*.

65. *See generally Federal Practice, supra* note 34, § 3828.

66. In addition, 28 U.S.C. § 1610, concerning the attachment of and execution upon a nation-state's property, might also need to be amended to reflect the addition of model 1605(a)(7).

67. Only the subsection labeled "(7)" constitutes a proposed legislative revision. § 1605's title and § 1605(a)'s prefatory language (introducing all of the immunity exceptions) are taken from the existing FSIA.

68. See chapter 4 for the analysis of the tort exception.

69. See chapters 3, 8, and 9 for the demonstration that these norms are basic and obligatory.

70. See chapters 8 and 9.

71. The ILC's work is examined in chapter 8.

72. These norms are discussed in *id.*

73. 28 U.S.C. § 1602 (1982).

74. 28 U.S.C. § 1605(a)(2)–(4) (1982).

75. The FSIA does, however, govern and afford both federal and state court jurisdiction over nation-states, 28 U.S.C. § 1605(a). Under current law, jurisdiction is rarely exclusive in the federal courts over nonstate and nation-state defendants in cases having international components, see chapters 1, 2, and 4. For that reason, none of our model revisions create exclusive federal jurisdiction.

76. The availability of constitutional arising-under jurisdiction in human rights and terrorism cases, even in the absence of alienage or diversity jurisdiction, is examined in *supra* notes 21–30 and accompanying text.

77. See chapters 8 and 9 regarding the ordering of international norms and the implications of this ordering.

78. See chapters 8 and 9 for these discussions.

79. See chapter 5 regarding this limitation on the political question doctrine.

80. See *supra* notes 62–63 and accompanying text.

7. Federal Courts as Global Actors

1. *Filartiga v. Pena-Irala,* 630 F.2d 876 (2d Cir. 1980).

2. See introduction for a description of the cases under consideration.

3. Of course, securities cases not so factually confined to domestic acts and actors can raise questions about jurisdiction under international law, see *infra* note 25 and accompanying text.

4. *See generally* I. Brownlie, *Principles of Public International Law* 298–320

(3d ed. 1979); O. Schachter, *International Law in Theory and Practice* 240–65 (1985); Akehurst, "Jurisdiction in International Law," 46 *Brit. Y. B. Int'l L.* 145, 152–257 (1972–73); Bowett, "Jurisdiction: Changing Patterns of Authority over Activities and Resources," 53 *Brit. Y. B. Int'l L.* 1 (1982); Harvard Research in Int'l Law, "Jurisdiction with Respect to Crime," 29 *Am. J. Int'l L.* 435 (Supp. 1935) [hereinafter Harvard Research]; Mann, "The Doctrine of Jurisdiction in International Law," 111 *Recueil Des Cours* 1 (1964).

5. *Restatement (Revised) of Foreign Relations Law* § 402 [hereinafter *Restatement*].

6. L. Henkin, R. Pugh, H. Smit & O. Schachter, *International Law* 823 (2d ed. 1987) [hereinafter *International Law*].

7. That the two systems are distinct does not undercut the idea that nation-states are normally at liberty to recognize domestic remedies for international law violations. The two systems can be separate, and yet one can implement the norms of the other, see chapters 2 and 3.

8. See chapter 9. See chapter 2 regarding how the international order is no longer composed exclusively of nation-state actors.

9. *Restatement, supra* note 5, § 401 comment b.

10. See *supra* note 6 and accompanying text.

11. § 402 of the *Restatement, supra* note 5, identifies the contacts that support domestic prescriptive jurisdiction; those contacts generally correspond to the sovereign interests that the jurisdictional principles encompass. But § 403 goes on to provide that that jurisdiction should not be exercised when "unreasonable." Although multifaceted, the reasonableness standard basically evaluates the quantity and quality of the forum nation-state's interests in an offense against those of other nation-states. When two sovereigns could each reasonably exercise authority over an actor or an activity, but their prescriptions conflict, the forum nation-state should defer to the other sovereign when the latter's interest "is clearly greater," § 403. A similar contacts/reasonableness approach to adjudicative jurisdiction is contained in § 421. Some comparison may be drawn here to the *forum non conveniens* doctrine, see chapter 5. We omit a more detailed description of §§ 402, 403, and 421 of the *Restatement* because the universality principle under §§ 404 and 423 will instead prove most relevant for our purposes, see chapter 8.

12. See chapter 9.

13. Prescriptive and adjudicative authority under the universality principle, as found, respectively, in §§ 404 and 423 of the *Restatement, supra* note 5, is not limited therein by a reasonableness standard or by a balancing of sovereign interests.

14. *See generally International Law, supra* note 6, at 821–23; Fitzmaurice, "The General Principles of International Law Considered from the Standpoint of the Rule of Law," 92 *Recueil Des Cours* 1, 218 (1957); George, "Defining Filartiga: Characterizing International Torture Claims in the United States Courts," 3 *Dick. J. Int'l L.* 1, 19 (1984).

15. *See generally id.*

16. Fitzmaurice, *supra* note 14, at 218.

17. Mann, *supra* note 4, at 73.

18. *See generally* Maier, "Extraterritorial Jurisdiction at a Crossroads: An Intersection Between Public and Private International Law," 76 *Am. J. Int'l L.* 280 (1982).

19. *Id.* at 280.

20. See chapter 2 regarding nonstate actors' rights and responsibilities under public international law. *See generally* R. Folsom, M. Gordon & J. Spanogle, *International Business Transactions* 11–13 (1986) regarding nation-states' participation in international business transactions.

21. That numerous treaties regulate public issues has already been well demonstrated; that new treaties also address private issues is exemplified by the prominent United Nations Convention on the International Sale of Goods, Doc. A/CONF. 97/18, Annex I.

22. *Restatement, supra* note 5, § 403 comment f. The principles may even support civil jurisdiction in some cases where criminal jurisdiction would be lacking, *see id.*

23. *Id.*, § 404 comment b.

24. *See, e.g., Tel-Oren v. Libyan Arab Republic,* 726 F.2d 774, 781 (D.C. Cir. 1984) (per curiam) (Edwards, J., concurring) (expressly suggesting that the universality principle applies in civil terrorism case), *cert. denied,* 470 U.S. 1003 (1985); *Von Dardel v. Union of Soviet Socialist Republics,* 623 F. Supp. 246, 254 (D.D.C. 1985) (explicitly finding that the universality principle applies to both civil and criminal cases), see chapter 8.

25. Of course, in the antitrust and securities contexts, foreign sovereigns have often reacted negatively to the United States' extension of its jurisdiction particularly under the objective territorial principle or the effects doctrine. *See generally* Davidow, "Extraterritorial Application of U.S. Antitrust Laws in a Changing World," 8 *Law & Pol'y Int'l Bus.* 895 (1976); Jennings, "Extraterritorial Jurisdiction and the United States Antitrust Laws," 33 *Brit. Y. B. Int'l L.* 146 (1957); Note, "The Judicial Role in Extraterritorial Application of the Securities Exchange Act of 1934: Vesco," 4 *Ga. J. Int'l & Comp. L.* 192 (1974). That adverse foreign reaction has usually not depended upon whether the United States' regulations were applied in criminal or civil cases.

26. See *International Law, supra* note 6, at 822.

27. The theoretical issue of whether the jurisdictional principles either limit or authorize domestic authority relates generally to the *Case of the S.S. Lotus (France v. Turkey),* 1927 PCIJ Ser. A. No. 10, 2 Hudson, World Ct. Rep. 20. The international tribunal there considered whether nation-states are free to extend their extraterritorial jurisdiction (or, for that matter, to do anything) unless specifically limited by international law, or whether nation-states cannot extend their jurisdiction (or act at all) without specific authorization from international

law. The court chose the former viewpoint (so sovereign jurisdiction theoretically exists unless the jurisdictional principles limit that authority), but the case's import remains debated. *See* O. Schachter, *supra* note 4, at 240–42.

28. Bowett, *supra* note 4, at 2.

29. *See generally* the sources cited in *supra* note 25. Various well-known cases, particularly in the antitrust context, have explicitly or implicitly drawn upon international law's jurisdictional principles. *See, e.g., Timberlane Lumber Co. v. Bank of America,* 549 F.2d 597 (9th Cir. 1976); *United States v. Aluminum Co. of America,* 148 F.2d 416 (2d Cir. 1945).

30. See *supra* notes 22–23 and accompanying text.

31. I. Brownlie, *supra* note 4, at 299.

32. *See, e.g., supra* note 24. See chapter 8.

33. Since international law's jurisdictional principles apply to civil cases, they are relevant even when a nation-state is sued. As vehicles to assess domestic civil authority, the jurisdictional principles are valuable evaluative tools irrespective of the defendant's identity. Within the United States, the jurisdiction that the Foreign Sovereign Immunities Act of 1976 (FSIA) permits over nation-states, see chapter 4, generally does not exceed the domestic authority that the jurisdictional principles permit. So, in general, when federal courts have authority under the FSIA within the domestic system, they also have authority under the jurisdictional principles within the international system.

Before exercising such jurisdiction in international cases, the forum sovereign should normally be mindful of the interests of other sovereigns. And foreign sovereigns obviously have a significant interest in any case in which they are the defendant. But federal courts should not decline to exercise their jurisdiction in all cases against nation-states; doing so would strip the federal judiciary of all authority over cases against nation-state actors. Federal courts may provide a more objective evaluation of whether the foreign sovereign's behavior was lawful, as compared with allowing the sovereign to judge itself in its own legal system.

Particularly when the FSIA (as written or if amended) permits federal jurisdiction over a human rights or terrorism case, and particularly when the universality principle supports that jurisdiction, federal courts should usually not agree to let the case be adjudicated instead in the sovereign defendant's home court. This conclusion is dictated not only by the importance of adjudicating human rights and terrorism cases, but by the fact that the universality principle does not require the forum sovereign to balance its interests in a case with those of other sovereigns, *see supra* note 13 and accompanying text. Indeed, since universal jurisdiction, uniquely, does not require any link between the forum sovereign and the offense, a very strong presumption should exist that that jurisdiction should be exercised whenever available in human rights and terrorism cases against both nonstate and nation-state defendants.

34. M. McDougal, H. Lasswell & I. Vlasic, *Law and Public Order in Space* 748 (1963).

35. *Liu v. Republic of China*, 642 F. Supp. 297 (N.D. Cal. 1986).

36. *de Letelier v. Republic of Chile*, 488 F. Supp. 665 (D.D.C. 1980).

37. *See generally* 1 C. Hyde, *International Law* 798–800 (2d ed. 1945); 2 J. Moore, *A Digest of International Law* 202, at 243–55 (1906); O. Schachter, *supra* note 4, at 254–58. The "effects" principle is another name for the objective territorial principle. The "subjective territorial" principle provides jurisdiction when an act is commenced within the forum nation-state, but consummated elsewhere.

38. This might remind one of *Persinger v. Islamic Republic of Iran*, 729 F.2d 835 (D.C. Cir. 1984), see chapter 4, which did not uphold FSIA jurisdiction over the parents' claim for emotional distress suffered in this country from their son having been held hostage in Iran, despite Judge Edwards's partial dissent and although the objective territorial principle might arguably have supported the court's international jurisdiction in the case.

39. *See* O. Schachter, *supra* note 4, at 245, *see also Restatement, supra* note 5, § 402 comment g. *See generally* Paust, "Federal Jurisdiction over Extraterritorial Acts of Terrorism and Nonimmunity for Foreign Violators of International Law Under the FSIA and the Act of State Doctrine," 23 *Va. J. Int'l L.* 191, 202 (1983). Recent human rights and terrorism treaties and recent federal legislation implementing the terrorism treaties expressly support legislative and adjudicative jurisdiction under the passive-personality principle. *See, e.g.*, the treaties and federal criminal laws that are discussed in chapters 3 and 8.

40. *Filartiga*, 630 F.2d at 876.

41. *See* Brownlie, *supra* note 4, at 303–4; O. Schachter, *supra* note 4, at 245; Akehurst, *supra* note 4, at 157–59; Harvard Research, *supra* note 4, at 543–61.

42. *See, e.g., United States v. Layton*, 509 F. Supp. 212, 216 (N.D. Cal.) (holding that protective principle, among other jurisdictional principles, supports adjudicatory jurisdiction in prosecution of terrorism), *appeal dismissed*, 645 F.2d 681 (9th Cir.), *cert. denied*, 452 U.S. 972 (1981); Paust, *supra* note 39, at 209–11. A perusal of the legislative histories of 18 U.S.C. § 1116 (Internationally Protected Persons), § 1203 (Hostage Taking), and § 2331 (Terrorist Prosecution Act) discloses important explicit and implicit reliance upon the protective principle; those statutes were partly passed to implement the terrorism treaties.

43. *Tel-Oren*, 726 F.2d at 774. The court held that it was without subject matter jurisdiction under federal statutes, and the per curiam opinion did not reach the issue of whether the court had authority under international law's jurisdictional principles.

8. Universal Jurisdiction

1. See chapter 7. The present chapter draws upon Randall, "Universal Jurisdiction under International Law," published originally in 66 *Tex. Law Review* 785–841 (1988). Copyright 1 1988 by the *Texas Law Review*, reprinted by permis-

sion. In certain instances, however, this chapter revises the author's previous writing and ideas on the universality principle. Other commentaries giving primary attention to the universality principle include Cowles, "Universality of Jurisdiction over War Crimes," 33 *Calif. L. Rev.* 177 (1945); and Sponsler, "The Universality Principle of Jurisdiction and the Threatened Trials of American Airmen," 15 *Loy. L. Rev.* 43 (1968).

   2. See chapter 7.

   3. See *id.*

   4. *Filartiga v. Pena-Irala*, 630 F.2d 876 (2d Cir. 1980). See chapter 2 regarding *Filartiga*.

   5. *Id.* at 890.

   6. *United States v. Layton*, 509 F. Supp. 212 (N.D. Cal.), *appeal dismissed*, 645 F.2d 681 (9th Cir.), *cert. denied*, 452 U.S. 972 (1981).

   7. *Layton*, 509 F. Supp. at 223. Since the terrorism was committed by a United States national and against United States officials, the court opined that the nationality, passive-personality, protective, and objective territorial principles offered jurisidictional support in the case, in addition to the universality principle, *see id.*

   8. *In re Demjanjuk*, 612 F. Supp. 544, 555 (N.D. Ohio) (determining that Israel's jurisdiction to prosecute a concentration-camp guard "conforms with the international law principle of 'universal jurisdiction'"), *aff'd sub nom. Demjanjuk v. Petrovsky*, 776 F.2d 571, 582–83 (6th Cir. 1985) (the guard's acts were "offenses against the law of nations or against humanity" and Israel or any sovereign "may undertake to vindicate the interest of all nations by seeking to punish the perpetrators of such crimes"), *cert. denied*, 475 U.S. 1016 (1986). *Demjanjuk* essentially held that the United States could extradite an alleged Nazi prison guard, known as Ivan the Terrible, to Israel because Israel possessed and wanted to exercise universal jurisdiction over the defendant. For a more detailed discussion of the case, see Lubet & Reed, "Extradition of Nazis from the United States to Israel: A Survey of Issues in Transnational Law," 22 *Stan. J. Int'l L.* 1 (1986); Reiss, "The Extradition of John Demjanjuk: War Crimes, Universality Jurisdiction, and the Political Offense Doctrine," 20 *Cornell Int'l L. J.* 281 (1987). The United States also could have assumed universal jurisdiction over Demjanjuk.

   9. *United States v. Yunis*, 681 F. Supp. 896 (D.D.C. 1988). The defendant's constitutional rights were later addressed in 859 F.2d 953 (D.C. Cir. 1988).

   10. *Yunis*, 681 F. Supp. at 901. Since several United States citizens were on board the flight, the passive-personality principle also supported federal court jurisdiction, *see id.* at 901–3.

   A few other recent cases that refer to the universality principle include *Tel-Oren v. Libyan Arab Republic*, 726 F.2d 774, 781, 788 (D.C. Cir. 1984) (per curiam) (Edwards, J., concurring) (voting to dismiss the terrorism case, but making several references to domestic jurisdiction over extraterritorial offenses under the universality principle), *cert. denied*, 470 U.S. 1003 (1985); *Von Dardel v. Union of Soviet Socialist Republics,* 623 F. Supp. 246, 254 (D.D.C. 1985) (referring to the "concept of extraordinary judicial jurisdiction over acts in violation of significant international standards . . . embodied in the principle of 'universal' violations of international law").

11. *See, e.g.,* 131 Cong. Rec. S8999 (daily ed. June 27, 1985) (statement of Senator Specter, "Today's international criminals have left the high seas for airplanes and trucks loaded with explosives. But the threat posed by terrorists is just as universal as that once posed by pirates, and, like piracy, terrorism should be prosecuted as a 'universal crime' against humanity").

12. According to § 404 of the *Restatement (Third) of Foreign Relations Law* [hereinafter *Restatement*], all nation-states have prescriptive universal jurisdiction over offenses such as "piracy, slave trade, attacks on or hijacking of aircraft, genocide, war crimes, and perhaps certain acts of terrorism." Under § 423, all nation-states have universal adjudicative jurisdiction over the same universal offenses. This chapter focuses mostly upon adjudicatory jurisdiction.

13. 1 L. Oppenheim, *International Law* 609 (8th ed. 1955). Pirates were considered *hostis humani generis* — the enemy of mankind — at least as early as the seventeenth century; *see* Dickinson, "Is the Crime of Piracy Obsolete?" 38 *Harv. L. Rev.* 334–39 (1925). But Professor Cowles indicates that universal jurisdiction over piracy dates back to at least the sixteenth century and derives from the treatment of brigands as the enemies equally of all nation-states; *see* Cowles, *supra* note 1, at 181–94.

14. *See United States v. The LaJeune Eugenie,* 26 F. Cas. 832, 843 (C.C.D. Mass. 1822) (No. 15551) ("no one can doubt . . . that vessels and property in the possession of pirates may be lawfully seized on the high seas by any person, and brought in for adjudication"). *See also* M. Sorensen, *Manual of Public International Law* 365 (1968); 1 H. Halleck, *International Law* 54 (3d ed. 1861). For a modern judicial statement concerning universal jurisdiction over piracy, see, *e.g., United States v. McRary,* 665 F.2d 674, 678 n.8 (5th Cir. Unit B), *cert. denied,* 456 U.S. 1011 (1982).

15. Regarding the first view, *see United States v. Smith,* 18 U.S. (5 Wheat.) 153, 161 (1820); *The Law of Nations* 389–90 (H. Briggs 2d ed. 1952); Sponsler, *supra* note 1, at 45–47; Treves, "Jurisdictional Aspects of the Eichmann Case," 47 *Minn. L. Rev.* 557, 570–72 (1963). Regarding the second view, *see* Harvard Research in Int'l Law, "Draft Convention and Comment on Piracy," 26 *Am. J. Int'l L.* 739, 760 (Supp. 1932). In part, this second view is premised on the positivist notion that only nation-states are the subjects of international law; individuals cannot violate international law because they have no legal personality under the law. Hence piracy, under international law, simply permits each nation-state to penalize individuals who violate substantive *domestic law.* See chapter 2 regarding the contrasting idea that individuals can be held responsible for violating international law.

16. M. McDougal, H. Lasswell & L. Chen, *Human Rights and World Public Order* 354 (1980).

17. At least in the criminal context, debate over the two theories has been short-circuited in the United States because there is no federal common law of crimes. One cannot be prosecuted in a federal court for either domestic or international acts unless a federal statute recognizes and defines the person's offense; *see United States v. Hudson & Goodwin*, 11 U.S. (7 Cranch) 32, 34 (1812). Whether piracy is a domestic offense or an international offense is thus unimportant because a defendant must still be charged with having violated the federal piracy statute; *see* 18 U.S.C. § 1651 (1982). *See generally Restatement, supra* note 12, § 404 reporters' note 1. In the civil context, the debate between the two theories of piracy may possibly have theoretical interest because there is civil liability for federal common law torts.

18. The high seas exclude any nation-state's internal waters and territorial seas. Under article 3 of the 1982 United Nations Convention on the Law of Sea, *done* Dec. 10, 1982, *reprinted in* The Law of the Sea, U.N. Doc. A/CONF. 62/122, U.N. Sales No. E.83.V.5, at 3 (1983) [hereinafter 1982 Convention], a nation-state is generally permitted "to establish the breadth of its territorial sea up to a limit not exceeding 12 nautical miles." The 1982 Convention is not yet in force, but represents customary law, *see infra* note 34 and accompanying text, and will imminently enter into force. Universal jurisdiction apparently exists over piratical acts occurring in the exclusive economic zone. *See generally* B. Dubner, *The Law of International Sea Piracy* 18, 157–59 (1980); Oxman, "The Third United Nations Conference on the Law of the Sea: The 1976 New York Sessions," 71 *Am. J. Int'l L.* 247, 259–68 (1977). The exclusive economic zone "is an area beyond and adjacent to the territorial sea" that "shall not extend beyond 200 nautical miles from the baselines from which the breadth of the territorial sea is measured," 1982 Convention, *supra*, arts. 55, 57, at 164.

19. J. Brierly, *The Law of Nations* 304–6 (6th ed. 1963).

20. *Id.* at 306–7.

21. *See* O. Schachter, *International Law in Theory and Practice* 245 (1985). Floating-territorial jurisdiction is a variation on the territoriality principle, see chapter 7.

22. Harvard Research, *supra* note 15, at 831 (translation of German treatise).

23. H. Wheaton, *Elements of International Law* 193 n.83 (R. Darra 8th ed. 1866) (editor's footnote). *See also* 2 G. Hackworth, *Digest of International Law* 681 (1941) ("By committing an act of piracy, the pirate and his vessel ipso facto lose the protection of the State whose flag they are otherwise entitled to fly").

24. J. Brierly, *supra* note 19, at 307.

25. *See* 1 L. Oppenheim, *supra* note 13, at 609; Lenoir, "Piracy Cases in the Supreme Court," 25 *J. Crim. L. & Criminology* 532, 535 (1934–35).

26. Harvard Research, *supra* note 15, at 825. Apart from vessels never registered, the only other arguably stateless vessels may be those sailing under the authority of two or more nation-states and duplicitously using different flags for

advantage; *see United States v. Marino-Garcia,* 679 F.2d 1373, 1378–79 (11th Cir.), *cert. denied,* 459 U.S. 1114 (1983).

27. Harvard Research, *supra* note 15, at 825. For background on the Harvard Research undertaking, see Kenny, "Manley O. Hudson and the Harvard Research in International Law 1927–1940," 11 *Int'l Law.* 319 (1977).

28. 1982 Convention, *supra* note 18, art. 104, at 34.

29. *See Bonnet's Trial,* 15 *State Trials* (Howell) 1231, 1235 (Am. Vice Adm. 1718) ("As to the heinousness or wickedness of the offence, it needs no aggravation, it being evident to the reason of all men"); Harvard Research, *supra* note 15, at 743.

30. *United States v. Brig. Malek Adhel,* 43 U.S. (2 How.) 210, 232 (1844).

31. B. Dubner, *supra* note 18, at 45. Professor Dickinson aptly concludes: "So heinous is the offense [of piracy], so difficult are such offenders to apprehend, and so universal is the interest in their prompt arrest and punishment, that they have long been regarded as outlaws and the enemies of all mankind. They are international criminals. It follows that they can be arrested by the authorized agents of any state and taken in for trial anywhere. The jurisdiction is universal." Dickinson, *supra* note 13, at 338.

32. 1982 Convention, *supra* note 18, art. 105, at 34 (emphasis added).

33. *Done* Apr. 29, 1958, 13 U.S.T. 2312, T.I.A.S. No. 5200, 450 U.N.T.S. 82 [hereinafter 1958 Convention].

34. *See Restatement, supra* note 12, pt. V introductory note (United States and most nation-states view bulk of the 1982 Convention to represent custom binding upon them even apart from the Convention). The *Restatement* identifies piracy as one of the offenses that the universality principle permits the United States and other nation-states to define and adjudicate, *id.* §§ 404, 423. Since most nation-states will be bound by the 1982 Convention directly or under customary law, we do not further discuss issues concerning nonparties' jurisdictional rights.

35. See chapter 7. *See also supra* note 2 and accompanying text.

36. 1982 Convention, *supra* note 18, art. 101, at 34 (emphasis added). *See also* 1958 Convention, *supra* note 33, art. 15, at 2317, T.I.A.S. No. 5200, at 6, 450 U.N.T.S. at 90. If this definition is considered in light of the two major views of piracy, *see supra* notes 15–17 and accompanying text, either it defines the acts that constitute piracy as an international law violation, over which universal jurisdiction is permitted, or it only identifies those acts that are subject to universal jurisdiction as domestic law offenses. See Harvard Research, *supra* note 15, at 749, 769, regarding the disagreement over piracy's definition prior to the 1958 and 1982 Conventions.

It is noteworthy that piracy under international law is not necessarily identical to piracy under the domestic law of the various nation-states. Sovereigns possess universal jurisdiction only over those specific acts that international law defines as being piratical. If individuals commit acts constituting piracy under domestic law but not under international law, the forum sovereign must rely upon a jurisdictional principle other than the universality principle; *see S.S. Lotus (Fr. v. Turk.)*, 1927 P.C.I.J. (ser. A.) No. 10, at 70 (Sept. 7) (Moore, J., dissenting); Harvard Research, *supra*, at 749–65. That specific situation could not arise in the United States because piracy, under the federal statute, is "defined by the law of nations," 18 U.S.C. § 1651 (1982); but the domestic law of other nation-states might define piracy more broadly than does international law.

37. See, *e.g.*, "Pirates Reportedly Kill 130 Vietnam Refugees," *N.Y. Times*, May 7, 1989, at A12, col. 3; "Pirates Attack Vietnamese," *N.Y. Times*, Nov. 9, 1986, at A9, col. 1.

38. See *N.Y. Times*, Oct. 9, 1985, at A10, col. 1; *N.Y. Times*, Oct. 10, 1985, at A11, col. 1.

39. The modern universal jurisdiction over hostage taking is discussed in *infra* notes 105–44 and accompanying text.

40. For a thoughtful assessment of this point, see Note, "Towards a New Definition of Piracy: The Achille Lauro Incident," 26 *Va. J. Int'l L.* 723, 743–51, which concludes that the *Achille Lauro's* hijacking did not constitute piracy under international law because the Palestinians did not act for private ends and the *Achille Lauro* incident involved only one vessel and piracy requires an attack from a ship against another ship, *id.* at 747–48.

41. *See, e.g.*, B. Dubner, *supra* note 18, at 162–63; Crockett, "Toward a Revision of the International Law of Piracy," 26 *De Paul L. Rev.* 78, 84–87 (1976); Note, *supra* note 40.

42. *See* O. Schachter, *supra* note 21, at 262.

43. M. Hudson, *Cases and Other Materials on International Law* 367 (3d ed. 1951).

44. *See, e.g.*, Treaty for the Suppression of the African Slave Trade, Dec. 20, 1841, 92 Parry's T.S. 437, 441 [hereinafter Suppression Treaty I] (providing ships of war with special warrants and orders to search merchant vessels suspected of trafficking in slaves); Treaty for the Suppression of African Slave Trade, Apr. 7, 1862, United States–Great Britain, 12 Stat. 1225, 1225–26, T.S. No. 126 [hereinafter Suppression Treaty II] (providing that certain vessels of each nation could visit merchant vessels of the other and search them according to specific rules).

45. *See, e.g.*, Suppression Treaty II, *supra* note 44, art. 4, at 1227, T.S. No. 126. Most of the treaties creating mixed tribunals are no longer in force. *See Restatement, supra* note 12, § 522 reporters' note 3.

46. *E.g.*, General Act of the Conference of Berlin, Feb. 26, 1885, art. 9, 17 Hertslet's Commercial Treaties 62, 67 (1890), *reprinted in* 2 *Key Treaties for the Great Powers* 880, 887 (M. Hurst ed. 1972).

47. O. Schachter, *supra* note 21, at 262.

48. *See* M. McDougal, H. Lasswell & L. Chen, *supra* note 16, at 484–90 (1980); Bassiouni & Nanda, "Slavery and Slave Trade: Steps Toward Its Eradication," 12 *Santa Clara Law.* 424 (1972).

49. *See, e.g.*, Suppression Treaty I, *supra* note 44, art. 1, at 441 ("[Their] Majesties . . . declare [slave] traffic piracy").

50. The issues of whether a party had universal jurisdiction over a nonparty's slave-trading national and whether a nonparty had universal jurisdiction over slave traders might be analyzed under the approaches used in *infra* notes 117–44 and accompanying text.

51. *See* 1982 Convention, *supra* note 18, art. 110, at 35 ("[A] warship which encounters on the high seas a foreign ship . . . is not justified in boarding it unless . . . the ship is engaged in the slave trade").

52. *See, e.g.*, Convention to Suppress the Slave Trade and Slavery, Sept. 25, 1926, 46 Stat. 2183, T.S. No. 778, 60 L.N.T.S. 253; Protocol Amending the Slavery Convention, Dec. 7, 1953, 1 U.S.T. 479, T.I.A.S. No. 3532, 182 U.N.T.S. 51; Supplementary Convention of the Abolition of Slavery, the Slave Trade and Institutions and Practices Similar to Slavery, Sept. 7, 1956, 3 U.S.T. 3201, T.I.A.S. No. 6418, 266 U.N.T.S. 3. Professor Bassiouni suggests that these treaties have cumulatively resulted in "slave trading [being] recognized as an international crime falling within the universality theory," Bassiouni, "Theories of Jurisdiction and Their Application in Extradition Law and Practice," 5 *Cal. W. Int'l L. J.* 1, 54 (1974). *See generally* Bassiouni & Nanda, *supra* note 48. The notion that slave trading violates international law may also draw general support from major post–Second World War human rights documents that address individual liberty and freedom; *see, e.g.*, *Universal Declaration of Human Rights*, G.A. Res. 217, art. 4, U.N. Doc. A/810, at 73 (1948).

53. The slavery conventions cited in *supra* note 52 do not explicitly confer universal jurisdiction over slave trading. Professor Bassiouni's position seems to be that the widespread attempt to abolish slavery and to designate slavery as an international offense permits universal jurisdiction over slave trading, either under customary law or general principles of international law; *see* Bassiouni, *supra* note 52, at 54. According to Professor Sorensen, even if the modern slavery and other human rights conventions by themselves do not explicitly establish universal jurisdiction over slave trading, "[i]n view of the extensive treaties seeking to wipe out slave-trade, it is possible that international customary law would today sustain an assertion of universal jurisdiction with respect to this offense," M. Sorensen, *supra* note 14, at 366.

54. See chapter 7. *See also supra* note 2 and accompanying text. An analysis of modern universal jurisdiction under the Apartheid Convention is postponed until *infra* notes 104–44 and accompanying text.

55. O. Schachter, *supra* note 21, at 262.

56. See chapter 7. *See also supra* note 2 and accompanying text.

57. *See*, respectively, Aug. 8, 1945, 59 Stat. 1544, E.A.S. No. 472, 82 U.N.T.S. 280; 59 Stat. 1546, E.A.S. No. 472, 82 U.N.T.S. 284 [hereinafter IMT Charter]. For discussions of the war crimes trials, see Cowles, "Trials of War Criminals (Non-Nuremberg)," 42 *Am. J. Int'l L.* 299 (1948); Taylor, "Nuremberg Trials—

War Crimes and International Law," 1949 *Int'l Conciliation* 241; Wright, "War Criminals," 39 *Am. J. Int'l L.* 257, 275–79 (1945); Zeck, "Nuremberg: Proceedings Subsequent to Goering et al.," 26 *N.C.L. Rev.* 350 (1948).

58. This phrase derives from the Moscow Declaration, 9 Dep't St. Bull. 310, 311 (1943), signed by Roosevelt, Churchill, and Stalin. The Allies relied upon the Declaration when selecting the individuals to be tried by the IMT, *see* Taylor, *supra* note 57, at 249–56.

59. C.C. Law No. 10, which created and regulated the zonal tribunals, was promulgated by the four zone commanders in Berlin on December 20, 1945, "to establish a uniform legal basis in Germany for the prosecution of war criminals and other similar offenders, other than those dealt with by the International Military Tribunal," Control Council Law No. 10, 3 Control Council, Official Gazette of the Control Council for Germany 49, 52 (Jan. 31, 1946) [hereinafter C.C. Law No. 10], *reprinted in* 1 *The Law of War: A Documentary History* 908 (L. Friedman ed. 1972).

60. *See* Taylor, *supra* note 57, at 255–56; *see also* Cowles, *supra* note 57, at 301.

61. For valuable discussions of the Eichmann trial, see Baade, "The Eichmann Trial: Some Legal Aspects," 1961 *Duke L. J.* 400; Fawcett, "The Eichmann Case," 38 *Brit. Y. B. Int'l L.* 181 (1962); Schwarzenberger, "The Eichmann Judgment," 15 *Current Legal Probs* 248 (1962); Treves, *supra* note 15. For an account of Israel's prosecution of Demjanjuk, "Ivan the Terrible," a former Nazi guard at a concentration camp in Poland, see "Israel Indicts Man in Treblinka Case," *N.Y. Times*, Sept. 30, 1986, at A3, col. 1; *see also* Lubet & Reed, *supra* note 8. Relatedly, see *Restatement, supra* note 12, at § 404 reporters' note 1, regarding France's 1983 prosecution of Claus Barbie, a Gestapo officer, for crimes against humanity.

62. See Horwitz, "The Tokyo Trial," 1950 *Int'l Conciliation* 475, 494–97.

63. *See* IMT Charter, *supra* note 57, art. 6, 1547; C.C. Law No. 10, *supra* note 59, art. 2, 1, at 50–51. The IMT Charter and C.C. Law No. 10, however, did not contain verbatim definitions of those offenses. C.C. Law No. 10 also identifies as a crime "[m]embership in categories of a criminal group or organization declared criminal by the International Military Tribunal," art. 2, 1(d), at 51. For discussions of the offenses that the International Military Tribunal for the Far East prosecuted, which were similar to the offenses that the IMT prosecuted, see Horwitz, *supra* note 62, at 484–87. For discussions of the offenses that other tribunals prosecuted, see Cowles, *supra* note 57, at 301; Zeck, *supra* note 57, at 380–84; Note, "Review of International Criminal Convictions," 59 *Yale L. J.* 997 (1949). The term *war crimes* will sometimes be used to include all of three primary Axis offenses; the term *war criminals* will refer to all of these offenders.

64. Wright, *supra* note 57, at 283. Supreme Court Justice Robert Jackson, who served as the United States Representative and Chief Counsel to the IMT, compared the Nazi offenses to piracy because both are essentially forms of "illegal warfare," Trial of German War Criminals, S. Doc. No. 129, 79th Cong., 1st Sess. (1946) (opening address by Robert N. Jackson); *see* Sponsler, *supra* note 1, at 49–50.

65. Fawcett, *supra* note 61, at 204.

66. Trial of German War Criminals, *supra* note 64, at 2.

67. *See* Cowles, *supra* note 1, at 194 ("[T]here is often no well-organized police or judicial system at the place where the acts are committed, and both the pirate and the war criminal take advantage of this fact, hoping thereby to commit their crimes with impunity").

68. "International Military Tribunal (Nuremberg), Judgment and Sentences," 41 *Am. J. Int'l. L.* 172, 216 (1947) [hereinafter *IMT Judgment*]. The IMT's entire proceedings exist in a twenty-five-volume compilation, *The Trial of German Major War Criminals* (1946–1951). Although the passage in text comes from the *IMT Judgment*, other postwar tribunals expressed that same viewpoint. *See generally* J. Appleman, *Military Tribunals and International Crimes* 267–69, 291–300, 306–11 (1954). Nevertheless, some observers maintain that the postwar tribunals were not created legitimately and were "born of no lawful marriage," April, "An Inquiry into the Judicial Basis for the Nuremberg War Crimes Trial," 30 *Minn. L. Rev.* 313, 318 (1946).

69. *Demjanjuk*, 776 F.2d 571, 582 (6th Cir. 1985) (referring particularly to the IMT and zonal tribunals), *cert. denied*, 475 U.S. 1016 (1986). One scholar has stated that the postwar tribunals established "war crimes charges as the chief example of the modern application of the universality principle," Sponsler, *supra* note 1, at 53.

70. For example, the IMT simply asserted that its charter created and defined its jurisdiction, which was thus "decisive, and binding upon the Tribunal," *IMT Judgment, supra* note 68, at 216. Certain zonal tribunals also claimed that C.C. Law No. 10 justified their jurisdiction. Of course, without further elaboration, asserting jurisdiction based simply upon the legislation that created the IMT or the zonal tribunals would be insufficient. That assertion begs the preliminary question of whether the Allies had legislative jurisdiction under international law to enact the IMT Charter or C.C. Law No. 10. *See* Carnegie, "Jurisdiction over Violations of the Laws and Customs of War," 39 *Brit. Y. B. Int'l L.* 402, 414–15 (1963). The tribunals also indicated that belligerent sovereigns had previously assumed military jurisdiction over enemy soldiers and officers who violated the laws of warfare, *see, e.g., IMT Judgment, supra* note 68, at 216–17, but that jurisdiction had been used when the forum sovereign had direct connections with the offenses under the territoriality or passive-personality principles.

71. That argument is explained and supported in Kelsen, "The Legal Status of Germany According to the Declaration of Berlin," 39 *Am. J. Int'l L.* 518, 518 (1945), but criticized in R. Woetzel, *The Nuremberg Trials in International Law* 76–83 (1960); Carnegie, *supra* note 70, at 418–19; Schick, "The Nuremberg Trial and the International Law of the Future," 41 *Am. J. Int'l L.* 770, 770–94 (1947).

72. *IMT Judgment, supra* note 68, at 216 (emphasis added).

73. Carnegie, *supra* note 70, at 415. Carnegie acknowledges that that interpretation is not necessarily conclusive.

74. The memorandum provides: "[I]t is . . . possible and perhaps . . . proba-

ble, that the [IMT] considered the crimes under the Charter to be, as international crimes, subject to the jurisdcition of every state. The case of piracy would then be the appropriate parallel. This interpretation seems to be supported by the fact that the Court affirmed that the signatory Powers in creating the Tribunal had made use of *a right belonging to any nation,*" The Charter and Judgment of the Nuremberg Tribunal 80, U.N. Doc. A/CN.4/5, U.N. Sales No. 1949V.7 (1949) (memorandum submitted by the secretary general) (emphasis added).

75. 11 *Trials of War Criminals* (1946–1949) 757 (U.S. Mil. Trib.—Nuremberg 1948) [hereinafter *Trials War Crims*]. A condensed version of *List* is reported at 15 Ann. Dig. 632.

76. *List,* 11 *Trials War Crims, supra* note 75, at 1241 (emphasis added).

77. *Id.* at 1242. The tribunal may have been tacitly referring to the numerous war criminals returned to Germany for prosecution after the First World War, who received, at most, minimal sentences.

78. *Id.*

79. *Id.* at 1235.

80. Because the tribunals did not usually render a full written judgment, the references to the universality principle are actually found in reports of the cases. The United Nations War Crimes Commission prepared these reports largely "on the basis of shorthand and other notes taken at hearings" by the lawyers and judge-advocates who were present, 1 *Law Reports of Trials of War Criminals* ix (foreword) (1949) [hereinafter *L. Rep. Trials War Crims*].

81. 1 *L. Rep. Trials War Crims, supra* note 80, at 35 (Brit. Mil. Ct.—Almelo 1945).

82. *Id.* at 42. The report mentioned two other jurisdictional grounds regarding the Dutch civilian's murder: Great Britain's interest in punishing those who victimize an ally's national under a type of passive-personality rationale, *see also* Carnegie, *supra* note 70, at 417–20, and Great Britain's possible assumption of the jurisdiction that Germany would have had under the nationality principle.

83. 1 *L. Rep. Trials War Crims, supra* note 80, at 93 (Brit. Mil. Ct.—Hamburg 1946). A condensed version of *Zyklon B* is reported at 13 *Ann. Dig.* 250.

84. *Zyklon B,* 1 *L. Rep. Trials War Crims, supra* note 80, at 103.

85. *Id.* at 103.

86. 1 *L. Rep. Trials War Crims, supra* note 80, at 46 (U.S. Mil. Comm'n—Wiesbaden 1945).

87. *Id.* at 53.

88. *Eisentrager,* 14 *L. Rep. Trials War Crims, supra* note 80, at 8 (U.S. Mil. Comm'n—Shanghai 1947). A condensed version of *Eisentrager* is reported at 14 *Ann. Dig.* 213.

89. 14 *L. Rep. Trials War Crims, supra* note 80, at 15 (footnote omitted).

90. Carnegie, *supra* note 70, at 423 (emphasis added); *see also* Sponsler, *supra* note 1, at 49–50.

91. *Attorney General of Israel v. Eichmann,* 36 I.L.R. 18 (Isr. Dist. Ct.—

Jerusalem 1961), *aff'd*, 36 I.L.R. 277 (Isr. Sup. Ct. 1962). An unofficial translation of the district court opinion, prepared by the Israeli government, is available at 56 *Am. J. Int'l L.* 805 (1962). The Supreme Court opinion is also available at 45 Pesakim Mehoziim 3, *published in part in* 2 *The Law of War: A Documentary History* 1657 (L. Friedman ed. 1972).

92. Lippman, "The Trial of Adolph Eichmann and the Protection of Universal Human Rights under International Law," 5 *Hous. J. Int'l L.* 1, 2 (1982). *See also* Treves, *supra* note 15, at 558. The so-called final solution was a plan to evacuate and exterminate some eleven million Jews and others.

93. *See Eichmann*, 36 I.L.R. at 273–76 (Isr. Dist. Ct.—Jerusalem 1961), *aff'd*, 36 I.L.R. at 342 (Isr. Sup. Ct. 1962).

94. *Eichmann*, 36 I.L.R. at 25, (Isr. Dist. Ct.—Jerusalem 1961).

95. *Id.* at 26.

96. *Id.* at 50.

97. *Id.* at 26.

98. *Eichmann*, 36 I.L.R. at 299 (Isr. Sup. Ct. 1962).

99. *Id.* at 304.

100. Israel initially claimed that volunteers, not Israel Security Services, commited the kidnapping. The Israeli government, however, apparently did authorize and supervise Eichmann's kidnapping; *see* Lippmann, *supra* note 92, at 6 n.28. *See generally* H. Arendt, *Eichmann in Jerusalem* 219–31, 240–45 (1963). Israel "expressed the hope that Argentina would overlook this violation of its sovereignty given 'the special significance' of bringing to trial the man responsible for the murder of millions of Jewish people," Lippman, *supra*, at 7 (footnote omitted) (quoting a *note verbale* sent by the Israeli government to the Argentine government, 15 U.N. SCOR Supp. (Apr.–June 1960) at 31–32, U.N. Doc. S/4342 (1960)). The Security Council passed a resolution requesting, in part, that "the Government of Israel . . . make appropriate reparation in accordance with the Charter of the United Nations and the rules of international law," 15 U.N. SCOR Supp. (Apr.–June 1960) at 35, U.N. Doc. S/4349 (1960). Israel and Argentina eventually issued a joint communiqué, indicating that they had "decided to regard as closed the incident . . . which infringed fundamental rights of the State of Argentina." The joint communiqué is reprinted in M. Pearlman, *The Capture and Trial of Adolph Eichmann* 79 (1963).

101. *See supra* note 100. Much scholarly attention has already been paid to unlawful seizure and irregular extradition, which obviates the need here to consider Eichmann's kidnapping at greater length. *See, e.g.,* Abramovsky & Eagle, "U.S. Policy in Apprehending Alleged Offenders Abroad: Extradition, Abduction, or Irregular Rendition?" 57 *Or. L. Rev.* 51 (1977); Feinrider, "Extraterritorial Abductions: A Newly Developing International Standard," 14 *Akron L. Rev.* 27 (1980); Garcia-Mora, "Criminal Jurisdiction of a State over Fugitives Brought from a Foreign Country by Force or Fraud: A Comparative Study," 32 *Ind. L. J.* 427 (1957); Morgenstern, "Jurisdiction in Seizures Effected in Violation of Interna

tional Law," 29 *Brit. Y. B. Int'l L.* 265 (1952); O'Higgins, "Unlawful Seizure and Irregular Extradition," 36 *Brit. Y. B. Int'l L.* 279 (1960).

We may briefly compare the capture of Eichmann with that of other universal offenders. Seizing Eichmann within Argentina's actual territory is more of an affront to Argentina's sovereignty than seizing a pirate vessel flying Argentina's flag on the high seas. In addition, nation-states have often seized pirates as a preemptive measure against future acts of piracy. Conversely, the immediate capture of Eichmann in peacetime was unnecessary to prevent him from committing additional war crimes. The conventional wisdom is that the kidnapping of a war criminal violates the second sovereign's territorial rights, although some United States officials have recently suggested that such territorial violations are justified in order to capture terrorists. *See, e.g.,* 132 Cong. Rec. S1382 (daily ed. Feb. 19, 1986) (statement by Senator Specter); 131 Cong. Rec. S9430 (daily ed. July 11, 1985) (statement by Senator Specter). For recent related commentary on the legitimacy of the United States' interception of the Egyptian aircraft carrying the *Achille Lauro*'s hijackers, see, *e.g.,* Note, "An Analysis of the Achille Lauro Affair: Towards an Effective and Legal Method of Bringing International Terrorists to Justice," 9 *Fordham Int'l L. J.* 328, 334 (1986).

102. Eichmann, himself, did not have any claim based on Israel's violation of Argentina's territorial rights. Only Argentina could assert that international law violation: "[T]he violation by one country of the sovereignty of another is susceptible of redress as between the two countries and cannot vest in the accused rights of his own," *Eichmann,* 36 I.L.R. at 70 (Isr. Dist. Ct.—Jerusalem 1961).

Under Israeli *domestic* law, the "irregularities" of Eichmann's apprehension did not entitle him to challenge the court's jurisdiction on the basis of a violation of his individual rights, *see id.* at 59–71 (Isr. Dist. Ct.—Jerusalem 1961). In this regard, the Israeli law is consistent with the United States' well-known (and often-criticized) *Ker-Frisbie* doctrine, which holds that irregularities in the defendant's procurement do not violate due process, assuming that the defendant receives the necessary procedural guarantees once within the sovereign's jurisdiction; *Frisbie v. Collins,* 342 U.S. 519 (domestic-interstate seizure), *reh'g denied,* 343 U.S. 937 (1952); *Ker v. Illinois,* 119 U.S. 436 (1886) (international seizure). One might argue that abducting defendants violates their individual rights under international law. *See, e.g.,* Feinrider, *supra* note 101, at 35–46. Even if that is true, however, there is little actual support for the idea that the defendant's remedy would be to divest the court of jurisdiction. *See generally infra* note 163 and accompanying text regarding a defendant's procedural rights.

103. *See, e.g.,* Green, "The Maxim Nullum Crimen Sine Lege and the Eichmann Trial," 38 *Brit. Y. B. Int'l L.* 457, 463–68 (1962); Treves, *supra* note 15, at 586–91. The *Eichmann* courts justified their usage of the protective and passive-personality principles because Israel is "the State of the Jews" and "the sovereign State of the Jewish people," and there is a "very special tragic link between the Nazi crimes" and "the establishment of the State [of Israel]," *Eichmann,* 36 I.L.R.

at 52–53 (Isr. Dist. Ct.—Jerusalem 1961). Another justification was that the "whole political landscape of the Continent of Occupied Europe" changed after the war, including "the very identity of previous states," *Eichmann*, 36 I.L.R. at 55 (Isr. Dist. Ct.—Jerusalem 1961).

104. *See supra* note 99 and accompanying text. The *Eichmann* case was decided after the enactment of the Geneva Conventions and the Genocide Convention. The language of those treaties, however, particularly the Geneva Conventions, suggests that they were not retroactively applicable to Eichmann's behavior. The implications of all of these instruments for the universality principle will be discussed next in text.

105. See introduction, notes 13, 15–16, 18–21, for full citations to these treaties. See chapter 3 for an examination of these treaties within the domestic legal order.

106. Geneva Convention I, art. 2, at 3116, T.I.A.S. No. 3362, at 1, 75 U.N.T.S. at 32; Geneva Convention II, art. 2, at 3220, T.I.A.S. No. 3363, at 1, 75 U.N.T.S. at 86; Geneva Convention III, art. 2, at 3318, T.I.A.S. No. 3364, at 1, 75 U.N.T.S. at 136; Geneva Convention IV, art. 2, at 3518, T.I.A.S. No. 3365, at 1, 75 U.N.T.S. at 288.

107. Grave breaches are identified in Geneva Convention I, art. 50, at 3146, T.I.A.S. No. 3362, at 34, 75 U.N.T.S. at 62; Geneva Convention II, art. 51, at 3250, T.I.A.S. No. 3363, at 34, 75 U.N.T.S. at 116; Geneva Convention III, art. 130, at 3420, T.I.A.S. No. 3364, at 106, 75 U.N.T.S. at 238; Geneva Convention IV, art. 147, at 3618, T.I.A.S. No. 3365, at 104, 75 U.N.T.S. at 388. The category of grave breaches has been expanded by the Protocol Relating to Victims of International Armed Conflicts, *opened for signature* Dec. 12, 1977, art. 85, 16 I.L.M. 1391, 1427, *reprinted in* 72 Am. J. Int'l L. 457 (1978). The United States and most other powerful nation-states are not parties to the Protocol. *See generally* Bassiouni, "Repression of Breaches of the Geneva Conventions Under the Draft Additional Protocol to the Geneva Conventions of August 12, 1949, 8 *Rut.–Cam. L. J.* 185, 197–201 (1977); Solf & Cummings, "A Survey of Penal Sanctions under Protocol I to the Geneva Conventions of August 12, 1949," 9 *Case W. Res. J. Int'l L.* 205, 221–40 (1977).

108. Geneva Convention I, art. 49, at 3146, T.I.A.S. No. 3362, at 34, 75 U.N.T.S. at 62 (emphasis added); Geneva Convention II, art. 50, at 3250, T.I.A.S. No. 3363 at 34, 75 U.N.T.S. at 116 (emphasis added); Geneva Convention III, art. 129, at 3418, T.I.A.S. No. 3364, at 104, 75 U.N.T.S. at 236 (emphasis added); Geneva Convention IV, art. 146, at 3616, T.I.A.S. No. 3365 at 102, 75 U.N.T.S. at 386 (emphasis added). The parties must also enact legislation necessary to provide effective domestic penal sanctions for grave breaches of the Conventions, *id.* The Geneva Conventions give very little guidance concerning violations of nongrave offenses, requiring only that the parties "take measures necessary" for their suppression, *see id. See generally* Bassiouni, *supra* note 107, at 196.

109. Hostage Convention, art. 8(1), at 1460 (emphasis added). For very similar provisions, see Torture Convention, art. 7(1), at 1032; Internationally Protected

Persons Convention, art. 7, at 1981, T.I.A.S. No. 8532, at 1981, 1035 U.N.T.S. at 170; Montreal Convention, art. 7, at 571, T.I.A.S. No. 7570, at 571, 974 U.N.T.S. at 182; Hague Convention, art. 7, at 1646, T.I.A.S. No. 7192, at 1646, 860 U.N.T.S. at 109. The offenses that these multilateral conventions (and the Apartheid Convention) address may be somewhat derivative of earlier offenses that were subject to the universality principle.

110. Persons charged with the offense of apartheid "*may* be tried by a competent tribunal of any State Party to the Convention which may acquire jurisdiction over the person of the accused or by an international penal tribunal." Apartheid Convention, art. 5, at 246 (emphasis added).

111. *See* O. Schachter, *supra* note 21, at 262. *See also* Carnegie, *supra* note 70, at 407–8. For the idea that the treaties might arguably be interpreted without reference to the universality principle, see *infra* note 115 and accompanying text.

112. See chapter 3.

113. *Von Dardel v. Union of Soviet Socialist Republics*, 623 F. Supp. 246 (D.D.C. 1985). See chapters 3 and 4 regarding *Von Dardel*.

114. *Von Dardel*, 623 F. Supp. at 254. In demonstrating its universal jurisdiction over offenses against internationally protected persons, the court did not specifically quote the convention's extradite-or-prosecute language, but drew support from the *Restatement*, *supra* note 12, § 404, which does refer to that language, *see* reporters' note 1, and which provides that the universality principle applies to both the criminal and civil contexts, *see* comment a. See chapter 7 regarding civil international jurisdiction.

115. *See* O. Schachter, *supra* note 21, at 263 ("In other words, the conventions include (by implication) advance waivers of jurisdictional claims among the parties").

116. *See supra* notes 108–10 and accompanying text. The remedy for such a treaty violation may be difficult to formulate. See generally Slomanson, "I.C.J. Damages: Tort Remedy for Failure to Punish or Extradite International Terrorists," 5 *Cal. W. Int'l L. J.* 121 (1974).

117. Indeed, the international consensus condemning these offenses would likely cause most nation-states to applaud any sovereign's judicial redress of such offenses. If the defendant's nation-state of nationality protested such judicial redress, others might conceivably view that nation-state as approving of the defendant's offense or as even having authorized the offense's commission. A protest to another sovereign's domestic jurisdiction would most likely be made by the defendant's nation-state of nationality, as in *S.S. Lotus (Fr. v. Turk.)*, 1927 P.C.I.J. (ser. A) No. 10 (Sept. 7). Possibly, however, the nation-state where the offense occurred might also want to exercise jurisdiction and might protest the forum sovereign's universal jurisdiction.

118. All treaties presumptively do not bind nonparties, *see* Vienna Convention on the Law of Treaties, May 23, 1969, art. 34, U.N. Doc. A/CONF.39/27,

8 I.L.M. 679, 693 (1969) [hereinafter Law of Treaties Convention], and one could hypothesize examples in which South Africa would protest a party's jurisdiction over acts of apartheid or in which Libya would protest jurisdiction over terrorism.

119. *North Sea Continental Shelf Cases (W. Ger. v. Den.; W. Ger. v. Neth.)*, 1969 I.C.J. 4, 42, see chapter 3. *See also*, Law of Treaties Convention, *supra* note 118, art. 38, 8 I.L.M. at 694; *Restatement, supra* note 12, at § 102, reporters' note 2. Whether nation-states view particular treaty rules as giving rise to customary norms is also relevant; *see* Akehurst, "Custom as a Source of International Law," 47 *Brit. Y. B. Int'l L.* 1, 43–49 (1977).

120. *See generally* O. Schachter, *supra* note 21, at 263–64.

121. *See* Charney, "The Persistent Objector Rule and the Development of Customary International Law," 1985 *Brit. Y. B. Int'l L.* 1; Stein, "The Approach of the Different Drummer: The Principle of the Persistent Objector in International Law," 26 *Harv. Int'l L. J.* 457, 481 (1985).

122. *See* Stein, *supra* note 121, at 479–81.

123. *In re Barcelona Traction, Light & Power Co. (Belg. v. Spain)*, 1970 I.C.J. 4, 32 (Judgment of Feb. 5).

124. See chapter 9.

125. *See, e.g.,* 18 U.S.C. § 1116 (1982) (terrorism — internationally protected persons); 18 U.S.C. § 1203 (Supp. II 1984) (terrorism — hostage taking); 49 U.S.C. § 1472(n) (1982) (hijacking).

126. *See supra* note 118 and accompanying text.

127. The conventions' very language illustrates that they were intended to have a broad multilateral, not a restrictive, application. Indeed, the treaties were drafted with some reliance upon the universality principle, *see infra* note 135 and accompanying text, which would have probably been unnecessary if the parties viewed the treaties as merely creating jurisdictional rights and duties among themselves pursuant to an agreement; *see also supra* note 115 and accompanying text.

128. Generally, under international law, extradition is regulated by a treaty or, in the absence of a treaty, by discretionary comity considerations utilized by some nation-states; *see* M. Bassiouni, *International Extradition and World Public Order* 6–23 (1974). The suggestion that nonparties might have a customary law obligation of extradition would thus represent a significant developement in the law. The United States specifically might challenge that development because it normally treats extradition as a matter directly governed by treaty.

129. *See* Message to the Senate Transmitting the Convention Against Torture and Other Inhuman Treatment or Punishment, 24 Weekly Comp. Pres. Doc. 642 (May 20, 1988).

130. *Cf. supra* notes 121–24 and accompanying text (exceptions to persistent objector's ability to protest judicial redress against its national when fundamental norms are at issue).

131. O. Schachter, *supra* note 21, at 263 (emphasis added).

132. The introduction's full citations to these instruments indicate that the United Nations adopted these treaties. The overwhelming majority of nation-states are parties to the Geneva Conventions and have direct obligations under those treaties. Our analysis of nonparty jurisdiction thus has more practical import for the treaties other than the Geneva Conventions.

133. S.C. Res. 579, U.N. SCOR (2637th mtg.), U.N. Doc. 85–38352 (1985), *reprinted in* 25 I.L.M. 243 (1986).

134. Those two treaties were produced by the International Conference on Air Law, held under the ICAO's auspices.

135. Regarding the Hague and Montreal conventions, see Abramovsky, "Multilateral Conventions for the Suppression of Unlawful Seizure and Interference with Aircraft Part I: The Hague Convention," 13 *Colum. J. Transnat'l L.* 381, 395–98 (1974); Ambramovsky, "Multilateral Conventions for the Suppression of Unlawful Seizure and Interference with Aircraft Part II: The Montreal Convention," 14 *Colum. J. Transnat'l L.* 268, 287–93 (1975). Regarding the Internationally Protected Persons Convention, see U.N. Doc A/9127 (28th Session, Item 90 of the Provisional Agenda) at 7, 13 (Aug. 28, 1973) (comments and observations on the draft articles as prepared by the International Law Commission); GAOR, Vol. III Verbatim Records of Plenary Meetings, Sept. 18–Dec. 18, 1973 & Sept. 16, 1974, at 29–30 (Dec. 14, 1973). Regarding the Hostage Convention, see 35 U.N. GAOR Annex 2 (62d mtg, Agenda Item 113) at 3, U.N. Doc. A/C.6/34/SR.62 (1979). Regarding the Apartheid Convention, see 27 U.N. GAOR Annex 2 (2004th mtg. Agenda Item 53) at 145–47, 168 U.N. Doc. A/C.3/SR. 2004 (1973); U.N. Doc. A/ 8768 (27th Session, Item 50(d) of the Provisional Agenda) at 9–10 (Sept. 14, 1972). Regarding the Torture Convention, see 29 U.N. GAOR Annex 3 (44th mtg, Agenda Item 99) at 8, 13 U.N. Doc. A/C.3/39/SR.44 (1984). Regarding the Geneva Conventions, *see generally* Carnegie, *supra* note 70, at 406–8.

136. Those doctrines will be discussed in chapter 9 to help demonstrate broad structural changes in the world legal order.

137. *See* G.A. Res. 95, U.N. Doc. A/64/Add. 1, at 188 (1946).

138. *Id.* The ILC was established by G.A. Res. 174, art. 1, U.N. Doc. A/519, at 105 (1947). *See generally* I. Sinclair, *The International Law Commission* (1987).

139. U.N. Doc. A/CN.4/25 (1950) (containing the first Draft Code), *reprinted in* [1950] 2 *Y. B. Int'l L. Comm'n* 249, 277. *See generally* Ferencz, "Current Developments—The Draft Code of Offences Against the Peace and Security of Mankind," 75 *Am. J. Int'l L.* 674 (1981).

140. *See generally* B. Ferencz, *An International Criminal Court, A Step Toward World Peace* 79–90 (1980); A. Sottile, *The Problem of the Creation of a Permanent International Criminal Court* (1966); Green, "An International Criminal Code—Now?" 3 *Dalhousie L. J.* 560 (1976); Johnson, "The Draft Code of Offences Against the Peace and Security of Mankind," 4 *Int'l & Comp. L. Q.* 445 (1955); Schwarzenberger, "The Problem of an International Criminal Law," 3 *Current Legal Probs* 263 (1950).

141. *Report of the Commission to the General Assembly*, 31 U.N. GAOR Supp. (No. 10) at 175, U.N. Doc. A/31/10 (1976), *reprinted in* [1976] 2 *Y. B. Int'l L. Comm'n* 95, 95, U.N. Doc A/CN.4/SER.A/1976/Add.1 (pt. 2).

142. *Id.*, [1976] 2 *Y. B. Int'l L. Comm'n* at 95–96.

143. *Restatement, supra* note 12, at § 404 reporters' note 1.

144. See chapter 9.

145. *See supra* notes 55–90 and accompanying text.

146. *See supra* note 137 and accompanying text.

147. G.A. Res. 96, U.N. Doc. A/64/Add.1, at 188 (1946).

148. See introduction, note 14, for full citation to this instrument.

149. *See Genocide Convention,* art. 1, at 280.

150. *See id.* art. 2, at 280.

151. *Id.* art. 6, at 282.

152. Fawcett, *supra* note 61, at 206.

153. Carnegie, *supra* note 70, at 408 (emphasis added). Although describing this view of article 6, Carnegie does not appear to adhere to it. Baade, *supra* note 61, at 418, and Lasok, "The Eichmann Trial," 11 *Int'l L. & Comp. L. Q.* 355, 364 (1962), espouse this view.

154. *See* Fawcett, *supra* note 61, at 205–6.

155. *Eichmann,* 36 I.L.R. at 39 (Isr. Dist. Ct.–Jerusalem 1961).

156. Regarding the *Eichmann* case and universal jurisdiction, *see supra* notes 91–104 and accompanying text. The Genocide Convention, however, might not have retroactively applied to Eichmann's acts, *see supra* note 104; the Convention thus might have been irrelevant to Israel's preexisting customary universal jurisdiction. Regarding *Demjanjuk* and the *Restatement, see,* respectively, *supra* notes 8, 12 and accompanying text.

157. See chapter 3 regarding the Covenant.

158. *See* Covenant, art. 2(3).

159. *See supra* notes 55–90 and accompanying text.

160. *See* O. Schachter, *supra* note 21, at 264. See *supra* text accompanying note 136 for definitions of *erga omnes* and *jus cogens.* See chapter 9 for an elaboration of those terms.

161. *See generally supra* notes 137–43 and accompanying text.

162. Dinstein, "Terrorism and War of Liberation: An Israeli Perspective of the Arab Israeli Conflict," in *International Terrorism and Political Crimes* 155, 164 (M. C. Bassiouni ed. 1975).

163. *See generally* O. Schachter, *supra* note 21, at 265. Universal jurisdiction raises two concerns as to the defendant's rights. The first relates to the procurement of defendants, particularly the occasional kidnapping of individuals in the criminal context. An extensive literature has already analyzed the defendant's rights in such situations under both domestic and international law. *See, e.g.,* Feinrider, *supra* note 101, at 35–46; Comment, "Jurisdiction Following Illegal Extraterritorial Seizure: International Human Rights Obligations as an Alter-

native to Constitutional Stalemate," 54 *Tex. L. Rev.* 1439, 1462–70 (1976); *see also supra* note 102 and accompanying text. The second concern relates to the procedural rights and safeguards that the defendant receives once a trial has begun. The Covenant establishes a minimum set of international procedural guarantees. *See* Muhammad, "Due Process of Law for Persons Accused of Crime," in *The International Bill of Rights* 138 (L. Henkin ed. 1981). In the United States, defendants, of course, would benefit from the Bill of Rights. Both of these procedural concerns have more import in the criminal that in the civil context.

9. The Human Rights Paradigm

1. See chapter 8.
2. R. Neustadt & E. May, *Thinking in Time* xv (1986). Randall, "Federal Questions and the Human Rights Paradigm," 73 *Minn. L. Rev.* 349, 421–24 (1988), contains a preliminary and skeletal attempt to posit this chapter's thesis.
3. Our discussion of the medieval system, the Thirty Years War, and the Peace of Westphalia draws upon D. Manland, *Europe at War 1600–1650* 179–90 (1980); R. Mowatt, *A History of European Diplomacy 1451–1789* 104–22 (1971); A. Nussbaum, *A Concise History of the Law of Nations* 86–125 (1947); D. Ogg, *Europe in the Seventeenth Century* 118–82 (8th ed. 1961); *The Thirty Years War* (G. Parker ed. 1984); J. Polisensky, *War and Society in Europe 1618–1648* 17–35 (1978); *The Thirty Years' War* (T. Rabb ed., 2d ed. 1981); IV *The Cambridge Modern History* 395–433 (A. W. Ward, G. W. Prothero & S. Leathes eds. 1906); C. Wedgwood, *The Thirty Years War* 445–84 (1961); Falk, "A New Paradigm for International Legal Studies: Prospects and Proposals," 84 *Yale L. J.* 969, 975–87 (1975); Gross, "The Peace of Westphalia, *1648–1948,*" 42 *Am. J. Int'l L.* 20, 24–30 (1948); Lane, "Demanding Human Rights: A Change in the World Legal Order," 6 *Hofstra L. Rev.* 269, 269–76 (1978).
4. Falk, *supra* note 3, at 980; *see also* Gross, *supra* note 3, at 28.
5. Bull *Unam Sanctam* on the Plentitude of the Papal Power, *reprinted in Church and State Through the Centuries* 89 (S. Ehler & J. Morrall eds. & trans. 1954).
6. *Id.* at 90.
7. *Id.* at 91.
8. Falk, *supra* note 3, at 981. *See generally* J. Strayer, *On the Medieval Origins of the Modern State* 49–56 (1970).
9. J. Strayer, *supra* note 8, at 57.
10. *Id.*
11. *See generally* sources cited in *supra* note 3.
12. Gross, *supra* note 3, at 28. *See also* A. Nussbaum, *supra* note 3, at 86–125; Lane, *supra* note 3, at 271–76. *See generally* D. Manland, *supra* note 3.
13. *See* Treaty of Westphalia (1648), *reprinted in* I *Major Peace Treaties of Modern History* 7 (F. Israel ed. 1967).

14. R. Falk, *A Study of Future Worlds* 59 (1975) (emphasis in original).

15. *See* H. Grotius, *The Law of War and Peace* (L. Loomis trans. 1949, 1st ed. Paris 1625). *See generally* A. Nussbaum, *supra*, note 3, at 96–112; Lauterpacht, "The Grotian Tradition in International Law," 1946 *Brit. Y. B. Int'l L.* 1. A. Nussbaum, *supra*, at 112–25, also discusses influential commentators other than Grotius.

16. *See* Falk, *supra* note 3, at 984–85.

17. *See* Bull *Zelo domus Dei* condemning the Religious Clauses of the Peace of Westphalia, *reprinted in Church and State Through the Centuries, supra* note 5, at 194.

18. Gross, *supra* note 3, at 28. *See also* Falk, *supra* note 3, at 982 (describing Westphalian peace as the "decisive juridical event").

19. T. Kuhn, *The Structure of Scientific Revolutions* 10 (2d ed. 1970). Significant responses to, and critiques of, Kuhn's work include B. Barnes, *T. S. Kuhn and Social Science* (1982); G. Gutting, *Paradigms and Revolutions* (1980); *Criticism and the Growth of Knowledge* (I. Lakatos & A. Musgrave, eds. 1970); Shapere, "The Structure of Scientific Revolutions," 73 *Phil. Rev.* 383 (1964).

20. See T. Kuhn, *supra* note 19, at 10–11, 23–24. *See generally id.* at chaps. 1–3.

21. *Id.* at 92.

22. *See id.* at chaps. 7 and 12.

23. *See generally id.* at 66–91. Kuhn's response to charges of "glorifying subjectivity" is contained in *id.* at 186, 191–205.

24. T. Kuhn, *The Essential Tension* 294 (1977). Kuhn attempts to clarify "paradigm" in chapter 12 of that book, which is somewhat duplicative of his same effort in postscript to T. Kuhn, *supra* note 19, at 174–91.

25. T. Kuhn, *supra* note 19, at viii.

26. *Id.* at 175 (emphasis added).

27. T. Kuhn, *supra* note 24, at 294.

28. T. Kuhn, *supra* note 24, at 297; T. Kuhn, *supra* note 19, at 182.

29. T. Kuhn, *supra* note 19, at 186–91.

30. *See generally id.* at chaps. 6 and 7.

31. T. Kuhn, *supra* note 24, at 295 n.4.

32. *See* T. Kuhn, *supra* note 19, at 78. *See generally id.* at chaps. 6 and 7.

33. *See generally id.* at chaps. 6 and 7.

34. H. Arendt, *On Revolution* 21 (1963). *See also id.* at 36.

35. *Id.* at 35. *See generally id.* at chap. 1.

36. *See* Falk, *supra* note 3, whose discussion of Kuhn, originally part of his Sherrill Lectures at Yale University, has benefitted the present chapter. Professor Falk has republished that discussion in a new book, *Revitalizing International Law* (1989), at chap. 1. Those lectures, however, were not specifically concerned with the domestic adjudication of international human rights, but more generally with the role of international law and lawyers in overall global reform; this is connected with Falk's work on the World Order Models Project (WOMP). *See*

R. Falk, *supra* note 14. For applications of Kuhn's work by legal scholars in other contexts, see, *e.g.*, Casto, "The Erie Doctrine and the Structure of Constitutional Revolutions," 62 *Tulane L. Rev.* 907, 909–11 (1988) (discussing *Erie*'s transformation of federal common law as representing a Kuhnian revolution); Spann, "Secret Rights," 71 *Minn. L. Rev.* 669, 701–21 (1987) (discussing paradigm shifts in the language and logic of individual rights). *See also* Kaye, "The Logic and Antilogic of Secret Rights," 72 *Minn. L. Rev.* 603, 618–19 (1988) (responding to Spann).

37. Falk, *supra* note 3, at 975; *see also id.* at 976–77.

38. *See supra* notes 5–8 and accompanying text.

39. *See generally* J. Bassett, *The League of Nations* (1928); G. Scott, *The Rise and Fall of the League of Nations* (1973); F. Walters, *A History of the League of Nations* (1960).

40. Those instruments actually predated some documents of surrender. See chapter 8 regarding the IMT Charter and C.C. Law No. 10.

41. *See* Glueck, "By What Tribunal Shall War Offenders Be Tried?" 56 *Harv. L. Rev.* 1059, 1059–60 (1943); Levy, "The Law and Procedure of War Crime Trials," 37 *Am. Pol. Sci. Rev.* 1052, 1062 (1943). War criminals returned to Germany for prosecution after World War I were, at most, given minimal sentences, see chapter 8 regarding *In re List*.

42. "International Military Tribunal (Nuremberg), Judgment and Sentences," 41 *Am. J. Int'l L.* 172, 221 (1947). See chapter 2 regarding legal personality, which also drew upon this passage.

43. Those offenses refer, respectively, to crimes against peace and crimes against humanity, see chapter 8.

44. Universal Declaration of Human Rights, G.A. Res. 217, U.N. Doc. A/ 64/948 at 71 (1948); International Covenant on Civil and Political Rights, see introduction, note 12, for citation and chapter 3 for discussion; International Covenant on Economic, Social and Cultural Rights, December 16, 1966, G.A. Res. 2200 Annex, 21 U.N. GAOR Supp. at 49 (No. 16), U.N. Doc. A/6316 at 490. *See generally* Henkin, "Introduction," in *The International Bill of Rights* 1 (L. Henkin ed. 1981).

45. See introduction, notes 13–16, 18–21, for full citations to those instruments and chapters 3 and 8 for examinations of those instruments.

46. This phraseology draws upon Leo Gross's statement in *supra* note 18 and accompanying text.

47. This phraseology draws upon Hannah Arendt's statement in *supra* notes 34–35 and accompanying text.

48. *See* Falk, *supra* note 3, at 978 (discussing cultural indices of global reform).

49. *See supra* notes 16–17, 23 and accompanying text.

50. Falk, *supra* note 3, at 979.

51. *See supra* note 21 and accompanying text.

52. Lockwood, "The United Nations Charter and United States Civil Rights Litigation: 1946–1955," 69 *Iowa L. Rev.* 901 (1984); *see also* Christenson, "Using

Human Rights Law to Inform Due Process and Equal Protection Analyses," 52 *U. Cin. L. Rev.* 3 (1983).

53. *See generally* Kuhn, *supra* note 19, at 187–91. The reference to the "medium is the message," of course, draws upon M. McLuhan, *Understanding Media* (1964).

54. *Filartiga v. Pena-Irala*, 630 F.2d 876 (2d Cir. 1980). See introduction and chapter 2 regarding *Filartiga*.

55. *See* Statute of the International Court of Justice, June 26, 1945, art. 34, 59 Stat. 1055, 1059, T.S. No. 933 (only nation-states may be parties before the tribunal, with limited exceptions for international organizations).

56. The Optional Covenant on Civil and Political Rights, G.A. Res. 2200, 21 U.N. GAOR Supp. (No. 16) at 59, U.N. Doc. A/6316 (1966), established a Human Rights Committee, and a party to the Optional Protocol may agree to allow the committee to consider human rights complaints from individuals subject to that party's jurisdiction. In its current limited subscription and application, however, this institution should not yet be equated with a global forum for individual complaints. *See infra* notes 59–61 regarding other international and regional human rights fora.

57. *See generally* Scelle, "Regles Generales de la Paix," 46 *Recueil de Cours* 1, 358–59, 421–27 (IV 1933) (describing dual and multiple functions played by single institutions in particular domestic and international contexts). Of course, our use of *dedoublement fonctionnel* refers to a domestic institution acting as an agent of two legal orders, rather than to an institution playing dual functions in a single system.

58. Reisman, "Through or Despite Governments: Differentiated Responsibilities in Human Rights Programs," 72 *Iowa L. Rev.* 391, 395 (1987). Professor Reisman, however, stresses the limits of functional doubling, *id.* at 395–97.

59. *See generally* Drzemsczewski, "The European Human Rights Convention: Time for a Radical Overhaul?" 10 *B.C. Int'l & Comp. L. Rev.* 9 (1987); Jenson, "The Impact of the European Convention for the Protection of Human Rights on National Law," 52 *U. Cin. L. Rev.* 760 (1983); Robertson, "The European Court of Human Rights," 9 *Am. J. Comp. L.* 1 (1960); Sherman, "Procedural Decisions of the European Court of Human Rights: A Comparative Study," 8 *Brooklyn J. Int'l L.* 309 (1982).

60. *See generally* Buergenthal, "The Inter-American Court of Human Rights," 76 *Am. J. Int'l L.* 231 (1982); Buergenthal, "The American and European Conventions on Human Rights: Similarities and Differences," 30 *Am. U. L. Rev.* 155 (1981); de Branches, "The Inter-American Court of Human Rights," 30 *Am. U. L. Rev.* 79 (1981); Lockwood, "Advisory Opinions of the Inter-American Court of Human Rights," 13 *Den. J. Int'l L. & Pol.* 245 (1984); Vargas, "Individual Access to the Inter-American Court of Human Rights," 16 *N.Y.U. J. Int'l L. & Pol.* 601 (1984); Witten, "International Decisions, Velasquez Rodriguez Case," 83 *Am. J. Int'l L.* 361 (1989).

61. *See generally* Gittleman, "The African Charter on Human and Peoples' Rights: A Legal Analysis," 22 *Va. J. Int'l L.* 667 (1982); Neff, "Human Rights in Africa: Thoughts on the African Charter on Human and Peoples' Rights," 33 *Int'l & Comp. L. J.* 331 (1984); Okere, "The Protection of Human Rights in Africa and the African Charter on Human and Peoples' Rights: A Comparative Analysis," 6 *Hum. Rts. Q.* 141 (1984); Umozurike, "The African Charter on Human and Peoples' Rights," 77 *Am. J. Int'l L.* 902–12 (1983).

62. T. Kuhn, *supra* note 24, at 294.

63. See chapter 8.

64. Concerning the *Barcelona Traction, Light & Power Co. (Belg. v. Spain),* 1970 I.C.J. 4 (Judgment of Feb. 5). See Randall, *supra* note 2, at 419–21, for the author's prior examination of the *erga omnes* and *jus cogens* doctrines, from which the present discussion draws.

65. *Barcelona Traction,* 1970 I.C.J. at 33 (dictum). The court's overall opinion, however, contains some ambiguity regarding the *erga omnes* doctrine. *See* O. Schachter, *International Law in Theory and Practice* 195–99 (1982).

66. *Barcelona Traction,* 1970 I.C.J. at 32.

67. *Id.*

68. Vienna Convention on the Law of Treaties, art. 53, U.N. Doc. A/CONF. 39/27, 8 I.L.M. 679, 698–99 (1969).

69. An authoritative list of *jus cogens* norms is nonexistent. Nevertheless, that *jus cogens* norms overlap with *erga omnes* obligations is illustrated by Schwelb, "Some Aspects of International Jus Cogens as Formulated by the International Law Commission," 61 *Am. J. Int'l L.* 946 (1967), and Whiteman, "Jus Cogens in International Law, with a Projected List," 7 *Ga. J. Int'l & Comp. L.* 609 (1977). For a recent, valuable study of *jus cogens,* see Christenson, *"Jus Cogens:* Guarding Interests Fundamental to International Society," 28 *Va. J. Int'l L.* 585 (1988). *See generally Committee of U.S. Citizens Living in Nicaragua v. Reagan,* 859 F.2d 929, 939–42 (D.C. Cir. 1988); Note, *"Jus Cogens:* Compelling the Law of Human Rights," 12 *Hastings Int'l & Comp. L. Rev.* 411 (1989).

70. *See, e.g.,* L. Tribe, *American Constitutional Law* §§ 16–7 to 16–12 (2d ed. 1988) (discussing impact of differentiating fundamental rights from other rights on equal protection model).

71. *See generally,* Lobel, "The Limits of Constitutional Power: Conflicts between Foreign Policy and International Law," 71 *Va. L. Rev.* 1071, 1134–50 (1985); Meron, "On a Hierarchy of International Human Rights," 80 *Am. J. Int'l L.* 1 (1986); Weil, "Towards Relative Normativity in International Law?" 77 *Am. J. Int'l L.* 413 (1983).

72. *See Banco Nacional de Cuba v. Sabbatino,* 376 U.S. 398, 428 (1964) ("[t]he greater the degree of codification or consensus concerning a particular area of international law, the more appropriate it is for the judiciary to render decisions regarding it"); R. Falk, *The Role of Domestic Courts in the International Legal Order* 9–10 (1964) (arguing that greater international community

support for particular concern should lead courts to greater willingness to adjudicate in that area).

73. *See* O. Schachter, *supra* note 65, at 195–201, 340–42; Schwelb, "The Actio Popularis and International Law," 2 *Israel Y. B. Hum. Rts.* 46, 55–56 (1972).

74. *See supra* note 31 and accompanying text.

75. *Tel-Oren v. Libyan Arab Republic*, 726 F.2d 774 (D.C. Cir. 1984) (per curiam), *cert. denied*, 470 U.S. 1003 (1985). See introduction and chapter 2 regarding *Tel-Oren*.

76. *Tel-Oren*, 726 F.2d at 823 (Bork, J., concurring).

77. See chapters 2 and 3.

78. See chapter 2.

79. Falk, *supra* note 3, at 978.

Conclusion

1. *Filartiga v. Pena-Irala*, 630 F.2d 876 (1980).

2. 1 A. de Tocqueville, *Democracy in America* 330 (H. Reeve trans. 1961).

3. *Talamini v. Allstate Insurance Co.*, 470 U.S. 1067, 1070 (1985) (Stevens, J., concurring) (footnote omitted) (criticizing sanctions against lawyer when appeal suffered jurisdictional defects).

4. *Tel-Oren v. Libyan Arab Republic*, 726 F.2d 774 (D.C. Cir. 1984) (per curiam), *cert. denied*, 470 U.S. 1003 (1985).

INDEX

About the Author

Kenneth C. Randall is Vice Dean and Professor at the University of Alabama School of Law. He joined the Alabama faculty in 1985 and was named Vice Dean in 1989. His teaching and research areas include international and constitutional law.

Library of Congress Cataloging-in-Publication Data

Randall, Kenneth C., 1956–
    Federal courts and the international human rights paradigm / Kenneth C. Randall.
        p.   cm.
    Includes bibliographical references.
    ISBN 0–8223–1038–4
      1. Jurisdiction — United States.   2. Human rights — United States.   3. Jurisdiction (International law).   4. Human rights.   I. Title.
    KF8858.R35   1990
342.73′085 — dc20
[347.30285]   90–2877
                                        CIP